W9-BBW-655

Adolescent Portraits

Adolescent Portraits

Identity, Relationships, and Challenges

ANDREW GARROD
Dartmouth College

LISA SMULYAN
Swarthmore College

SALLY I. POWERS
University of Massachusetts

ROBERT KILKENNY
Harvard University

ALLYN AND BACON
Boston   London   Toronto   Sydney   Tokyo   Singapore

Managing Editor: Susan Badger
Senior Editorial Assistant: Laura Lynch
Production Editor: Lisa Feder
Editorial-Production Service: York Production Services
Cover Administrator: Linda Dickinson
Cover Designer: Suzanne Harbison
Manufacturing Buyer: Louise Richardson

Library of Congress Cataloging-in-Publication Data

Adolescent portraits: identity, relationships, and challenges/
 [compiled by] Andrew Garrod . . . [et al.].
   p. cm.
 Includes bibliographical references (p.   ).
 ISBN 0–205–13344–4
 1. Adolescence—Case studies. 2. Adolescent psychology—United
States—Case studies. I. Garrod, Andrew,
HQ796.A3343 1992
305.23'5—dc20   91–24518
                                                                          CIP

Printed in the United States of America

10 9 8 7 6 5 4 3 2 1   96 95 94 93 92 91

Contents

PART TWO
Relationships   165

PART THREE
Challenges   229

CHART 1 • Cases Categorized by Theme

Theme	Case No.
Careers	5: Distilling My Korean-American Identity 6: I Reconcile the Irreconcilable 14: Forever an Awkward Adolescent
Child abuse	4: Someday My Elders Will Be Proud 13: The Simple Beauty of a Conversation
Disabilities	13: The Simple Beauty of a Conversation 14: Forever an Awkward Adolescent
Drugs/alcohol	2: Working Through My Adolescence 4: Someday My Elders Will Be Proud
Eating disorder	10: Guilt Was Everywhere Around Me
Ethnicity	3: Running Hurdles 4: Someday My Elders Will Be Proud 5: Distilling My Korean-American Identity 6: I Reconcile the Irreconcilable
Family relationships	3: Running Hurdles 4: Someday My Elders Will Be Proud 7: To Be the Best 8: A Step in the Only Direction 9: Becoming Comfortable with Who I Am 10: Guilt Was Everywhere Around Me 14: Forever an Awkward Adolescent
Peer relationships	1: Courting Danger 2: Working Through My Adolescence 3: Running Hurdles 4: Someday My Elders Will Be Proud 5: Distilling My Korean-American Identity 7: To Be the Best 8: A Step in the Only Direction 9: Becoming Comfortable with Who I Am 11: No "Boring Little Friends" 12: Loving Women 13: The Simple Beauty of a Conversation 14: Forever an Awkward Adolescent 15: Proud of the Strength I Had
Pregnancy/abortion	7: To Be the Best 15: Proud of the Strength I Had
School Problems	13: The Simple Beauty of a Conversation 4: Someday My Elders Will Be Proud

CHART 1 • Cases Categorized by Theme (Continued)

Theme	*Case No.*
Sexuality	2: Working Through My Adolescence
	7: To Be the Best
	8: A Step in the Only Direction
	12: Loving Women
	15: Proud of the Strength I Had
Women's identity	1: Courting Danger
	11: No "Boring Little Friends"
	12: Loving Women
	15: Proud of the Strength I Had

Acknowledgments

The following students provided editorial and research assistance on the book: Jay Davis, Patrick Lynch, Theresa Shay, James Stascavage, Lisa Wilson, and Samantha Zee. We thank them for their skill and energy throughout the project. We also appreciate the faculty research grant awarded by Swarthmore College in support of the project and the comments on many of the cases provided by Stephanie Beukema, Assistant Dean at Radcliffe College.

The cases in this book are the words of college students who have taken our courses, individuals who were willing to share their life experiences with many outsiders. Although we cannot thank them by name, we wish to acknowledge their personal strength as well as the time and energy they invested in this project. In addition, we want to recognize the many students who worked with us on cases that have not been included in the book; they, too, gave a tremendous amount of themselves as we worked to shape the final manuscript.

Adolescent Portraits

Introduction

Overview: The Study of Adolescence

The way in which we view adolescence depends, to a large extent, on our perceptions of human nature and the relationship of the individual to society. Those who study adolescence today draw on past perceptions but also bring a new set of lenses to the field. Many have begun to realize the diversity that characterizes their individual subjects and the difficulty in generating theory that captures their experiences. Using the lenses of class, ethnicity, race, and gender, they work to describe and explain the complexity seen in adolescent thought, behavior, and relationships.

Twentieth-century understanding of adolescent development has some of its roots in earlier studies of human development (see Elder, 1980; Muuss, 1988; Sisson, Hersen, & Van Hasselt, 1987). The first consideration of adolescence as a separate stage of life is often attributed to Plato (1921) and Aristotle (1941), both of whom described the adolescent as unstable and impressionable. They suggested schooling for girls and boys that would shield them from society and help them develop the self-control and reason that characterizes a mature individual. In the Middle Ages, the prevalence of Christian views of human depravity and of knowledge as external to the individual led to a less developmental perspective. Children and adolescents were seen as miniature adults who had to be socialized into acceptance of adult roles, values, and beliefs (Muuss, 1988).

John Locke and Jean Jacques Rousseau helped to restore society's belief in the qualitative difference between children and adults. Rousseau, in particular, emphasized a process of development during which innate knowledge and character unfold throughout childhood and youth. In *Emile*, Rousseau presented his view of this process and the role of society in nurturing and schooling young people as they develop into responsible citizens. Rousseau attributed different natural characteristics and social roles to males and females and suggested that, while the process of development is similar for both, schooling toward the end product differs as a result of their divergent natures and responsibilities.

1

In the nineteenth century, several social and intellectual movements influenced perceptions of human nature and adolescence. Charles Darwin's *The Origin of Species* included humans as a part of the natural world, providing a more biological and evolutionary view of human development and growth. The Industrial Revolution led to a gradual deemphasis on the family's role in socialization for work and relationships and a discontinuity in an individual's experience of home and work. Accompanying movements such as child labor laws and compulsory schooling contributed to society's perception of a phase of development between childhood and the assumption of an adult role in society, a phase that G. Stanley Hall named "adolescence" in 1904 (Bakan, 1972).

Hall (1904) described adolescence as a key stage of life in the evolution of the mature individual. Drawing on Darwin's work, he postulated a scientific theory of recapitulation in which the individual develops through stages that parallel those of human civilization. Like Rousseau, he saw development as a natural, largely innate process that could be guided and supported by society. Hall characterized preadolescence as the "savage" stage in the life of the individual. Adolescence followed, a transitional period to adulthood filled with contradictory emotions and behaviors: selfishness and altruism, sensitivity and cruelty, radicalism and conservatism. Through the struggle of adolescence, the individual is reborn, a new self is created, ready to assume a role in modern society.

Hall's work has influenced the study of adolescence through the twentieth century, but it has also been modified and challenged over the years. While Freud and those whose ideas developed from his work (e.g., Blos, 1962; Erikson, 1968; A. Freud, 1946) continued to focus on biological imperatives and their influence on the individual's psyche in the process of development, others began to take a more sociological perspective on adolescence. The work of Margaret Mead (1958) and Ruth Benedict (1950) suggested that society determines the behaviors, roles, and values of its adolescents. Others focused on the effects of social disorganization, social class, and social institutions on the life of the adolescent, documenting the role of environment in the shaping of experience (e.g., Hollingshead, 1949; Havighurst, Bosman, Liddle, Mathews, and Pierce, 1962). In the 1950s, studies of adolescence tended to emphasize the role of the peer group and the uniqueness of the adolescent experience; adolescence was seen as discontinuous with both childhood and adulthood. Adolescents had their own culture, comprised of a unique language, patterns of interaction, and beliefs.

While events of the '60s contributed to this perception of an adolescent subculture, they also led those who study adolescence to focus on the intersection between the life course of the individual, the age cohort, and the historical context within which the individuals act (Elder, 1980). Some researchers and theorists, following Mead's emphasis on cultural influences on adolescence, focused on the social-historical context of adolescent development. They challenged Hall's view of adolescence as necessarily stressful by examining continuity and change in adolescent behavior over time. Other began to reexamine the period of adolescence within the context of an individual's lifespan. Research in child and adult development and in ego, cognitive, and moral development led to an understanding of adolescence as one of a sequence of life stages during which the individual addresses key issues such as identity, autonomy, attachment, and separation. The emphasis in this work has been on phases or stages of development that cut across social, historical, and cultural boundaries (e.g., Erikson, 1968; Kohlberg & Gilligan, 1972; Piaget, 1972).

Some of the most recent work in the study of adolescence has challenged approaches that emphasize either socio-cultural determinism or universal developmental theory, suggesting that understanding adolescence involves a consideration of how social categories such as race, class, and gender interact with processes of individual development (e.g., Berry & Asamen, 1989; Gilligan, 1982; Josselson, 1987; McAdoo & McAdoo, 1985). The historical and cultural context is important in understanding adolescent experience, but it may not be sufficient to explain an individual's behaviors, beliefs, and sense of self. Stage and phase theories of development tend to overgeneralize from small, nonrepresentative samples and often ignore key variables such as race and gender that have a profound impact on an individual's experience and identity. The study of adolescence, then, has become more inclusive in terms of who is studied, what questions are asked, and how experience is analyzed. It has also become more complex, as we take a range of variables and contexts into consideration when examining individual development.

Even as researchers and teachers try to understand the multiple aspects of each individual's identity, the context within which American adolescents develop continues to change, further complicating the picture. Adolescents in the 1990s grow up in a society that takes technology and global communication as givens. On a large scale, this adolescent cohort's historical and cultural context is one in which international shifts toward democratic governments and market economies mean changing relationships between the United States and former Cold War antagonists. Increased international communication will lead to greater knowledge and understanding of other people around the world and, perhaps, to greater interdependence. Closer to home, these adolescents experience a society that is working toward greater acceptance of diversity—one, for example, in which women and minorities strive to define and work toward their goals while simultaneously trying to change society. Although they are growing up in decades of change and progress, today's adolescents also face persistent social problems: educational systems struggling with declining enrollments and shrinking resources, urban (and some suburban and rural) communities focusing on teenage drug use and the spread of AIDS, and a resurgence of racial and ethnic questioning and occasional violence. The social questions and issues that surround them demonstrate to today's adolescents that society does not have all of the answers and that it often seems to lack the direction and commitment needed to find them.

Research in the past twenty years has also refuted the "storm and stress" model of adolescent development which grew out of Hall's work. This approach sees adolescence as a time of severe turbulence, during which relationships disintegrate as the individual rebels against internal and external value systems (e.g., Blos, 1962; A. Freud, 1946, 1958). In contrast, more current work in the field emphasizes continuity and renegotiation as processes that characterize adolescence. "Normal" adolescent development encompasses a wide range of experiences, including a variety of family structures, sexual experimentation and orientation, and ethnic and racial exploration. Although some adolescents may experience more environmental stressors than others during these years, they occur within a meaningful personal and social context for that individual. Researchers have come to accept many variations within their definitions of normality in adolescence.

The Case Study Approach

Those of us who teach courses in adolescent development continue to search for materials that address our students' lives and illuminate emerging approaches in the study of adolescence. Such materials help students learn what past and present theorists and current research have to say about the adolescent experience and engage students in asking questions about those theories and approaches as well as their own lives. We want our students to be thoughtful and critical participants in the study of adolescence, contributors to our growing understanding of how this phase of life relates to the larger life cycle.

The authors of this book found this kind of material in a book called *Experiencing Youth*, first published in 1970 by George W. Goethals and Dennis S. Klos. We used this book in our own study of adolescence and have since incorporated it into the courses we teach. *Experiencing Youth* is a set of first-person accounts written by undergraduate and graduate students (the latter appear primarily in the second edition) that highlight key issues in adolescent development: autonomy, identity, and intimacy. These cases demonstrate how powerful narrative can be as a way of examining individual lives within a framework of theory and research on adolescence.

By listening to the voices of individual adolescents, students and teachers of adolescent development can gain a greater understanding of the issues facing some of today's adolescents. Case studies illustrate the complexity of the individual experience and the interactions among an individual's needs, ideas, relationships, and context. Each case, taken alone, helps us begin to know one more adolescent and his or her experience; taken together, the cases provide a rich overview of the field of adolescence. Through them, students come to a greater understanding of key theorists and current research findings as they examine patterns in their lives and the lives of others. We are indebted to Goethals and Klos for helping us and our students learn the value of the case study.

Despite the strengths of *Experiencing Youth*, we felt a need for cases that reflected the experiences of today's adolescents — their social and historical context, their diversity, their concerns — and for theoretical frames that reflected more recent work in adolescent research. In this book, we build on the model provided by Goethals and Klos, bringing together the voices of students in our own classes and some key theories and approaches used in the study of adolescence. Each case in this volume was written and revised by an undergraduate or very recent graduate, most of whom have taken a course in adolescent development.

Although it is never possible to be completely representative, we chose students and cases with the goal of achieving a cross section of ethnicities, class backgrounds, and experiences. The book includes cases written by first-year college students who reflect primarily on their early adolescent experience and by students who have recently graduated from college and look back on those years as well. Case No. 1 was written by a first-year student; Case No. 15 by a sophomore, Case Nos. 2, 3, 6, 8, 10, and 13 by juniors; and Case Nos. 4, 5, 7, 9, 11, 12, and 14 by seniors. Of the fifteen case writers, eleven are white, two are African American, one is Native American, and one is Asian American. Nine are women and six are men. Case writers come from the West, Midwest, South and East; from urban, suburban, and rural environments; from more and less privileged backgrounds; from single and two-parent homes; from situations that have stimulated reflection and those that have allowed the writers to develop without thinking deeply about the implications and meanings of their actions and ideas. Although we have included each case under a major topic (as listed in the Table of Contents), each case addresses a number of issues. The charts at the end of the Introduction provide a guide to the themes present in each case, as do the abstracts at the beginning of each case.

How to Use the Book

The cases are about adolescents, and the majority of participants in the discussion are either adolescents themselves or are just finishing their adolescence. Whether or not it appears on their faces, this material does resonate with some fact of their own lives.

(Discussion leader)

The most essential characteristic of a good discussion group is, in my mind, a lack of tension and a sense of trust which enables all members of a group to feel happy about speaking. It is easy to feel overwhelmed having just read a case: Thoughts such as, "What right have I to be 'judging' this individual? Is my point valid or simply naíve? Do I trust the other members of the group enough to say this?" rise in one's mind.

(Student)

The cases included in this book have been chosen for their representative nature, which means that the students who read them will relate to them in a variety of ways. Successful use of this kind of case demands a classroom in which people feel that they are safe, respected, and heard. One way to establish such an environment is to acknowledge the strength and resilience of the people who wrote the cases and to help students do the same. The authors of these cases found writing a valuable process in examining their own experience; through writing they have opened up a part of their lives to others. If we can help our students listen to and respect this process, we can create a classroom in which they, too, can share and examine their own experiences in light of the cases read and theory studied.

Cases, because of their personal nature, often evoke strong reactions from students. We have found it useful to prepare students for the possibility of this kind of response in advance, explaining that case studies may illuminate aspects of their own experiences that they find uncomfortable. One way to work with intense student reaction is to emphasize the need for students to examine themselves, their reactions, and how they relate to the case writer. The goal is not to judge the writer, nor the student who responds to that writer, but to find patterns in their experiences. The classroom teacher may also want to identify opportunities and resources within the college or university community that can help students address issues of concern that may arise within (or outside of) their classroom experience.

Although the case study approach emphasizes the primacy of listening to adolescent voices, we believe it is important that students have a theoretical context within which to explore what they hear. We have provided two theoretical frameworks for use with these cases. First, at the beginning of each major section — identity, relationships, and adolescent challenges — we offer an overview of some of the major theory and current research in that area. For example, the introduction to the Identity section reviews key theoretical and research findings and suggests ways in which they are reflected in the cases that follow. Second, four experts in the field of adolescent development offer interpretations of three cases in the book, providing both a model for approaching case analysis and an application of relevant theory to that case.

Use of the cases and this theoretical material will depend in part on the structure of the course within which they are read. In general, the cases seem to be most valuable when discussed in small groups, although they can be integrated effectively into other formats as well. In large classes or lecture courses, students can be asked to form groups in which they apply and critique ideas presented in lecture through case analysis. The teacher of a large class might also refer to a case to illustrate lecture material, or could have students write about a case outside of class to allow them to explore course material on their own. Students can be asked to examine the case through the lens of several theorists, looking for patterns that may support or challenge the works they have read previously. The "expert" pieces following Cases 1, 8, and 13 can be used as examples of this kind of analysis. Students can also be asked to try a range of approaches in examining cases. For example, they might try a clinical approach that looks for symptoms and patterns of behavior, or an interactive approach, such as that described by Carol Gilligan (in this volume), that focuses on finding the relationship between the reader and writer and the selves they project. The cases can therefore be used to help students engage in learning both the *content* of adolescent developmental theory and the *processes* used to examine actual adolescent experience.

This book can be used as a supplemental text, paralleling and support-ing a traditional adolescent development text. It can also be used as the primary text in a course. In the latter situation, the approach might be more inductive: Students would read a case, looking for patterns and asking questions about the writer's and their own experience that would lead them to formulate ideas about adolescent development. Though theoretical read-ing and background would be necessary in support of this approach, the cases themselves become the focus. Students work to find out how the writer sees himself or herself, using relevant theory and an awareness of their own responses as lenses for doing so. Discussion of the cases could again emphasize content as well as different approaches to analysis.

Engaging with the Text

As the student who speaks at the beginning of the previous section suggests, reading through a case the first time can be an overwhelming experience. What follows is a set of suggestions that can help students prepare for effective discussion of the issues within the text. Some of the suggestions may also help students pull together their ideas following a case discussion, integrating what they have said and heard with theoretical reading and/or their own experience. Neither students nor professor need clinical training to make effective use of case analysis; the personal and revealing nature of the cases can be used in many ways to further understanding of the adolescent experience. The following list is far from exhaustive; it is meant to provide an initial set of ideas from which further possibilities will develop.

1. Goethals and Klos (1976) suggest that students read through a case several times. The first time, they should summarize the writer's perspective, trying to minimize their own tendency to judge or impose a point of view on the writer. The second reading focuses around a question or questions (either provided by the teacher/discussion leader or generated by the student) that allow the reader to collect information to support or challenge a theory or generalization.

2. Gilligan also suggests that students read through a case several times. The focus of each reading differs significantly from that suggested by Goethals and Klos, however; Gilligan's emphasizes a gradual identification of one's own perspective and the reader's engagement in a relationship or dialogue with the writer.

3. Some discussion leaders have found it helpful to begin a session by having students list the major facts of the case as a springboard to discussion. This approach may help students move away from their personal reactions to the case and discuss it first on its own terms.

4. Another way to begin a discussion session is to have all students write down questions related to the case, in particular those they want to discuss in class. Students share these with the group as a way of beginning a conversation about salient aspects of the case.

5. Students can be asked to write about a case in ways in which help them explore its key ideas and their own responses to those ideas. They might, for example, write a dialogue between themselves and the writer, focusing on a particular issue of asking questions about what is and is not in the case. This kind of assignment (which could be done prior to or in class) asks students to put themselves into the writer's world and to examine how they feel and respond to that world.

6. Students can also be asked to write a case describing an aspect of their own adolescent experience. The case could include analysis, or students could be asked to write the case first and then analyze it using the approaches that have been modeled in the class. They might also be asked to write a comparison of their own experience and that presented in one of the cases they have read.

7. Comparison can be a useful tool in discussion of cases. If, for example, the class has been discussing adolescent sexuality, students might read two cases and discuss similarities and differences in the authors'

approaches to issues in their lives, the origins of those similarities and differences, and how they as readers respond to the different approaches the writers have taken. We have provided a list of films that can also be used as cases for this kind of comparison (see Film Reviews).

One typical student response to cases is to question the "normality" of the case writer, focusing on what appear to be extreme or unusual circumstances in his or her life. Students should be encouraged to trust the case writer, understanding that each author presents reality as he or she knows it. At the same time, students need to question the writer, asking what he or she might have left out of the case and why. They can also learn to move away from the categories of normal and abnormal, or perhaps to expand their perception of normality, by concentrating on the characteristics of the case as it is without judging or categorizing the experience. Normal development takes a range of guises as adolescents move toward adulthood. Each case reflects a single individual's experience, yet it also represents patterns of experience and response that may be shared by others.

Students may also react by sharing personal experiences that relate to the case just read. As we have suggested, a discussion leader must work to hear and validate each person's experience, but must also find ways to help individuals relate their own lives back to the case and issues under consideration. Without the connections, the discussion can become a series of unfocused personal anecdotes; with the connections, students may find that they learn more than they thought possible from a single case.

> I think case discussions jumped the furthest when one member would entrust the group with something personal and valuable from his/her experience or knowledge. Other members were therefore encouraged to share their more private views, and the discussion penetrated the case much more deeply.
>
> (Student)

First person accounts created by students of the same age as the intended audience have proven to be, in our experience, a remarkably effective way of helping students examine critical issues in adolescence and assess the power of theory to illuminate what appears idiosyncratic or general in adolescent experience. Because the case writers in this book represent diverse backgrounds and present a range of concerns, they allow us to examine both the individual in his or her context and the patterns that prevail across time and place. By listening to the voices of the adolescents themselves, we can better understand their lives and the place of adolescence in the lives of others.

PART ONE

Identity

Theoretical Overview

The nine cases in the Identity section of this book show a pattern of a struggle for meaning and a quest for wholeness. Within the categories of gender, work, values and ideology, ethnicity, and sexuality, the adolescent writers wrestle with important choices—who they want to be, how to relate to others, what values should guide them, and what their place is in various spheres of their lives. Though the content of the autobiographies may differ from case to case, the reader will see they share common explorations and preoccupations with the self, the self in relation to the self, the self in relation to the other, and to the broader society. We offer here a framework for approaching the cases in this section.

Erik Erikson (1968), who has helped shape our understanding of identity, proposed a detailed and widely applied psychosocial theory of identity development. Convinced that the study of identity is as crucial to our time as the study of childhood sexuality was to Freud's, Erikson forged a radical rethinking among psychoanalytic theorists about ego structure and the role of culture and environment in personality development. As is inevitable, his writings have, over the last decades, been expanded (e.g. Marcia, 1967), and debated (e.g. Gilligan, 1982) by a succession of theorists, some of whom have significantly broadened his theory's applicability. Its general acceptance, however, remains widespread, and his ideas form the foundation of the psychological approach we take to the cases of this section.

When asked to describe his adolescence, one of our students recently wrote: "I don't know where it started and have no more idea if it's ended. Something inside of me tells me I'm in transition between something and something else, but I don't know what." In transition between two "somethings," this young man is not at all sure where he has come from and even less sure of his destination; he is Kurt Lewin's (1939) "marginal man," uncertain of his position and group belongingness. As an adolescent, he is in a stage of his life in which pressures, both internal and external, to define himself become simultaneously impossible to ignore and impossible to satisfy. He is working to establish a self-concept while at the same time realizing that this concept is changing as rapidly as he can pinpoint it. Like Lewis Carroll's Alice, he may well reply to the question: "Who are you?" posed by the Caterpillar, by saying "I, I hardly know Sir, just at present—at least I know who I was when I got up this morning, but I must have changed several times since then." In Erikson's terms, the adolescent has entered a psychological moratorium—a hiatus between childhood security and adult independence.

Adolescence is a critical stage in the individual's development. Adolescents are intensely aware of how they are seen by others—aware, as V.S. Pritchett (1971) observes, that "other egos with their own court of adherents invade one's privacy with theirs." It is a time in which the values and perspectives of others become clearer to the developing mind. The adolescent must first attempt to evaluate his or her different options— different ethical positions or religious beliefs, acceptance or rejection of societal norms, attitudes toward sexuality, ideological stance in relation to family and friends—before he or she can choose among them. In this sense, the search for identity is not only the process of molding an image of oneself—it is also the attempt to understand the fundamental components of the clay that will be used.

The ego of childhood, strengthened by identifications with significant others and by growing mastery of the tasks of school and family life, will no longer hold; the challenge now for the adolescent is a creative synthesis of past identifications, current skills and abilities, and future hopes—all within the context of the opportunities the society offers. This challenge is made immeasurably harder because of the technological society we live in, in which multiple roles and careers tantalize us with choice. Mead (1930) suggests it might be easier to live in a society in which roles are inherited through birth or decided by gender! Yet the autonomous creation of identity, the redefinition of one's relationships, the crystallization in various domains of a sense of who one is, what one stands for, and how one relates to the world, is the critical task of the developing adolescent.

Erikson's theory of ego identity formation focuses on the concepts of ego-identity, the identity stage, and the identity crisis. He defines identity as "the capacity to see oneself as having continuity and sameness and to act accordingly. It is the consistent organization of experience." As Côté and Levine (1987, p. 275) point out, there are two dominant characteristics defining the concept of ego identity: (1) the sense of temporal-spatial continuity of the ego, a requisite indicator of ego identity (Erikson, 1964, pp. 95–96), and (2) the self-concepts (the configuration of negative identity elements) that unify individuals' experiences of themselves during interaction with the social world. "The development and maintenance of the sense of ego identity is dependent upon the quality of recognition and support the ego receives from its social environment" (Côté & Levine, 1987, p. 275). In contrast, those who have challenged psychosocial notions of identity have suggested that we should think of defining identity in terms of the individual's connections/relationships in the world and see the individual as embedded in the social context rather than outside of it.

The concept of the identity stage introduces us to the notion of ego identity formation and the process by which identity is transformed throughout the life cycle. Erikson held to the epigenetic principle of development in which "anything that grows has a ground plan, and that out of this ground plan the parts arise, each part having its time of special ascendancy, until all parts have risen to form a functional whole" (Erikson, 1968, p. 92). The stages are not merely passed through but instead add cumulatively to the whole personality; Erikson saw the quest for identity and the crises that it often produces as the defining characteristics of adolescence. His psychosocial stage theory is founded on the belief that life is composed of a series of conflicts that must be partially resolved before the developing individual can move to the next one. He proposes eight general stages of conflict: trust vs. mistrust, autonomy vs. shame, initiative vs. guilt, industry vs. inferiority, identity vs. identity confusion, intimacy vs. isolation, generativity vs. stagnation, and integrity vs. despair (Erikson, 1968). Following psychoanalytic theory, these stages appear in sequential order but are never completely resolved. The formation of ego identity does not then take place only in the identity stage; the degree to which one satisfactorily resolves the identity crisis is heavily dependent on the resolutions to the challenges of the first four stages in Erikson's eight-stage life cycle theory. Each item exists "in some form," Erikson tells us, before its decisive and critical time normally arrives (Erikson, 1968; pp. 93, 95). That is, there are identity elements in all preceding stages (just as there are in the succeeding stages), and if the conflicts in these earlier stages are concluded satisfactorily, the healthy development of the ego is more probable; if the conflicts are resolved unsatisfactorily, negative qualities are crystallized in the personality structure and may impede further development.

The psychosocial moratorium—a time of deferred choice—is the period in an adolescent or young adult's life for resolving the identity crisis. It is a time when role experimentation is encouraged and where there is little expectation that the individual will commit to permanent responsibilities or roles. The identity crisis "is precipitated both by the individual's readiness and by society's pressure" (Erikson, 1980, p. 130). The age at which the identity crisis occurs may vary "according to such social structure factors as class, subculture, ethnic background, and gender" (Côté & Levine, 1987) or socialization factors such as child-rearing practices and identification with parents (Jordan, 1971). The moratorium must end, with the experience of role experimentation complete and the achievement of a resynthesis of positive identifications that enable the individual to find "a niche in some section of society, a niche which is firmly defined yet seems to be uniquely made for him" (Erikson, 1968, p. 156). This niche is dependent on the adolescent's feeling that commitment in the areas of values, vocation, religious beliefs, political ideology, sex, gender role, and family lifestyle are accepted, settled, and expressions of personal choice. Other more critical theorists, Jackson, McCullough, & Gurin (1981) for example, have suggested that the option of having a moratorium and being in a position to choose in the area of commitment are limited by social, political, and economic structures and dominant ideologies.

Allied with Erikson's faith in ego identity is his understanding of the difficulty with which adolescents must create and maintain this identity. Identity confusion, and the resulting identity crisis, result from the individual's inability to understand the "mutual fit of himself and the environment—that is, of his capacity to relate to an ever-expanding life space of people and institutions on the one hand, and, on the other, the readiness of these people and institutions to make him a part of an ongoing cultural concern" (Erikson, 1975, p. 102). Feeling pressured by society and his or her own maturation to choose between possible roles even as personal perspectives are rapidly changing, the identity-confused adolescent experiences a confusion that challenges his or her ability to form a stable identity.

Erikson believes that the success with which the adolescent resolves these crises is extremely important for the eventual achievement of intimacy with others. It is only through the commitment to sexual direction, vocational direction and a system of values that "intimacy of sexual and affectionate love, deep friendship and personal abandon without fear of loss of ego-identity can take place" (Muuss, 1988, p. 63). Identity achievement, as opposed to identity confusion, allows the individual to move smoothly from preoccupation with the inner core of identity to exploration of the potential roles this self will play in intimate relations with others.

Erikson's construct of identity versus identity confusion has been expanded by James Marcia (1966, 1980). Marcia, whose work on ego and identity development began with his dissertation "Determination and Construct Validity of Ego Identity Status" (1966), establishes two concepts already mentioned by Erikson—crisis and commitment—as the determining variables in identity achievement. "Crisis refers to times during adolescence when the individual seems to be actively involved in choosing among alternative occupations and beliefs. Commitment refers to the degree of personal investment the individual expresses in an occupation or belief" (Marcia, 1967, p. 119). Using these variables as the determining standards, Marcia breaks Erikson's fifth stage down into four sub-stages: identity diffusion, identity foreclosure, moratorium, and identity achievement.

The identity-diffused individual is characterized by having neither an active involvement in the search for identity roles nor a commitment to any of these roles. He or she is not questioning alternatives. At this point, the adolescent is like James Joyce's Stephen Daedalus, "drifting amid life like the barren shell of the moon." Identity foreclosure is characterized by commitment without crisis; that is, the individual has chosen a set of values or ideological stance, most often that of his or her parents or valued others, without examining these values or searching out alternatives. In moratorium, on the other hand, the individual is in the midst of the crisis, actively questioning and searching among alternatives, without any commitment to one option. He or she is exploring possible alternatives, but temporarily unable to commit to one or the other. In achievement, the individual has experienced the crises of moratorium, and has successfully made a commitment. Identity achievement is most often attained in the college years, with moratorium and diffusion characteristic of earlier adolescence (Santrock, 1990). It should be pointed out that differences exist between societies and between groups and individuals within societies in the length of the sanctioned intermediary periods, the psychosocial moratorium (Manaster, 1989). Also, those not afforded the time or opportunity to engage in identity seeking may well not undergo an identity crisis in adolescence or young adulthood.

Adolescent identity formation also varies, as has been suggested by Signithia Fordham (1988) and Janie Ward (1989), in accordance with the ethnic background of the individual. In her examination of black identity formation, Fordham considers the phenomenon of "racelessness." She explores the relationship between group (black) identity and academic success, and concludes that there are one of two paths followed by black adolescents. Some respect an "individualistic ethos," disregarding their mandatory membership in the black group—a path which may lead to academic success. Others consider this to be "selling out" and espouse the "collectivistic ethos" of their minority group in order to avoid becoming "nonblack," although they may sacrifice academic success in the process. Ward (1989) examines identity formation in academically successful black female adolescents and discovers that racial identity formation is compatible with academic accomplishment. Considering not only the factors of beliefs, values, attitudes, and patterns of family socialization, but also "the girls' own subjective understanding of the role that race plays in their lives" (Ward, p. 217), she concludes that racial identity must be considered in order to gain a complete understanding of identity formation.

Other theorists, among them Miller (1976) and Surrey (1984), have suggested that theories of identity development have been theories of separation and autonomy rather than connection and relationship. They believe that whereas adolescent boys seem concerned with separation and individuation, adolescent girls create identity more in connection to peers and members of their families. Carol Gilligan (1982) writes of her reservations about Erikson's theory in *In a Different Voice*. Gilligan points out that Erikson recognized sex differences in identity development and discussed how for men identity precedes intimacy and generativity in the optimal cycle of human separation and attachment, but for women these tasks instead seem to be fused (the woman comes to know herself through relationships with others). Erikson, nevertheless, retained the sequence of identity preceding intimacy. The sequencing of Erikson's second, third, fourth and fifth stages, Gilligan suggests, little prepares the individual for the intimacy of the first adult stage. "Development itself comes to be identified with separation, and attachments appear to be developmental impediments, as is repeatedly the case in the assessment of women" (Gilligan, 1982, pp. 12–13).

An alternative perspective on the process of identity development in adolescence, then, focuses on the examination of the individual in context. Development is thus seen as a process of renegotiating relationships, redefining oneself in relation to individuals and social groups (family, ethnic group, class, gender) of which one is a part. Along these lines, the reader may follow Carol Gilligan's approach to examining "Courting Danger" (Case No. 1) and focus on how the writer represents his or her *self* in the larger narrative, how the *self* is seen in relationships, and what words, themes, and images are repeated. Such an approach acknowledges that the narrator is speaking, constructing a meaningful account of his or her life.

In the nine cases that make up the Identity section of this book, we include, in addition to the sexual and gender aspects of identity development, cases that address three other aspects of identity development — work, values and ideology, and ethnicity. Any one writer may well focus on a particular area of identity formation. We encourage the reader to examine these autobiographies through a consideration of the following questions. What roles do issues of trust, autonomy, initiative, competence, and identity play in each person's case? Within what contexts does the author define himself or herself? What relationships and connections contribute to his or her sense of self, and how are they changing? Advisable, too, is an exploration of identity status—the evidence of crisis and/or commitment—in relation to each case, an approach similar to that followed by Ruthellen Josselson (1987) in *Finding Herself: Pathways to Identity Development in Women*.

Whatever theoretical perspective one adopts, and we suggest an eclectic approach, the essential components are a simultaneous discovery and creation of self leading to a deepening self-understanding. We believe the cases in this section capture that process in both tone and substance. In each case there is a greater sense of understanding and acceptance of oneself at the end than at the beginning. Each author makes clear that the process continues, but they seem here to have reached at last a plateau from which they can look back and survey their progress. Readers may do well to suspend somewhat their theoretical assumptions while reading a case, lest they miss the sheer spectacle of lives unfolding. Though different identity theorists provide a useful framework for interpretation of these cases, the best of them are but a scaffolding for understanding. We should try to listen first to each author in his or her own terms, to see the authors' evolution through their own eyes. In the unique and intimate details of their individual lives we can discern the outline of a universal struggle to identify our true selves. Your readings here should influence your understanding of theory at least as much as theory influences your reading.

CASE 1

Courting Danger

A 19-year-old English woman describes her coming of age in the context of a private British girls' school. She enters puberty as a vulnerable and uncertain young woman, torn between compliance with her family's standards of propriety and her own need to crash through what she perceives as the stagnation and regimentation of her life. She finds a haven in an art class where her teacher demands that students break the rules and go beyond conventionality into creativity. This adult validation of her unspoken belief that she is emotionally suffocating gives her the courage to trust her own intellectual, emotional, and physical instincts. She begins to see her needs as having at least as much validity as her parents' expectations of her. The world of intense peer friendships begins to open to her and with it comes a sense that she is attractive and capable in her own right and can make her way in the world on her own terms.

I still have not fully resolved why, at the age of 13, I stood in the corner of a chilly classroom and calmly took off all my clothes in front of twenty or so of my peers. It was a cold, crisp day and I remember watching goose pimples form on my very ordinary legs. There was absolute silence in the room as I carefully undid the buttons and stepped free from our horrible green uniform. The school sweater and skirt lay crumpled round me and my little white panties circled my feet. I felt a strange lack of emotion or horror at what I had done: my eyes stared blankly back at the girls' uncomprehending eyes and I stood straight and certain. I was very white, very cold, very vulnerable, but very unemotional. Puberty had barely hit me: my breasts were still small and unformed and any waist, as yet, unidentifiable. There was nothing special about my body — I certainly had nothing either to show off or to hide.

I was not aware of doing this for anyone in particular: the girls present in the room were acquaintances rather than friends or enemies, and none knew me that well. The seconds passed slowly; I wanted to ensure that everyone had the opportunity to recognize what I had done. Was it merely the first raw shock of adolescence causing me to act in such an "odd" way?

Was this simply a new awareness of the body and an expression of awakening sexuality? What was I trying to say and why did I have to resort to such lengths to make my point? I heard the delayed reactions—"Melanie, *what* are you doing?" and "Hey, Emma, come and see this, will you?"—and felt as if I wasn't there at all. I was completely isolated from my body—my pale limbs really had nothing whatsoever to do with me. I have no recollection of dressing again: all I have is that frozen moment when I see myself from an outsider's point of view. I see the goose pimples on my legs as if I were another person looking at this "freak" from substantial distance. In the weeks to come, my mind would be filled again and again with images of that small figure standing alone in the shadowy corner.

As I started writing this paper, I had no real idea of where it would lead or what, if anything, would be the cohesive factor pulling my adolescence together. Of course the stripping incident had an impact on me—for one, I had never before done anything "unacceptable" in the eyes of society. However, how would all the other ensuing things that mattered to me fit in with that one isolated happening? Many hours of contemplation have led me to believe that stripping was perhaps a first cry to establish who I was—to find some kind of wholeness in my muddled mind. It was a bold statement in order to dare myself, and others, to think about me in a new, and in many aspects, scary way. Although I never did anything quite as "dramatic" again, I see many of the other things that I subsequently describe as further attempts to clarify who I truly was. Things have been painful and often incomprehensible; I have faced an eternal struggle between solidifying my own individuality and maintaining connections with others important to me. As I stood shivering and exposed in that classroom, I still remember realizing that this was the first time that I had been truly "alone"—there was something intangible separating me from "the rest."

A few other crazy things also happened that year. Surrounded by several friends, I stripped down to the waist on the exposed playing fields (faint half-broken voices echoed in the background from the neighboring boys' school) and returned to math without my underwear on. I did cartwheels between the desks in history lessons when the teacher's head was turned, almost longing for her to catch me and punish me. I threw my shoes out of third floor windows in the midst of physics lessons and watched them tumble into the out of bounds quad where no girl was allowed to trespass. I leaned over the banisters on the top floor of the school until I was nearly vertical with my head below my feet pointing skyward. That entailed going right to the brink of my physical capabilities and I trembled at the fact that one slight loss of concentration would result in paralysis or death. I was courting danger, but there was something else going on too—falling from those banisters was the only way I could imagine of doing something truly irreversible, permanent, strangely beautiful, and perfect. No one would be able to brush that off lightly or complain that I could have done it better. It was an absurd thought, but it appealed to the part of me that was wanting some kind of permanence and perfection. There was little, if any, *acceptable* logic behind these acts: I never thought of the reaction my peers would give and never planned my actions in advance. I just knew that I was never caught or upbraided, and that each time I tried a new escapade, I was in part attempting to have my sense of justice restored: why was I never punished when others so frequently were?

My friendships were, at least superficially, unaltered by my "demonstrations," and there was no noticeable stultification or intensification in my relationships with the rest of my peer group. They certainly regarded me as "weird" and unusual, but, fortunately, I had just enough "normal" endearing qualities to allow me to stay within the realms of their conforming cliques.

Thus began my adolescence in a flurry of self-exposure. I have always been a very shy and vulnerable person, and it has therefore taken me some time to understand why I did things so blatantly *obvious*. I pondered earlier that stripping was maybe the first glimmer of a search for identity. But why did I have such a need to make myself noticed and distinctive when, at the same time, I shied away from drawing any degree of attention towards myself? To begin to answer this question, I shall have to explore my intense feelings of self-doubt and low self-esteem.

Ever since I can remember, I have felt a fraud. I usually surpassed my schools' and my parents' expectations and failed to achieve my own. Often things have been easy academically, but from age 7 onwards teachers have said, "You must be prepared—in your *next* school, things won't be like this. You'll suddenly find yourself a small fish in a very big pond." The problem is that whenever I moved into another academic environment, I was *still* considered a success—still a "big fish." I always fear that the next time will be the one—the next time I move on I'll be exposed for who I really am. Suddenly all these grand perceptions of me will be crushed. When in a new setting, I am often convinced that everyone else is more socially and intellectually capable than I. The more "successful" I become, the more inadequate I feel: *why* can people not see my limitations when I find it so easy to fault myself and not live up to my own expectations? Although my drive for perfection means I often fail in my own eyes, to others, I have *never, ever* failed. That is absolutely terrifying; I feel I have come so far now that if I do stumble in front of others, it won't merely be a fall, it will be tumbling right over a precipice. Paradoxically, although I don't really value external praise for my success, I still yearn to be reassured and affirmed; I need to be told I am achieving even though I can never fully hear it. And paradoxically also, my perfectionism is complemented by an awful self-sabotaging urge: one part of me seems determined to teach me how to fail in front of others. How can I relate my arrogant perfectionism — which is unable to accept my mediocrity — to my severe lack of self-confidence and feelings of inadequacy?

Sadly, the conscious and logical mind often cannot explain my thoughts. Much of my fear of being a fraud is, I know, irrational, yet I still find it painfully difficult to acknowledge that *really* I am okay. Underneath all this self-doubt, there is something worth valuing. The world of green uniforms was a private girls' school where my scholastic achievements were particularly highlighted (we were valued for what we could *do* rather than who we could *be*). I was the model "do-er," and how I hated it. Thus all my shoe-throwing, clothes-stripping, cartwheel-turning were, in part, attempts at throwing off the role that had been cast in marble for me — that of the good, obedient, successful student. For far from giving me a feeling of pride, achievement, and worth, my role as a "good girl" was making me feel more and more isolated, empty, and disoriented. They were measuring my worth totally on a scale of tangible success. This had two major implications in my eyes: (1) any part of me that couldn't be measured on that scale — that is, who I was as a *person* — was inconsequential and worthless, and (2) since I had no true belief in my own intellectual and creative talents, I was certain that I was the largest con artist ever. I became increasingly shocked that I did well in exams; I rationalized it by saying that exams were simply a "knack" that I was fortunate enough to possess.

My ability to analyze myself and spot my fallibilities fits in very well with the general ambience of my family and house where intellect and reasoning is very much admired and where action fades into the background. My family has always been stable and permanent in my life. My relationship with my sister Sarah (two years younger) is particularly untroubled. I have always been very fond of, and protective towards, her; she is a very imaginative and almost unworldly girl who seems to exist for much of the day on another planet. Her naïveté and innocence occasionally irritates me, but usually I am amazed and impressed that she has reached midadolescence so pure, old-fashioned, and untainted by the grubbiness of the world. She very much looks up to me and is ever so proud of me. She is incredibly shy in front of other people; I worry about her low self-esteem (it runs in the family, I think to myself, wryly) and the fact that it is very difficult for her to live up to what she perceives as my enormous successes. Her own very special talents and strengths are unfortunately not as obvious as my damned ability to pass exams with flying colors. It makes me furious to think that my success damages not only me (in a topsy-turvy way) but poor Sarah as well.

Both my parents completed higher education and it was a matter of course that I would do the same. My father is very proud of my academic successes and both my parents nourish and encourage "intelligence." Thus our house is very nurturing to all cerebral functioning. However, because all four of us are shy—we all find listening so much easier than asserting ourselves—I have always believed my affective and social development to be rather stymied at home.

My father especially has a fear of emotions and instability, and he copes by being the most centered and unflappable person I know. Life for him is divided into organized, categorized sections. People, time schedules, objects, relationships, and events all have a defined place in his hierarchical scheme. His constant companion is a big scribbling diary incorporating every aspect of his life. Birthdays, for example are slotted in with an "A" alongside—"A" stands for annual event; "wash sox" has a "3W" (for three times a week), and emptying the vacuum cleaner has an "M" for monthly. Everything is crossed off once it has been recognized (Christmas Day is lined through early on in the morning—thank goodness that doesn't need to be thought of for the rest of the day). He was "green" decades before the concept of "greenness" had even filtrated our society; wrapping paper has always been ironed and the scotch-tape removed by steam so that it can be used again; baths are always two inches deep to conserve water. I see him now, bending over the pine kitchen table and wielding a paper knife and the tissue paper in which wine is wrapped. He folds the paper and carefully cuts it up into six-inch squares that can then be used for toilet paper. My mother always has to rush around the house before our (infrequent) visitors arrive to remove tell-tale signs of "eccentricity." Our attic is filled with eighty or so identical, numbered boxes which contain all that we don't need on a day-to-day basis. When we need to put up the Christmas decorations, I simply look on his handmade index under C for Christmas, notice subsection 1 (decorations as distinct from wrapping paper) and know that all I require is in box 53.

For years it was wonderful for me to be able to believe that life was simply a question of putting numbers on boxes and letters in diaries: it was very reassuring to see a means of control. Although I have never been physically tidy, perhaps some of my mental perfectionism was derived from observing my father's amazing exactitude. He has managed, somehow, to exist throughout his life in this manner, but I gradually became aware of many uncategorizable things. I couldn't just compartmentalize people or feelings—that would be denying their very interconnectedness with other people/feelings—and thus I had to reject my father's philosophy. Nevertheless, I still had to live in a house where emotions were kept very much under control and social interaction was treated as nonessential. I believe my father could exist perfectly well by communicating with no one but the rest of his family. People really are a terrible burden to him, probably because they are unpredictable and tend to resist simplistic categorizing. He gets on very well with strangers when he has to, but can go months without getting in touch with any of the few friends he wishes to keep. He is a very private, mysterious man, and I wish I understood better his way of thinking. He adores my mother and is very fond of both my sister and me but could not recognize that I needed to be meeting new people, talking with my peers about new things, going to parties, and doing all the other 'foolish' things that adolescents so desire to do. I think that because I was so successful in the things that were of paramount importance to him (academic work, musical achievement, being a "nice and polite" daughter), he assumed that my social skills were just as advanced.

He regarded nights out with my friends as a waste of time and would usually say no in answer to my supplications. I think his objections to my socializing also implied a real concern with protecting me from the irrational, dangerous world. I found it poignant when he gave as a reason for his negative reaction, "Your mother would be worried out of her mind if you just waltzed off into the night"; of course my mother would be anxious, but the truth was it would be *he* who would be more frantic. As I grew older, I often did not even bother to disturb the family's harmony and ask to go out when I knew they would not approve of the occasion; I thereby forfeited many evenings with my friends to which I felt entitled. I think this issue became somewhat enlarged in my mind: I was convinced both that my father wanted to keep me under lock and key, and that he would never listen to me. In reality, I often didn't even voice my needs to give him a chance to hear me.

In connection with this, I was becoming more and more concerned about my ability to relate and communicate with others—particularly those of the opposite sex. I have always been scared of "maleness." I choose that word carefully; I am not afraid of men as individuals, but I am certainly uneasy about the whole concept of masculinity. I find it difficult to pin down this fear, but I suppose it must be at least tenuously connected to many things: my fear of my father's categorizing, the fact that I never had brothers and their friends round the house, my eleven years in an all-girls' school, my father's lack of social interaction with anyone but his family, and my belief, between the ages of 14 and 17, that I was profoundly repellent and that no man would ever look twice at me as a possible friend, or—God forbid—girlfriend. It was a short step from my shameless undressing in the classroom to a state of shameful embarrassment about my physical presence.

Trapped in a world of school girls where physical beauty was the prime standard by which to judge and compare peers and where the most complimentary adjectives were *fashionable, trendy*, and *slim*, I longed to exist in some dark cupboard where my vulnerability would be invisible. The ultimate aim was to be "trappable"—worth trapping by a member of the boys' school over the wall. (It has always amused me that the school proudly regards itself as very feminist when we as pupils held such conventional and degrading notions of the function of females as simply an object of desire and adjunct to males). I suffered acutely because I knew that I didn't quite live up to the cliques' standards of fashionable, trendy, and slim. I have vivid recollections of nearly our entire class of thirty-two sitting in lines during lunch breaks comparing the various merits of our shapely and shapeless legs. There were two marks out of ten: one for length and another for "general impression/shape." I, too weak to protest at such behavior, was an unwilling participant. I remember being relieved, and also disappointed, that I was classed as a "double five"; thank goodness I was within the realms of leg normality, but, yet again, I wasn't going to make it into trappable class.

I wasn't really that concerned with my legs: there were, for me, far more worrisome things to think about. I hated my hair, detested my glasses, and was ashamed of the braces on my teeth. For several months, much of my energy was devoted to feelings of physical inadequacy. I defined myself by how others would regard me — and since I was sure that to others I was ugly, awkward, and gawky, I didn't end up with a very strong self-image. Those were days of torment and despair, of hours in front of the mirror trying on every conceivable combination of clothes to make me look the least objectionable. I would curse the inane values against which I was powerless to resist: I knew most of the standards set amongst my peers were insubstantial and trivial, but I was caught up in them all the same — I wanted, and needed, to belong. My early flouting of their rules of normality by undressing in front of them had given way to a desire simply to fit in.

I was desperately trying to define my own identity but was failing so miserably that I turned to others to help me unify my sense of self. My time of conformity was dark indeed, since I had no real core to my being and all was fragmented and amorphous. In addition, I was suffering from bouts of incapacitating depression — day after day of black woodenness and despair. I was sure that if someone were to open me up they would find absolutely nothing there — if such things as souls existed, I wouldn't have one. I would wake in the morning with nothing but a dull headache filling my entire being, and often I would cross off the hours left before I could get into bed again and escape into the oblivion of unconsciousness. I would long with all my feeble heart to sleep for six months so that I wouldn't have to face any of the awful and draining responsibilities that I saw my life entailed. Depressions were deepened by awful feelings of guilt and remorse: What right had I to be feeling this way? I was physically healthy, had a loving family, did very well at school, was treated by all as someone with abundant reasons for having high self-esteem and self-worth. It was plain contrary of me to feel I had a right to suffer. The very fact that I didn't think I had a right to my depressions made them seem all the more immovable and permanent. I remember gazing from a top story window at school (only yards away from those treasured banisters where I had hung so precariously two or three years earlier) and imagining what would happen if I threw myself from it. I saw my body banging heavily through the air and landing on the lawn below. What glorious peace and permanence that would bring—no more mundanities of everyday existence and no more people making me feel so scattered and disjointed.

I would cry monotonously and regularly, both at home and school. My sobs would be silent to the world but huge and deafening to myself. All I could see were the long days stretching effortlessly and emptily to the end of time. How could I possibly fill them, and what good could I do anyway? My family of course sensed that I was not at my happiest, and made a special effort to be understanding, warm, and trusting. However, I was so good at constructing a façade—a semblance—of okayness for the outside world that soon they too began to believe that everything was just fine and treated me accordingly. As I became increasingly competent at maintaining this veneer of togetherness my internal screams shrieked louder and louder, and I felt I must surely be smothered by this dual existence.

But it would be wrong and misleading to pretend that my adolescence was simply month after month of despair, separateness, confusion, and fragmentation. Now I regard all that blackness as a positive force in my development—I *was* thinking, questioning, and acknowledging that everything wasn't all just "fine, fine, fine." I was being torn and stretched, twisted and distorted—but this was a molding into something new and fresh. Indeed I experienced moments of great lucidity and joy between those weeks of deadness. For a few fleeting seconds, existence would seem purposeful and comprehensible. Often it would be merely the tilting of a head, a certain shadow on the sidewalk, a few piano notes caught in the stillness—suddenly I would sense an acute beauty in life that would be almost too expansive to hold inside me. I would struggle to hold onto that sensation for I knew that I was filled with something precious and valuable; my sense of self then was strong and constant.

The depressions began to wane with my first glimmerings of meanings in the world; this coincided both with my achievement of a satisfactory physical identity and with my escape from the acceptance of others' definitions of me. Actually, my transition from—what I considered—a dowdy, gauche 16-year old to a presentable, even perhaps attractive woman, was the one fairy-tale-like thing that has happened in my life. In the space of one short evening I threw off the shackles of physical insecurity that I had been carrying with me for so long.

Everyone had been talking about the school ball weeks in advance, a joint occasion with the boys' school. All of a sudden I was filled with a crazy and wild desire to make an impact at this silly occasion. I was sick to the back teeth of losing at games where others had made the rules; if I couldn't make my own rules, then at least I'd beat them at their own game. If the aim was still to be eminently trappable, then I would do all I could to be as ravishing as possible. I think my intense desire to succeed made things fall into place—how otherwise could it have chanced that I was to have my braces taken off, contact lenses fitted and my hair cut all the weekend before that damned dance?! I riffled gleefully through all the dresses hanging in the shops the Saturday before and chose the brightest I could find. The "in" color that winter was black, and so I chose crimson. I still remember the sensation when I pulled the red satin over my head and felt its smooth coldness over my flushed skin.

That night my faith in the world and myself was unshakable. I stood before the mirror with my glasses gone, my hair sleek and sophisticated, teeth proud and white, and that wonderful dress hugging me close in all its glory. Somehow, without my acknowledging it, I had become someone reasonably all right to look at after all. I stood there for several minutes: gradually it dawned upon me that that strange figure in the shadows was a woman, and that woman was me. There was no longer any need to separate my psychological and physical selves: I hugged myself, reveling in that wholeness. That was the real moment of Epiphany: the rest of the evening was perfect but predictable. Everyone was amazed at the "transformation"; by the end of the evening I was satiated with declarations of approval. I danced and danced and smiled and wept. At long last I had no cause or need to feel inferior: conversely I had no desire to live up to some ideal of perfection. I was *there:* concretely and earthily there. I actually *felt* my feet aching and I laughed in the knowledge that for once I wasn't "floating all over the ceiling" (as I so often tend to do when I feel ungrounded and unsure) and that I had overcome the enormous hurdle of denying my own physicality in a matter of hours.

To this day I have not had a close or intimate relationship—platonic or sexual—with a man. Despite my acceptance of the interdependence of my physical, emotional, and intellectual self and my newly found physical self-confidence, I still feel unprepared and nervous about tackling a close relationship with a male. Remnants of my own fear as a sexual being remain, and as time goes on, I feel relatively less and less experienced in comparison with others. That is not to say that I do not have strong sexual drives or fantasies; even now I occasionally wonder (1) does everyone else think about sex as much as I do? and (2) are other women just as obsessed with the muscles in a man's legs and bum when he walks? Even after one brief introductory meeting I have a distinct and vivid memory of the exact shape of a man's lower body. Faces may fade; legs do not.

Anyway, I have not yet found anyone with whom I feel I can develop a strong feeling of trust. My vulnerability still makes me terribly wary of revealing parts of my psychological or physical self. I kiss and pet as required, but I am never fully at ease—I can never lose myself in the experience alone and never shrug off the question, "Is this right; am I doing OK; is this what's supposed to happen; is this what I'm required to do?" I feel the hands on my back and glimpse my slip rising up by thighs and think "Is this actually me here — are these my hands, my lips, *myself?*" I search for some ideal notion of that overused word "fulfillment" and all that seems to happen is a taste of soggy mouths and sweaty skin.

Occasionally I wish for a constant boyfriend. People cannot understand why I don't "go out" with someone; many of my friends go from one long-term relationship to the next almost without pause. But I still have to find someone with whom I want to make some kind of commitment. I cannot see the point of dating just for the sake of it; I cannot afford to expend a lot of energy on a relationship I don't care about. I have no wish to give a lot of myself to someone I don't truly respect. Thus most of the time I am happy with my decision not to fall into a relationship to be like my peers; I like being free and I am thankful not to be called so-and-so's "bit." I used to believe that vulnerability was the only thing holding me back. "If only I weren't so shy," "If only I didn't worry so much about being wounded." Now, however, I have come to cherish it as one of my inherent strengths. I believe vulnerability has made me all the more sensitive to the vagaries of both myself and others, and I feel that it has helped me to be more self-questioning and willing to take risks. Life for me has never been solid or secure, and so I am all the more aware of what a "risk" is, and how exposed I am to change and new circumstances.

When, at the age of 14, I suddenly found myself immersed in art, its teacher, and the fellow students, I found it incredibly exciting to explore a new part of myself. Art wasn't something I could automatically do and it was wonderfully refreshing to grapple with something that couldn't be classed as "right" or "wrong." In addition, no one had preconceptions of my ability, and I had no one to live up to but myself. However, at the beginning it was not art *per se* that thrilled me; it was the art teacher, Ms. Madeleine Tremayne, in all her strange, beautiful mystery.

To me Madeleine is quite unforgettable. I don't quite know where to start—she is still such an important element of my life that I find it difficult to see her objectively, and I feel a strong obligation to portray her as well as she deserves to be presented. Every moment she is *alive*—questioning us, herself, events, imaginings—and I think it is this constant searching for some kind of ultimate truth of faith that makes her so exciting. It is almost possible to feel the zone of her impact and influence; to my unformed mind this "magnetic field" was fascinating and mesmerizing. She drew people towards her—they would come with love and hate but never with indifference.

I would be painting and slowly my paintbrush would droop and my wrists go limp. I would turn and look — trying to identify what on earth made this woman special. Her uniqueness definitely had something to do with her physical presence and aura — there was a steeliness *and* a softness about her — but I think ultimately her great strength was both her integrity and her sense of risk-taking inherent in her teaching style. Every day she would come in with some new theory about "life's rules" — mingling Buddhist meditation with astrology, reincarnation with existentialism. She did not talk for her own benefit — I am sure she was trying to get us to think about life and art in different and often unconventional ways. Her own life was hardly rosy even now (I remember her saying, "Life's no less shitty to you even when you have got bits of it worked out"). She would ask for our advice and cherish our support when life was being a "real bugger." We would sit enraptured by this woman who actually considered *us* worthy enough both to share her life experiences and to nurture her in crisis. She would also listen limitlessly to our own tales of conflict and confusion and seemed to posses infinite quantities of compassion, empathy, and suggestions. She forced us to look at what we were creating for ourselves, and pushed us into a new state of awareness and responsibility for our actions.

"It's no good thinking that it's always the other person's fault when things go wrong for you, Melanie," she would say, skewering me onto the wall with the intensity of her gaze (escape or evasion was never possible). "You're always going to be part of the equation when other people are involved, and so you have to work out what you're doing to cause this response." I would look at her feeling peeled and exposed. How did she always know exactly what was happening for us?

"You're still being a victim of your fate instead of an instigator. You *do* have the means to control rather than to be manipulated. In the meantime, instead of faffing around and 'floating around on the ceiling,' put some of this anguish into your picture and give yourself twenty minutes to get emotion into those contorted figures. You see, that's what art is — a means of showing *yourself,* a vessel in which to pour your soul. If you have nothing to show, then all we get is a cluster of meaningless, empty lines. And if I were you, I would go home tonight and meditate for half an hour — you clearly haven't been doing that, have you? Your aura's all over the place." (I would admit that I hadn't been meditating: it was impossible to lie to her.) "And ask yourself why your parents aren't hearing you. The blame's not necessarily entirely theirs. Are you really speaking to them, or are you simply talking in a half-hearted way? By the way, I've just noticed: that tiny bit of blue in the center is really singing; you're beginning to understand the pictorial tension. Maybe something is moving inside you after all."

Madeleine was the one member of staff who acknowledged passion, insecurity, and sexuality — both in herself and in her pupils. She recognized our adolescent turmoils as healthy, joined in with our wildness, rejoiced at our unpredictable inflammability, and treated us as sexual beings. Other teachers denied us the right to be disruptive, sexual, and confused; she loved us for what and who we were and knew that all our "madness" could be harnessed to improve our art. She would stride into the room saying, "Come on. Figure drawing — we're really going to get the hang of internal form today. I want you to see the model as monumental." We looked at the 11-year old posing in front of us in her green school uniform, her legs skinny and her breasts flat. Monumental was not the word that would have automatically jumped to mind.

"Her legs must be solid — they've got to be big enough to support her. Imagine her as a baronial hall: overwhelming the paper, spilling over. You must be like a little ant crawling around her. If you get this going, you're going to be creating masterpieces — I'm telling you, the experience of drawing magnificently is way, way better than sex. I'm completely serious — so let that be an incentive to you!"

My instinct believed that in the chaotic art room my battered soul could be rebuilt, and that here what I had to give would be valued. For those brief months during my last two years, Ms. Tremayne and the other three members of the art class provided in abundance all the love, frustration, inspiration, and despair that I needed. For good or bad, everyone else — parents, other friends — faded into the background. Although I had always managed to be fairly popular with my peers (even without reaching the upper echelons of "cliquedom"), I had never before felt a real sense of belonging or connecting. It was with joy that I heard Madeleine talking of:

"Our raft. Our raft's sinking. We've got to support each other. We're all in the middle of this bloody great ocean and the only way we can keep above water is to paddle like mad *together*. It's no good you all standing in your separate corners beavering away at the old still life." All four of us turned, looked at each other guiltily, and dragged the easels closer together.

"The great thing about learning art together is that you pull everyone else along. We create a pool of energy and everyone draws from it. No more of this trying desperately to be better than everyone else. If you're doing awfully, just be grateful that Sophie over here is making up for you."

Art became the focus and the purpose of our passions — a means of catharsis and purging and an outlet for all my emotional and sexual frustration. At home suppers were still pedagogical affairs, but at least now filled with a sense of excitement; my family could recognize that something was happening to me even if they did not fully approve. They realized that I was living in another world, but still struggled to make me hold onto the image of a loving, considerate daughter. After one particularly lengthy argument between my father and me, he said quietly, "Oh, don't be silly, Melanie — just try and be more demure. That's what you should be aiming for —

everyone values demureness and femininity." At that moment I was at last able to conceptualize and clarify one of the primary struggles in my development: I was becoming a woman but was fighting tooth and claw against that image of "womanly goodness and obedience." I wasn't only trying to throw off my role as "good student": I was aiming to get to the much bigger issue of what it is to be feminine. I hated the vice-like grip of the word *demure.* Why had I stripped naked, why had I hated those "marks out of ten for leg shape" discussions so much, why was I unhappy with the power wrapped in the words *fashionable* and *trappable?"* My fight was *against* the whole belief of girls being quiet, predictable, and dainty. Even when I had joined in that game by going to the Ball, it was in a red, angry dress which defied conventional notions of prettiness. I was just learning how to express my darkness and energy through some creative channel, and the last thing I needed to hear was that I should be aiming towards some traditional notion of femininity.

At last I was destroying the semblance of "good girl/good student" and starting to unleash my hidden and suppressed anger. I felt as though I were bringing into the light a half of me which had been hidden and etiolated for years. Occasionally I would stand back, look at my picture, and be amazed that it was the product of my own hand: did I really have that much blackness and badness in me? It was both liberating and terrifying to be able to see art revealing some of my murky depths. Even so, still I felt choked: if the right point were tapped I would be faced not with a slow welling up of emotion but a full-scale avalanche of desires/bitterness/half-formed needs/unresolved fears . . . It's a good job that we learned how to do "anger release."

It was a muggy summer's day — the sort of day when one's pores feel saturated with humidity and nothing much seems to be happening. Madeleine was getting fed up with our slowness to get down on paper "what was really happening for us":

"Is this what you really want to say about yourselves through art? All I can see at the moment is a namby-pamby schoolgirl picture — you're painting the wallpaper and thinking about the next tea break at the same time. Do you really want your pictures to look so flabby? I want to see something "yummy": I want it to look so good that I could eat it. Find the "wow" effect — do anything but make bloody sure that it's strong enough to knock off anything beside it on the wall. Where's the internal form? The heart? The passion? I want to be *convinced.* "

For once, none of us could respond to her exhortations, and so she led us — Jessica, Joanna, Sophie and me — downstairs to the deserted gym. The school was almost empty since it was after four o'clock, but there was a badminton practice going on in the next-door hall. Madeleine was completely fair: each one of us was free to leave at any point and we certainly felt no obligation to do what she was suggesting. As I sit here typing, I can still recall the touch of those faded mats as we unpacked them and piled them a foot high; I still see the dust motes hanging in the gym; I still sense that tension of nervousness and expectancy as we stood round those mats waiting to begin. Madeleine began talking in a slow, calm voice:

"OK, now, I am trained to do this, so you don't need to feel in any way that I am merely experimenting or messing around. I want you all to watch closely and give me energy as I go first. I'm not going to do it fully since none of you would know how to replenish my energy if I let myself go completely."

As usual, my brain understood some of her meanings but not all. What was all this talk of energy and replenishing? What was she actually going to do? I could feel myself beginning to "float on the ceiling" — as I am still wont to do when apprehensive — and I struggled to get both my feet back on the ground. I watched her take off her cardigan and expose her lithe, strong arms and artist's hands. She knelt in front of the heavy pile of mats and locked her arms together by grasping her hands firmly.

"In order to keep me going, I want you all to say insistently something that really pisses me off. I always hate it when people tell me to calm down and so I want you to say just that. 'Calm down!' — again and again. I'm going to shout back 'Shut up.' OK?"

She gave one of her enormous, reassuring smiles to each one of us in turn. Everything sounded perfectly run-of-the-mill and ordinary. I wondered how she was possibly going to get angry in the middle of a school gym at 4:30 on a Monday afternoon with no real provocation. As I pondered, her face changed: there was absolute focus and concentration, and she started to radiate an almost tangible sense of drive and life force. We felt the tension enveloping us, saw the old, overused mats and heard childish voices from the badminton room. Suddenly there was a whisper of the unknown and the irrational. Madeleine raised her arms high in the air and — Jessica walked out. Her face was filled with an awful fear — perhaps a fear of seeing anger, exposing a weakness, overturning some stable notion of the world? We turned and watched her slam the door, and then drew closer together.

Madeleine didn't break concentration even for Jessica. As if wielding an axe, she raised her arms in a great arc and hurled her full body weight onto the mat. In the same motion she let out a huge and gut-felt cry, "Shut up." The two words lost all meaning as they penetrated the lofty hall. Again and again she drew herself up and thundered back down as we began the slow provocations of "Calm down. Calm down." Her body and voice worked rhythmically; she was both brutal and graceful as the energy surged through her and exploded on the mats. For the first few seconds I was paralyzed by shock and fear. I watched the muscles trembling in her strong arms, the hair in her armpits glistening with sweat, the skin stretching over her temples and the blood flowing to her lips. Gone were all vestiges of what society so admires and needs: control, etiquette, niceness, and obedience. The figure before me had stripped all our superficial coverings away and taken us back to our brutal and real nakedness. So this is humanity: this is what we all so desperately try to cover with manners and social graces. This untamed beast in all of us. My fear subsided and I looked with admiration at the power curving through my teacher and snarling in her throat. What on earth would a "full" anger release have done to me?

It was hard not to feel overwhelmed and self-conscious as I knelt down and gazed at the mats before me. Why did I have to be the first one after Madeleine? I tried to empty my mind but I could not shut out the sound of girls screaming in the next hall. What if they look through and see us here? How could this be explained to 12-year olds? I focused on my charcoal-covered jeans and swept the hair out of my eyes. Delaying tactics. I felt an absurd desire to rush out of the room into the sunlight.

"Come on, Melanie," I whispered to myself. "Don't let yourself down; if you get this, think of how much you'll move. Even if you can't do it for any other reason, do it for your picture. Your picture needs it; you need it. Don't think about inhibitions, don't think about what society wants. Come *on*, Melanie." Part of me reeled with the thought of exposing the power within me — acknowledging in public the strength of my dark side. I struggled, finally overcame that fear, lifted my arms, and began. As though from a great distance I heard them shouting — shouting the very phrase my father uses which drives me to distraction. "Don't be silly, don't be silly, don't be silly." I registered Madeleine's voice strong against the rest and shouted back with all the power I could muster, "No!" It wasn't very much of a word, but it was all I could manage. I felt vibrations in my throat and gradually everything — the badminton game, the dusty hall, my friends — became lost, and I was overtaken by wild instinct. I was sucked up into a glorious unity and was expressing that deep and unheard wholeness. As I struck the mats, I had no awareness of my hands growing numb with pain and my voice growing hoarse and incoherent. There was only a sensation of deep and exhilarating release — something was at last pouring from me and I was cleansed and revitalized. I have no idea how long I managed to carry on; slowly the presence of my friends reasserted itself and I collapsed onto the mats, drained and limp. My hands were burning and my throat parched.

I lay there feeling like a newborn babe and recalling the temper tantrums of my childhood years. When had I last been able to express emotions physically? Had I really been keeping so much inside for so long? Madeleine's olive arms extended towards my white ones and swaddled me in a blanket. I curled over onto my side; Madeleine's breath was hot on my back as she drew me near and held me close, one arm pressed onto my lower spine. My ability to hear seemed to have vanished temporarily and her voice sounded thick as she spoke: "That was good, did you feel good? It was wonderful seeing what no one has seen of you for such a long time. Just lie still—stay still. I'm holding you like this to create a big circle of energy so that my energy can flow back into you. I'm going to refill you. This is, in many ways, the most important part: it's essential that you have someone to give back what you just gave out. I'm trying to make myself as open as possible."

I murmured in reply and felt her body strong and warm beside me as I began to expand and re-inflate. I lay quiet and clean amongst the marks made by years of scuffling feet and sweaty toes. The minutes passed and I began to experience a magnificent sense of power and liberation: all the matted junk had been cleared away from my inside and I felt ready to begin again. I saw my big picture—the culmination of our five years of learning with Madeleine—waiting for me. Its primary function was to express, in any way I wished, what really concerned me at that moment in time. Easily six feet long and filled with agonized, contorted horses and humans, it had become nightmarish and abstracted. I was trying to express the enormous conflicts raging inside me, but still couldn't quite get the dynamics working. I had been feeling for the past two weeks as though I were hitting my head over and over against the ceiling.

Ten minutes later (the mats put away and my friends gone home—they were going to do their anger release next week) I swept along the corridor feeling as though I were running on air. I saw exactly what I had to do to make that picture work. It was growing dusky outside and the janitors were beginning to thump around with mops and buckets in the next room. I picked up my pastels and felt entirely alone. The anger release had filled me with such energy that I was sure I could carry on all night if I had to. Taking courage in both hands, I obliterated all the flashy, superfluous marks, rubbed over all the superficial highlighting, erased all parts which were just trying to make me look like an "expert" artist. What would be left? My throat was dry and scratchy and my fingernails filled with the grease of oil pastels. After two hours I stood back, terrified that I had destroyed it all: had I simply gone overboard with this "anger" and killed everything? My eyes skimmed the image; to an outsider the board looked a mass of messy and unintelligible marks. I exhaled noisily: to me the picture, although now stark and unpolished, had jumped forward more in this one night than it had for the past two weeks. A force was moving within it—oh the joy that that brought. So this is what commitment feels like. I rested on my haunches and thought: this is the first time I have really exposed my anger; this is the first time that I have really experienced commitment to anything. As I sat in that gloomy room, art and that picture were the most important things in my life. Take that away and my life would be meaningless.

By deliberately evading mundanities and trivia by condemning them as the antithesis of art, we had entered a dream world where creativity, irrationality, and insubstantiality flourished. It was by no means a stable and realistic existence, but it came at a vital time in my life — all at once no one was forbidding me my rights to feelings of insecurity and inadequacy. I was actually being allowed to ask "What really matters to me?" instead of having to maintain a pretense of okayness. Wow — my art actually improved each time I realized and accepted some previously hidden weakness. The world for me extended not much further than the ends of my finger tips; anything beyond my reach seemed distant and relatively unimportant. I was concerned with how I fitted into life's workings, not how the great impersonal world functioned by itself. I was completely wrapped up in the personal, and set great store on the value and effect of emotion. I began to shun all people — including my father — who appeared to exist without them. Emotion gave my life at that time color and excitement. Experiences were heightened simply because I felt them so keenly; my newly formed relationships were stronger because they were born through feeling. All seemed intense and vital because my spirit was at last being succored whilst my cerebrality and cold intellect were being starved. At last I was a "do-er" no more.

Unleashed from the restrictions and pressures of cliques, I formed my first real friendship with one member of the art group in particular. Jessica is an extremely powerful, exciting, obsessive, and invigorating woman. She was all that I had been aspiring to be: strong in her convictions, sensitive in her vulnerability, creative in her unpredictability, and powerful in her femininity. She was also incredibly unstable, and there would be days when she was beyond us all — uncontrollable, mad, and irrational. Although she was sensitive and vulnerable, she couldn't really get in touch with her feelings so that she could express this insecure and compassionate side: witness her inability to participate in the anger release. I saw these hidden emotions lurking within her and I longed to tap those resources.

I loved her as I wanted to love myself. My deep compassion for her was intense and exclusive; I didn't have much left to give to other people. Jessie, because of her own need for companionship and security, transferred much of her love onto me. We succored and nourished each other with our crazy devotion. I experienced moments of liberation and commitment that I have never since transcended: both of us were managing to get over our great fear about exposing and trusting, and we knew that there was much invested in our "other half." But this progress was made painfully; our friendship developed most rapidly at times of suffering.

One rainy afternoon I picked up the phone and I heard her voice devoid of any panic but with a hardness and a tension which meant she was in one of her mad days. Never, till now, had she been able to come to me during one of her deepest crises (she would simply retreat into herself), and I was therefore exhilarated and terrified.

"Mel, Mel . . . um . . . is there any way you can come over?"

"Right now?" (Thoughts fluttered through my mind; two papers to be in the next day, a major piano concert that coming week, my father's refusal to let me out since I was under "such pressure." I had to go; I just had to.)

"Yes. It's that . . . well . . . it's just me. I don't know . . . what's happened."

I placed the phone on the receiver, having assured Jess that I would be over as soon as I could. I faltered on the threshold of the kitchen where my parents were sitting. What do I say—that my friend needs me, that my papers don't matter? I had to find some strength to center my energy so that I could not fail.

"Um, Mom and Dad . . . well, actually, Jessie's just rung. She's desperate and she's come to me for help. I have to be with her. I know you'll understand—and understand how much Jessie means to me." I looked at them, amazed that I was for once being open. As I looked, I suddenly saw their love for me in their eyes. I *did* know at the moment that they would understand: why had I always been so afraid of enunciating my needs to them before?

An hour later, I was sitting with Jessica in her room. Of course my parents hadn't thought my papers more important than the bonds of a friendship. On the train I had experienced a new self-confidence: I had come to understand my parents better, and we had opened a new line of communication. Even so, as I stepped into the room my confidence evaporated. Jessica was there but not there: she seemed abstracted from life itself. How the hell could I reach out to her? She was sitting on her bed, her face white and unmade-up and her expression fixed. She looked as though she were made of clay; nothing was going to give. Around her, on the paint-stained rugs, lay half-finished self-portraits, sinister abstracts, angry figure drawings. Her full-length mirror had been propped up against a cupboard. Suddenly there were dead and heavy words amidst this chaotic silence.

"Thanks Mel. Thank you." I looked at her, trying to convey by my eyes what my mouth couldn't express. No, that's inaccurate: I didn't even know exactly *what* I was trying to convey. All I wanted was to make some kind of connection with her.

"I was sitting . . . I was sitting in front of my mirror for ages. I wanted to try and get my self-portrait more intense and mysterious."

Was this some kind of explanation? Terrified, I picked my way across the floor and sat down at the end of the bed. There was something almost inhuman about Jess's lack of emotion and the hardness in her voice. Where had she retreated this time? Do I talk, or sit silently and use my body energy to empathize with her? I had never before been in a position when such responsibility was falling on my shoulders—Jessie had come to *me*.

Again she spoke—continuing the monologue, "And I looked, and after a while, after I had sat there for ages, there was nothing there. I looked in the mirror and—I had disappeared—there was just a crazy head there. Desperate—I couldn't find myself anywhere—I had vanished.

I glanced at her self portraits—wild eyes, pained cheeks—and back to her own impassive, motionless face. "Maybe we should go for a walk," I suggested pathetically. At least then we could get out of this claustrophobic room and maybe the fresh air would help me clarify what I could do to help her. I led her out into the drizzle and felt as though there were a ghost walking beside me. Impulsively I turned towards her and hugged her stiff and cold body close and hard. I felt the energy in my gut and stomach, and tried with all my force to transfer some of it to her. I could feel myself wanting to cry—wanting to show some emotion myself if she couldn't. My knuckles turned white, and Jess's head drooped onto my shoulder. Suddenly she was limp all over, but still no outburst of feeling came.

We carried on walking, and slowly her voice rose in a whisper, a monotone. It came in fragments: her intense fears about not growing up to be a great artist, the terrifying agony when she feels she "must have vanished." Her days of utter irrationality when she cannot even remember the words with which to have a conversation, the spiderlike fatality of her attraction which draws people towards her only for her to suck them dry, her uncontrollable tantrums. I heard her words and wept inside; my best friend had at last removed her "I'm okay" façade and I loved her all the more for entrusting me with the blackest parts of her character.

What did I say in those next two or three hours before I led her home? I know that I was trying desperately to allow her to let something break inside her. This deathlike passivity seemed so unnatural and unhealthy. I myself felt very strange: I had never—even momentarily, as now—been in a "dominant role" in any relationship, and I struggled to relax. Gradually I managed to forget myself and focus entirely on Jessica. As we tramped homeward through the dismal rain, I began to feel the first flames of energy licking through Jessie's body. She had lost that hardness, but I had to acknowledge that Jessie could not, and would not, recognize her emotions that night.

It was with trepidation that I glimpsed her dark head bent over a book in class the next morning. She looked up, gazed at me and looked down again; I glimpsed serenity in her eyes. Was this a good sign? Do I stay here or do I leave her to her own intimate thoughts? She lifted her head again and tears were trickling down her face. She did not even attempt to brush them away. I watched the pure clean sorrow in her face and felt real warmth in her pale hands as I grabbed them. I had never seen even a hint of a tear in the past and now she was crying openly and beautifully before me. I could feel in those tears the outpouring of all the tension and deadness of last night, and I rejoiced that Jessica had at last let down her final and most firmly established mask — her mask which stated proudly, "Nothing can get to me: my emotions are totally under control." In the following weeks, our friendship blossomed even further since the remaining few barriers against intimacy had been destroyed. Well, temporarily at least.

You see, this sharing of our lives couldn't last for ever. We began to come into school wearing the same clothes without even realizing it, and started using each other's mannerisms and vocabulary. We began to function interdependently — almost as one person. In effect, we were each other's life-support machines. The nature of our union became symbiotic: our combined power was so strong that it was uplifting to exist as one, rather than to return to our separate loneliness and lack of security. Writing this now, our relationship seems unhealthy in the extreme; the emotions and intensity invested in the relationship were comparable to those in a love affair. But at that time, it was wonderful to know, for the first time, that what I had to give was valuable. The sense of standing alone and being somehow separated was temporarily extinguished.

But the very closeness that was our strength also engendered in me seeds of envy and mistrust. Art, the common ground on which we both stood so firmly, provided the means for comparison. Which of us had more talent? Which of us had greater depths of character to nourish our creativity? The competition inspired our art and put an invisible, paper-thin divide between us. Also, I began to fear that she didn't need me as much as I thought she did. She seemed scared of our closeness, and I sensed that maybe she was starting to reject me. Her periods of withdrawal returned, and in the holidays she would go weeks without contacting me. I would often call her but she was nearly always out with her boyfriend Andrew (was she substituting our interdependence for a new interdependence with Andrew?) and rarely got back to me. Was it possible that she had sucked me dry and was now discarding the empty shell? I hated myself for thinking that, and so whenever she did either write or phone I would forget all my doubts and everything would be wonderful once more. Even so, it was becoming increasingly complicated: Jessie was now deeply attached to Andrew, and therefore there was a third variable to be considered.

I struggled constantly to give the two of them enough room to grow. Whenever the three of us were out with other people, I knew that it was Andrew's, and not my right to be with Jessie. But still Andrew felt in competition with me for her trust and companionship. Jessica is a very striking woman, and I knew he was very proud of her and felt I had no right to claim her. The strange thing is that she defies all standard definitions of femininity — there is something distinctly masculine (if we can call characteristics "masculine" and "feminine") about her "grit" and stubbornness. I would stand there and think: my "best" friend is at the same time the male ideal image of sexual beauty. How does that affect me; *where* does that leave me?

Although one of Madeleine's axioms rang constantly in our ears—
"When you feel you can't exist without someone/something, then that is the
time to give him/her/it up"—neither Jess nor I had the strength to make a
real split. Our partial separation had to be forced by the physical dividers of
leaving high school and beginning our separate lives. I wonder now: was it
right of me to expect such loyalty from her? Was it right of me to sacrifice
so much of myself for her (even now I forgive her every time she "forgets"
about me or treats me in an off-hand way)? I remember Madeleine's words
clearly, "It's no good thinking that it's always the other person's fault when
things go wrong for you, Melanie. You have to work out what you're doing
to cause this response." Much of my ongoing doubt therefore stems from
myself: is my concept of friendship too intense and distorted? What was *I*
doing to make Jess shy away? Even now I am reluctant to admit the close of
that chapter in my life of which I was so desperately fond. In my turbulent
and joyful "art phase" it was so clear that I was developing and learning.
The storms of mid-adolescence—with all their agonies and their ecstasies—
are over and I now face a period of consolidation rather than complete
reformation. It's harder now: I have to look very carefully indeed to
identify the few millimeters' progress that I aim to advance each day.

But there have been gains: partially freed from ties with Jessica and
the art group, I have been able to re-incorporate and reaccept my family.
Although I had managed to break down the fear of communicating openly
with them during my time of intense friendship with Jessica, I still wasn't
treating them as an integral part of my life. My *real* life was my hours spent
in the art room: coming home was like having to return to a hotel to sleep
and recuperate for the next day. Now, my eyes are free to observe my
parents and accept them both as parents and as people in their own right.

The turning point arrived in the form of my first major piano recital.
The two weeks preceding this event I had stayed home with my mother and I
had felt a real strengthening of bonds between us as we entrusted each other
with our intimate selves. On the day of the concert itself, she couldn't eat
one thing; it was almost as though she was going to be playing and not me.
My father had been like a shadow during this time; he was often there but I
never really acknowledged his solidity.

The hundreds of hours of practice for my recital condensed into one
short evening. Those rare moments of happiness when I'm playing well—
when I feel that I *have* achieved my full potential, and near perfection
doesn't seem *quite* so impossible—were quickly over and I was standing
bowing. At first I could focus on no one, but then I spotted my father's
snowy hair near the back (at the back so as not to distract me). In between
bows I strained to see them all clearly. I blinked rapidly and caught my
mother's beautiful joyful face and the tears in Sarah's eyes. Thank God I
had played my best. I felt on top of the world. Then I saw my father's strong
hands clapping and—my father was crying. My father was *crying* because

of me. He was being more damned emotional than anyone else in the entire room. I snatched back a sob in my own throat and clutched the bouquet closer to my chest.

I had been so critical of my father's categorizing, and yet I had neatly classified him as "not able to have emotions." I remembered Jessica's tears and now I experienced the same joy as I had done then. What tears could do to me! As I lay in bed that night, I knew my eyes were opening to the world; with a sharpness in my chest I realized that my father, and indeed all other people to whom I am closely attached, are infinitely more varied and magical than I had previously been willing to admit. As I lay there in the darkness, I again felt that degree of separateness that I had experienced in that drafty classroom several years ago. But this time I wasn't scared; although there was a thin line separating me from "the rest," there was also a thin line separating each individual from "the rest." (What is "the rest" anyway? Surely it is merely a collection of struggling, lonely souls.) It was incredibly comforting to know that I would never be able to understand fully the workings of someone else—people could never be truly figured out. They would always be able to shock me by their inconsistencies of behavior. One person would cry or one person would strip naked and someone else's notion of the world would be overturned. Yes, it was wonderful to be able to perceive at last each person's own, precious uniqueness and complexity.

Yesterday I was strolling along the sidewalk. It was quite a nice day and my glance fell on my elongated shadow gliding along beside me. I paused: that was *my* shadow. I could never get rid of it, add to it, swap it with someone else, or change its fundamental characteristics. It would always be mine. Just as my "Melanieness" will always be mine. I had never formulated that thought quite so clearly—no matter whom I get involved with, what I do with the rest of my life, there is absolutely no way that I can ever change or add to my shadow. There will always be just one. The only companion it will have is me. I carried on walking and heard a voice inside me: "We must die alone: we *shall* die alone. *We* are our own constant companion. Surely therefore we must learn to live and stand alone." Just as I was about to go inside into the gloom I heard my voice again, "Here I am, whole, eager, vulnerable, and alone. I'm walking alone. I'm existing alone. And I'm *living* . . . not merely surviving."

Carol Gilligan: Response to Melanie: Reflections on Case No. 1

Ourself behind ourself, concealed---
Should startle most---

Emily Dickinson

I felt as though I were bringing into the light a half of me which had been hidden and etiolated for years.

Melanie

I am listening to Melanie, tuning my ear to her voice, letting it enter my psyche, picking up its resonances, its familiar themes and cadences, and also its distinctiveness, its Melanieness. Because Melanie's voice is my guide, taking me into the realm of her psyche and leading me across the terrain of her adolescence. Preparing to speak in response to this voice, I take my bearings by asking four questions about myself and also about Melanie: who is speaking? in what body? telling what story about relationships — from whose point of view or from what vantage point? in what societal and cultural framework? And I realize that I am familiar with the fugal structure of Melanie's composition — the two-part invention or the counterpoint of Melanie's narration where one voice begins with a startling story about self-exposure and disconnection (from her body, from herself, from her feelings, from others, and from the society in which she is living) and then, midway through, a second voice enters — picking up the themes of self-exposure, relationship, and challenge and telling a vibrant story of living in intense connection with herself and others.

This doubling of voice and vision — this telling of two stories simultaneously that are fundamentally at odds with respect to the portrayal of self, relationship, and reality — is a familiar landmark of girls' adolescence because it is a creative solution to what Melanie describes as a "painful and often incomprehensible" problem: the seemingly "eternal struggle between solidifying my own individuality and maintaining my connections with others who are important to me." This split between "self" and "relationship" is psychologically painful and also incomprehensible because it marks the taking of self out of relationship, paradoxically for the sake of maintaining relationships as well as for the sake of solidifying one's self. With this withdrawal of self from relationship, the moving life of relationship stops. The voice of the opening section of Melanie's self-portrait — in portraying a self feeling all alone and disconnected and relationships that feel inauthentic or fraudulent — bespeaks this stillness and this disjunction.

For the opening voice is a voice that is in some odd relation to Melanie — an observing "I" who speaks about herself from somewhere outside of her body, who is preoccupied with questions of judgment (is she ordinary or special, a con artist or an artist, a fraud or a person of worth and value), who stands alone — apart from "the rest," and who speaks in partial quotation, as if taking on some foreign language ("odd," "freak," "unacceptable," "alone," "weird," "normal," "big fish," "successful," "doer," "knack," "intelligence," "maleness," "categorizing," "trappable," "fashionable, trendy, and slim," "togetherness," "separateness," "fine, fine, fine").

This is the no-voice voice in which psychology is commonly spoken — a voice that speaks as if it is disconnected from a person and a body, which tells a story about relationship that is at its center a story about separation, within a setting that is supposedly culture-free or universal. And in this voice Melanie tells what is, to psychologists, a familiar story of female adolescence: about self-sabotaging urges, feelings of worthlessness, a drive for perfection, intense self-doubt, a wooden depression, suicidal impulses and gestures, poor body image — all in a girl who is physically healthy, doing very well in school, who has a loving family, who is treated by all as someone with abundant reasons for feeling good about herself, who is the daughter of highly educated parents — a girl who is musically gifted and living in the midst of educational and economic and racial privilege.

Melanie, however, portrays herself as a weary survivor of a relational struggle — wanting to expose herself but also wanting to stay in connection with others who are important to her. This crisis of connection is accompanied by a feeling of seemingly hopeless relational impasse: to be with others she has to cover herself with "our horrible green uniform" and to free herself means to be at odds with other people — angry, passionate, and presumably too sexual, dressed in red at a dance where everyone wears black. In her most direct answer to her opening question as to why she took off her clothes in the chilly classroom, Melanie says "It was a bold statement in order to dare myself, and others, to think about me in a new, and in many ways scary, way." This healthy, if dramatic, act of resistance to her pervasive experience of disconnection, is, as she says, the beginning of her move to join her "psychological and physical selves," and to connect her thoughts with her feelings. Melanie seeks to bring herself into her relationships—at first by expressing her point of view on what is happening and thus revealing her experience of the world in which she is living.

Because, like a member of the underground, Melanie has become facile "at constructing a façade—a semblance—of 'okayness' for the outside world," so convincing that "they too began to believe that everything was 'just fine' and treated me accordingly." But the psychological darkness that encroaches on Melanie—the incapacitating bouts of depression and the feelings of emptiness—comes from her sadness about living in such isolation and her uncertainty in this radical aloneness as to who she is and what is reality. Her "veneer of togetherness" covers over and muffles "internal screams which shrieked louder and louder," leaving Melanie feeling that she "must surely be smothered"—kept from breathing, kept from speaking, physically and psychologically dying. The more she sees herself fitting into the roles that have been cast in marble for her—"good girl/good student" and also "loving/considerate daughter"—the more she feels "isolated, empty and disoriented": disconnected from others, drained of feelings, without a soul, and out of touch with reality.

But this is only half of the story. Midway through her chronicle of despairing choices (between being true to herself and appearing perfect in the eyes of others) Melanie suddenly backtracks and retells her story, beginning now at the age of 14 rather than 13 and changing the location from the chilly classroom where she stood all alone in a shadowy corner to the art room where she "suddenly found [herself] immersed in art, its teacher, and the fellow students." The catalyst for this transformation is Ms. Madeleine Tremayne, and the medium is genuine connection or real relationship.

The shift in Melanie's voice is striking as the remote "I" (or eye) of the first section who *looked at* and *spoke about* her in ways that ultimately were terrifying, holding up an image of perfection that, like virginity, could be lost irretrievably with one false step or careless moment, gives way to an "I" immersed in feelings, in art, in herself, in her teacher, and finding it "incredibly exciting," "a deep and exhilarating release" of creative energies that had been bottled by concerns about perfection and overbearing judgments. Rejoicing at being able "to grapple with something that couldn't be classed as 'right' or 'wrong'," Melanie now is able to take risks which are developmentally essential, because imperfection no longer means "failing in front of others," or "tumbling right over a precipice," or losing everything.

The quotations drop off as Melanie no longer struggles against the voice of constraint but instead is drawn by her teacher into an experience of alive and moving relationship. Lapsing briefly into the voice of the first section, she attempts to be dispassionate and to judge Ms. Tremayne "objectively," feeling at the same time "a strong obligation to portray her as well as she deserves to be presented." But this voice now sounds stilted and artificial, remote and judgmental, and Melanie quickly shifts into a language that is for the most part free of quotation, grounded in her own strong feelings and thoughts rather than "floating on the ceiling," and a voice that bespeaks living in a world of emotional generosity, joy, pain, and abundance rather than a world that is sparse, spare, and judgmental.

Again Melanie feels peeled, exposed now by the eyes of her teacher who wants to see her, who wants to be with her, who calls on her to speak the full range of her feelings with unmodulated intensity: to show her passion, her insecurity, her sexuality, her confusion, her anger, her desire for closeness, her wildness, her power, her weakness, her love of her artwork, her inflammability, her wish to be alone with her painting, her relief at being comforted—in short, her humanness. The "madness" that previously had seemed so dangerous and disruptive now could be "harnessed to improve our art." Art was "a means of showing *yourself*, a vessel in which to pour your soul."

It is essential to stress the relational context in which this self-exposure takes place and to note that what Melanie refers to as her teacher's "uniqueness" and "her great strength"—"her integrity and her sense of risk-taking inherent in her teaching style"—was her readiness to bring herself into relationship with her students. The risk Madeleine took was the risk of relationship, exposing herself, peeling herself, revealing her vulnerability— her ability to be wounded or her humanness, her imperfection, her need for closeness, for comfort, for nurture, and also her irritation, her impatience, her steeliness, her anger. Her listening, compassion, empathy, and suggestions seemed infinite—abundant and limitless—because they were given so openly, so freely. Here Melanie could expose herself and release her feelings without feeling herself "silly" or finding herself all alone and abandoned. And this release is carried in Melanie's language as she actually feels feelings ("I felt choked") rather than thinking about what she must surely be feeling ("I must surely be smothered by this dual existence").

In the world of the art room where Madeleine and the other students "provided in abundance all the love, frustration, inspiration, and despair that I needed," Melanie felt for the first time "a real sense of belonging and connecting." On this raft where they were "paddl[ing] like mad together," she was "at last able to conceptualize and clarify one of the primary struggles in my development: I was becoming a woman but was fighting tooth and claw against that image of 'womanly goodness and obedience.' "

In "the chaotic art room" where Melanie's "battered soul" could be rebuilt—where what she had to give "could be valued," where she "felt a real sense of belonging or connecting," and where she experienced "the joy" of "learning together . . . [and] creat[ing] a pool of energy"—Melanie speaks about becoming a woman, having to fight against being trapped in the conventions of "femininity," and having to speak back in anger to the voices that say everything is fine, nothing is wrong, calm down, don't be silly.

> Much Madness is divinest Sense---
> To a discerning Eye---
> Much Sense---the starkest Madness---
> 'Tis the Majority
> In this, as All, prevail---
> Assent---and you are sane
> Demur---you're straightaway dangerous---
> And handled with a Chain---
>
> Emily Dickinson

When I become confused in listening to Melanie is when she refers to the vibrantly colored interior of her self-portrait as "a dream world," "insubstantial," "unrealistic," "unhealthy," while calling the shadowy outer story of aloneness and separation reality—the way "we must live," and the way, she implies, she shall live in order to ensure her survival. Because in doing this, Melanie covers over problems of relationship that she has revealed and gives up both a healthy resistance to disconnections that are psychologically wounding and also a political resistance to an order of living that denies the "interconnectedness [of people and feelings] with other people/feelings." Thus Melanie moves from the healthy resistance that opens her narration into the political resistance that characterizes her "turbulent and joyful art phase"—the resistance that, with Madeleine's encouragement, leads her to speak openly of her desires to her parents, and then, finally, to what is clinically known as a psychological resistance: a reluctance to know what she knows, about belonging and connection, about passion, commitment, closeness, love, pain, and struggle.

This pattern, whereby a healthy resistance to disconnection turns into a political resistance or open struggle for honest relationship, which then is under pressure to turn into psychological resistance—a reluctance to know what one knows, reflects girls' sense at adolescence of coming up to a chasm: the place where their experiences in living divide from what is generally taken to be or socially constructed as reality. Melanie, for example, "gradually became aware of many uncategorizable things. I just couldn't compartmentalize people or feelings—that would be denying their very interconnectedness with other people/feelings—and thus I had to reject my father's philosophy." And yet, "I still had to live in a house where emotions were kept very much under control and social interaction was treated as nonessential" — the house she grew up in.

Which brings me to the silence — the fact that her mother says nothing, has no voice. Madeleine speaks, Jessica speaks, Melanie speaks, her father speaks, the girls in the opening classroom scene speak, but not her mother. Like Jessica who looked and looked and "couldn't find myself anywhere — I had vanished," Melanie's mother has disappeared or appears only as a pale shadow of Melanie ("it was almost as though she was going to be playing [the piano] and not me"). And their relationship, said to be intimate and trustworthy, is overshadowed by Melanie's father who, in the end, cries at her near-perfect performance.

Whether this assent on Melanie's part to the ideal of perfection and the conventions of femininity that she had resisted is sanity or madness remains in question. Her mother silently models capitulation as Madeleine had exemplified resistance, and perhaps Melanie's relationship with Jessica serves as the passage leading away from intense and powerful relationships with women that now seem to her "unhealthy in the extreme" and toward the overriding claims of the patriarchy — "I knew that it was Andrew's, and not my right to be with Jessica. I had no right to claim her." Melanie's questions: "How does that affect me; *where* does that leave me," orchestrate the ending.

Moral language returns to cover the loss of relationship and to justify giving up a way of living that was "joyful and turbulent," that "chapter in my life of which I was so desperately fond . . . [when] it was so clear that I was developing and learning." With her "eyes opening to the world," Melanie comforts herself with the realization that she is safe from detection ("there was a thin line separating each individual"; "people could never be truly figured out,") and also with the recognition that notions of the world can be suddenly overturned by crying or sudden nakedness. As her sentences shorten and relationships dwindle to a shadow, the words "never," "ever," and "always" convey her sense that what was moving within her has come to a stop ("there is absolutely no way that I can ever change or add to my shadow, there will always be just one"). Living away from her art world and also from her family and her country, she is now her only companion. In the end, the voice that spoke earlier in partial quotation now speaks in full regalia: "We must die alone: we *shall* die alone. *We* are our own companion. Surely therefore we must learn to live and stand alone." And yet, going into the gloom, Melanie hears "my voice again" — speaking as if from some underground cavern: "Here I am, whole, eager, vulnerable and alone. And I'm *living*: not merely surviving." Like many adolescent girls, she is surviving in the underground, has gone into hiding.

My sensitivity to the disjuncture in Melanie's narration between the first person "I" and the cultural "we"—this chasm between experience and "reality"—comes from the fact that although I am much older and grew up in a different country and in a different family and culture, I too am a woman, was also a girl, and like Melanie, I know standards of physical beauty, the voice of the father, the lure of perfection, the realization that this is deadly, the feeling of being a fraud, the persona of "good girl/good student," the feeling of "being smothered by this dual existence," the split between self and relationship and the urgency to heal that division. And, like Melanie, I too have experienced passion, insecurity, sexuality, wildness, confusion, abundance, "a real sense of belonging [and] connecting," joy in being in it and "paddling like mad together," the power of "unleash[ing] hidden and suppressed anger," the feeling of being choked by the fear that "if the right place were tapped I would be faced not with a slow welling up of emotion but a full-scale avalanche of desires/bitternesses/half-formed needs/unresolved fears," a tendency to "float on the ceiling" when apprehensive and a struggle "to get both my feet back on the ground," the feeling of vibrations in my throat, of "deep and unheard wholeness," the comfort of being drawn near and held close, of taking in the energy of others, the exhilaration of discovering "what really matters to me," of realizing and accepting weakness, of knowing love and closeness instead of having to stand alone and maintain a façade of "okayness."

Melanie, with the discerning eye of an artist, the ear of a musician, and the candor of one who is willing to undress in public, has drawn an exquisite and powerful portrait of adolescence—psychologically compelling, beautifully rendered, and in the end deeply unsettling, because she covers over what she has revealed. Like a painter working in oils, she layers her canvas by telling two overlapping stories about her adolescence. And the resonance of her voice comes in part from the dissonances between these stories and the way in which she is thus able to convey what otherwise, perhaps, cannot be heard or spoken: that her adolescence at once fits into the models of adolescent development that she has studied and deeply calls into question the models. Her readiness at the end to fit herself into a simple story of developmental progress and in doing so perhaps to perform for her father or reassure him that she is alright, that what has been lost is inessential, is what I find distressing. As I listen to the silent aligning of her first person "I" with an unspecified "we" intoning aloneness, I find myself wondering what Melanie might say if we were able to talk with one another directly.

CASE 2

Working Through My Adolescence

In this case, the 20-year old author describes his experience working at a local art film theater in early adolescence. As the only child of parents who married and had him before entering college, he was expected early on to "pull his own weight," and learned the independence that would carry over into his work experience. By far the youngest employee at the theater, he finds that he can play "little brother" while being exposed to a range of people and experiences he would not otherwise have encountered. The movie theater serves as an arena outside of the home in which he gains self-confidence and develops a sense of responsibility, and where he begins to experiment with drugs and sexuality. At the same time, he is a "model" student and family member. His feelings of self-confidence and self-knowledge are challenged by his realization that his overdependence on drugs affects his relationships with women and other aspects of his early college experience. This case study explores the author's sense of leading two lives and of his more recent attempts to reconcile them.

To set the scene: it is 12:30 on a Saturday night. I am working at the Palace Theatre while "The Rocky Horror Picture Show" plays in the background. It is my first job, and I am excited to be there. After all, I am 14 years old, handling lots of money, candy, and late-night zaniness every weekend. I am the youngest worker there, but because I work hard my age isn't often remarked upon. Furthermore, I don't look 14, with my wide shoulders and 5′10″ frame, my well-spoken manner and air of confidence. And I don't worry too much about being younger — I simply do what I have been raised to do: be responsible and work hard.

I was raised to work hard, since hard work is what has kept my family together from the start. I am an only child, the son of parents married at age 18. My mother and father had been dating a few months when my mother became pregnant with me. My parents were high school seniors at the time, and I can imagine the leaden feeling in their stomachs as they faced the reality of this unplanned pregnancy. The circumstances have been described to me in snatches, small bits so as not to flood the memory with pain. My mother told me that I wasn't the reason for their marriage — a catalyst, but not *the* reason. Neither of them would have been comfortable with a forced marriage. Their options were limited: they could get married, and face the tremendous pressures of a young marriage, or my mother could go away and have the baby with relatives, away from the eyes of friends and neighbors. Abortion was not an option due to the limited resources available in my state. So they thought and cried about it and decided to get married and try to make it work.

Both sets of parents were extremely disappointed and angry. The extended family's anger did not help the situation any; now my parents were scared *and* alone. My father's parents were especially hard hit, since they, too, had faced a similar problem at age 20. They had gotten married, but theirs was not a happy union: there was a lot of bitterness and anger between them, which my father had seen all of his life. To see their son repeating their mistake was hard for them to handle. Their disappointment was multiplied by my father's academic success up to that point. A good future was in store for him if he played his cards right. He was president of the Honor Society, a scholarship recipient, and the vessel of his parents' dreams. They were angry about his predicament, furious with my father's failure, and they gave him only minimal help. There was no emotional support from my father's side of the family.

My mother's situation was different, but no less difficult. While not the academic superstar that my father was, she worked hard and took college prep classes. She has told me that every year she had to go and argue with her guidance counselors to be allowed to take those college prep classes. In a way, her pregnancy confirmed the low expectations that her guidance counselors had for her. As for her family, it appears that they kicked her out. Through their accounts I have vicariously experienced the coldness and anger that they faced from both sides.

My parents' marriage required a complete renegotiation of expectations, dreams, and lifestyles. I feel that my father had to change his expectations the most, having been a high school superstar looking eagerly towards college. My mother had less to prove, but less to fall back on. She was the only one convinced of her own abilities. Together these young people entered college as married freshman, with a child on the way. I arrived in February and was an ever-present reminder of the reality of the situation. Despite living in college housing, my parents had to work all of the time. Whoever was not in class or at work was taking care of me. There was never enough money, time, or energy for my parents to relax while our family was young. Never enough of the things which make college fun.

So long as I can remember, my parents have always placed a lot of confidence in me. Their confidence came with the responsibilities which they gave me. As soon as I was able, I was asked to do my share in our household. Anything that I could contribute lessened the overwhelming amount of work my parents faced. My first responsibility was to take care of myself. I was a latchkey kid during grade school, taking care of myself after school. This self-monitoring allowed my mother to finish her classes and student teach without worrying about being home in time to meet me. Being a latchkey kid was the first responsibility I remember having, and while I was helping my parents out, the confidence they had in me was clear in their choice to leave me alone during the afternoons.

The effect of placing their confidence in me at a young age can be seen to this day. In my household I am accustomed to being held accountable for my actions, as well as being responsible for my share of the housework. When I first spent the night at a friend's house, I noticed that his mother never asked him to clean up after himself, or share the cookies with all of the family. By seventh grade I had realized that I did much more housework than any of my male friends and most of my female friends. Yet I am glad that I learned how to be responsible as a young boy, for I also learned about the corollary of responsibility—the promise of freedom.

For me, our household philosophy meant several things. First of all, I was expected to think as a member of the household, and not as a boarder. If there was work to be done, I should do it, without complaint, as a natural reaction to my commitment. Some of my friends' families were set up with the mother doing the housework, the father making the money, and the kids just being kids. With my chores and self-regulation, and two working parents, the same rules did not apply in my household. But if the rules weren't the same, neither was the way in which I was treated. My responsible nature won my parents' respect and earned me more understanding for my occasional youthful indiscretions, without which this narrative would be entirely unbelievable. Moments of poor judgment, like the time that I did a forward somersault in the family room, kicked the TV with an awkward foot, knocked over the flower vase on top of the TV, and blew up said television. Rather than telling me how awful and immature I was, my parents told me to go outside and play. In retrospect I think their understanding was due in part to their respect for me, which gave them the understanding that this was an isolated incident and not a typical stunt. Hearing how some of my friends were put down by their parents for being lazy or immature, I was glad for the way my household was set up. To this day, however, one will never find flower vases on our television.

By the time I was 12 or 13 years old, my responsible nature had won me a bigger share of independence than that which my friends enjoyed. My parents did not question every decision I made; instead they trusted that I had thought out my choice and would accept the consequences. I was not forced to take music lessons against my will, although my father had been; my stabs at adolescent romance were not overly lampooned as immature; and my school life was my domain. I enjoyed this relationship with my parents, and the faith they had in me gave me a lot of self-confidence. Their faith also allowed me a lot of room for self-expression. I could stop playing the saxophone if it sounded like a moose's mating call to me, since my feelings were considered valid. I could be very silly without worrying what my parents would think, since they knew the depth of my responsible nature. Their faith, however, was tested when I was 13, and a friend of the family offered me a job working at his movie theater.

I was in the seventh grade and in braces when he asked my parents, with my eager approval, if I would help him deliver schedules for upcoming movies and events. They consented to the proposal after some thought. If there was to be a good entry into teenager work, this was it: working for a friend of the family in a simple job. I felt as if I had been offered the chance of a lifetime. I rode around in the back of a gutted-out Volkswagon van, not noticing the severity of the accommodations – due to my euphoria I never felt a bump. When it came to working, I was enthusiasm incarnate, a teenage whirlwind running, literally running, from door to door. I acted as if I had received a great honor to be able to deliver movie schedules. It seemed a task of almost heroic proportions – defying large dogs, paranoid residents, and the imminent clumsiness of a 13-year old frame were just some of the dangers I faced. I jumped whole flights of stairs, and mastered a certain way of throwing the schedules so that they landed face-up. My first day at work was tiring, not for me, but for those who watched me be so energetic.

That day of delivering schedules began my involvement in one of the most important experiences of my life, for having impressed the owner with my speed and eagerness, I was adopted into the Palace Theatre organization. My parents' decision had opened the door to a whole new set of experiences, and the lessons I had learned in our household had primed me for success.

The Palace Theatre was an old-fashioned movie house which sported a brass rail balcony and showed movies in a double feature format. It is best characterized as a repertory/art film theater, showing Hollywood favorites, foreign films, and midnight cult classics. My parents and I were regulars there, and our affiliation with the theater certainly influenced their decision. My parents' knowledge and affection for the theater was important, since the place had a bad reputation. It had previously been owned by hippies and was associated with drugs and loose morals. My friends' parents thought that by allowing me to work there, my folks were throwing me into a den of corruption. In casual grocery-store conversation, they often commented so. My mother had to deal with my peers' parents, all of them at least eight or ten years older than she, and their condemnation of the decision to let me work. Both of my parents stood firmly behind their decision and never showed any sign of wavering.

So I worked. After my debut as a schedule deliverer, I was asked to help clean up the theater on weekends. During seventh and eighth grade, besides my standard school subjects, I learned all of the intimate details of broom. I graduated from my household responsibilities to a larger scale of work. Instead of cleaning my bedroom, I was cleaning up a 400-seat theater. Hard work took on a new meaning as I worked against the mess and chaos created by "The Rocky Horror Picture Show."

I could only imagine what happened during the film, since I had never seen it, but being confronted on a Sunday morning by a floor covered with rice, playing cards, toasted bread, and toilet paper gave my imagination room to roam. When I finally saw "Rocky Horror" a few weeks after I began cleaning, the reality of it was stranger than any scenario I could have dreamed up. All sorts of people, hundreds of them, came dressed up like it was Mardi Gras. They carried bags of rice, squirt guns, toast, and bags of assorted projectile goodies. As I watched the movie I was engulfed in an audience participation event of cultish proportions. At different points and lines in the movie, members of the audience shout responses and humorous profanities in response to the character's lines and queries. At other intervals they cover their heads with newspaper as a massive water gun fight erupts, mimicking the storm in the movie. Still other moments call for flying toast and toilet paper to soar through the air. I was enthralled by the film and its consuming atmosphere, but not pleased with the aftermath and the way it shaped my Sundays.

But I wouldn't have traded places with any of my friends who played outside on Sunday afternoon. I was having a lot of fun, working with other teenagers in a whole different world. As a matter of fact, many of my friends wanted to join me at work; there was definitely a Tom Sawyer phenomenon, a romantic notion about working in a theater. I myself won't deny the real romance of the Palace. The balcony, the loud stereo sound system, free candy, soda, change for video games, movies—for a young adolescent the Palace had it all.

The most important thing that the Palace offered me, however, was an extended family which I didn't have at home. Most of my co-workers were four years older than me, 18 when I was 14. The Palace was the center of their social lives, since they were all close friends and the Palace was an exciting place. The theater had a homey feel to it, since there was almost always friends hanging out while others worked. And if we were a family, I was certainly the little brother. They even called me Little B, a way of commenting on my position in the "household" (and differentiating between the four or five Bs who worked there).

I was forever being wrestled, chased, and wrangled into doing extra work — the life of a little brother. One of the favorite pastimes of the theater family was getting into each other's business. I could never have a date without it being commented on and joked about. I often took my dates to the Palace, with all of its secret spaces and the dark and romantic balcony. My love life was a favorite topic at the Palace, with its share of embarrassing moments for myself. Moments like being caught half naked in the back stage dressing rooms, caught in the heat of my eighth grade mating dance.

But if the Palace gang observed my romantic development, they also helped prompt it. My co-workers were my role-models, both good and bad. By interacting with 18-year olds on a regular basis, it was inevitable that I would use them as a standard, and reach for their level of maturity. After all, at work I had been admitted into a circle of older people, and in a way this signaled my acceptance as a 14-year old who was mature enough to enter the 18-year-old strata. For anyone who is growing up, maturity is the goal, a prize to be attained. It was my goal, too.

From early adolescence on, I was thought of as a mature young man. I did all my chores, got good grades in school, and never got into any big trouble. Being a good kid and not causing trouble are the two most important measurements of maturity. I lived up to everyone's expectations, and then some. But I think it was my intelligence and the lessons of my upbringing which led to my fulfillment of adult expectations. I was used to working hard and doing a good job. And I had learned that if I did a good job I would be trusted with a greater share of freedom. That was the way I considered maturity when I was younger, as a social contract. If you do this, you get that.

In my free time, away from adults, I played and acted like a child. I was a silly boy. The Palace was the perfect place for me to express both my more adult and more childlike sides. Our cleaning work was often interrupted with play. We played tag with rolls of toilet paper, long white ribbons trailing behind. Once or twice we turned off all of the lights and threw a glow-in-the-dark frisbee around. The more usual form of recreation was our spontaneous concerts on stage. The theater had an excellent sound system, and we fueled our cleaning efforts with really loud music. Sometimes the pull of the stage would overcome us, and we would perform. Brooms became guitars, and "Rocky Horror" costumes were pulled out of the dressing rooms. In a few seconds we were all transformed into superstars, as we air-jammed our favorite songs. Our all-time classics were "Won't Get Fooled Again" by the Who, "ABC" by the Jackson Five, and the tasteless "Big Bottoms" by Spinal Tap. We played our hearts out on the stage. I share these antics with you in order to dispel any notion that I actually was mature. I knew *how and when to act maturely*, but I still had a lot to learn. Since my sense of maturity was very circumstantial, that is, about when I needed to be mature or not, I learned about maturity as I faced new situations at the Palace. One particular incident stands out in my mind, when I was taken to task for not living up to the expectations which accompanied being a mature worker.

The scene: 2 A.M., the abandoned lobby of the Palace, during "Rocky Horror." I sat in the warm ticket booth, watching the lobby while the movie played. Or rather I alternately watched the lobby and the insides of my eyelids. I was very sleepy. My boss suddenly appeared before my groggy eyes, quite irate with my sleepiness. He proceeded to berate me for not looking cheerful and businesslike at 2:00 in the morning. From his point of view, boss to worker, I was not living up to his expectations. In my mind, I was thinking, "Give me a break! I'm 14 years old! I'm in eighth grade! What did you expect?!?" He told me what he expected. When dealing with customers you have to be at your best. You're not at home. You're getting paid for this. At the time, his speech was very upsetting, almost unfair. Who was he to expect so much of me?

After my anger and upset due to this conflict had passed away, I thought more about what he had said. I thought about his image of a good worker, and his image of me. I wondered if he had forgotten how young I was, and if he had overstepped his bounds by having such high expectations of me. In reviewing the incident, it became clear that my boss *had* forgotten how young I was. He certainly wasn't treating me like a 14-year old whom he expected to be less mature. No, he had the same expectations of me which he had of all the others. The same adult expectations of worker cordiality that he demanded of the other older workers were demanded of me.

Suddenly I realized that this interaction was not an indictment of my immaturity, but rather a pronouncement of my mature image. He *did not* think of me as a 14-year old! This was made clear by his expectations. And it made sense, since I did the same work as the others, with an equally high level of efficiency and energy. The realization that my boss did not consider me as a 14-year old had amazing consequences. It was like getting your eighth grade CAT tests back and scoring "college level" in reading. The incident with my boss and my subsequent realizations made me conscious of the fact that people considered me to be as old and mature as my 18-year-old co-workers.

My image as an older teenager, maybe 16 or 18, was helped by a host of personal traits. I was an intelligent young man who spoke easily to adults, without the paralyzing self-consciousness which impairs many adolescents. I was physically larger than many of my same-age peers, with wide shoulders and a deep voice. I also had a knack for thinking practically and handling problems easily. The last, and perhaps most important factor contributing to my older image, was that I was very responsible, and carried out my duties competently. After the confrontation with my boss, it was apparent that all of these qualities spoke louder than my biological age, and it was clear that I was being judged by my appearance and performance, and not some age measurement. The realization that I had successfully, unconsciously projected the image of an 18-year old gave me a lot of confidence.

But what did all of this mean in my life? In simplest language, it encouraged me to grow up a little faster and involve myself in some of the activities that my 18-year old friends were engaged in. They were my role-models, and their actions functioned as a subtle encouragement to do the same. They were my standard. Most of my male friends from the Palace were college freshmen, eager to meet women and explore the realm of sexual activity. Don was particularly libidinous, taking great pride in the length of his penis. There is a Palace legend of a great showdown between him and Adam, but the result is fogged in a haze of drunken, inaccurate measurement. The openness of sexuality, this phallic exuberance if you will, was a central component in the male experience at the Palace, a topic of continual joking and question. Once I began seeing girls, I was often quizzed on my sexual progress by the men at the Palace.

Another aspect of their involvement with women was commitment, and longer term relationships. Having had more experience with dating, they had longer relationships than most of my same-age peers were having. My contact with the examples at the Palace helped shape my notions about relationships and sexuality. I had never had a BIG TALK with my dad, but my Palace peers educated me by example. In retrospect I am surprised that my parents and I didn't talk about sexuality more, but they did give me a book. Maybe they didn't want to talk about it, since it was an especially sore subject with them. Anyway, the characteristics of my Palace peers' relationships with women influenced my eighth-grade interaction with girls, by informing my ideas about sexuality and commitment as I became involved in my first relationships.

The place to meet girls in eighth grade was school. At the beginning of eighth grade, having come from a smaller public school, a feeder school, into a huge sea of adolescent hormones and strange faces, I would characterize my social situation as "King of the Geeks." I was the coolest of the geeks, geeks being smart, weird, nonathletic types who had not entered into the ranks of the popular. I sat at the far end of the geek table in the cafeteria, closest to the "cool" tables, in a very hierarchical set-up. With the confidence gained at the Palace, however, I was primed to make the jump from "geek" to "cool." With a self-awareness about the effect of appearances gained at the Palace, I made the connection between fashion and social strata. Just as by acting mature I was considered mature at the Palace, so perhaps by dressing cool I would be considered cool. I put my theory into practice by adopting the oxford shirt and upturned collar look of the cool kids.

Amazingly enough, my theory worked. It seemed as if the lesson I had learned at the Palace could be widely applied: appearances were very important in creating an image. After a month or so of dressing cool, I found myself being eyed by a girl from the cool group. She was very nice, an intelligent talkative girl who also gave me the chance to enter the popular crowd. With the confidence I had gained at the Palace, and the lessons I had learned from my male co-workers in mind, I entered into an eighth-grade romance. I was to go out with this girl for nine months, practically an eternity by eighth-grade standards, and it was in this relationship that I first had sex.

Our relationship was even more passionate than the average horny eighth graders. This was the result of the precocious maturity which both of us brought to the match. She came from a very social neighborhood where kids start dating early, in fifth or sixth grade. I came from the Palace, my special realm of social interaction, and brought to the relationship my vision of a long-range commitment. There was the sense that both my girlfriend and I were growing up faster than most of our friends, and we formed a relationship which was very mature for 14-year olds. I forgave her the time that she messed around behind my back, and she was happily surprised by my faith in her. She brought a willingness to explore our sexuality together. She encouraged me to explore her body and the pleasures associated with it, while I encouraged her to think of our relationship as a long-term thing. Together we said "I love you" for the first time, and together we made love for the first time.

I was pretty nervous when we first had sex. I had good reason to be nervous too, considering the way my parents had been put in a difficult situation by their lovemaking. There were signs of a family curse in the air, what with both my father and grandfather impregnating their girlfriends premaritally. Despite the lack of a BIG TALK, my household had an implicit message for me: be careful. And I was; I always used a condom. But I still had to get over my nervousness, and I can see how three subtle pressures helped me make the choice to have sex. First of all, all of my male role models at the Palace were openly sexual, and I did want to be like them. Secondly, my girlfriend's willingness and desire to make love were very influential. I remember almost backing out when we were about to have sex, and she told me straight out that she wanted me to make love to her. That was a pretty powerful pressure. The third influence was more general—the adolescent desire to explore the mysteries of being adult, and the actions and privileges associated with maturity. When all these factors came into play within the course of our six-month-old relationship, the result was the mutual loss of our virginity.

Having sex for the first time didn't change much. I guess I was still a little nervous, because we did not proceed to have sex all of the time; in the course of the next three months we only made love twice more. What was more important was my discovery of the powerful sexuality within me. In the course of our relationship, I got in touch with my sexual feelings, and was able to express them. In this way, my early sexual experiences helped to shape my future sexuality, which continued to be a powerful force. It takes a powerful force to make me ride my bike six miles uphill to see a girl, as I did in eighth grade.

Throughout the course of my first serious relationship, I continued to work at the Palace. Between these two simultaneous events, I increased my self-confidence weekly. In my relationship I was loving and being loved for the first time, and just having a relationship gives you confidence that you aren't an ugly pimply nosed geek. Being in a relationship is a sign of success, just like a promotion, an acknowledgement of your worth. At work, I was also being acknowledged, as I moved up from cleaner to usher and finally to assistant manager by the summer before ninth grade. I was regularly responsible for lots of money, crowd control, and the nightly running of the theater. As my job experience expanded, I got more practice in public speaking, problem solving, and organizational tasks. All of these tasks require a high level of self-confidence: one cannot move a grouchy, chaotic crowd into the rain without a confident presence. In order to get anyone to do anything, you need to seem like you know what you are doing. To my mind, the measure of this ability is confidence. And I had it.

Others seem to think I had it too. It is interesting how this period of precocious autonomy affected my relationship with my parents. As I worked at the Palace, confident in my own abilities, my parents became less and less mothering. (By mothering I mean a certain mode of close-watched connection between parent and child.) The early decision to trust me as a latchkey kid had evidenced the fact that there was not enough time or energy for a full-time mother. Once I began taking care of myself after school, my mother finished school and started her job as a teacher, solidifying a two-job household. As I learned to take care of more and more of my needs, the duties of my parents became less and less, and they took on the role of providers and advisors, rather than keepers. As advisors, my parents usually waited for me to bring things up for discussion. So if there was no glaring need, and no manifestation of a desire to talk about it, a subject would not be freely discussed in my household. Sometimes the distance between mother/father and advisor can be great.

In retrospect, I can remember several situations in which my parents probably should have said more than they did. Like the time that my dad found a condom in my jeans' pocket as he did the wash. Rather than taking the opportunity to talk about early sexuality, he just "hoped I was being careful." Other times when I was caught drunk, my parents didn't talk to me about it, but let me get out of it without discussing it. Without reprimanding my parents for bad parenting, I am suggesting that I would have benefited from more parental involvement. I can easily understand why they trusted me so, but when the trust became an unquestioning confidence, some of my faults grew into problems.

Without the direct supervision/intervention of adults either at home or at work, I found myself becoming involved with both drugs and sexuality. I became exposed to marijuana at both school and the Palace during my freshman year. At work many of the workers and regular patrons smoked dope, and the Palace was a safe, dark, and hassle-free environment to try marijuana. I could hide my pipe and stash at the Palace, and spend my stoned hours safely inside the movie theater.

At school, I was also setting up a safe environment by gaining the confidence of the adults. As a freshman I ran for class president, and won. I continued my involvement in student government throughout high school, eventually becoming the president of the student body in twelfth grade. My work in student government had much the same result of my chores at home, earning me a greater share of trust with my handling of responsibility. By the time I met some "stoner" friends at school, I had established myself as a mature young man in the eyes of the teachers. This image was to ensure that no adult ever thought I was stoned. Within this safe reputation, I began to explore marijuana use when I was 15.

Smoking pot was an activity which linked my Palace existence and my social life at school. I would go out and smoke pot with my school friends on Friday night, and then smoke more at work on Saturday night. My school friends often met me at the Palace, with its free candy and soda, and its safety. I used the theater as my home away from home, where my friends and I could party without the fear of getting caught. With all of the worries gone, smoking dope was a fun thing to do, with its wild times and altered state of mind. I loved climbing out on the roof of the theater, forty feet up, and relaxing in the sun with a beer and some pot. The abundance of intoxicants was certainly the result of my collegiate co-workers, for whom beer and dope were readily available. Again, by working and growing up at the Palace, I was steeped in the attitudes and actions of my co-workers. When I found a group of friends at school who were also into partying, I connected to my same-age peers.

I continued to smoke pot throughout high school. I also continued to be an Honors student-class-president type who was the opposite extreme from a stoner. For me, there was no opposition. I saw the two sides of myself, the Honors student and the stoner, as the two sides of the freedom and responsibility of maturity. Since I was successfully negotiating my duties as student and class president, I had earned a certain amount of freedom. My student government advisor gave me a permanent hall pass, allowing me to walk freely around the school. I used the pass to do my government work, organizing dances and Homecoming and whatnot, as well as to leave campus for McDonald's or to go get stoned. My permanent hall pass was formal acknowledgement of the freedom that comes with responsibility.

My parents never caught on to my regular pot smoking. Even when another parent called my house to tell my mother that he had heard his son saying how he could buy pot from me, my mother dismissed his claim. "Oh, no," my mother said, "you must be mistaken. Bill gets associated with that stuff because of where he works. The theater has a bad reputation, you see, and . . . ." I was out back, shitting bricks. When my mother came outside and saw me upset, she commented on how frustrating it must be to be falsely accused of pot use. "Yeah, it sucks . . . ." I said, shocked by her near-sightedness. Yet I did not leave much for her to see. I was careful to use breath mints and to wash my hands after I got stoned, and I usually came home from partying after they had gone to bed.

Since no one caught on, I became more and more involved in marijuana use. During the summer after freshman year in high school, I was almost always stoned. Stoned and free and doing my own thing. I used to get stoned before I did almost anything. Get stoned and play basketball. Get stoned and go to classes. Get stoned and lie in the sun. Get stoned for no reason at all. Just like some friends always go to Friendly's for ice cream, me and my friends always got stoned. By the time I entered college, I was getting stoned way too much. I began to see it as a problem.

Looking back, I do recall three of my closest friends talking to me about marijuana. These friends were the three women with whom I had gotten very close in high school. I went out with all three of them, at different times throughout high school, and they knew me better than anyone else. From these three women came the first criticism of my pot use. Their experiences with me both physically and mentally, in school and at parties, left them with a total picture of me which showed some inconsistencies between my responsible image and my irresponsible behavior, between my natural silliness and my desire to get stoned. They would talk to me about their feelings, but I didn't consider what they described to be inconsistencies, simply different sides of myself. I was very confident, perhaps too confident, that I knew what was going on. In the course of my relationships with women, however, I discovered I was not as mature as I thought I was.

My eighth-grade experiences had allowed me to discover my own sexuality, and I was very comfortable with it. For me, sexuality was a natural means of expression, and with my charm and intensity I often found myself becoming very passionate with young women in high school. I would get myself, and my partner, into intensely physical situations early on in our relationships. In retrospect, I know that I was unaware of what sexuality meant to the women I was fooling around with. In my mind, it was simply fooling around. I wanted to express myself physically with these women, but I was unaware of their needs, or unwilling to admit them to myself. In other words, I was a prick. I would mess around with someone, naked by candlelight one night, and then act as if it was nothing special. I wasn't acknowledging the emotional needs behind their physical expression. They would feel used and angry, and I would be angry at their anger, thinking it was the woman who was being immature. Nice male bullshit, huh?

By the time I graduated from high school, none of those three women were talking to me any more. One of them was so angry that she took a cassette tape I had given her, threw it into the road, ran over it ten times, back and forth, and shoved the broken mess of tape into a manila envelope and left it on my doorstep one Tuesday morning before school. I did not expect such anger, and I did not understand it. I didn't see the cassette tape incident as an indictment of my immaturity but rather as a sign of hers. After all, lots of adults were telling me how mature I was, at work and in school. It is memories like that of the broken tape which make me realize that I was not as mature as I thought I was.

As I entered college, my most intimate feedback from my most intimate friends told me that I needed to do some thinking. By this point the Palace had been closed for a year and a half. No longer did I have that safety net, that other arena to act in. Now I was alone, going off to college, and leaving behind broken relationships and anger. But I didn't leave it all behind. I carried a lot of guilt and self-critical anger inside of me, astonished at how immature I had been.

I had always been very introspective and self-critical of my actions, but until this moment I had continued to be confident in my introspection and feel good about myself. Now I felt that I had failed my own test, miserably. This feeling of failure, and my guilt about hurting my past girlfriends, fueled my harshest self-criticism yet. In response to my strong feelings of guilt, I decided to refrain from any sexuality during my freshman year, in order to clear my head and think. My first priority, then, was to reconsider my sexuality, and the way in which I expressed it. After a long time thinking, I decided that the safest thing to do would be to let my partner, whoever it would be in the future, initiate any sexual activity. I decided that my sexuality had to be contained, and it was a year or so before I felt ready to date women again.

As sophomore year in college began, I got involved in my first relationship after that long hurt. It was also during sophomore year that I began to see my pot smoking as a problem which needed to be dealt with. It was always in a relationship in which the pot smoking became a problem, because if you are stoned and your date isn't, the conversation, and the whole relationship, tends not to go well. Pot creates a distance, since the other person doesn't know when you are stoned, or if she does know, she may be resentful of the difference, resentful about the choice you have made to be different than her. Now I was finally beginning to understand.

My understanding about how pot can be a problem came at the time when I began to make all of my own decisions. I was deciding what courses to take, which interests to pursue, and what activities to engage in. Pot smoking became an activity like any other, with a cost and a benefit. For the first time, I began to realize how high the costs of smoking pot were. Now I don't mean that I was worried about cancer or mutated babies—it was simpler than that. Pot smoking as a habit can take up a lot of time. Being stoned began to feel like a waste of time, now that I was making all of my own choices. So during my sophomore year, I made a new choice—to cut back on my pot smoking.

This choice was harder than it sounds, since I had set up a friend network in which pot smoking was a regular activity. With my decision to smoke much less marijuana, I was afraid that it meant seeing less of my friends. I felt a lot of pressure to remain where I was, a pressure emanating from a fear of change. From a fear of losing friends. Slowly I thought the whole thing out, and realized after a few despondent days that I needed some help. I couldn't talk to my parents about it. They knew nothing about it, and when I would begin a conversation intending to tell them about it, I would invariably chicken out, and cast my troubles upon girls or something else. They were not the resources to tap for this problem. At first this angered me, but since then I have talked to them about it. In our talks I have realized that they are not the people to talk to about this part of my life. They have no experience with marijuana, and no desire to banter with me about it. To them, it's just bad.

So I decided to go and see counseling on campus. It was helpful just to go and admit that I had a problem. By admitting it, I was telling myself that I had something to work on, in much the same way that I worked on containing my sexuality. Counseling confirmed this feeling, telling me to treat each incident individually, without a past and without a history, and make my decision based on what I want there and now. Since what I want is to be free to engage in a variety of activities, without the eight-hour time loss of marijuana, pot smoking has fallen from among my favorite activities.

By that time, the end of my sophomore year, I knew that I couldn't just wish marijuana away. It was something I would have to work on, like an alcoholic, for the rest of my life. I came to understand that problems have to be worked out slowly, without the haste of extreme decisions. I had also come to realize that I had been too extreme in "containing" my sexuality. I had learned the dangerous outcome of my decision to banish my sexuality during the summer after sophomore year, when I felt attracted to a woman, and she to me, but I could not find my passion anymore. I did not trust myself to even kiss her. This was a very empty feeling. It seemed as if I had taken a step backwards rather than a positive movement towards growth. As I spent some time getting in touch with my strong feelings again, I came to see that just hiding my feelings and depending on the other person was an extreme, and immature, strategy. There was no way for me to keep learning how to express myself in relation to others so long as I didn't allow myself any chance at expression. Guilt and confusion were the result of my disowning my own strong feelings.

So I decided to repossess my sexual feelings again. I needed to be honest, to myself and to my future lovers, and talk out my feelings with them. Being honest about my feelings unlocked my sexuality again. I acknowledged my strong feelings, and began to reintegrate them into my current, junior-year relationship. My partner and I have talked out our feelings about sharing the responsibility for our sexuality and our self-concepts concerning sexuality. This open communication has been very successful; we both know where we stand and how our partner feels about the relationship and our mutual sexuality. Being honest to myself and to my partner turned out to be a very positive way to clear up that confusion and work it out together.

This more realistic approach to my problems was helpful in dealing with my sexuality and my pot smoking. These were both things to be worked on, without going to extremes as I usually did. I now feel that the extremes I would to go were a sign of my immaturity. Now I am much gentler with myself, talking things out with my girlfriend, and not whipping myself into submission with guilt or ideals. No, maturity seems to be a process of realizing what you need to work on, and working gradually towards change. An acknowledgement that I was not perfect, not totally mature, was a first step towards maturity.

I still look back to my days and nights at the Palace as the place where it all began. This case study has helped me to integrate other factors, such as my home and my social life, into that picture. I participated in several arenas simultaneously, as we all do, day to day. Maybe it was the novelty, the difference, the movies, and the good times which lead my mind back to the Palace. Perhaps it was a den of corruption in some people's eyes, but for me it was a safe place, a loving place, with a group of friends whom I shall never forget. I have attempted to share some of my feelings and experiences, without moralizing, although some of my decisions seem to veer towards conformity. No, all of my decisions were my decisions, made from my beliefs and my feelings. If this case study prompts reaction, so be it. But I'll have no moralizing!

CASE 3

Running Hurdles

This autobiography focuses on the author's determination to over-come obstacles in the way of becoming a doctor. She describes a regimen of self-improvement begun in junior high school and carried on through college. Though she has many successes along the way, her status as a pre-med student in a highly competitive college brings her up against the fact that she cannot maintain the high grades she had been used to in high school. She also reconsiders her single-minded striving for academic achievement as she becomes active in demon-strating against racism on her campus. Though shaken in her belief in herself, she invokes religious faith as the means for survival. Her experiences at college emerge as a means for her to take a larger perspective on the philosophical notion of the good life and the meaning of personal success. Though her ambition remains, she moves toward a deeper understanding of her own fallibility and a spiritual acceptance of life outcomes beyond the grip of self-determination.

> I don't feel no ways tired,
> I've come too far from where I started from.
> Nobody told me that the road would be easy,
> but I don't believe He brought me this far to leave me.

As I think about the words in this gospel song, I can only look upon my past with relief and anticipate the future with hope. I ask myself what it is that has guided me to this, my junior year in college and my twentieth year in the world. The answer is, in short: motivation, hard work, deter-mination, love, and, of course, God. There have been frequent ups and downs—times when I did much soul-searching. During these periods I learned to dig deep. I tried to understand why what was happening at that particular time was so important to me and then plan my future course of action accordingly. I was not always sure that the steps that I was about to take were the right ones. However, I did know that no matter what the outcome, there was a lesson I could learn. Often there were tears that could flow river-deep. Nevertheless, I knew that I would never give up on a dream, for my faith and hope reached far into the sky. Barriers became temporary hindrances which, once overcome, would make me a true victor — fit and able to handle future problems.

My mother often explained to me that I must never let others set limitations for me. She said that if I believed with all my heart that I could do something, I shouldn't let anyone tell me that I can't — at least not without giving it a try first. She added that only God knew what was to become of my future, not men. My mother believed in me and, more important, I believed in myself. I started to read books on how to succeed in high school and, using a self-teaching guide I got at the thrift store, I worked hard on doing algebra problems. Despite the teacher believing I was not yet ready for the challenge of the algebra course, I took the class in the summer and got an "A"! This experience helped me to learn a lesson of self-confidence and determination that I have never forgotten.

In high school I encountered new battles. Even though I had an "A" average and was taking a couple of honors classes, I realized that my English class was far from honors level. I remember talking to a teacher who said that the level I was on was *average*. That was difficult for me to accept. My eighth-grade teacher once said, "You should always strive to be above average and should never let anyone consider you as average." Oh, no, I was not going to let someone look down his nose at me; I was just as capable of excelling as anyone else!

I used another self-teaching guide to aid me in preparation to take a placement exam to move to a higher level class. My book bag went with me everywhere: on long trips to grandma's, to my parents' meetings, to church, and even on the way to shopping centers. During this time people thought of me as a "little brain." I didn't pay much attention to this, because the only thing that concerned me was getting ahead. I was not going to let those who teased me distract me from the tasks which would one day help me to become a great doctor. I knew that once I had accomplished my current academic goals, I would have time to move on to other things. Sure enough, I was put in a higher level English class after passing a placement test.

Having realized that I was academically sound, I then went out for track where I made only a small contribution, but I still remained dedicated. I enjoyed getting to know upperclassmen on the team, and I began to look forward to going to practice. I felt that by talking to older students I was taking a sneak preview of possibilities for my own future. More and more I wanted to complement my academic success with other types of accomplishment; therefore, I added reducing my hurdle times to my list of goals. The feeling of being down in the starting block, waiting for the gun to sound, gave me a sense of perfect concentration. I was filled with excitement as I cleared the hurdles and passed the finish line. I was inspired by the senior awards ceremony where I saw students acknowledged for their outstanding achievements in academics and athletics. I wondered if the same types of honors were to be a part of my future.

In my sophomore year I challenged myself by taking mostly gifted and talented courses. My enrollment in these classes was a result of careful planning. Freshman year I had looked through the course guide and noted all the honors courses that I wanted to take before I graduated. I talked to teachers about the courses well ahead of time to see how I could best prepare. If I was to be a doctor, I knew that I would have to start working at it then. While I still continued to play sports, I managed to keep my priorities straight and maintain an A average. However, that year I failed the state writing test. I cried, and I never told my friends because I knew that I was the only one who could correct the problem. Because passing the exam was a graduation requirement, I had to figure out my next plan of attack. Recalling that some members of my family couldn't read or write very well, I knew it was important for me to work hard to overcome these deficits in my basic skills. With all this in mind, I worked diligently and passed the test the next time.

I didn't have a sibling at home to whom I could express my frustrations. Because my brother was ten years older, I didn't get to know him well until he was in high school. The next thing I knew, he left home, got married, and had kids. The good things in life always seemed to be at the *next* stage of life or educational level. My boyfriend was the only person other than my family members with whom I felt comfortable sharing my goals, dreams, and frustrations. I never thought that my friends at school could understand my tendency to think so far into the future. They knew that I did well in my classes, but they really didn't know how hard I worked and why. Jason, however, was aware that I wanted to be a doctor and that it was my first priority. I had fun like everyone else, but whenever I had the chance, I read books on study skills or about being successful. Jason and I became very close, probably because he was a little older and was thinking about life plans as well. I learned to trust him in a way that I had not known before. I learned to love and to be loved, and thus felt good about myself. Jason was there for me throughout many ups and downs until my senior year.

Stories about how difficult it had been years ago for blacks to obtain education of any sort made me strive even harder towards my goals. I knew that my grandmother, as brilliant as she was, didn't have much education. Even though she was the most insightful and loving person that I had ever known, it hurt me to know that she did not have the same opportunities that I had. It was almost as if she, along with many others, had been cheated out of something that they rightfully deserved. Although no one in my family ever pressured me to set high standards for myself, I knew that they hoped that I would succeed. Through much support and encouragement, they made me believe in myself to such a degree that I felt nothing was impossible for me to obtain. I never wanted to let opportunities pass me by; so many people had sacrificed so much so I could have them. Deep down inside, I knew I was able to overcome academic obstacles just as my family members had endured hard times in their lives. My family has always stressed that God made it possible for them to overcome prejudices and other barriers they encountered. I knew that if I continued to encounter academic stumbling blocks, I needed God to guide me through any problems that I might encounter.

During my senior year in high school, I spent most of my free time in the lab at the state university. Having participated in a fellowship program the previous summer, I developed a project that I could work on independently for a science research class. I had a key to the lab and was allowed to work there whenever I could. During the times that I processed rat nerve tissue until midnight, Mom or Jason stayed in the lab with me. Having such strong support from the people I cared about was crucial; I was able to develop the self-confidence and skills which made my interest in science increase. Filled with energy and enthusiasm, I felt a sense of satisfaction in knowing that my classwork had some practical applications in the real world. As senior year came to a close, I had succeeded in meeting most of my academic goals. I presented my project at a science fair and gained assurance that my skills in science were apparent in the work that I produced. I received many awards and scholarships at the senior awards ceremony which made both my parents and me proud. However, in spite of all this success, I had failed to strengthen my relationship with God. I realized this to be true when I became haunted with both Jason's words, "You need to have God in your life," and a recurring nightmare. The nightmare horrifies me today as much as it did years ago. I dread the thought that my fate in the nightmare could ever take place. If by chance it did happen, I would know that I was in Hell or some other inferno.

In my nightmare, I find myself on a ship looking out at a dirty brown-grey body of water divided by a large brick wall. Boundless, the wall stretches as far as I can see up into the sky and out in every other direction. As I look into the water, I notice an object floating in its center. A strong and powerful force then pushes me forward, making my body press close to the ship. As the pressure intensifies along my upper spine, I begin to feel weak against the force, but somehow dominant over the unknown floating object. As the force increases, I am able to dive in the water and swim toward the object. Swimming fast causes my back to ache and arms to tire. Each stroke, though painful, seems to take me closer to the object. However, this feeling changes after about a minute. Suddenly it seems as though the object is moving away from me and towards the brick wall, which now seems more vast and blocks all light. I try to swim faster, but it does not seem to make much difference in the distance that I am from the object. Tired and puzzled, I stop swimming and reach out towards the object expecting to grasp nothing. Immediately I feel myself sinking. There is nothing that I can do to save myself; therefore, I take one last look at the object and the brick wall. I have arrived at the end of my journey.

As I now look back upon the dream, I can understand why I consider it infernal. In my interpretation of the dream the ship that I am standing on is my home. The force coming from my home represents my parents and other role models. They are trying to lead me toward the distant object symbolizing my goals. Those who support me are trying to make me see that my goals are real and obtainable. Their belief in me gives me confidence to dive into the world, symbolized here by the water. Unfortunately, once I am on my own, I begin to take on too many tasks without really knowing what I am getting myself into in the long run. As I begin to think that I am reaching my goals, I find out that times have changed. My goals are leaving me and are about to crash into a brick wall. I begin to believe that my goals are now unobtainable, but I reach out in vain, feeling that I still might have some dominance over them. After doing this, I begin to sink into the lower parts of the world. By losing hope of obtaining goals, I become a victim of my own efforts. Because of this, I enter the bottomless lower world which is indeed Hell.

My worst fear has always been to have goals and not be able to obtain them. At the time when I had the nightmare, I never considered the possibility that it could come true, nor that God was a possible savior. I had not yet found the connection between my goals and Him. It was only while in college that I began to understand what a relationship with God could mean. Before then, I remained confused about how he would affect my personal development.

I am the daughter of a preacher. Though my father works many long hours in the church each week, he also has another occupation to help support us. As a preacher's kid (P.K.'s, we call ourselves) I came face to face very early with many special expectations and problems. Most of the time I was puzzled by church members' inconsistencies and seeming hypocrisy. The biggest problem was watching people criticize one another. Being present at most of the church events, I became increasingly aware of jealousy. I have seen people upset with others for holding a particular office in the church, for singing too many solos, for dressing differently, and even for trying to become "buddy-buddy" with the pastor and/or his wife. This has always bothered me because, in seeking to learn more about God, I became more and more confused by the actions of those who claimed to be Christians. Inconsistencies became increasingly apparent as I became aware of these people's testimonials about how much the Lord had done for them.

How could it be that these people could be so unkind to one another? Weren't these people supposed to be kinder than those who were in the "world"?

I became even more confused when it came down to matters concerning my father. I felt severe pain whenever I heard someone say something bad about my father. I became very bitter towards these people, mainly because I would hear these comments behind my father's back, yet see them smile to his face. I wondered how these Christians could be so cruel. Wasn't my father a servant of God? Did he, as their leader, deserve this treatment? I remember overhearing one particular woman challenge my father's judgment. I was hurt, for I truly believed that my father would not intentionally do anything that was wrong; however, I realized that my father was still human. I knew that he was not God and was only a messenger. Let me say that I never have been close to my father, probably because deep down I wish that he was perfect and all that the church members think he ought to be. For most of my life I have seen Dad in two lights, the one who I knew through his thoughts in his sermons, and then as the man I could never open up to about my feelings. I love my father, but I have always wished that we had been able to communicate more as I was growing up and to know each other more personally. Instead, I became quite close with my mother, since she had stayed home to raise me.

There came a time when I could not merely rely on my family's opinions or views of God. I began a search to find out who God was for myself. My freshman winter in college was the first time that I learned to depend truly on God. This was because I found myself walking around in disbelief at actions going on about me. There was an incident in which a black professor was harassed, insulted, and tape recorded without consent. I remember seeing a terrifying picture of the professor on the front page of an ultra right-wing newspaper on campus. The photo, taken in the heat of fury and chaos, angered me just to look at it. I thought the newspaper staff had gone too far this time. It was not the first time that this professor had been harassed. Because of its history of articles negatively portraying blacks and other minority groups, I suspected that racism was involved. However, it was not purely a white-versus-black issue; it was also about threatening one's dignity and reputation as a type of sophomoric blood sport. I was sick and tired of seeing articles in that newspaper that tried to make blacks seem inferior. I was tired of these pompous guys acting as if only they knew how things should be. With some self-proclaimed authority they figured that they could say or do anything they wanted and get away with it, hiding their racism behind the smoke screen of freedom of the press. What was so scary and almost intimidating was the paper's persuasive style; many people could read it and say "Yeah, that's a good point." A little serious thought and consideration of undertones would reveal that something was wrong. Unfortunately, the newspaper's writing style swayed quite a few people into believing that its presentations were accurate and true.

This and much similar outrageous racism on the part of the newspaper turned my resentment into a force which propelled me to protest. I began to participate in rallies, to picket stores advertising in the paper, and to express views and concerns in ways that were unthinkable for me before coming to college. The people to whom I felt closest during that time were those engaged in these activities with me. I felt a common bond with them because we were working for the same cause. While walking on campus, I was always on guard, just waiting to hear someone talking about the incident with that professor, or to see someone stare at me or the ribbon symbolizing black liberation pinned to my jacket. The air was filled with bad vibes.

Living next door to one of the newspaper's editors made those days much more trying. One day as I was studying at my desk, I heard a loud conversation going on just outside my door about the "reactionary blacks blowing things out of proportion." This comment presumably was made in response to student protests and TV and newspaper reporters flooding the campus. I was struck motionless at my desk. I felt trapped within the confines of my room. I was tense and angry and full of pain and frustration. I badly wanted to go out there and give an argument that would put all those men into a state of awe and speechlessness. It angered me even more when they spoke of the Afro-American Society and its predominantly black dorm. They put everything down, yet admitted that they had never stepped foot inside the building. I doubt if any of them even had a black friend. I wondered how such otherwise intelligent people could be so closed-minded and ignorant about others. Every time I heard the pipsqueaky voice of one young man who was talking in the hallway when the comments were made, I became extremely annoyed and angry. I was frustrated because, although I was angry at the students for being so uninformed and insensitive, I also was disappointed with myself for being so bothered by their actions. I longed to be stronger.

Dorm events didn't end there. Every day as I passed my editor-neighbor's door there were mean and degrading statements written about minority groups and feminists on his memo board. It would include things like: "No radicals, feminist witches, black racists, or gays wanted." With each glance, I wanted to rip the board down, or just scribble on it. I wanted to kick that stupid door—do something that showed that someone was not afraid of him or his malicious words. Something, however, always restrained me. No matter how great my resentment, I told myself I could not stoop to the level of that hateful young man who lived in the room next door. I prayed that I might maintain my dignity and self-control. Each day my roommate (who was black) and I talked late into the night about everything that was happening and our growing concerns. I always felt like a captive in the dorm, for even these private conversations were whispered so that none of our white neighbors would hear what we said. We were not really afraid of what might happen if others heard us, but we didn't want to run the risk of having our comments misinterpreted or purposely distorted.

It was during the days of protest that I began to understand the pressures upon people in the civil rights struggles of the '60s. More than twenty years later, effort to correct situations of injustice continued. My uncle told me before I went to college, "Always remember where you've come from, where you're going, and who and what has helped you to get where you are and hope to be." There is no way that I can ever forget or ignore my past or the problems that still exist today.

During those days, I spent my mornings in class and my afternoons and nights protesting. I studied during any free moment I had. It was hard to do, but I had put protesting high up on my list of priorities. This was in spite of the fact that I knew other freshmen who had been asked to take a one year leave to reevaluate their goals after a poor performance first term. I had to do what seemed right at the time. I worked hard to do the best I could in my classes—I had tutors and went to see my professors regularly. I was glad they all were understanding and knew the position I felt obligated to take. My Chinese language professor asked me to see him after class one day. He said he knew that I was involved in the protests and wanted to know how I was doing. We talked for quite a while and both of us had teary eyes. I could tell that he cared and that what was happening was affecting him too. He was willing to work with me to make my classwork more manageable during this period. I knew that he and other professors understood the situation, and many were actively involved in the protests. For example, I met an English professor while we were both out picketing. He chatted with me then and whenever I saw him throughout the rest of the term.

I really valued the friendships that developed during the days of protesting. It seemed rare to find people who would *really listen* to what you had to say: not just hear your words but not your meaning. This was because we discussed, in addition to the incident with the black professor, many issues about student life which came to the surface. For example, many whites wondered why blacks seemed to separate themselves at dinner. Blacks wanted to know why we so often had to take time away from studying to protest things which shouldn't be happening in the first place.

In the midst of all the confusion, I learned to pray continuously. My time in prayer seemed to be the only time when I was at peace and the only thing that gave me strength to make it through the day. At the end of the term, in a class where I was the only black, we had a discussion about all the things that had happened. After hearing the comments about the "typical black" (which I didn't know existed) as well as some other radical and conservative views from my classmates, I felt obligated to say something.

Before I did, however, I prayed briefly that I would be understood and not just heard. After stating my opinion and feelings, I thanked God for making me stronger that term than I ever had been in my life. From that day onward, I valued my college more than before because it had, however unintentionally, taught me to communicate with people from a wide variety of backgrounds and outlooks. It is only too bad that it took a crisis for people to start expressing their true feelings and concerns.

As I started to develop new friendships in college, I tended to share only parts of me, almost like a puzzle. Each piece would fit well with certain individuals, and not so well with others. I learned how best to mix and match those pieces so as to get along with different types of people. No matter how great the differences are between people, there has to be a common ground somewhere. It is unfortunate that a person's skin color, religious beliefs, nationality, or difference of views can sometimes distract us from other traits he or she might possess which could bring us closer. My friends who are Jewish, gay, foreign, and Caucasian have helped me to recognize the basic good in everyone.

Though I value the relationships I have with others outside my race, just as I do those within it, my four closest friends are black. They have seen me both at times when I was bubbling with energy and stressing-out over something. There are few other people I feel are trustworthy enough for me to open up to. I can't imagine what my life at college would be like without them, because they have not only been friends since I arrived on campus, but have also been family. Combined, I can say they know almost as much about me as I do. It was really strange when I went abroad one term and did not have them to lean on. However, I did get to know God as a friend who would be wherever I went.

In the summer after freshman year, I was able to go abroad for the first time in my life. Looking back, it seems evident that in Taiwan I learned more about myself than I ever thought possible. This knowledge helped me to gain increased confidence and direction. Most importantly, I became close to God in a way that I had never known. By taking classes and having Chinese roommates, I was able to learn a great deal about the language, lifestyles, and traditions of the people. I felt so at peace at this Christian university because religion seemed to be a part of many people's lives. I was able to respect those who were of different faiths because they were not ashamed to express their beliefs in any setting. All these things made me eager to develop my own spiritual life.

On my nineteenth birthday I was awakened by an alarming announcement recounted here from my journal:

> I heard something or a voice say "You are going to die young." What a scary thought to wake up to on your birthday. I don't know if it was my conscious self, the end of a dream, or God. All I know is that I

won't forget these words ever. I must take each second seriously, and value it, because the next moment is not promised. New doors will open up to me, and I must be sure to live as a Christian and take advantage of those gifts. I don't want to separate myself, I just want to be me—a goal-oriented, religious, and successful person. It's not ambition, for sometimes that's bad. It is determination to do the very best I can. As long as I follow God's word, there is nothing that I can't do. No matter how short a life I live, I must be first and foremost thankful to God who gave it to me. I hope that I make the right decisions and can in some way be a positive influence on someone else. I love the Lord and pray that he will always be with my family and me. . . .

Praying continuously, I came to know God as my personal savior. I did whatever the holy spirit led me to do, and reaped many blessings because of it. I was unafraid to go in any church on the island and sit down. I jumped on buses, and trusted that whoever I met would help me reach my destination. Listening to the English translations of the sermons at the chapel made me believe in the power of God that was touching my life halfway around the world. I never felt alone or afraid because I knew the Lord was watching over me. I continuously thanked God for the blessings that he had bestowed on me each day.

As my faith grew, I also looked to God for direction with my future. By taking the time to be still and listen for an answer, it was revealed to me that I would spend my life going to different countries and helping people with their health problems. Afterward, I would spread the word about the goodness of God and His ability to make all things possible. Having been given this awareness of my destiny I felt fulfilled and content. I knew where I was headed and felt happy about the enormous possibilities for growth in my work in serving the Lord. Soon, I began to meet missionaries who were doctors and other health care workers. After talking with them, I couldn't wait to get home and share the news with others about my future career.

When I returned to college in my sophomore year, I was on a spiritual high. I worked with the chaplain and for the first time realized what a wonderful calling my father had. I couldn't think of anything more satisfying than dedicating one's life to God. As I continued to think about my future in health care, I became obsessed with the idea of doing everything I could to make God proud of me. Gradually I spent more time thinking about the future and less time in my daily devotions without fully realizing that I was doing so.

As the year progressed, I started to feel empty and unsatisfied with my academics. I initially thought it was because of the difficulty of college; it never occurred to me that God was trying to tell me something. I was reminded of the picture that my high school guidance counselor tried to paint for me of what life at a highly competitive college would be like. She told me to imagine the smartest person in my most difficult class who seemed to get A's without really working hard for them. I should then think of a school where almost everyone was that type of student. She said that she knew that I got where I was (at the top of my class) by working extremely hard and by putting in extra time, and that was an accomplishment in itself. She warned me, however, that it might become unfulfilling or burdensome later. I found it difficult to accept that what I had always taken pride in (working hard) was now something that might not lead to success in the future. Once again in my life, someone was trying to discourage me from getting ahead. By reading extra books, doing additional problems, and asking about the practical applications of the course in class, I felt I was preparing for my future as a physician. That was my motivation, so although I was competing with people who caught onto some principles quicker than me, my concern was not with them, but with my goals.

As a college student I am beginning to see that perhaps Mrs. Riley was right in warning me about what I was going to be up against. I know that I have potential to succeed, so I have worked extremely hard in my classes and met with professors, obtained advice from grad students, had a tutor every term, and frequently met with my pre-med advisor and the academic skills director. Regardless of my efforts, my academic standing is not high. I have become disgusted with the grading system at my college. First of all, the science courses are graded on a curve. I hate to always have to compare myself to the mean, or actually all the other students in the class. I despise that since learning is something that I feel is very personal. If my grade falls below the mean, my attitude toward the class changes. No longer is my emphasis on doing the best I can on an exam, but instead it is on getting at least the mean. I realize now that I was lowering my standards and settling for doing about the same as everyone else.

For the first time in my life, I have become accustomed to C's and being a satisfactory student. I have had professors say to me "C's are not bad. You'll still get into med school." By being on a campus where my right (or any other minority's) to be there is continuously being questioned, I have come to realize that it is necessary to excel and get A's and B's. Otherwise, people will doubt my credibility, and even worse, my ability.

It has been difficult for me to accept doors being closed due to the G.P.A. I remember that when invitations were sent out to students in my class to discuss the honors program as well as internship opportunities, I wasn't invited. Many people asked me why I wasn't there. Since I always walked about with a positive attitude, was involved in a professional society, and knew many important people on campus, they assumed I was somewhere near the top of my class. I couldn't really answer them because the pain I felt was unimaginable; I knew that I should have been there and I felt left out. As a result, I had to make a special appointment to discuss these programs. It hurt to realize that I had learned about them not because the college thought that I should know about them, but because of my own efforts. My mom always told me that sometimes you have to make things happen for yourself. I had to work very hard to get into higher levels of English and math years ago, so I naturally continue to seek out people and opportunities now that I am in college. I try to overcome any obstacles in my path, for my success has always come about because I have refused to settle for anything — regardless of the situation.

It was at a national youth leadership meeting in high school that I realized the true leader in me. Since that time I have been coming up with ideas of things I'd like to do. A while ago I developed a project that would try to encourage middle school students to become interested in science through role models. This project meant a lot to me, for I knew from personal experience that when you talk to people who are where you want to be, you begin to believe that you really can get there, too. During breaks, I had always called physicians, med students, or anyone else in health care who could tell me about the field and steps to get into it. In turn, I often spoke to students at different churches to try to get them interested in continuing their education. I believed these things could keep dreams alive for someone.

After spending a couple of months meeting with different people who could give me ideas about how to get my project started, I was just about ready to get it off the ground. I had a meeting with my former professor and friend, whom I always go to when there's something on my mind or a new thing I'm interested in doing. After he agreed to help me carry out the project, I said to him, "I know that there still might be some trouble getting funding to do this, since my grades could be stronger." When I told him my standing, the expression on his face was that of shock and disappointment. He suggested that perhaps I should try to constrain my ideas until I was in a position in my life to make the greatest contribution. He went on to say that he knew that I was going to make great changes one day, but all good leaders need a solid background. It was his wish to see me concentrate my energies on improving my grades, so I could get into the best medical school in the country. Though I did not doubt his sincerity, I felt all alone and stripped of the very thing that had made me feel so fulfilled for so long — a project that would spark energy and enthusiasm in kids who, like me, may have to overcome many academic obstacles. What would I do now? I left that office and tried to come to grips with the fact that things don't always work out as planned.

In the next term, I tried to concentrate more on my studies. After laying my project aside for a while, I became confused about where my life was headed. Some mornings I would lie in bed wondering why I should get up. Why should I put myself through so much pain for so little gratification? Why couldn't I stop school, get a job, and do whatever I wanted? Even though these thoughts kept running through my mind, I knew that they wouldn't make me happy. I always felt a great sense of accomplishment and joy when I worked in the lab all night, completed a paper or problem set, or developed ideas for the future. These things made me see that academics were a necessary part of my life.

At the term's closing, I felt drained of all energy. I had hit a burnout point. It was during these days of physical and emotional strain that I realized I had been leading a life that was not dependent on God. For many months I had been taking my life into my own hands. Because I wanted to take advantage of anything associated with being a doctor, I rushed through the first half of college. There were many warning signs and people telling me to slow down, but I overlooked them or simply regarded them as more barriers that I had to overcome. It never occurred to me during that stressful time that perhaps God was trying to tell me that great things can be accomplished only through His will. Attainment of my goals will not come through my efforts alone; only He possesses the master plan for my life. I had to take some time off from school in order to understand at last that if I was to *succeed*, I needed to turn over my life to God and let Him choose my path.

Presently, my attention is focused on increasing my happiness, flexibility, and spirituality. I no longer take for granted the relationships I've had or lessons learned. After breaking up with my college boyfriend, I realized that too often I have let my goals draw me away from those whom I love the most. I can become so involved with what I am doing that I don't give others the time to show me how they feel about my actions. I need to take time out to listen to others. I realize that my friends have always been there for me when I needed them. Therefore, I have no real reason to believe that they will disappear if I allow them to see my innermost fears of not being able to obtain the very high goals I set for myself. Often they have been the ones who have given me happiness and support that I couldn't find elsewhere.

It has been this type of support that has helped me to see my potential and to go after my goals with an almost uncontrollable desire. It is only after reading the biographies of those who have inspired me in the past that I now realize they achieved success by hard work *and* strong spiritual beliefs. They were all happy people, who had endured pressures, by trusting that God would lead them through those times. Even though I have overcome barriers in the past, I have always carried a bit of resentment towards those things or persons who I felt caused them. I should have actually been thankful for them, since God had control over my future and knew what was best.

My first response to any advice conflicting with my goals has been to first regard it as a barrier, and then try to see what *I* can do to prevent it from having a negative effect. I need to spend more time praying to God to see how *He* wants me to deal with the situation. I know He is able to do this because while I was abroad it was from His word that I received direction in all parts of my life. I long to have this type of relationship with God again.

While growing up I used to wonder how God would influence my life. I have heard some older folks say that He is a "heart fixer, a way maker, and a mind regulator." God is able to be all these things for me. My life is in God's hands, and it is through His guidance that tomorrow's joy, treasures, and perhaps even a medical degree, shall be mine. I am so glad God forgives those who, like me, make the mistake of vainly trying to completely control their own lives. I truly believe the message in the words of the gospel song I have paraphrased in the first person to fit my own story:

> I know somehow, and I know some way,
> I'm gonna make it!
> No matter what the test, whatever comes my way,
> I'm gonna make it!
> With Jesus on my side, things will work out fine!

CASE 4

Someday My Elders Will Be Proud

This Native-American woman recounts her experience of living in two worlds. She describes how her mother raised her and her three brothers after her father abandoned the family when she was quite young. These circumstances, along with abuse at the hands of her uncle, leave lasting emotional wounds she will not address until much later. While firmly rooted in and proud of her Native-American culture, she becomes a scholarship student at an elite secondary school. Her family's relative poverty and the condescending attitudes of her classmates further feelings of self-doubt, low self-esteem, and ethnic inferiority. Her transition to college does not succeed; she turns to heavy drinking, fails academically, and returns home. She gets a job working with troubled Native-American adolescents, and through helping the self she sees in them, she finds a purpose in returning to college.

I grew up in Bismarck, North Dakota. My parents met through a relocation program. Relocation attempted to assimilate Native Americans into urban life from their reservation or tribal communities. The goal of the program was for an individual to gain economic self-sufficiency by means of a vocation or technical school education. My parents were in just such a program in Denver, Colorado, where they met and married. That is where my three brothers and I were born. My mother, a Cheyenne, was 22, and my father, a Blackfoot, was 21 when they had me. I am the oldest.

My father ran back to his reservation in Montana before my youngest brother was born. I must have been almost 4 years old. I have no concrete memories of him. My mom says that he taught her how to take care of me, because she didn't know that much about babies. He began drinking when I was born, and he was a womanizer. Soon his drinking got out of control. Despite her problems with our dad, Mom would always tell us how he loved my brothers and me and that he was a good father to us. Whenever he came home we would run and crawl all over him. We never saw him again after he left Mom and us behind. Dad died on the reservation when I was 7 years old, from alcoholism. He was only 28. I don't remember exactly when Mom told us, but it held no meaning. It seemed that he had already died when he left.

By the time I was 6, my mother had moved to Bismarck, where many of her relatives and immediate family lived. We did this because family was important to her tribe, and they would help us as much as they could. Initially we lived off welfare and the help that our relatives could give us. My mother decided she didn't want us to live like that forever. She wanted to be a good example for the four of us, so she worked during the day and went to school at night to get her bachelor's degree in social work at the state university. We grew up in a single-parent family with the benefits of an extended family.

Mom worked through temporary services at factories, and we got some monetary help from our father's Social Security benefits after he died, food stamps, and AFDC. We were very poor. We went to garage sales, Salvation Armies, and Goodwills for most of our clothes, furniture, and toys.

During those years when my mother pushed herself, my brothers and I were watched by one of my mom's younger brothers. She had no choice; he needed a place to live, and we needed a babysitter. I think he was in his 20s. He stayed with us from the time I was in first grade, until I was in the sixth grade. He was always there after school when we came home. He taught us good things, like to stick up for each other when we used to get chased home from school by the white kids, and not to be afraid of fighting for ourselves.

However, our uncle was alcoholic and had a violent streak in him. We became convenient scapegoats for him when he was sober or drunk. Even though my mom forbade him to drink in her home, he still did. There are lots of stories about how we couldn't wear shorts because the belt or switch marks were too vivid. He never hit us when Mom was home. When he did whip us, he'd say to us after he was finished, "You'd better keep your mouths shut and not tell your mother." And we stayed silent.

It was for stupid reasons that we got whipped. Who moved his magazine, who messed up the kitchen, who lost his sock and where was it? Who did it? Guilt, innocence, truth, right, wrong, what did any of that matter? It meant nothing. We could have been perfect children but that wouldn't have changed anything. We learned to clean the house as soon as we got home, and maybe it was good enough, maybe it wasn't. We learned to hide in our rooms until Mom got home. We used to be mean to our dogs, and sometimes to each other. He made everything seem our fault.

Why didn't we say anything? I don't know. I remember one time how our uncle picked up my brother Lance by the hair, and Lance was screaming. I never felt so helpless. I was mad, but I was afraid too. I knew it was all wrong, but I was glad in a way too, because it wasn't me. Mom kicked him out finally when I was in the sixth grade. All that mattered to us then was that he was gone. I still remember the relief I felt.

Why so long to get him out? Mom had to know. All I can think of is how her tribe is strongly patriarchal; men rule the home, and women must listen to and abide by what their brothers say. You never tell them that they're wrong; it would be disrespectful. In the traditional way, uncles are a second father to their nieces and nephews. Alcoholism ran through her side of the family and our dad's. I know that our two uncles had a violent father and uncle too. Those behaviors were probably passed on, and were allowed to continue because men have so much power to do what they want. Mom hadn't quite broke out of that mindset when our uncle was living with us, and she tried so hard to make our lives better at a cost to hers. I couldn't really be angry at her, because I remember how she tried to make us happy.

When I first started actively remembering everything that our uncle did to us, I hated him. I was glad that he couldn't hold a job, that he had a rotten marriage, that his own kids were uncontrollable and spoiled, that his drinking gave him critical liver and heart problems. But I tell you, it's strange. He loves us. I'm not going to live fueled by hate, and so I tried to understand what there was in him and his life that let him beat four little kids. He never had it easy himself, and he is the one who has to live with what he's done. He doesn't need another person who hates him, or another part of his life to make him more bitter.

Many of our relatives on my mother's side lived in Omaha. Lots of these relatives were members of the newer religion, Native American Church. NAC integrates Christianity, adapting to urban life by getting an education or keeping a job, and being aware of what's good and beautiful in life, in other people, and in yourself. At least that's what it means to me.

An NAC meeting lasts throughout a night; you pray for whoever the meeting is for, including your family. You get no sleep, people sing "hymns" that are in the native language, and you eat a bitter-tasting cactus called peyote. The old school relates the Bible to life, and others talk about what their elders told them about being good people. People talk about how to cope with problems, talk about why things are the way they are, how you can look at your misfortunes, and how we must appreciate and recognize the good that we have. They talk about humbleness and realizing that so much of what we deal with will pass in time. It was there that I felt awe for wisdom and reasoning.

We drove back to Nebraska frequently for NAC meetings and for traditional religious ceremonies, where we prayed and made offerings to the gods and spirits, holding feasts and dances to honor what was being done for the people. We used to travel around the surrounding states for powwows — intertribal gatherings where dancers and singers from different tribes got together to dance and visit with one another. We also stayed with close relatives with whom my mother's generation had grown up. They told us stories from long ago, and they fed us and took us along with them in their areas. The four of us liked going out of town; our world was not defined by the city.

When I finished sixth grade at the public school, Mom had me tested for a private school that an uncle's wife highly recommended. They wanted me to go to a school better than the public junior high. I was accepted and given a scholarship, and when seventh grade came around I went there. At the time, I didn't want to go. I wanted to go on with my friends to the public junior high.

I remember feeling that I didn't fit in, and being apprehensive. It was an affluent Episcopalian college preparatory school, grades K–12. It wasn't race that made me an outsider, though there were undercurrents of it. If anything, it seemed to be worse in grade school, where my brothers and I had come home crying, until they told us to fight and stick up for each other. I'd say that poverty made me an outsider.

The first day an English teacher had us write essays on the furthest place in the world we had been. After we finished, we placed them up on the bulletin board. I wrote about Nebraska, and when I looked at the other essays, I saw people saying, "I've been around the world on a cruise ship." A larger majority than I could have imagined said countries in Europe, California, all over. Showing off seemed to occupy a great deal of time at school.

Kids were mean there, not physically, but with their words. "*Who* does your shopping for you? You've *never* been to the Calhoun Club? *Where* do you get your clothes from? You mean you *haven't* been out of the U.S.? You *rent* your home? You mean you don't get an *allowance*?" I couldn't have what they had or really understand the importance of it all, and I felt it acutely. There were the times when I would be talking with someone, and instead of listening to whatever it was I was saying, they'd be staring at my clothes.

It wasn't anything that my family or relatives understood. We all knew that it was a good thing for me to go to school there; they wanted us younger kids to be able to work at jobs we wanted and not struggle like they had. Being poor was awful, the bills were too many and too much. I knew all of that in a vague sense way down, and I suppose that's why I stuck it out. But still, it didn't help me in dealing with the daily questionings or scornful looks from my peers. When they did that, I just looked away or down, shoulders slumped, because I felt self-conscious.

Learning the stuff from the books wasn't ever really hard; it was just memorizing most of the time. So I'd memorize and forget everything later.

Mom made sure that I did homework when I was home. She always used to say to us how important school was, because if we had it, life wouldn't be so hard for us as for her generation. If anything, the material was boring. I noticed that the kids were highly conscientious about doing their work. Grades mattered to them in a way I never really understood. Mom never said to me, "Jean, I want you to get A's," and she never acted disappointed when I didn't get an A. All Mom ever said was, "Did you try?" and that was enough. The other kids did their work because they wanted a good grade. For me, it was a way out.

The only way I could figure out to make things better was to bug Mom incessantly about clothes. She tried her best, but it wasn't good enough in my eyes to catch up to the other kids. So I started stealing from stores and from unlocked lockers at school. And then it happened; I got caught. I felt hunted, and I knew the other kids would really talk. "Can you believe what she did?" Most of all, I knew that I would hurt Mom. That's what mattered the most to me. I got suspended for a couple of days. When my mom and I came in to talk to the middle school director, and I was asked "how come?" I ended up crying, and talking about how people called me names, looked at me funny, and that I couldn't take feeling bad about myself anymore. I hadn't realized that those things preyed on my mind, that they hurt, and that's why I was stealing.

So Mom and I went home and she talked with me. She said that it was wrong to steal, and that it reflected on myself and the kind of upbringing I had. She said how it was easy to steal, it was cheating, and that it was hard to tell the truth and live by it. She said that we all make mistakes and that it was all right. "Just learn something good from this." And then she talked to me about the things that I had been called. "They're wrong and cruel and do not know you or your strengths. They're just a bunch of kids." I knew what I had done and felt ashamed about myself, but she made me believe in her love and in myself. From Mom, I learned to be compassionate.

I think I learned that I couldn't be myself at that school. I had to be like the other students to be happy there; I had to be rich and snobby. Because of my family's poverty and our tribal gatherings, I couldn't be like them. Not really anyway. Most of the time I was bored, or distracted by home. So what if the football team lost? So what if you're pissed off because you can't talk on the phone past 8:00? What kind of problems are those?

I felt that I had to put on airs, or have a dramatic life that people would be interested in, otherwise I was a lonely person. I needed to find a niche somehow, somewhere. So for about two years, somewhere between eighth and ninth grade, I became a liar. I made up the death of a relative, talked about things like drinking, or weed. I told people that I was part Greek. I quit when someone asked about my Greek grandmother. I knew what a lie it was, and I thought to myself, what about your real grand-mother? Why can't you be proud of her and everything back home? It was like I had erased her life, said it was nothing by making up another woman who never even existed. I knew something was really wrong with me then. I cringe at the pitiful person I was. I see why I did what I did, but still. . . . I decided that never again would I lie like that, because it takes away from the truth of my life. It's "cheating." Parts of my life were ugly, and not understood, but it was mine. My life was no less important than my schoolmates'. Life can't be for everyone what it is to the affluent or sheltered, and none of that makes them better than those less fortunate or different.

By this time I realized how hard it was for my mom to support the four of us on her own. I know the bills and our teenage wants that got more and more expensive were getting to her. She would lash out at us about "never being satisfied" or about not helping enough around the house. She used to point out our faults to us, not in a nice way, during those times. For myself, I cowered during those times when she lost her temper. I couldn't help it. But it wasn't anything like those times with our uncle when we were kids — I understood why she was frustrated and yelling. Even so, Mom always came through for the four of us. She would tell us how smart we were, and how strong we could be. If we did something wrong, she would understand what drove us but always tell us to learn from it all.

There were other times when we went to an NAC meeting, powwow, lodge feast, or a meal with the relatives. I loved all those things. I didn't think about why I felt that way, all I did was feel good. I remember being back at school in the ninth grade after one weekend when we'd been to a powwow. I was in math class, looking around and listening, but my atten-tion kept fading. I kept staring out the window, remembering. We had been to Canada, and the powwow was by a huge network of lakes. During one of the breaks, my brother and I had gone out onto the lake on a motorboat. He killed the engine in the middle of the lake and we were drifting; we could see the powwow ground, all the campers, smell the fires, hear the singing, see dancers walking around in bright colors, shawls and bustles, people laughing.

We tried to start the engine, but it wouldn't, and we had forgotten to bring oars along. We were drifting farther and farther away to the opposite shore, and right before we got tangled in the reeds by the shore, we tried one last time to start the engine. It started, and we were laughing, and the wind whipped our hair back as he gunned the engine. We sped around for awhile like that, and when we got back, we had a good story to tell.

People were always teasing each other about something. That's what I liked, laughter. At night you could see all the stars; coffee tasted the best when it got chilly after the sun went down. The smell of a wood fire was always around too, and you were up late and probably tired, but you were having a good time, so it didn't matter. Out of the four of us, I liked to dance the most. When I was small, I used to dance until I had blisters and they would make me rest for awhile.

No one at school though would know what in the world I felt good about, or why. I felt caged. What did I care about a logarithm? I was disgusted when I kept hearing three girls across the aisle talking about the teacher, how nerdy she looked, and wasn't John hot, he just broke up with his girlfriend.

Reconciling school, our trips, and home life was hard. Keeping up with us and the bills was hard on Mom, and she was alone. Even though she finished up at college and got her degree, $18,000 a year didn't go far enough for the five of us. Mom was always stressed, and then there were the four of us being adolescents going through all of our stages. Sometimes I wasn't the nicest person, and got mad or upset when I couldn't do something because we didn't have the money. I would act like it was all Mom's fault. My brothers Rick and Lance were starting to hang out with the crowd at school that smoked weed, skipped school, and acted tough. Lance tried to run away one time when our uncle who used to live with us threatened to beat him up if he kept on smoking cigarettes.

My youngest brother Bill went to school with me. My other two brothers went to the public high school. They also tested for our school when they finished sixth grade, but there weren't any scholarships for them. By the time they were offered one, Mom couldn't swing it. As it was, the school was always hounding her to pay up. If she had paid on time, we would have gone without food, and probably heat and electricity too. Most of me wishes that my other two brothers could have gone to school with us, but part of me feels so glad they didn't. Basically, I didn't want them to feel bad about themselves. I know life would have been "easier" for them, but do years of ridicule have to go along with it?

By the middle of the ninth grade I developed some friendships. I found it easier to talk to other new students. For the first time in two years, I had friends. Most of the time our talks revolved around classes, boys, how hard track practice was. I liked it.

I think that high school for Bill and me was a time where we numbed ourselves to being poor, and to forgetting the Cheyenne and Blackfoot ways. It was easier that way. It seemed that we had to learn to be one way at school, and another at home; but it was hard, how are kids supposed to do that? I went unwillingly to family functions. My family didn't see that much of me the last two years of high school. I was involved in sports, stayed over at friends, or talked with them on the phone incessantly. I didn't want to hear about how far we were behind in bills anymore. School was easier because it was shallow. I could handle talking about classes, etc., but I couldn't do anything to help Mom or not make us poor.

By the time I was a junior, my brother Bill was in the upper school too. Only thing is, I didn't like him that much, because I saw things about myself from his behavior. He looked down on our family for being poor; he was ashamed. School and the people in it were the most important to him. I saw it in him when he brushed my mom aside. She was trying to tell him something, and he answered in a condescending voice to her. I was angry at him for not respecting everything she had done for us. He paid more attention to his friends than family. He said derogatory things to my other two brothers like, "Oh, what do you know?" and after awhile they'd say things about our "rich private school." He looked down on them, and I thought, my God, it was only luck that got Bill and me in; it wasn't Lance's or Rick's fault they had to go to public school.

By the time it came around to applying for schools I had a sneaking suspicion that I had neglected something really essential by ignoring as best I could home and the tribes for so long. I applied to colleges because it was what everyone else did. I did fairly well on the entrance tests, had a good grade average, and got recommendations from teachers who liked me. When I applied to school, I applied to out-of-state schools because I wanted to see what it was like elsewhere. The whole process was funny, because I had all these ivy league schools interested in me. I didn't really care about going to a top school, but most of the other kids did, and a lot of them did double-takes when one of my friends teased me loudly about Harvard calling for me. I liked the school I'm at now the most because it had a Native American Society. I knew that I would need some connection to my background to help me out in school without my family or relatives.

Again, my relatives and mother were encouraging. I'll amend that. Everyone but the traditionals were glad for me. As a young woman, I should have been starting a family, not running across the country for four years. They never actually said anything, but when Grandma told them, they'd look away, or talk about something else. In my eyes, going to college wasn't going to make me less Indian, or forget where I came from. If anything it would enhance it.

It used to bug me sometimes when Grandma would say where I was going, because the way she said it would make other people jealous of me. Lots of people she told this to had kids in state schools or community colleges, and I felt bad because they were just as good as me. I didn't want people to be envious, or think that I was snotty. There were a lot of relatives like that, who were proud of me, but I hated it when they would announce where I was going; they didn't always mention that Sue was doing something really good for herself by going into the Marines, or that Bob was a supervisor in a plastics factory. They weren't any less than I was; in fact, the things they did demanded so much more.

Graduation was boring, and I wasn't crying like most of the other students were. I just remember being glad that school was finally all over with. I wouldn't yearn for my years in high school, and I wouldn't miss most of the people there.

My family brought me to the airport. Mom, Grandma, Grandpa, two uncles, two cousins, and my brothers were there. They took all kinds of pictures, me and brothers, me and my cousins, me and Mom. I said goodbye to my brothers, and Mom was crying. She tried not to, but I knew she would miss me. And all of a sudden, I knew that I would miss her too. It startled me. I had tears in my eyes and was biting my lips, and Grandma said, "You're going away to do a good thing. Nothing bad has happened. We don't have to cry." They called my name as I boarded, and I turned as they snapped a picture. I sat in my seat and looked out the window, crying. This man tried to make small talk with me, until he saw me crying, then he let me alone. The plane started to go towards the runway, and I looked at the terminal, and there they all were, standing and waving. I could still see Mom crying. Love. I was leaving love.

I was excited about going to school, partly to be on my own, but I thought because it was college, people would be wise and mature, that there wouldn't be the cliques like in high school. I was wrong. It was freshman week, and most of the people were *just like* my high school peers. I was horrified. I couldn't get into the class spirit, I didn't like my roommate, I didn't like most of the bubbleheads I met. I didn't really feel my purpose in being there — except possibly to meet all the self-important people and party as much as I could. It was a time when I had to stand on my own and rely on my strengths. The only thing was, I didn't know what my strengths were. It didn't feel like I had any.

I was sitting alone one night that first week looking at the stars, like I used to at powwows or in Nebraska. All of a sudden I had a tight feeling in my chest, and I said aloud "Why am I here?" I felt like walking into the woods and crying, because I didn't want to go through a repeat of being new, like when I started private school.

This is what I did my first term at school: I went to math class for the first week, I went to English for the first half of the term, and to my third class maybe once a week. I drank whenever I could. I remember being three or four papers behind in my English class. I read the books I had to; I just couldn't sit down and say something about the topic questions. I sat in front of a computer, and for the life of me, couldn't think of a damned thing to say about Conrad's imagery in the *Heart of Darkness* and its effect on the reader. I went to math for the first three classes, and it was all review, from like the eighth grade. The thing is, I always hated math. It was my earliest class, and I didn't feel a compelling need to wake up and go to it.

When I drank too much, I would end up crying and babbling. One time I was at a fraternity, looking at the mob of people dancing, watching people weave in and out among the tightly packed basement to get a beer, and I saw people jumping up and down and crowing with triumph about a beer pong game when a cup got knocked over. I was supposed to be having a good time. I ran out and stood under a pine tree, fists bunched up, crying for my relatives. I was always embarrassed about crying or babbling like that, and would act like I had never done it the next day. I was homesick, more than I had thought possible, but I didn't know it. I felt empty and knew something was wrong with me because I should have been having the time of my life. After all, I was young and at college.

People tried to help me. Friends would ask if I'd gone to class, if I'd caught up in math and English. I'd say no, and they'd say, "Jean, you've got to or you're going to be in trouble." I'd laugh, or say nothing. I got called in by my freshmen dean, and he asked how come I was having trouble. I said I didn't know. I was nervous and afraid of what he'd say to me. He said, "You went to a private school, you did well there, you are more than capable of doing well here. You're messing up. Why aren't you doing well?" I didn't say anything. He asked if I was homesick, and almost sobbing, I said yes. He told me that I had to go to classes, and that I could do it. I walked out of there, and composed myself. Crying, what good did it do anyway?

I used to talk with my mom about once every week. She always asked about the people who I was meeting. So I'd tell her about the people I hung out with, what we did or talked about — except the drinking parts. Mom hated to see any of us ending up alcoholic. She asked about classes, and I'd say that they weren't going so well. She'd ask about how I was doing, and I'd say, "I don't know, Mom, not so good." She always said "You can come home if you want to Jean. You know that. We want you to be happy."

Somehow I imagined that if I had a boyfriend, everything would be okay. I had met this Native-American guy my freshman week. I went looking outside of myself for what I lacked. I liked it that he still had close ties to his tribe, that that was where he drew his strength from. I had spent the night with him a couple of times after parties during the weekend. Platonically, I mean. We spent most of our days together. People were always wondering if we were ever going to get it together. I wondered too.

John came up and said he wanted to talk. I had had a knot of anxiety and yearning in me, and it loosened up. He said something about wanting to wake me up with a kiss when I had slept in his room, taking it slow, how he had fun when we were together, and that he respected me. But it was almost like he was dictating a letter to me or something. Maybe I should have gotten up and gone to him when he finished talking. Instead, I said that I needed to go to the bathroom, because I really did.

When I came out, he had gone downstairs, and I felt disappointed. He ended up drinking until he passed out, and then I knew that we didn't have anything. I felt immensely alone, and sad. The next day we studied together, and that was it. He wasn't very talkative. We went back to his room, and he said I would probably hate him, because he had decided to get back together with an old girlfriend, and that he didn't want to date someone who wasn't Navajo. I told him I hoped it worked out for him, and felt surprised that I meant it. But that was the last straw for me, and I set myself on the path of self-destruction. I just drank whenever I could, tortured myself with dreams of getting him back, and forgot completely about classes.

The end of the first term came, and finals. I wouldn't get up to go to my math final. Why go? I was going to fail anyway. I still needed to finish three or four papers, and I hadn't done my term paper for my third class.

I got a call over break, and my dean said that I had been suspended. So when I went back to school it was to pack. Dimly, I regretted it. I had been on my own out there, and I was just beginning to see that there was a lot I could have done, such as pulling my act together, being independent, and maybe learning to loosen up with people my age and have fun.

Mom was supportive of me, as were most of my relatives when I got home. I didn't really know what to do with myself in terms of getting a job, or going to the state university. I didn't really feel like doing anything. For about three months I stayed home a lot, cleaned, cooked, hung out with Mom and my brothers. I tried to escape from thinking about myself and what I would do. The only things I made an effort for were to go to Nebraska with my grandmother and to go to as many NAC meetings and powwows as I could.

I started to drink on the sly. I'd drink when there wasn't anything for me to do, or just to liven things up. One time, I had been slipping into the bathroom to take a shot of vodka every now and then, and I got carried away. My brother Rick told mom that I was acting weird, and I remember sobbing as she rubbed my back. The next morning I woke up, and I thought, "Oh my God, what have you done?" I felt apprehensive, I couldn't remember anything, and I couldn't really believe that I had gotten stinking drunk like that.

Mom came home, and this is what she said: "Jean, you can't do this to me. This happened to your dad. If something happens to you because of drinking, I'm going to feel really bad. What's the matter? Why are you doing this?" And I didn't know what to say. But I realized that the parents are supposed to die first, not the kids. I saw in her face that Mom knew that she couldn't help me. I had to help myself, and drinking like there was no tomorrow wasn't going to do it. I saw how my not thinking had led me to so many things, and that somehow I needed to make sense of what was bothering me. I said how sorry I was, and for the first time in my life, I meant it.

So I enrolled in a religion and psychology class during the evenings and I got a job tutoring math and English at an inner city alternative high school for Indians. Most of these students were from the reservation and had come from North and South Dakota, Nebraska, and Montana. Indians flock to Bismarck for jobs or for excitement. Most of us are poor, lots are alcoholic, and many come from dysfunctional families. What smacked me in the face was seeing that abuse was a way of life, the only way of life they knew and accepted. Their education: poverty, alcohol, drugs, emotional, physical, and sexual abuse.

There was a girl named Sharon who did her work and was quiet. When people picked on her she would cower. When she was called on in class her voice shook and she wouldn't look up. If I told her she was smart or looked pretty that day, she'd say, "No I'm not." If she had to ask me for some help with some problem she'd say, "I'm so stupid, I can't do this." I heard Sharon's boyfriend sneering, "Why am I even with you, I could have any woman I want." Sharon said, "I'm sorry, please don't be mad. I'll be how you want me to be." When I heard that I winced and ran into the bathroom. I tried to block out the echoes of her beseeching him. Those were my words whenever anyone was mad or displeased with me. I knew how that felt in your gut.

They had nothing. So those that still had any fight left in them latched on to being tough, independent, and reckless, all for pride. Everyone needs something. I don't know why the kids talked to me and told me about their lives so much. I don't know why they picked on almost all the other teachers and aides (to their faces most of the time) and left me out of their ridicule. Maybe it was because at 19 I wasn't that much older than them. Or because I was Indian. I liked to laugh with them or tease them when I could. And when they talked to me, I listened, because what they were telling me about was their lives.

All I could say to them was, "It doesn't have to be that way, you know." Those kids are the trapped, the bereft, the haunted. They are the reason I came back to college. I have to find a way to open up a life and world outside of their childhood so that they can at least get through high school and get an adequate education, one that prepares them for college. I have to find a way that doesn't make them feel ashamed about their pasts. I want to change the schools somehow. Schools and your success in them determine what kind of life and career you're going to have. I see so many kids weeded out, and it has nothing to do with their intelligence. Why is the path through high school to college so narrow?

Working helped me decide what to do with myself in terms of college. Since my return, I have done fairly well in classes. I still have problems in making myself go to classes on a regular basis and doing all the reading that I'm assigned. I'm more caught up in my family life and what goes on there than in my studies or the issues at school.

I don't aim for straight A's, but for learning what I can that will be useful to me when I go into education, or what will help me understand people in general. I also try to learn as much as I can about the culture here, what kinds of ideals and standards motivate the students and professors. It's still a pain a lot of the time, because for all the advantages that most students have here while growing up, and for all their intelligence, there's an incredible lack of compassion or understanding that there are people who live hard, hard lives. Their worlds and lives are closed, too, and it disheartens me lots of times. Sometimes I think that academic knowledge is how they gauge the wisdom and respect of one another. It's something I don't understand, because what does academic knowledge have to do with what we are as people? As far as I can see, wisdom has nothing to do with books and theories.

For awhile when I first came back, I joined a coed house, but I found that I still drank a lot to pass the time. I was hung over at least three times a week. I drank so much that I ruined something in my body. Now, when I have more than three beers or mixed drinks, I'm hung over really badly the next day. Luckily, I only get carried away once or twice a year like that. Now, I'll have a beer with dinner once or twice a month, and that's about it. I don't really miss it because I finally figured out that drinking solves none of my problems. It only wastes my time.

Since I have been back I have been an active member of the Native American Society and have lived at the Society's house whenever possible. It feels like a home. Most of my friends are Native American, not because I'm prejudiced, but because I'm much more at ease with them. I am still really quiet and shy when I first meet people, and I avoid at almost any cost participating in class. Just this past year I decided that I couldn't always be like that, and for now that's enough. I also fell in love for the first time. We were together for two years but broke up three months ago. It was so hard — it still is.

Peter accepted me for who I was, faults and all. He used to say that he wanted the two of us to be able to do what we both wanted, and then be able to tell each other about it all. But I didn't know how to accept myself, and I demanded so much from him. It was as if I expected him to make up for things lacking within myself, within my life. Now I know that there's no one in the world that can do that for me but myself. Until I met Peter I was always lonely. With him I learned how to actually reach out to another person instead of being someone who just dreamed about love. He reached out to me and I learned to trust.

One time I went out with a high school friend, and she was talking about how her father went to meetings for abused children and children of alcoholics. She named off all the symptoms that these children have. And you know, as she listed off the characteristics, she described me. I sat there with my mouth open, and it felt like I had been punched in the stomach.

I saw a lot of the abused child behaviors in myself throughout the whole time Peter and I were together. It's like there was a lightness in me after I realized it. Even when I was with Peter I often felt hopeless and depressed. I was always afraid he would leave me. I never understood what he saw in me, so I would try to be what he wanted. I couldn't stand getting into fights with him, and if I was ever mad at him, I'd sulk around and keep it in because I was afraid to express it. I was so insecure with myself. Things would build up, and when we finally got it out in the open, I wouldn't even know myself what I was mad about. Somehow I felt inarticulate and that I didn't even have the right to be mad. I still have some of these tendencies.

I see how I turned him into a kind of addiction and couldn't give him what he gave me, love and acceptance. When I told Peter about the fact that my brothers and I had been abused, and that I wanted to do something about it, he held me. My voice was shaking, and I could barely get across what I had found out. Peter asked if I felt like crying, and when I said yes, he said, "come here" and hugged me. But I couldn't cry. And when he asked how I felt, I said I felt ashamed. He said, "Oh babe, you don't have anything to be ashamed about. It wasn't your fault." And then I cried.

As time went on, when we were apart I became more and more insecure. I demanded that he put me at ease and hounded him to keep me a part of his life. I smothered him. Slowly, I lost confidence in myself and in him. Then I knew that I had a long, slow battle to feel good about myself and to not revert to my victim reaction. Oh God, I just wish we had met years from now when I was normal. I wish I had not been abused. But that is not going to change the past. I need to deal with how things are now, and slowly get rid of the things from my childhood. At least now I am aware, unlike many people who never have an inkling about what beneath it all is really bothering them.

Graduation is finally in sight. I plan to go on to graduate school for Indian education. I want to work in curriculum and administration, but I will probably teach first so that I can get some practical experience. I find that because of my experiences away from home I've gotten a lot of perspective that has, in the end, allowed me to appreciate my heritage. I will always do my utmost to keep family ties, NAC, traditionals, and powwows in my life. I want all that, or something like it, for my children.

I've learned to think about myself as important and to know that I have strengths. I'm finally starting to be at ease with myself and with other people, and I look forward to the person that I'm becoming. It's been a long, slow haul. When I walk down that aisle for graduation I want my relatives to be there with me, and I'll walk proudly. I would do everything over again. I wrote this poem which speaks for me and for others:

> *I wear a coat. I wear tennis shoes.*
> *I play a game and I am winning.*
> *I go to school. I feel the worth*
> *in the knowledge of my relatives.*
> *I play the game, I do not live it.*
> *Knowledge from all areas . . .*
> *My thought, my hope:*
> *someday that all my elders will be proud*
> *respectful of the little ones who follow them.*
> *I dream . . . to make a way for the small ones not yet here.*
> *The younger ones to play the game in a skillful manner.*
> *In a way that I never could.*
> *It is our wish, it is our wish.*

CASE 5

Distilling My Korean-American Identity

This Korean-born American recalls a pervasive desire as a child to go unnoticed, not to stick out due to his "almost fetishistic desire to be 'just an American teenager.' " He asks, "How could we expect non-Koreans to ignore our racial differences if we ourselves did not?" He comes to feel that his drive to blend in has suppressed his own personality to the point that upon entering college he finds himself knowing his new friends better than he knows himself. The shock of this self-recognition causes him to undertake an active "identity distillation" in order to find his real self hiding within the faceless persona he had worn during high school. He takes the opportunity of a new social environment at college to explore the duality of his Korean-American self. He also uses this period to rethink his image of himself as a "science person" and to redirect his intellectual interests into areas he had never before considered.

I am a Korean American. More accurately, I am an American with a limited Korean background. I lived in Korea until I was 4 years old. I don't happen to remember anything of the Korea I experienced before moving to the States, apart from some vague images. Maybe that has something to do with the fact that I don't speak the language well anymore. All my experiences way back then were defined by and framed within the Korean language. But since my mind now seems to operate only in English, I can't remember my early Korean experiences—except in a vaguely imagistic way. The several times I have returned to Korea, I felt completely the foreigner, and Korea seemed for the most part unfamiliar to me.

This is not to say that being ethnically Korean meant nothing to me in my childhood, during my adolescence, and even now. Being Korean has always been significant to me. But the nature of that significance has varied immeasurably across different periods of my life. As an adolescent, being Korean meant being different. I attended a small private school in the

Midwest. I was not the only Asian in the school, but Asians constituted only a small minority of the student body. I never encountered or perceived any racist attitudes at the school. No, the real effect being Korean had on me was not a product of others' direct perceptions of me, but of my own perception of others' perceptions.

Everyone knows that no adolescent wants to stick out in a crowd. The desire to be "normal" may just be the *sine qua non* of adolescence. Being a member of a minority group made it hard for me, as an adolescent, to avoid feeling like I "stuck out." Being Korean was a liability that I felt I had to overcome; I thought that others were constantly conscious of the fact that I was Korean and therefore different in some way. And although being "different" isn't bad per se, being "different" is not usually desirable to an adolescent, and it certainly was not desirable to me. I didn't want to be different, but because I couldn't do anything about it I avoided calling attention to myself. My logic must have been that if people didn't notice me, then they wouldn't notice my differentness. If people didn't notice my differentness, then I wouldn't feel it, either. I guess that is how I explain to myself how I got to be a "quiet" person.

But somehow, I did wish that more people *knew* me. I resented the fact that people saw me as "quiet" — and not much else. I wasn't a "nobody" in my high school class — that would have been hard in a class of twenty. I did well academically, and people seemed to know that. But being labeled "smart" was never of much satisfaction to me. Being the one to get the highest score on the calculus test did not seem to me to reap many benefits. It was just another label. So I was quiet — but smart, too. And that's how people would talk about me. If only people really knew me, I thought to myself, they would see me not just as a quiet (but smart) person, but as a regular three-dimensional individual. The paradox, though, was that although I didn't want to be known only for being nonnoticeable, I did not want to be different from everybody else.

Today, being Korean has a significance to me that differs greatly from the significance it had when I was a teenager. As a teenager, I felt that I was first and foremost an American, and that my Korean background was only of marginal importance in my personal makeup. I tended to believe that the impact on me of being Korean extended only as far as my physical characteristics. My parents often exhorted me to recognize that I should not and could not ever deny my Korean-ness. My parents wanted me, I think, to not just accept the fact that I was Korean, but to embrace it. But I always thought they had it all wrong. As an adolescent, I simply wasn't interested in my ethnic roots. I wanted to ignore them. Besides, I rationalized, race was something to be downplayed and minimized, not highlighted and brought to the surface. After all, wasn't the ethos of the late '60s, the age into which I was born, that each of us should celebrate the bonds that tie us all together, and not the differences that distinguish us? And perhaps most importantly, I asked myself, how could we expect others (i.e., non-Koreans) to ignore our racial differences if we ourselves did not? My adolescent preoccupation with, or quest for, inconspicuousness blinded me to any satisfactory answer to this last question. As an adolescent, I could not reconcile my almost fetishistic desire to be "just an American teenager" with any sort of conscious, positive recognition or affirmation of my cultural and ethnic roots.

By the time I got to college, I was beginning the long hike up and out of the murky depths of adolescence, facing concerns that I had never before confronted. During my first month at school, I met new people almost every day. I marveled at the excitement that I felt in suddenly finding myself surrounded by a thousand people, my classmates, whom I had never seen before, and who had never seen me. The primary task everyone seemed to be undertaking was to get to know everyone else, to find out as much as possible about as many people as possible — mainly by attending as many parties as possible. It was not too long before I realized that while I was trying to find out about others, all those others were trying to find out about me, too. But, my God, what *was* there to find out about me?

At the threshold between adolescence and whatever comes afterwards, I found myself paradoxically knowing my new friends virtually better than I knew my own self. I sometimes felt as if I were a completely uninteresting person. Not uninteresting in the sense of inducing ennui in the people I interacted with, but uninteresting in a broader and vaguer sense, in the sense that I had a hard time identifying those features about me that *defined* me as *me*. On reflection, I guess I could say that I had been altogether too successful in my adolescent struggle and quest for qualified anonymity. I saw that it was time, then, for me to undo much of what I had done during my adolescence. So I started engaging in a process of discovery which finally allowed me to leave adolescence behind, a process I refer to as the "personal identity distillation."

The way I conceive of it, the process involves the boiling off of the "solvent" of one's personality, that is, all the "stuff" that coexists with a person's individuality, but that doesn't comprise or constitute it. As more and more of the "stuff" boils away, the residue that remains becomes more and more salient and knowable. It is this residue that defines and constitutes a person's identity; the residue is the material which allows individuals to be distinguished from each other in some substantive way. The residue, the end product of the distillation process, is a person's identity in its pure form. Before the distillation, identity is "dissolved" and therefore hidden, secret, invisible. Before distillation, it's hard to really know how one person is different from the next, just as it's hard to tell the difference between water containing dissolved salt and water containing dissolved sugar. But after the distillation, the residue become tangible and directly viewable.

The point of the process is not to find out that "everyone is different." In identifying the residue of your personal distillation, you may consider important, that, in fact, your "residue" has much in common with someone else's "residue." Paradoxical as it sounds, that commonality may help you conceptualize or may even comprise part of your personal identity. Thus, for example, Korean-ness might be a constituent of my identity, although obviously, I'm not the only one who's going to have this constituent. In the context of the rest of the factors that make up my identity, though, the single factor of Korean-ness might mean one thing to me and quite another to someone else.

An interesting weakness of the distillation metaphor is that the idea of a substance being distilled out of some solvent suggests strongly that the substance was "there" all along. The metaphor of distillation suggests that the residue of the process—identity—is simply *discovered*. But in fact, one doesn't just discover one's identity. I would suspect that the real process of getting to know your identity involves as much an element of creation as it does of discovery. The very act of searching for one's identity may in fact unavoidably affect what one "finds" and what one chooses to jettison.

In essence, what happened after I got to college was simply that my adolescent quest for "sameness" (qualified anonymity) was replaced by a new quest—a quest for individuality and identity. While I stubbornly denied my "Korean-ness" throughout adolescence, I felt almost compelled to examine it once I got to college. I needed to know whether being Korean really was an essential part of my own being, or whether that part of me could just be boiled off. I ended up going back to Korea for a summer to find out. I participated in an intensive language program at Yonsei University in Seoul geared primarily toward Korean Americans like me. That summer, aside from learning to speak Korean a lot better, I learned a great deal about what Korean-ness meant to me. I learned that Korean-ness certainly was not the center of my being; but neither was it at the outer fringe. But the important point for me was that I had finally put an end to contending that being Korean meant *nothing* to me.

As an adolescent, it was impossible for me to give a satisfactory answer to the question I brought up earlier, "How could I expect others to overlook my Korean-ness if I myself did not?" Implicit in the question was a fear of being set apart from everyone else for my Korean-ness. The interesting thing, which I can only now see, is that by ignoring my own Korean-ness, I may have made it easier for others to look upon my Korean-ness in an undesired way. Because insofar as I refused to affirm Korean-ness as a part of my *personhood*, others may have had no choice but to regard my

Korean-ness as simply a matter of *race*. Perhaps that sort of status facilitated and engendered in others stereotyped or generic perceptions of what Korean-ness meant. If I had recognized Korean-ness as constituting a part of my identity, then maybe that would have pushed others to similarly perceive my Korean-ness as a part of my personality, a part of me to be confronted and accepted – or rejected – like any of the other aspects of my personality, and not as something that existed on a different plane from those aspects.

Part of my identity in high school was as a brain. The "brains" were the students who did well in science and math. If you happened to be a superb student in English, or history, or French – well, then, that was that. You were just good in English, or history, or French. Unless you were also highly proficient in one of the sciences or maths, you in no circumstances would merit characterization as a "brain."

My high school classmates tended to impute "brain" status to me, although in the end, I hardly think I deserved the label. Perhaps that's partly why I always thought of myself as a science person. I was good in the sciences; I was interested in the sciences generally; and I took it for granted that I would go to medical school and become a doctor, following in the footsteps of both my parents. In fact, I usually conceived of college as nothing but an unavoidable stepping-stone on the path to medical school, and medical school a similar step on the final path to doctorhood. But on reflection, I don't think my interest in becoming a physician really explains why I liked to think of myself as a science person. I knew even back in high school that one didn't have to be a science person to become a physician, and I did as well in English and French as I did in any of the sciences. Moreover, in terms of level of interest, I preferred English overall to the sciences. So, why, I've asked myself, didn't I think of myself as an English person, or more generally, a humanities person?

I think it's fair to say that most people want to have as rosy and flattering a conception of themselves as possible. I'm sure I did, and still do. In high school, it was flattering to me to be able to think of myself as an intellectually competent person. And, naturally, the best way to maintain that self-conception was to think of myself as a science person. Well, at least it was natural back in high school.

By the time I reached high school, I had been strongly ingrained to believe that to be intellectually competent – smart, a brain – meant largely one thing: to know "The Answers." If you were smart, you were privy to a relative abundance of answers. The sciences and maths – at least at the high school and perhaps even at the intermediate undergraduate level – were subjects well suited to the quest for answers, and seemed well suited to the conception that being smart and having answers meant one and the same thing. Being proficient in English provided no marker for intellectual competence; at least it didn't imply having lots of answers. So how could being good in English tie in with being smart? I resisted thinking of myself as an English person as opposed to a science person largely because that would have been incommensurate with a self-conception encompassing intellectual proficiency and academic commitment. It seemed to me that to conceive of myself as an English-person would have been to abandon any claim to intellectuality. I might have even thought that English-persons were people who couldn't hack it as science persons—"wimps."

When I first arrived at college, I intended to consign myself as a biology major. Biology, after all, seemed the subject logically prior to medicine. Then I went to a meeting for potential pre-meds. At this meeting, all of us doctors-to-be heard about the myriad courses prerequisite to taking the MCATs and being admitted to medical school. What surprised me, though, was the fact that one did not have to major in a science to go to medical school. What's more, I learned that well-rounded medical students were very much in vogue among medical school admissions committees. By all reports, medical schools tended to look *favorably* on candidates who majored in the liberal arts! This tidbit of information came as a revelation to me. I had been given the perfect opportunity, I thought. I could major in something other than a science and have a perfectly valid reason for doing so: it would be instrumentally useful! This was a perfect alibi. Yes—I was an English major, but only because majoring in English would make it easier to get into a top medical school! Mind you, the most important intended audience for this alibi was no one other than myself.

Armed with this strategic bent of mind, I groomed myself to become an English major. But then I encountered a significant obstacle. I found out that I didn't like the subject. Somehow, English classes just didn't seem to be all that I had cracked them up to be. I enjoyed the lectures, and I enjoyed most of the reading, but for some reason, I simply wasn't finding myself engaged in what I was doing. It's not that English bored me; it just seemed that everything was "made up." The primary texts of English—the poems, novels, etc.—seemed to me chronically indeterminate. One literary critic's interpretation of Yeats or Woolf seemed to me just as appealing as another's, and I personally could see no objective way of even comparing one against the other.

Freshman spring, I took an introductory course in philosophy. From day one, I was lured in and hooked. That introductory course in philosophy was the first college course I took that really and truly excited me. In fact, I think it was in that course that I for the first time felt the thrill of being stirred up by *ideas*. I remember actually feeling my heart race as the professor in the first or second class meeting began to schematize the questions that comprised the themes of the course. "What is knowledge? Is moral knowledge possible? Are there defensible arguments for the existence of a god? How do we know that anything exists? What does it mean to be moral? Why should people act morally? What is a 'mind'? What is the relation between mind and body?" And so on. As the professor presented the class with these questions — the kinds of questions that form the broadest basis of general philosophical inquiry — I felt overwhelmed. The questions startled me. It had never occurred to me during my eighteen years of existence that those kinds of questions could or should be asked. I was startled to think that for eighteen years I had never thought to grapple with a single one of those questions. Now, as I listened to those questions, I wondered why I never had. And I wondered how one could in any sensible way go about answering them.

I stayed with philosophy, and I ended up majoring in it. (Now that I look back, I think maybe I concentrated on philosophy too much — to the detriment of a more diverse learning experience.) But, for me, philosophy offered a middle ground between the "stone-cold hardness" of science and the "mushiness" of English. At least in a simplistic sense, argumentation in philosophy bowed to more or less objective (but not formulaic) standards of justification. I found that it was possible for an argument in philosophy to be just flat-out wrong (e.g., logically inadequate) in a way that an interpretation of or an argument about a literary text never could be. On the other hand, I discovered that in philosophy, unlike the sciences, even as a "novice" one could carefully read a classic piece of writing like Descartes' *Meditations* and, at least on a simple level, be able to find flaws and formulate substantively weighty critiques of the author's arguments. I found that to be enormously empowering. How exciting it was to be able to match wits (well, more or less) with the philosophers who had laid down some of the foundational bedrock of contemporary Western thought!

In the end, I became a philosophy person through and through. English? I abandoned it. Science? I abandoned it, too, for the most part. But I still maintain an interest in it. I took a course in the philosophy of biology and was deeply fascinated by it. I've come to realize that the body of knowledge we call science is really not so "stone-cold hard" after all. And after everything I've said, maybe I shouldn't say this, but sometimes I wonder whether the *real* reason I was attracted to philosophy was that I was good at it; the scope and depth of my insight in philosophy was far greater than I could ever have hoped it to be in science or English.

I've been talking at length about finding my identity, but I haven't yet mentioned the single most important event in my development as a person. At college, early in my junior year, I met the woman with whom I would promise to spend the rest of my life. Until I met Laura, I had never shared any significant part of my life with anyone.

I come from a pretty good-sized family. I have a brother and two sisters, all younger. My parents emigrated from Korea when I was 4.

Although they were brought up in Korea, my parents are quite liberal (culturally), and have become more "Americanized" than most other immigrant Korean parents I know. Our family is quite close, by most people's standards. Although my family is united in love and mutual care for one another's well-being, I don't think we share a mutual understanding of what goes on in each other's inner lives. We know about each other's physical lives (what we're doing at 8:00 tonight) but not about each other's mental lives (how we feel about what we're doing). I don't think I really comprehended what it means to share one's life with another until I met Laura.

You would think that, never having done so before, I would have had tremendous difficulty expressing myself in a personally revealing way to Laura. But just the opposite was true. After our relationship became serious, I was never afraid to divulge practically anything I felt to her, and I found myself divulging quite a lot, including most of what I've been writing about in this essay. As our relationship developed, events unfolded such that, finally, I felt the need to tell Laura something I had never told anyone, aside from my parents: that I loved her.

I believed that by telling her, I would be making myself vulnerable to complete emotional destruction. But I had to tell her, even though I was unsure whether she would tell me the same. On Valentine's Day, the moment came. I revealed to Laura that I had come to utterly depend on her for my happiness, and that I would be left immeasurably lonely by her absence. I told her that I loved her. Without hesitation, she responded in kind. What a breakthrough that was! At that moment, I should have realized, if I didn't, that I had radically departed from my life as I used to live it, and had entered a life in which I was no longer alone. For me, that moment of reciprocal communication of love between Laura and me represented the moment at which my identity intersected with hers. It sounds so cliché, but at that moment, each of us became a part of the other. For me, that meant that from that point on, I would never be able to understand my identity without considering what Laura means to me, and what I mean to her. Sometimes I think that, really, the only part of my identity that matters to me today is that part which encompasses what Laura means to me. Sometimes, I think my entire life revolves around her, and that everything I do is for the benefit of our life together.

I can't begin to accurately describe the empowering effect my relationship with Laura has had on me. My outward personality hasn't changed all that much, but I have come to believe that my life has significance. I mean something to somebody; I am irreplaceable in the eyes of somebody. Whereas before my relationship with Laura, my activities in life seemed somehow lacking in thematic integration, now they seem endowed with an undeniably unifying purpose.

Even my relationship with my family has changed because of my love for Laura. Because Laura has redefined who I am, I suppose it's inevitable that consequently, she has also redefined who I am in relation to my family. First of all, Laura described my family to me in terms that I could not possibly have used myself. I realized that my family was indeed a close-knit one, albeit one that is reserved in its display of sensitive emotions. I think the most important thing I realized about my family through Laura is that, although in some respects we do not explicitly share our lives with each other, we unhesitatingly make sacrifices in our own lives for the benefit of one another's lives; we share our physical and practical burdens, if not our emotional inner sancta. Most notably, I was astonished to realize the extent to which my parents had made sacrifices to make a comfortable life for us, their children.

My family accepted Laura into "the clan" about as readily as a family could be expected to. That fact is, to me, especially significant because Laura is not Korean. She is Italian. The topic of interracial marriages happens to be a major issue for my generation of Korean Americans. For the interracial couples I know, race is a nonissue, though. This was certainly true for Laura and me—that's partly why I've neglected to mention our difference in race up until now. In fact, I "forgot" that our relationship is interracial! But I consider myself lucky, because my parents never so much as hinted at disapproval of my plans with Laura. They repeatedly tell me, in fact, that they find it easy to conceive of Laura as "one of their own" daughters. Laura's own parents seemed also to be more than agreeable to our relationship. They expressed happiness at the fact that Laura had found "the right person"—for them that was enough.

It's ironic. The aspect of my adolescent life that was singularly the *most* affected by my Korean-ness, or more accurately, by my attitude toward my Korean-ness, was my social life, or rather its absence from my teen years. It wasn't *because* of my Korean-ness that I was no Casanova. At least I hope not. It was because of my *insecurity* about being Korean that being Korean was a factor at all. Part of the problem was that I feared rejection. But that's normal, isn't it? Everyone fears rejection to some degree. The *real* obstacle for me was a feeling of inappropriateness. I somehow felt that it was *inappropriate* for me to even "ask someone out" on a date.

I never really stopped thinking these sorts of thoughts until I became involved with Laura. It sounds so cliché to say "love conquers all"—but as far as I'm concerned, love not only conquers all, it overshadows it. Laura helped me to think about all of the things I've been talking about here. Her love for me erased all the insecurities I have ever had with my Korean-ness; without that love, I would never have been able to talk about much of what I have talked about in this essay. My personal identity may have been formed before I met Laura, but not until after I met her did I have the strength to face it.

CASE 6

*I Reconcile
the Irreconcilable*

This 20-year old African American describes his determination to be a leader of men. The death of his father when he was 8 led his mother to relocate the family to the South, where she had grown up and would now pursue a medical residency. Concerned about the lack of male influence in her son's life, she introduces the author to a number of institutions that are predominantly white and predominantly—or entirely—male: a military academy's summer camp; the Boy Scouts; a prep school. The author follows the pattern, joining a fraternity when he enters college. Active and successful in student government at college, he now has his eye on the presidency of the student body as he seeks to reconcile within himself those "seemingly contradictory experiences and paradoxes of race and privilege, disadvantage and advantage."

One of my first memories is my father teaching me how to spell my last name; "D-A-N-F-O-R-T-H," he would say over and over again, and I would repeat the letters until I had memorized them. My last name held a fascination for me. It is sufficiently rare so that I have never met a Danforth who was not in my family. I also was struck by the way that my family used our name; when they spoke it they always changed their tone, as if it was the most special word in the English language. Members of my family have always carried themselves with a certain sense of arrogance, and I do not mean this in a bad light. I have found that America's most successful blacks are rarely modest. Arrogance or cockiness is used as a sort of a drug to combat the sense of inherent inferiority that America places upon blacks. In my experience as a black person who deals in the white world, all of my peers who have demonstrated the so-called virtues of modesty and humility have, in almost every case, failed to achieve their desired goals.

From what my relatives tell me, my grandfather was an arrogant man. He was born in North Carolina into a family of land ownership that could also read and write. His father had attended college, graduating sometime before 1920. He went on to get a degree in dentistry and, like so many black men of his era, moved to the North. In the thirties, after a first marriage that failed, he moved to New York where he met and married my grandmother. He set up his dental practice and they had four sons; my father was the third of these. My grandfather would always make a distinction between other blacks and himself. As far as he was concerned, his education and profession put him in a separate class. He passed this attitude on to his sons to a certain extent. Although I never heard my father articulate this sentiment, I could tell the difference in the way that most other blacks carried themselves and the way that my father and his friends carried themselves. My parents' friends were all college-educated blacks who seemed to be still celebrating the gains of the 1960s, which is appropriate since they were the ones who had benefited the most. I was expected, as these people had done, to take advantage of the new-found educational and social freedoms to the fullest. This meant college definitely, and graduate school most likely.

When I was 6 my mother entered medical school. A few months later my father was hospitalized for cancer of the colon. My mother hired a live-in housekeeper to take care of my sister and me; we would have such help around the house for the rest of my childhood. When I was 8 my father died at age 41. My memories of this are images of lots of people being around the house for several weeks. I understood what had happened, but my father had been gone for so long in the hospital that the situation seemed somewhat removed from me. I do remember my mother's grief, but I was so young that my emotions were not developed enough to understand anything more than the concrete changes in everyday routine. My mother graduated from medical school and decided to pursue her residency in North Carolina where her mother and younger brother lived, and where she had grown up. I felt indifferent to the move except for the fact that I had just recently learned that North Carolina was a slave state, and I was wary that there would be racists down there. I was 9 years old.

My mother's family in North Carolina was quite different from my father's. My grandmother worked as a waitress in a downtown department store, my maternal grandfather was a mailman who died soon after I was born. My mother had grown up relatively poor, though not impoverished. I did not see much of my mother since she was completing her residency as a pediatrician. We lived in a suburban home in a predominantly white neighborhood that had a few blacks. The house was larger than our first home and better appointed. I attended the public schools but didn't like them at all. They were large and impersonal, and it seemed the teachers really didn't care about the development of students. One positive aspect was my inclusion in the district's Talented and Gifted Student Program. I also served as the treasurer of the elementary school's student council. In middle school I became involved in the public speaking program in which we would choose poems or speeches and practice for the countrywide competition at the end of the year. I won two years in a row, once in poetry and once in prose. During my time in public school in North Carolina, I felt awkward and out of place. There were no other kids in the school who had a similar background. My earlier exposure to white kids in Connecticut contrasted with the starkly segregated world of my North Carolina town. The other black students teased me for not speaking in the Black-English dialect. The middle-class white students did not really associate that much with the blacks. Maybe once a year I would hear an insult of "black boy" or an occasional "nigger." By the end of seventh grade my marks in school were dropping and I felt as if I was learning nothing. When my mother offered me the chance to go to private school, I jumped at it.

My mother was always afraid that my development would be adversely affected by having lost my father at such a young age, so she was determined to provide other strong male influences in my life. Partially as a result, I have always been exposed to institutions that were predominantly or entirely male. These include my attendance at a military academy's summer camp, the Boy Scouts, prep school, and my college fraternity.

My mother got the idea to send me to a summer military academy from my father's older brother, my Uncle Bill, whose son had also gone to this camp. I spent the four summers following my father's death at this military academy turned summer camp where all the traditional American values were stressed. We were awakened every morning by bugle and had to assemble in military formation. The days were filled with athletic events such as horseback riding, riflery, and archery. In the evenings we saw movies like *True Grit* and *Patton*. During these four summers I became accustomed to spending long periods of time in an entirely male environment. I also learned at an early age what it meant to be independent from one's parents. However, there were some corresponding disadvantages to the experience at the camp. It encouraged the boys not to be dependent upon parents or other adult figures, and to look with disdain at such needs for nurturance or guidance. Leadership and responsibility were emphasized at the camp. As each camper would return for another year he was moved up a notch in military rank. After four years I was made a second lieutenant. My duties included assembling my group of 100 campers, who would report to me and salute in military fashion. By the end of my last year I had become so enamored with the place that I wanted to return there and go to the military academy. My mother was not about to let me go that far.

When the decision came to send me to prep school, the fact that it was an all-male school did not matter. The school was undoubtedly the best college preparatory school in central North Carolina. The surroundings at

St. Andrews School were so much nicer than public school that I was too dazzled to worry about the lack of women. Also, the work was so much harder that I spent much more of my time studying than socializing. The structure and atmosphere of the St. Andrews program appealed particularly to the male psyche. Almost all of the teachers and administrators at the school were male, athletics were mandatory, and success in sports was heavily stressed. Time and again it was emphasized that we were the future leaders of our community. Since there was not a woman among us, this message also carried other connotations. As we entered the ninth and tenth grades, girls from our sister school, St. Anne's, began to attend classes with us. They came to St. Andrews to take math, science, and English, although we were not allowed to take such courses at St. Anne's, since it was generally thought that the girls' curriculum was watered down. There were only two or three black girls at St. Anne's, and my contact with any of them was rare. After five years of this situation, I became used to functioning in an all-male academic environment. It seemed perfectly normal to me to attend meetings or plan activities that were entirely devoid of any female participation.

My first day at St. Andrews was rather strange. I noticed first the difference in the way students dressed; they were all wearing pastel-colored "dress shirts." There were no blue jeans allowed, but the students did not seem to care. In class, I was struck by how much control teachers had over their students, who simply didn't act up as much. Out of my eighth-grade class of sixty-five, four of us were black. Three of us were new students and the other one, Jonathan, had been at the school since fourth grade. I ended up in the same class with him. Though he seemed pleased that there finally was another black person in his class, his attitude toward me was somewhat patronizing. He would constantly stress to me the difference between St. Andrews and my previous educational experience.

One day not long after I had first started at St. Andrews, the teacher arranged the seating. I ended up sitting next to a boy named Scott, a typical West End White kid. I noticed that he stared at me constantly. I got the feeling he was staring because he didn't think I belonged there; he did not stare at the new white student in the class who also sat near us. Another incident also clued me in to the way that things worked at that school. Members of the class had to give an oral presentation. One student named Ben gave his talk and he stuttered very badly. No one laughed or even flinched, and at the end he was congratulated as if he had given a flawless presentation. Next, a student named Louis went up to give his speech and he also stuttered badly. This time the members of the class chuckled and made faces. After the class most of the boys, including Ben, made fun of Louis. I questioned Jonathan about the double standard, and he explained to me that it was "not cool" to make fun of Ben because he came from a very wealthy and prestigious family, and his father was a respected alumnus. Louis, on the other hand, was Jewish, and his family owned a discount furniture store. Also, Louis had only been at the school for three years, whereas Ben had been at the school since kindergarten.

I soon came to understand that the boys of St. Andrews were taught that there was an ideal best exemplified by members of the community's elite society. These men were always white, always wealthy, and always Protestant. There was only one black teacher at the entire school, and he was too immersed in his religion to worry about social concerns. The only other blacks at the school were the kitchen and janitorial staff; not just particular members of the support staff were black, but the *entire* crew. The only white who worked for the school in this capacity was the supervisor. The students would always call these maintenance employees by their first names, no matter how old they were. The janitors would simply nod their heads in response. To call any other member of the staff by their first name would be grounds for severe punishment.

At first the students in my class did not know exactly what to make of the black students, but by the end of our first year opinions about us had begun to gel. Al was the most popular black member of our class. He was a gifted athlete and this immediately gained him considerable respect from our classmates. He was middle class and did not live in a very fancy neighborhood but every weekend a different white guy would invite him to spend the night. I was treated quite differently. In English and history classes I was beginning to show a remarkable amount of verbal ability. This shocked the other students in class; they had expected me to be slightly below par, at best. Another thing that shocked them was my accent. Within a year I had so immersed myself into the life of St. Andrews that I had donned a near flawless southern gentleman's accent. On the other hand, my athletic skills left something to be desired. The other boys dealt with this by coating me in humor. I began to notice that many of my habits were being ridiculed. This would continue in earnest until the tenth grade. I was constantly questioned as to why I did not possess greater athletic skill. When I showed skill in the classroom they said the only reason I did well was that I had somehow been able to shirk the curse of ignorance placed upon my race.

Early in ninth grade I was confronted with overt racism for the first time at St. Andrews. A student named Tim came up to me and for no reason said, "Nigger, nigger, why so tall? Nigger, where's your basketball?" He then proceeded to laugh and walk away. When I told another classmate about this incident he dismissed it as not being so much a racial attack as a personal one. He pointed to the fact that Al was one of Tim's best friends. I was later to find out that Tim said that he just wanted to see what my reaction was, and that he would never have done such a thing to a "normal" black person. When I went to my faculty advisor to explain my problem to him, he asked that I not tell anyone else and said that he would handle the problem himself. I never got any sort of an apology from Tim. During my freshman and sophomore years I was a target for racial harassment. Guys would say things to me just to get a reaction, and often I supplied them with it. During this period my grades, particularly in math and science, began to fall. I failed two terms of chemistry and one term of trigonometry.

During the last month of my sophomore year we held elections for junior class leadership positions. When the nominations came up for student council, a kid named Tom decided it would be funny to nominate me. There was no way that I could win since such positions were reserved for students who could act as role models. When the time came to give the speeches, I argued that the people who had held the positions of leadership so far had rested on their laurels and had looked upon their positions as honors rather than jobs. People were surprised by this tactic; it had previously been unspeakable to condemn our class leaders. When election day came I actually had much support. I won my position handily, to the surprise of the students, faculty, and administration of the school. I therefore found myself in a very different position to deal with my junior year, and my self-esteem rose considerably.

During the following summer I spent most of my time working-out in the school weight room and became close friends with Jonathan, the black student who had first greeted me in eighth grade. Now he had a new sense of respect for me due to my election as a class leader. Jonathan was the eldest son of wealthy physicians. His wealth did not in any way prevent him from acknowledging his black identity, and "blackness" was often a topic of conversation between us. By the time junior year began we were definitely the best of friends. Both of us had the desire to complete St. Andrews as successfully as possible, and we were willing to do anything to make this wish a reality.

As junior year began, I was hungry for opportunities to get involved. I entered the tryouts for the school's team for "Battle of the Brains," a TV quiz show in which area high schools competed in tournament-style competition. I did not make the competition team, but I did make first alternate, and I practiced with the team and went to all of the matches. The coach, Mrs. Morgan, took a personal interest in me and valued my capacity to learn and understand facts, especially in the area of history. By the next year I was to join the television team and I soon became a major force. Many people were surprised to see a black guy on the team from St. Andrews. We did very well, making it all the way into the semi-finals. I even sent my tapes to the admissions committees at the colleges I applied to.

I didn't really search for all of the activities that I became involved in. When sign-ups were announced for the Drama Club's play, Tom, the same guy who had jokingly nominated me for a position on the student council, took the liberty of signing me up. To the surprise of many, I actually went ahead with tryouts for the play. I became involved in several productions during the course of my junior and senior year, which brought me into contact with the women from St. Anne's for extended periods of time. Jonathan and I began to go to the parties of our wealthy, white friends. These parties were comprised of the "popular crowd" of the St. Andrews and St. Anne's students. These people began to take a new attitude toward me; I was no longer simply someone to make fun of. I had finally begun to turn my experience at St. Andrews into a positive one.

In the spring of junior year I found out that I was accepted by the AFS intercultural program and went to Israel to stay with a family for the summer. The group with which I traveled was a diverse mix of people from around the United States. About half of the students in the group were Jewish, and I was the only black. This was the first time I had come into close contact with people from all over the country, and I felt as if I had been living in a closet; the closed-mindedness of North Carolina had left its mark. We arrived in Israel and were taken to a youth hostel in Tel Aviv where we underwent further orientation. As we traveled around Tel Aviv, I remember feeling self-conscious because I was black, though this feeling left when I saw that there were actually a fair number of black Israelis. After I had been in the country for several days, my host brother, David, came to pick me up with a female friend of his. As I talked with them, I began to notice the differences between them and my peers at home; these people seemed to be a lot more mature and less materialistic. I also felt that they did not notice that I was black, or that if they did notice, it made no difference.

In all of my travels around Israel, I never felt that my race was an issue or a problem. I was referred to simply as an American. I remember only one conversation that concerned race. My host father had heard that things were pretty bad for black people in the United States and he asked me what my experiences had been. I told him that in my hometown there were still many problems that revolved around race. However, I explained that things were much improved since the days when my parents were my age. He replied that to his people, race itself meant nothing. He noted that when distinctions were made, they had more to do with religion than race. But what he told me and what I observed were two different things. The family that I stayed with were of European descent, and every once in a while they would make derogatory comments about Jews of Middle Eastern descent. I also saw the way Arabs were treated within Israel. Their neighborhoods were some of the most impoverished places that I had ever seen. And the Israelis to whom I spoke believed that if the Arabs wanted to live better they should go to another country. My eyes were opened to the fact that people could oppress others for reasons unrelated to race. I had heard that this happened around the world, but I had not seen it up close. I left Israel feeling that I understood much more that people had different perspectives on life, and that no one perspective was necessarily better than any other.

When time rolled around to start thinking about college, my initial reaction was to apply for early admission to the University of North Carolina. However, this attitude changed when I noticed that Jonathan was looking at an entirely different set of institutions. His football prowess, along with good grades, had assured him of acceptance to most of the Ivy League schools. This sparked my interest in these schools, and when it came time, I applied to them. Most of the guys in my class thought that I was taking a shot in the dark; there was no way that I would ever get in. In the end, however, I was successful and was accepted into every school to which I applied.

The reaction by some to my acceptance into a top college was that I would soon fail out or disappear into the woodwork. This seemed to be the attitude of the St. Anne's girl who was also accepted to the same college as I was. She had been part of the crowd that had given me such a hard time during high school. Whenever she and I would talk about heading off to college, she behaved as if the two of us were going to entirely different schools. I got the feeling that she could not imagine that our college experiences would be at all similar, primarily because I was a black student and could be expected to separate myself from the college mainstream. My stock did go up among the faculty of the school. I was encouraged warmly by faculty who had been cool toward me in previous years. The teachers even went so far as to award me an honor prize for outstanding citizenship at graduation, the culmination of two years of surprising people by succeeding where I was not expected to.

The fact that my Uncle Joe attended this same college has much to do with the attitude that I have developed toward it. Samuel Joseph Danforth, my Uncle Joe, was the oldest brother of my late father. He enrolled in my college as a member of the class of 1954. This was years before this college had any thought of diversity; there were only three blacks in his entire class. He even joined a fraternity. After graduating, he went on to medical school where he did well enough to earn a fellowship in research.

When first coming to college I sensed that, as a black student, I was expected to look upon the past of this institution as something that should be alien to me. I was supposed to reject its traditions and reactionary fraternity system. However, my family's connection did not allow me to take this stance to the extent that some of my fellow black students did. I was aware that in the past my college had many problems and prejudices; my uncle had been excluded from a fraternity that had an open policy of excluding blacks. However, I did not treat the past of this institution with the loathing which I sensed from other black students, and which I felt some administrators expected me to espouse. For some reason, I felt connected to that part of my college's past that my uncle represented. Part of this was a sense of pride in being a black second-generation Ivy-Leaguer, and a fourth-generation college undergraduate. For this peculiar reason, I wished to experience that side of college life that most black students feared or even hated.

I lived my freshman year with two roommates from very different backgrounds. Phil was from the Midwest; he came from a wealthy background and had attended an exclusive day school, as I had. Jim was more middle class, his father was a football coach, and he had come to college primarily as an athlete. Interestingly, I was the intermediary between these two. Phil and I shared the same tastes in clothes and had shared a similar educational experience in high school. Jim and I could talk about football, had similar attitudes toward women, and enjoyed rap music. Phil and I developed the closer relationship. Jim did not drink, and alcohol would soon become a large part of my life at college. I also found it difficult to discuss my career goals and plans with Jim; he knew little, if anything, about corporate law or investment banking. On the other hand, Phil's experiences and aspirations were more congruent with my own.

During my first term at college, alcohol became the means to purchase my popularity. This popularity would make possible attainment of most of my student leadership positions ranging from class council representative, student assembly representative, to class president. The College had a policy that excluded freshmen from the fraternities during their first term. As a result, wherever alcohol showed up, large groups of freshmen were sure to follow. One Friday a couple of my hallmates and I decided to buy a few cases and invite some people over. We set the beer out in a trash can with some ice and soon a crowd of about fifty to seventy had gathered in our hallway. Phil suggested that I go around and collect "chips" (small donations of one or two dollars to help defray the cost of the beer) and, as a result, I met more people in one hour than I had met during my entire first two weeks. Later, as people were beginning to file out, I heard people saying, "you guys are really ballsy" and "when's the next rager." We had these parties for the next six successive weekends. We started to buy our beer in kegs and people began to depend upon us for their weekly entertainment. Within three weeks our parties were 150 strong, and even upperclassmen were beginning to show up. I began to achieve widespread recognition, at first as the "big black guy who collected the chips." Eventually people whom I did not ever recall seeing before began to call my name around campus. I began to realize that if I had anything going for me, it was the fact that I had an image that stuck in people's minds.

Elections for class council were announced about the fifth week of the term. I decided to run and produced only one simple campaign poster. It used photographs from our several parties and the caption read, "Let's keep the tradition going." Therefore, in my first student government election I ran on a platform of "free beer" and parties. It worked, and I went to my first class council meeting the next week.

By the second term of my freshman year the fraternity system had become a major mental preoccupation of many of my fellow classmates, as well as myself. We had abandoned our weekly parties on the hall and had begun to consume beer at the expense of fraternity brothers. The Zeta Upsilon house had a reputation for being a haven for the wealthy and powerful. This reputation was taken seriously by the campus, and an article on this particular house had appeared in *Playboy* magazine just a year before. This did not intimidate me or my roommate, Phil. One Wednesday night early in winter term we went into the basement of Zeta. It was filled with about 30 guys wearing Brooks Brothers shirts with ratty jeans and dingy baseball caps. The Grateful Dead played in the background. I went over to a guy who appeared to be wearing a sweatshirt from one of St. Andrews rival schools. It turned out he had actually gone to Exeter, but he got excited when he found out that I had gone to a private school and he invited me to come back the next week.

Phil and I began to go to Zeta U on a regular basis. We became good friends with most of the brothers and we began to spend time outside the house with those guys whom we expected to become members of our pledge class. At the beginning of spring term, rush came around. Both Phil and I were let into the house and I began to spend all of my leisure time there. I would get up and go to class, eat, and then go straight to the house. For a relatively small fee each term, I would have all of the beer that I could drink, not only at my own house, but also at most of the other houses in the system. I began to partake of the system on a regular basis, but I did not feel that I would be any more productive if I was not in a fraternity.

The women who hung out at our fraternity were basically the female counterparts of my brothers. They were all white and wealthy and knew it. They were much more civil toward me than were the St. Anne's girls, but they were extremely image conscious. One thing that really struck me was the fact that I received odd looks from these people when they discovered that I was in Zeta U. I was the only black person in the house, and at many of the "social set" parties that I would go to, I would almost always be the only black person in the room. The one thing about the fraternity that would often cause me stress was the every-term chore of finding a formal date. Usually the only women who were interested in going were white sorority girls. I often shied away from asking black girls because I was afraid that they would not feel comfortable. I often had to reconcile within myself the fact that as a black person I belonged to this organization that made no effort to include blacks.

During the entirety of my sophomore year, I was the only black member of the house. When rush for the next class came along, I felt obligated to ensure that another black member got admitted. One black guy, whom I did not really know, rushed. When the time came for deliberations, I made a passionate plea for this person's acceptance as a member of the house. Several of the other brothers felt that I used "racial guilt" to force this member into the house. Therefore, they put pressure on me to ensure that person would become a good member. I felt that such an attitude was inherently wrong, but it is representative of what I have often had to deal with as a member of this fraternity. Even though I have been exposed to several incidents of racial insensitivity, to question these events usually brings about vehement denial of any racist motives. Often these incidents are passed off as jokes, or simply a matter of objective, intellectual fact. The style of racism may be different from the more blatant form I had to deal with at St. Andrews. However, the end result is the same; I am made painfully aware that I am different from those around me. One fear that I had when I joined a white fraternity was that I would be shunned by other blacks on campus, but this has not come about because I always made a point to speak to black students whom I know, especially when I am in the presence of my white friends.

The experience of being in a fraternity has opened my eyes to the true nature of this college. Though the administration preaches a "principle of community" that promotes the toleration and celebration of diversity, the student body is allowed to maintain an elitist structure. Most of the people in my fraternity are white and wealthy. The people that they eat with, socialize with, and compete with in athletics are also white and wealthy. I am the only black friend that most of these guys have, yet I do not bring them face to face with the poverty and injustice that most blacks must labor under. This causes me to wonder whether I am giving these people a false sense of security about their dealings with black people, and whether I should be more persistent in voicing black concerns in my dealings with my fraternity brothers. However, I believe that I should not seek to place a special burden upon myself to "educate" my white friends. To do so would reduce my ability to function and, hence, succeed.

Rushing my fraternity was rather easy; ten years in predominantly male environments allowed me to take to Greek life like a fish to water. By the beginning of sophomore year, as my skills as a student politician increased, I began to realize that it would be to my advantage to reassess my views toward women. I began to use the word "girls" less and use "women" more. My politician friend, Randy, persuaded me that my attitude was going to eventually get me into trouble. However, inherent in his criticism was a basic misunderstanding of why such attitudes had developed, his having always been in a coed environment where parity between the sexes was stressed. Even now, however, the part of student social life to which I belong is rather divided along gender lines. All of the major positions in student government, with one exception, are occupied by men.

So my involvement in a male-dominated environment still continues, though my awareness and perception of this situation has changed.

My career in student government has, in several ways, been tied to my fraternity experience. First, I realized that if I was to assert myself as a leader at the college, it would be necessary for me to join a fraternity, which had to be well respected and traditional. Second, my closest partner in student government was also a fraternity brother of mine. Third, my fraternity experience has constantly brought me into contact with more and more people. Being in a fraternity such as Zeta U also has an effect upon my campus image. Just as black print is most distinctive against a white background, I, too, stick out in my college environment. This makes me more recognizable and, hence, more viable as a campus politician. There are also some drawbacks to my unique position. There are many on this campus who thrive upon their differences with other people, whether they be racial, socioeconomic, or religious. Many of these people have used their situation to gain prominence and power within the community. To many of these people, I represent a dangerous element because I reconcile the irreconcilable. By virtue of who and what I am, a Zeta U, a class president, and a black person, I mix experiences and attitudes that many in this community contend cannot coexist. It is these attitudes that can eventually hinder my progress in this community, if anything can.

My associations with whites are a result of the institutions and experiences that I have been exposed to. I never set out with the purpose of associating myself with the wealthiest, "whitest" people that I could find. I do, however, show great discretion in choosing the educational and social institutions in which I become involved. Blacks have traditionally been excluded from such organizations, but in the late 1960s a conscious decision was made to allow blacks access to these places. This is the situation into which I was born. The earliest decisions about whom I would associate with were made by my parents. They decided to settle in a predominantly white neighborhood because of certain perceived advantages. These reasons further led them to place me in a white nursery school. As a result, I learned from earliest childhood to be most comfortable in a predominantly white environment. My parents saw no harm in this, since they understood that the recognition of racial differences would come with age.

The motivation for associating with whites was not a desire to stay away from blacks. The minute number of blacks at traditionally prestigious schools and organizations forced me to modify my patterns of association and socialization. I had to associate with Whites in order to have any social life at all. There are very few blacks who have shared my set of experiences, and to find someone similar to me who is black is rare. I guess that these shared contradictions and experiences form the basis of my friendship with Jonathan. Most of the time we spend together is consumed with the discussion of race and class . . . and women.

My relationships with women, or the lack thereof, are a result of my unique situation. Just as I am hampered by the lack of other black males who have shared my experiences, there are even fewer black females that I have come into contact with. This is not to say that I haven't met a few, but the field is very small. It is unrealistic to believe that I will be compatible with every upper-middle class black female that I meet. To limit my relationships with women to one race is therefore foolish for me. In dealing with white women, another set of factors comes into play. Even in the 1990s it is not fully acceptable to have interracial relationships, especially for those women who are conscious of their class and position. They care about what their peers will think, as well as their parents. This is especially true in a conservative town like the one I grew up in, or the small, sheltered community of my college. When I have tried to initiate such relationships, I have encountered the barriers that society has erected.

As I look beyond my upcoming final year at college (with an eye on the presidency of the student body) I feel I have a good idea of what it is that I have to overcome. I must be sure that I have reconciled within myself these seemingly contradictory experiences and paradoxes of race and privilege, disadvantage and advantage. I am a young black man, socialized by elite white institutions, very aware of the racism that surrounds me; yet my perspective on life is one of empowerment and unfettered opportunity. If I do not reconcile these contradictions, then those goals that I have set for myself shall be much harder, if not impossible, to reach.

CASE 7

To Be the Best

The author, now a college senior, grew up feeling that her parents' affection for her depended on her academic success. Acutely aware of their own humble origins, they stress the importance of getting ahead, instilling in Emily a strong competitiveness, the ethic of hard work, and the need to maintain a brave face regardless of the circumstances. Though successful academically and athletically in high school, Emily finds it difficult to make friends; her insecurity came across to her peers as arrogance. Her high school experience oscillates between bouts of depression and attempts to find sexual gratification. When she becomes pregnant in college she decides to have the child and marry the baby's Native American student father, in part because she sees enormous promise in this relationship. No longer supported financially by her parents, who are outraged by her decisions, Emily leaves college for a year to establish her independence for financial aid. When she returns she switches her major and career plans; free of her parents' "domination," Emily feels her adolescence has ended.

My parents are among the most mutually incompatible married people that I have ever encountered. My husband's parents, who are divorced, are perhaps even more incompatible than my own. Perhaps in some ways this is a good thing. We both got to see bad marriages in action and we are aware of many of the pitfalls that our parents were unable to overcome. We have clear examples of what one ought not to do. But it is difficult because we are both walking into unfamiliar territory in trying to build a lasting, strong, and supportive marriage. My marriage marks the end of my adolescence. It is the beginning of my adult life. Although I was only 20 when I married and 21 when my son Ian was born, youth had passed. For reasons that I will discuss later, the choice not to terminate my pregnancy demanded that I assume absolute responsibility for my life, as well as for the life of my son.

The drive to "get ahead" is something that was transmitted to me very strongly throughout my adolescence. I was always told, especially by my parents, that it was very important for me to do well, to get ahead, to carry the family forward on the path to success. I was always praised for doing well in school and criticized, particularly by my father, for oversights, mistakes, or failures. From earliest recollection my mother indoctrinated me with the idea of becoming a doctor and going to Harvard.

I'm not sure when I made the association between parental affection and my continuing success, but I do know that this link was well established by the time I moved to Maine in the eighth grade. It certainly was an effective goad to my working hard, with love and security riding on every test. However it was around the eighth grade that I began to experience episodic depressions and thoughts of suicide.

This depression problem is seasonal, with my worst depressions coming right around my birthday in late February or early March. My psychiatrist of many years believed my condition to be chemical in nature, although I have discovered over the years that intense frustration or deep unhappiness can trigger it as well. But all of this knowledge of my depressions was not to be had quickly. In the eighth grade I had no understanding and no control at all over episodes. It was like falling into a pit, or down a well. It hurt to get up in the morning and put on my clothes. It hurt to read or to think or do anything. I could not see anything worthwhile enough in my future to struggle any more. Death seemed like a blessed release from the dreadful efforts of living.

I didn't tell anyone about this problem until the winter of my freshman year in high school, when my mother reacted by getting me into psychotherapy. At the time I had no idea what a godsend my therapist would prove to be. I have no doubt that without his help I would not have survived adolescence. I am now able to recognize my depressions as they are only beginning, lessen their intensity, and shorten their duration, or I seek help from an outside source if I am not able to handle them on my own.

But it was a long hard battle. There are so many facets to overcoming depression that are all a part of living through being a teenager, developing a strong sense of who you are, learning to live with your emotions comfortably, learning to cope with your sexuality, realizing that it is okay to be different and not being ashamed of your differentness. I don't find it at all surprising that so many teens commit suicide. I find it surprising that so few do. Adolescence sucks.

Oddly enough, when I was going through all that insecurity for the first time, many people who knew me thought me to be the epitome of a well-adjusted, mature teenager who had a firm sense of self, and they tended to treat me accordingly. In many ways this made it very difficult to make friends in high school. I had never understood this at the time, but this past Christmas I hosted a get-together with my closer friends from those days and it became much clearer. All of the people I had over were shocked to find out that I had opted not to have an abortion and that I was married with a baby. From various things they said I was able to see that to them I had appeared to be the supremely confident, even arrogant, young pre-corporate type. None of them had the slightest inkling that I, too, had been as unsure as everyone else. I guess I was too good an actress for my own good.

As I said earlier, I am loath to place blame for my life on my parents, but there is one area in which I feel that my father justly deserves blame. He trained me not to cry. I can remember many occasions when my father would fly into a rage at the sight of my tears, saying things to the effect that I had better just suck it up because no one was going to take care of me, and that if I thought that womanish tears were gong to help me in life I was sadly mistaken, that people don't have any use for weak, whimpering women, and so on. Now I think that teaching children not to use tears as a weapon against their parents may not be a bad thing, but that teaching a young child that tears are inappropriate on all occasions is very much a mistake.

My father represses so many of his feelings that when he flies into a temper he loses all control. Usually these tempers are short lived, only long enough to throw something, slam something, or slug someone. For some reason many of his tantrums were directed at me. Over the years I don't think he hit me more than once a year, and up until the last time he never used his fists or caused me any serious damage. The last explosion occurred when I was 16, and up until then I had always felt that my mother would prevent him from ever doing me real harm.

This incident was quite different from the others in a variety of ways. First of all, my father provoked the conflict. In the course of making some point he commented on how, as a goaltender in youth, in soccer, years ago, I had looked really stupid on my first penalty kick. I was very hurt by this comment, since I had not understood the rule about not moving my feet until the ball was kicked, had never even seen a penalty kick taken, and had honestly done my best to make the save. I pointed these things out to him, restraining myself from tears and acting in the rational manner he preferred. He repeated and elaborated on the fact that I had indeed looked stupid in front of all those people. I insisted that I had not known what I was doing, by now noticeably upset. He maintained once again that I had looked stupid. I lost my control and screamed "I didn't know what the fuck I was doing," which I suppose was the only alternative to crying that I could think of. He lost it completely.

He came across the kitchen swinging. Being an athlete, I reacted quickly enough to shield my head with my arms and turn my more vulnerable areas away from his fists and towards the wall against which I was standing. He beat on my back very hard, cracking a rib. I remember my mother unsuccessfully trying to pull him off me, but finally he quit on his own. He immediately began to blubber and apologize. I felt as cold as ice and was hurting a lot.

I went and took a shower, leaving him crying and wailing to my mother. Several things were clear to me. He had no self-control, and my mother could not stop him from doing as he would. He was a big man and capable of hurting me again, perhaps even more severely. I had done nothing to warrant this beating. In fact, the entire incident was his fault. He had definitely provoked me into swearing, and not even the foulest of curses warrants a beating with fists. I was afraid, angry, and contemptuous of his infantile tantrum, so dangerous in the body of a full-grown man. And most of all I was determined that I would never be beaten in such a manner again.

I dressed in my bedroom and got my shotgun out of the closet. I found the shells and the slugs. I think I loaded the shells, which with the number-six shot I used for hunting grouse would have been unlikely to kill him even at close range, but I did not think of that at the time. I was unsure if I wanted to kill him or just blast the wall over his head as he came up the stairs to scare him out of ever beating me again. I sat on my bed with the loaded gun considering this.

I heard my mother come up the stairs (it's a really good thing I could hear the difference in their steps or I might have blown her away by accident). She came into my room and was very shocked to see the gun in my lap. I told her that I was going to kill him, that he was a maniac, and that I was going to be sure he never did that to me again. She left quickly. I heard my father leave the house, get in the car, and drive away. I guess she told him to get out of the house and stay away until I cooled off. The odd thing is that I was very cool and calm; I was just determined not to ever let that happen again. And I must say that it never did; he never so much as raised his hand to me again as long as I lived there.

I think the real crime of this episode was not that he beat me or that I seriously considered killing him but rather the fact that I had been unable to make the more healthy response of crying when what he said hurt my feelings. It was not for years afterwards that I learned how to cry in simple grief, hurt, or disappointment. I am sure that he has the same problem to a more severe degree, since it is almost impossible for him to express any emotion unless he loses control all together. I hope I can break the cycle of this kind of repression with my own son.

My mother and I were always very close until we fell out. She always did her best to encourage me in almost every pursuit. Not a game or a practice or any other endeavor of mine did she miss. Ballet recitals, school assemblies, soccer games, basketball games, track meets, school concerts, and on and on. The time she invested in me can hardly be overestimated. She was always there to cheer me on if I did well, and nag and carp if I did badly. I think that all of the things that she made it possible for me to do were things she would have liked to do if she had the chance. She had such an emotional investment in my success that she drove me to "be the best" all the time.

We fell out when, sometime during high school, I came to the realization that the thrill of being the best never lasted for more than an instant, and never served to make me feel better about myself. So I began, tentatively, to invest myself in things other than competition, like friendships. As a result, my mother felt betrayed and angry. Let me say that this experimenting with making new friends, mostly in my senior year of high school and in college, caused me to graduate second in my high school class rather than first, and merely maintain my state title in the high jump, rather than setting a new record. So I felt then and now that my mother's sense of betrayal at my slacking off was truly misplaced. I was hardly the loser she often represented me to be. It is only now, when I have just graduated with honors from college and have been accepted into a Ph.D. program at another Ivy League school, that she is beginning to be pleased with me once again.

The place where my mother made her fatal mistake in conditioning me to be the sort of yuppie automaton she wanted was in developing my sense of morality about sex. This was the chink in the conditioning that allowed me to get in touch with what I wanted and needed. Mom is, by her own reckoning, a frigid stick. She felt that it was her Catholic upbringing that made her ashamed of her own sexuality and unable to express herself sexually. She once told me that she didn't have an orgasm until after my brother was born (he is five years my junior). I asked her why she bothered to do it at all and she said it was her "wifely duty." Thank God and thank her that this was a legacy that she successfully prevented from reaching me.

But I don't think she realized that the consequences of raising me to feel good about my sexuality would probably lead to a fair amount of sexual experimentation beginning at an early age. It was only my fear of being branded a slut at school that kept my encounters to a minimum. I discovered that as long as you only sleep with boys who keep their mouth shut you can get laid and keep your reputation spotless. I told three guys that I was a virgin and two others that I had only slept with one other guy. High school guys in my school were much more likely to keep quiet if they thought that you were not a slut. A slut was someone who "slept around," which actually worked out to be someone who slept with a blabbermouth. One bad report and your reputation was finished.

Please don't let me mislead you. I never got as much sex as I wanted in high school until my senior year when I dated Brian for eight months. My encounters were mostly an assortment of one or two night stands with long dry spells in between. But I think that they are all important from the perspective I now have. My sexual experiences have been, without exception, growth experiences for me.

I was desperately horny during the entire period of time from the beginning of high school until I became pregnant at the age of 20. I have often heard men and boys speak about the intensity of their sex drives during that period of their lives, but I have seldom had even my good female friends admit that they share the same feelings of desperate compulsion. There was, however, a problem. None of the boys within my acquaintance were interested in me. I could see that they were going after girls who I thought were much less attractive than myself. I concluded that I actually had much less to offer than these girls who were managing to find boys. It may seem funny now, but at the time I was sure that I was doomed to live out my life as a lonely, unwanted, undesirable spinster.

So much was I caught up in this thinking that when I joined the track team in the spring I was oblivious to the interest of two of the senior captains and did not encourage them in any way. They were, after all, godlike senior captains of a varsity team and since I was horrible to behold there was no possible chance for me to capture their interest. One was not very aggressive when I did not encourage him. The other one exhibited more determination. I got to know Joe initially as a coach. I found him to be very entertaining because he had a keen mind and much experience (or so it seemed to me). I enjoyed his company a lot, but I did not consider him as a potential boyfriend because of my low self-esteem and his lack of height. I am a tall woman and he is a shortish man. I was sure that he was not interested in me except as a pupil or perhaps as a friend. Later when I began to think that perhaps he was interested in me, I wasn't sure what to do. So he courted me for most of the early part of the season with little or no encouragement. However, his pursuit, his back-handed compliments and various attentions, and his support in my athletic endeavors all conspired to make me think that perhaps there was one person who might find me attractive. It was a heady feeling, to think for the first time that I might not be as awful as I had previously believed.

Joe made his move on our way to an evening track meet some distance away from our school. He saved a seat for me next to him in the exclusive senior section at the back of the bus, and when we got to the meet he asked me to wait while everyone was getting off the bus. I began to panic. I had no idea what he planned to do. I wanted his attentions, but I was terrified with nervousness. What if I did the wrong thing and he lost interest? What the hell was I supposed to do anyway? I just say there, too scared to move. When we were alone on the bus he turned and hugged me. Then he turned my face towards him and kissed me very gently. It felt wonderful. So much better than I had ever imagined a first kiss would be. We stayed on the bus for a while necking. I don't remember how long it was, because I was on cloud nine. I do, however, vividly remember getting off the bus to rejoin the rest of the team, only to have them burst into applause as Joe and I approached them. Very embarrassing. I blush to this day remembering it.

My mind should have rung a warning bell when Joe offered to drive me home that night, but since he offered rides to other people as well I figured that nothing would happen. I was so tired and I was almost asleep when I realized that, having dropped off the other two people, he was driving away from my area of town. I started to get scared again. But I also remembered how good it felt that afternoon and how he hadn't been rough or anything. I decided to wait and see what happened, since I trusted him enough to know that if I said "stop!" he would. It turned out that because he went so slowly and made me feel so good I never did say stop. He stopped on his own just shy of actual intercourse, but not before he had fired me to previously unimagined heights of pleasure. And I was sorry that he stopped. Of course it goes without saying that I was not in the least concerned with issues of contraceptives or morality at the time; all I cared about was getting more. He fortunately had more wits about him and managed to get me calmed down, dressed, and back home before I had my wants fully satisfied.

After that night I was no longer shy or afraid. I wanted him worse than anything else in the world and I was determined to get him. So I said all the right things about not getting emotionally involved and having an abortion if I got pregnant and not expecting any happily-ever-after stuff. I lied my ass off. I said what he wanted to hear, or what I thought he wanted to hear, and in fairly short order it worked. I think he had reservations about my passion. Being Italian, he had a good-girl/bad-girl complex, where only bad girls wanted, enjoyed, and pursued sex, while good girls were sweet and virginal. But here I was, as virginal as could be before he got hold of me and now being very insistent about the fact that I wanted sex, and lots of it. He often lamented the fact that he had "corrupted a youth," and I think that it was this that made him stop seeing me not a week after we first had sex.

Of course I was devastated. By the time we broke up I was sure that I loved him and would love him forever. It was quite a blow to my new-found self-esteem. In fact, it returned my self-estimation to its previous level, except that now I knew that having had one man I could probably get another. But he was the only man I wanted. I pursued him fruitlessly for the remainder of the school year and for about a year afterwards whenever I had the chance, which wasn't often, since he was away at college.

I had pretty much decided to give up, even though I still wanted him, when his grandfather died during Christmas break of my junior year. I knew how he must be feeling, since my own grandmother had died just before the start of school that year, so I went to the funeral. While I thought

I went unnoticed, he showed up on my doorstep that night bearing a fruitcake for my mother and asking if I could come to his house to watch a movie he had just gotten. I went and he was able to weaken my resolve not to sleep with him, partially through charm and partially because I could tell how badly he was hurting even though he couldn't admit it.

From that time until Thanksgiving break of my senior year, I was his home town honey, which is to say that he slept with me sporadically during school vacations. We never called or wrote and I learned not to count on seeing him until I actually did. He didn't give me anything too satisfying in the emotional department, but even a little bit of occasional sex was better than none at all. But Thanksgiving that year I did not even get that from him, and being fed up I stormed over to his house, told him to get lost, and did not see him again until I resumed the acquaintance shortly before I left for college. I tried to arrange a rendezvous at college, but he didn't show up for it and I became in rapid succession hurt, depressed, and disgusted. I wrote him a "how could you do this to me — who the hell do you think you are" letter and resolved never to think about him again.

He called me during the winter of my sophomore year at college just after I had started seeing Jim, who is now my husband. Joe wanted to come up and take me out to dinner, and since Jim and I weren't exactly solid at this point, I agreed. But I was determined not to be had this time. Joe arrived and took me out to shop at a local mall. I looked at various pieces of junk, and resisted his attempts to buy them for me until he told me that he wanted to "atone for past sins" and didn't expect anything in return. I let him buy me two baubles and dinner at a local Chinese place, where he explained that he had come to realize that he had been a jerk most of his life when he woke up one day and had no friends. He said that he had spent the last few months going around trying to make amends with everyone he had alienated and that he hoped that he and I could just be friends. I was suspicious, but I said I would try. He disappeared again into that void from which he came, and I heard not a word until the following winter. I briefly debated inviting him to my wedding in November, but I rejected the idea as too awkward to carry out.

When he called next, I was married and pregnant, but I didn't tell him on the phone. He wanted to come up again and I said okay, but that I had some big news for him that I could only tell him in person. I must say that I relished the idea of getting such a good one-up on him, and his shock at the news was all that I could have hoped for. Since that time he has been most cordial to both Jim and me, inviting us down to see him and giving us many random gifts.

I am glad for what we had, but I am also glad that whatever winds of fate drew us together were strong enough to overcome my girlish determination and tear us apart, because we would have been miserable together on a more permanent basis. He is a good friend and a lousy boyfriend.

But, of course, there were others besides Joe. There was Phil right after my grandmother died in the fall of my junior year. We were drawn together by our losses. Phil's cousin was killed in an accident, and while he was trying to cope with that death he needed me and reached to me for comfort. But afterwards I needed and wanted more than he could give at the time, or perhaps ever. He was afraid of me, because I think he knew better than I did at the time that I would quickly outgrow my need for him. Or perhaps he was just an ungrateful jerk and I am merely sentimentalizing the brief relationship we had. In either case he ran away from me until I got the hint and left him alone.

There was Giorgio, who was an idealized notion of doing a dashing and romantic thing while at Harvard Summer School my junior summer, a one-night stand that was a way of proving my power and attractiveness and slapping Joe at the same time. Not that Joe ever knew or cared, but it was a way for me to prove to myself that I wasn't sitting around waiting for him without endangering my reputation at school.

There was Jason, whom I met at a convention of selected students in Washington, D.C. He was from Alabama and I was able to successfully charm him into writing me a very flattering letter after we went home. He was full of all that southern chivalry that I find very enjoyable, but he did try to force his advantage with me one night. He was a big football type, but I am also a big and fairly strong girl, so I managed to convince him that I really meant the "no" I gave him by throwing him across the room, after which he found me to be a rare Yankee lady and treated me with even more deference and respect. He was definitely an ego-boosting experience.

In my senior year I finally managed to find a boyfriend and have a nice high school relationship, complete with the prom and passing notes in the hallways and going out cruising around with a six-pack on Saturday nights. It was something that I had always aspired to and finally figured out how to make happen. His name was Brian, and he was rebounding off of the love of his life when she dumped him. She and he were much better suited than he and I were, but I did what I had to do to make the relationship work. He was a nice guy, simple and trustworthy. Unfortunately, he was not too bright. I had to learn to speak in words of less than three syllables and to enjoy listening to music rather than expecting to have a conversation, but it was fun. He had many friends and by dating him I got to know many people who were "cool," and they came to realize that I was not snotty the way they had always thought. I began to be included in a much wider social circle where I had always been excluded before. It was a confidence-building relationship for me. I broke it off with Brian as soon as he came back from a summer away because we no longer had anything in common now that the senior spring fun and track were over. I had done the boyfriend thing and now I wanted something more than just a warm body to go out with on weekends.

So now I reach the next big relationship, that of Ted. My relationship with Ted was very intense emotionally, perhaps as much so as was my relationship (if you can even call our on again-off again thing a relationship) with Joe. Perhaps it was simply the timing, coming as it did at the very beginning of college, right after Joe had blown off our date to meet at school. I'm not sure. What I am sure of is that Ted was representative of how my life might have been. Had I stayed with Ted I would have been the wife of a workaholic businessman, like my mother was before me. I would have married a man like dear old Dad. What I would have had with Ted was all my mother aspired for me to become.

The first thing that happened to me when I got to college was that I got very sick during the middle of tryouts for soccer. I missed most of the social activities of Freshman Week and got cut. It was a blow to my esteem, and I felt very awkward about making friends. I didn't like any of the people on my hall and didn't meet people in my classes. I happened into a date with Ted by accident, since he thought he was talking to my roommate when he called up and asked me out. He covered his surprise and took me out instead. A couple of dates later we were an item. Like most freshman relationships we were both lonely and insecure so far from all that we were familiar with, and we clung to each other as the only security in the world. We always ate together, studied together and, in short, were each other's only friend. We didn't make many efforts to make other friends because we didn't need to; after all, we had each other.

It was a pure fluke that we ended up joining a coed fraternity. We showed up at a pre-rush event, and all of the men in the house who were around at the time hastened to make me feel welcome, which was so flattering that I wanted to rush. I think in retrospect that this was the beginning of the end of Ted and me, because within the nest-like confines of our fraternity I would grow more and more confident. And Ted became more confining and boring in direct proportion to my increased self-confidence.

But at the time it seemed like an answer to my isolation. Our fraternity was fun on tap. When Ted and I moved into the house sophomore fall, we moved into the same room. I am glad that we did because it intensified my realizations of the problems in our relationship. Lest this account turn into a diatribe about how screwed up in the head Ted is, let it suffice to say that Ted had a GPA of 3.87, clean-cut good looks, conservative political views, absolutely no interest in any academic subject, and was very into the idea of S&M, with a heavy preference for being on the receiving end of pain. His concept of morality was simple: his family and his few friends were to be protected from harm, and everyone else was to be exploited as was necessary or desirable.

At first I did not realize the extent of his weirdness or how completely lacking in conscience he truly was. But as I gradually came to know him better I found that what he gave to me was not worth what I gave him financially, emotionally, morally, and finally physically. I resisted this at first, for after all, he was good-looking and had shown that he would make a lot of money when he was done with school. My parents liked him. He was safe and secure. But he made me miserable.

I didn't realize how miserable I was until he went home for Christmas and I was so relieved to have him gone. I was at school to train for track and I found living alone in our room to be pure bliss. I was able to get out and socialize with other people around the house for a change. But therein lies a tale, for one snowy night a day before Ted was to return I was overcome with lust for Jim. Never have I desired anyone so much as I did Jim, not even Joe at my most desperate. The feeling was so strong that I simply had to have him that night, or I would die. Perhaps what I experienced was what is politely known as love at first sight.

Now I should qualify this night of adventure with a few words about Jim. Jim is Native American and from Nebraska. Where he comes from men kill other men who sleep with their women. Jim is a sensible and pragmatic sort of guy who had no desire to get himself injured or killed over a one-night stand, so he tried to run away to avoid my determination to sleep with him. At first he left the house, but then decided to return. Then he set out to drink himself beyond the ability for activity of the sort that I had in mind, but fortunately for me the liquor ran out before his capacity for recovery. By this point he was too drunk to run away and too interested to drive me off with nasty words. He valiantly resisted temptation long enough to remind me of my long-standing relationship with Ted, but to no avail. I had my way at last.

But of course all nights end with The Morning After. I now had a problem. Ted was due to return that evening, and I had no idea what I wanted to have happen. I was guilty of violating one of my own notions of right behavior by cheating on Ted, but it was amply clear that I would do it again if I had the chance. I was horribly confused and unable to figure anything clearly, except for the fact that I did not want Ted to return.

Within a week of his return, I was certain that I no longer wanted a relationship at all with him, so much so that I told him and moved my stuff out of our room into another room in the house. It was an ugly time. Ted came unwound; I felt both guilty and angry. And, of course, Jim was there. I wanted to start seeing Jim on a regular basis, but Jim was not sure he wanted to have a steady relationship just then. It was all very confused.

Eventually everything settled down, except for Ted. Jim and I started seeing each other and it went along very well. Jim treated me better than anyone I had ever been with, and he was more interesting and fun than anyone else I had ever known. But it was hard for me sometimes because I still had a lot of bottled up resentment about my relationship with Ted.

I must admit I was glad when he left school at the end of the summer. In retrospect it is amazing that someone with whom I was very much in love could leave me feeling nothing but pity at best and stark contempt at worst. Ted is in some ways an issue that I have yet to resolve, but I am very glad that I had the courage to break out of that relationship when I had outgrown it. On the other hand I know that it was my leaving Ted that caused him to freak out. I knew before I left how dependent on me he had become, and sometimes I feel guilty. Other times I feel angry that I stayed with him as long as I did, and lost so much good time to grow at college. Most of the time, however, I try not to think of him at all.

Jim is not a man who can be slotted into a category. As a long-standing student of astrology, I place a great deal of faith in knowing how to deal with people by having a knowledge of a person's Sun Sign. I tend to generalize as well by class, where the person in question grew up, what their ethnic background is, and what religion or lack of religion they follow. But Jim defies these generalizations. Sometimes I think that defiance is the only way to describe him. Jim stands in defiance against the stupidity of the world as he sees it. And since there is a lot of stupidity in the world, he is a busy man.

When I first started "seeing" him, I was on the rebound in a big way. I was still very bruised from the whole Ted thing and needed a lot of reassurance. Jim was much more mature and far more experienced in real-life situations than any other man I had ever met. He knew everything from how one should deal with hysterical ex-boyfriends to how one went about hiring contractors. We were both officers of the house at the time and I came to realize that my upbringing as an aspiring pre-professional was very short on how to deal with things like leaky pipes and unplowed driveways. Jim always seemed to know how to fix things, but he never forced his ideas on me. He let me do my own thing and stood by to give assistance if I needed it and asked for it. I developed a great respect for his abilities, his sensitivity, and his tact.

But I also learned that he does not like to be crossed on issues that he perceives to be within his own domain of control. This is why bureaucracy drives him bats. He sees a situation in which things need to be done, and when he is willing to do them he does not for the life of him see why he should be told by other people how to go about it, or worse yet, have to fight against the rules, regulations and small-minded people in order to do what needs to be done. Since this seems reasonable to me, I don't have a problem. But as you can imagine, he gets into many tangles with administrative machinery. Sometimes I wish he would go with the flow a little more, but then again I am very glad that he doesn't. He has an amazing mind and can almost always outwit whatever bureaucracy stands in his way and make them rue the day they messed with him.

But lest you think that Jim is all fight and fire, let me hasten to add that he is very tender and romantic. I trust him unreservedly. He is a person of great moral integrity and would never sleeze around on me. I know that I can depend on him always. But there are many things that are difficult. We come from backgrounds as alien to each other as if we were from different countries. It can be difficult to bridge the gap, but time and experience have made it easier.

But I am skipping ahead of myself. Jim and I dated from the beginning of winter term until we were married in November of that same year. In early October I discovered, much to my dismay, that I was pregnant. I was working and living in an apartment off campus, and Jim was living on campus in the Native American house and taking classes. I suspected that I might be pregnant when I had an entire week of the worst PMS of my life only to have it go away without my period ever starting. This did not seem like a good thing, so I bolted off to the infirmary at school and found out the awful truth. The first thing I did was make an appointment to have an abortion and arrange for my school insurance to pay rather than my parents' insurance. But even in the daze that I felt in the time just after I found out, I was not completely convinced that having an abortion would be the best thing to do. I had always wanted to have children and, at some level, I was afraid that if I aborted this child I would be unable to have another since "the Gods do not shower gifts on those who reject them."

I was also afraid that if I had an abortion I would destroy the relationship with Jim out of my own feelings of guilt and remorse. I knew that deep down I wanted to have this baby, but I was unsure if I would be able to provide for him or her in the way I would like. So in planning how I would care for the baby if I did choose to go through with the pregnancy, I had to keep in mind that I might have to care for this child with little or no outside help. It therefore became of paramount importance that I be able to finish college. If it had not been possible for me to find ways of finishing my education with a baby, I know that I would have opted for the abortion.

There was also the easiness factor to be considered. It would be a hell of a lot easier to go with the flow, have the abortion, and carry on with my life as if nothing had happened. But I knew that this was impossible. I would despise and misuse the freedom of a lifestyle that was purchased with the life of my baby. I would hate myself.

To say that it was not an easy decision is to trivialize the anguish that I felt while I was grappling with this issue. I tried to pass the choice onto Jim, but he wisely declined taking responsibility for my decision. He assured me that he would love me as much and would be with me through it all either way, and refused to commit himself to the issue of abortion or not. He said that it was my child as long as it was in my body and so until birth the decision had to be mine alone.

He did add that should I decide not to have an abortion he would be totally against putting the baby up for adoption. If after the birth I wanted nothing further to do with the baby he would take the baby back to Nebraska and raise him or her with the help of his family. I could stay or go as I saw fit, but if the baby was born he would see to it that it was raised as a member of his family.

This helped me a great deal to know that I had more options than just that of an abortion. I knew that if I had the baby my parents would give me little or no help. Jim's mother Mary, on the other hand, was very supportive. I knew that in a worst-case scenario I would have Jim's relatives to depend on. But more than that, Jim's Indian relatives were thrilled with the prospect of having another baby to raise. There was no mistaking their delight, which was only slightly dampened by the lack of a marriage between Jim and me. There were some concerns that we would be unable to finish school, but beyond that there was primarily pleasure.

I finally reached a decision in the obstetrics office at the hospital. I had gone in to pick up some information about the medication I was taking for my asthma, since I was concerned about the possible effects on the baby. Had there been a danger to the baby I would have had an abortion rather than risk a deformed baby, but as it turned out there were no fetal side-effects, so I was back at go. A nurse overheard me discussing this drug with the receptionist and said that she had some time if I needed to talk about the whole thing. I will always remember her answer to me when I told her the main thing holding me back from going ahead with the pregnancy was my parents and how they would react. She said, "They will get over it." And I realized that she was right, that no matter how badly they took the news they would eventually get over the shock of it all.

Unfortunately, she has yet to be proven right. My parents lost all self-control and flew to pieces. My father called Jim a "cocksucker," and my mother wished me a miscarriage. They screamed and cried and threatened. They drove to school, I guess to try to bully me into an abortion. But Jim and I made ourselves scarce, so they eventually drove home to continue their miseries elsewhere. When it became clear to them that we were unwilling to change our minds they attempted to get a grip on their mouths and stop being so hateful, but the damage had already been done. Jim despises them. To his way of thinking, wishing a miscarriage on me is almost the same as killing our child. It is bad medicine. He has not yet forgiven, nor is he likely ever to forgive, my parents for the things they said during their tantrum.

The decision to have the baby and my parents' reaction to it served to sever forever the ties that still controlled me to a certain extent. It freed me from ever being worried about what my parents think of what I want to do. I am foolish enough to want their love and approval still, but never enough now to let myself do something I hate for their benefit. It is clear to me now that my parents are so emotionally retarded that I seriously doubt if they ever really loved or approved of me. Now that I am clearly far happier than I have ever been because of my decision, their continued animosity makes me question the depth of their capability for love and understanding. They cannot and will not see that one can be happy in not following the narrow path to yuppie happiness. Oh well.

During this same fall I discovered that I was learning disabled. I had been referred for testing by one of the deans because of difficulties I was having in one of my classes. The diagnosis of my dyslexia was a great relief. I had always been a terrible speller, and for years had been haunted by comments from my teachers about my sloppy work. Until I learned to write on a computer with a program to check my spelling, I never realized that I could write stories or papers that anyone would want to read.

But other symptoms of my disability were more difficult to realize until after my diagnosis. My tester recommended that I be allowed to take my exams in a room by myself and have no time limit. These two simple things have boosted my grades consistently by a solid letter, with no more studying on my part. Often I am able to finish within ten minutes of the time limit. But without the pressure of a time constraint I am able to write my answers with clarity and attention to detail, even if the spelling is bad.

Finding out about being dyslexic coincided with finding out I was pregnant, so it is natural that in rethinking my life I would also call into question my career path. Since my marriage distanced me so much from my parents' influence I was able to look more carefully at why I was pursuing medicine. Now I still think that being a midwife or an obstetrician would be a very fine and rewarding line of work, but almost all other branches of medicine seem either disgusting or boring. I also disliked about 90 percent of my classmates from my pre-medical classes. They seemed, for the most part, to be unthinking, uncreative automatons who follow all the rules and always color inside the lines. They also have little or no sense of morality, and I found this very frightening.

I was unable to return to school after my leave term in the fall when I married, because my parents would no longer foot the bill for my education. I had to leave school for one calendar year in order to be considered an independent student and receive financial aid. During that time I still was committed to being a doctor, but I had decided to change my major to something that I might enjoy more than geology. Since my favorite classes had been religion classes, I decided to try that as a major.

In fulfilling the requirements for my religion major, I found myself completely captivated by the material in my courses. I wanted to learn more and more. I have always been interested in religions different from my own Roman Catholic upbringing, and now I found that there were people who made a life out of studying religion and writing about it. It had never occurred to me that I might become a professor and spend my life learning about a topic that fascinates me. More than that, I found that I liked and respected my classmates and instructors and began to think that spending my life working with people of integrity and depth had a lot to recommend it.

The decision to pursue a Ph.D. in religion is one of the first milestones in my adult life. All the pieces fit together now: my marriage to Jim with all the warmth and love that we share, being free of my parents' domination, having the faith in myself to truly believe that I know what is best for me even if it is "the path less traveled," having the courage to face the possibility of future disappointments and not always be working backwards out of fear. It may not all work out as well as I hope, but I know that I can always make it better somehow if I want to.

I am not finished yet, by a long shot, but I am happy with how far I've come.

CASE 8

A Step in the Only Direction

This writer's central theme is coming to terms with being gay. The 20-year-old autobiographer recounts the emergence of homosexual longings in junior high school amid all the peer pressure toward heterosexual involvement. He has his first gay experience as a first-year college student, and he realizes that these feelings represent where he wants to go with his sexual life and that he must somehow come to terms with being gay in a straight world. He describes an excruciating coming-out scene with his parents that begins a period of coming-out to friends, though he avoids being openly identified as gay at his college because he perceives an anti-gay environment. He blames his parents for his reluctance to be more active in his advocacy of gay issues at his college. This resentment of his parents for their lack of true acceptance of his sexual orientation remains a powerful source of anger and insecurity for him, and it reflects his struggle to maintain both a sense of belonging and self-respect in a homophobic society.

"How can I study with *that* over there?" I asked myself over an open philosophy textbook. "Finals are coming so you'd better pay attention to your books and not to anything or *anybody* else," I warned myself. Still, I found myself rubbernecking awkwardly every time I heard one of the two doors at the west end of the study hall open. After reading the same paragraph about fifteen times due to my perpetual rubbernecking, *he* walked into the study room. Of course, I again awkwardly contorted myself in my chair in order to catch a glimpse of whoever may have entered the scene, and when I did this time, I found myself in a locked stare with a very attractive man. The stare which seemed to last for minutes could not have been more than a second and a half glance, but that was enough to make me forget about Mssrs. Kant, Hume, and Hegel.

Tim, as I later learned was his name, placed his things on the long wooden table right next to the door he had just passed through and sat down facing my back. I had to know if his glance was just casual or if it was more. I turned toward the clock and stole another glance at Tim. However, again, my attempt did not go unnoticed. Tim was waiting to meet my glance with his. My heart was racing! I was sure that everybody in the silent study hall could hear it pounding loudly in my throat. I could not keep myself from looking again, and I was greeted by an "inviting" glance. One time I was met by a rather forward raising of the eyebrows.

"Your attention please. The library will be closing in thirty minutes. If you wish to check out books. . . ." What was I going to do?! The library was closing, so I headed for the door — the door farther from me and closer to Tim. He had begun to pack up when I did, and he *just happened* to be at the same door at the same time that I was. He held the door open for me (literally and figuratively, as I'll explain later), and I passed within inches of him and choked, "Thanks."

"What's up?" he asked in a friendly voice as we headed for the stairs.

"Not a lot," I stuttered. "And you?"

"Where are you headed?" he answered with a smile.

My God. It was really happening. This beautiful man was making a pass at me. By the time we reached this point in our "conversation" we had reached the first floor of the library on our way toward the doors that lead to the west end of campus.

"Where are *you* headed?" I answered meekly.

"Would you like to go somewhere and talk?" he asked.

"Sure," I answered, choking on my heart.

Since that evening, I have had no doubt whatsoever about my sexuality. I am gay. I have always been gay. I will most likely always be gay. I am happy being gay. It is true that the fact I am gay creates some barriers in life for me, particularly in the political world and other professions. Also, the possibility of having a family is considerably decreased by the biological incompatibility with homosexuality. Finally, being gay has caused me to distance myself from people, like my family, to whom I would like to be closer. However, these are things that mean very little in comparison to the life I imagine if I tried to live a straight life as a homosexual. I couldn't live a charade like that. My happiness stems from my being me, and my being the only one who knows what is best for me. Homosexuality is not the cause of my happiness. My acceptance of it is.

But what about the first eighteen years of my life? Was I happy then? I will answer yes and no to this question. I answer yes because I was truly happy before my mind understood what it was to be sexual at all. When I did not understand sexuality (heterosexuality or homosexuality), I was ignorantly blissful. My troubles began when my body began changing and when my intellect began understanding those changes and the feelings they caused. Before I get into the inner conflict of my adolescence, let me say something about my early childhood.

I was the most self-confident child I knew. I wasn't afraid to say or do anything to anybody. In elementary school and in middle school I was always the "teacher's pet." Why shouldn't I have been? I was the model student: well-behaved, respectful, entertaining, and intelligent. It all came very easily and naturally. To behave in any other way would be to behave as I was not. As I look back on those years before high school, I see many things which I am now better able to understand.

In middle school I was very involved with the drama club. My singing voice is comparable to a cross between Elvis and Roger Rabbit, but I was always on stage in the school musicals. I was an attention "addict." My habit was more than adequately supported by the many attention "pushers" around me who were more than willing to give me a fix. I never had trouble dealing with people in the structured and regulated environment of school. However, out of the classroom I was out of my element and, therefore, a very different person. Still, I was very charismatic and self-confident until the subject of sex was brought up. I just couldn't participate in the "oogling" that my friends engaged in. I didn't find Danissa and her chest as inviting as everybody else did. John's conquest of Cindy wasn't the least bit interesting to me, particularly because I didn't yet have the sexual drive to engage in these behaviors myself. When I did develop this drive, I guess in eighth grade, I found myself equally disinterested in Danissa and her chest. Instead, I found myself very interested in Tony and his sharp features and muscular build.

Parties! I loved them then. I love them now. Soda and chips have been replaced by beer and more beer, but the idea of getting together with a group of friends (an audience) and sharing some stories and laughs is my favorite way to spend time. Well, maybe my second favorite way. Parties were great in middle school until I became sexual. An innocent game of spin-the-bottle among friends was a lot of fun. Actually, it seemed pretty inane to me. Why would anybody want to voluntarily enter a situation in which he or she would be forced to kiss somebody else? What was the big deal about kissing anyway? I must have played fifty games of spin-the-bottle, and not once did I get any pleasure from kissing. Kissing wasn't repulsive to me, but it wasn't attractive either, until I began to have sexual desires for men. I felt forced to play spin-the-bottle. If I didn't, I feared being labeled as gay. And I *wasn't* gay. That's what I told myself so often, in fact, that I actually believed it for a while.

Things got tougher, however, whenever one of my oversexed and underexperienced adolescent friends would suggest that we play a game of "French" spin-the-bottle. It sent a shiver up my spine and caused my stomach to contract to the size of a pea. They wanted me to put my very personal tongue into somebody else's equally personal mouth. No way! I wasn't even interested in putting my tongue in Tony's mouth. I don't know what I wanted to do with Tony. I think I just wanted to be with him, to

admire him, to touch him. I put my foot down when it came to institutionalized French kissing, and this seemed odd to everybody else. "Why
not?" my friends would ask. My answer was usually something like "I'll
only do that with somebody special" and not "It's gross and I'm afraid to try
it," which was the true answer. I laugh when I think of Susan (who later
earned herself the reputation of being the class slut) trying to teach me how
to kiss: "It's just like giving somebody a raspberry only into their mouth."
Ick!!! More than four years would pass before I had my "first kiss."
Needless to say, my attitude towards kissing is very different now.

Now, before I jump from middle school into high school, is the best
time to say more about the relationship between my twin brother and me.
First, I should note that I haven't told my brother Keith that I am gay. I do
not feel that close to him, nor do I feel that he would react in a positive way
to learning that his own twin brother, albeit fraternal twin brother, prefers
intimacy with men over sex with women. Also, I have respected my parents'
wish that I not tell my siblings about my homosexuality. Anyway, Keith and
I always got along, and we always fought. We were best friends and worst
enemies. In middle school we had different friends. He hung out with the
tough Neanderthal jock crowd. I moved in more civil circles. My friends
were students, actors, and other human beings.

Academically, I've always been a better student than Keith. I was
enrolled in my school's Gifted and Talented Students program. Keith, on
the other hand, excelled on the playing field, particularly the gridiron. I
participated in athletics, as well, although I disliked most team sports and
was equally as terrible at most of them. I even played full-contact football
until the end of middle school when everybody got big and I didn't. I know
that I only played in order to be "one of the guys." The pressure in my
community to be this way was tremendous. I needed to be accepted by my
peers, and the only way to do that was to appear to be like every other
normal heterosexual young man. This pressure existed even before I became
aware of my sexuality and was only exacerbated by my feelings of "abnor-
mality," which I suffered when I began to have sexual feelings for men.

When we entered high school, the tables had turned. Keith was more
relaxed and at ease than I was. I had a serious lack of self-confidence,
especially in the social sense. I wasn't comfortable. I just couldn't bring
myself to talk about girls and all of the other stuff that high school guys
talked about. My friends loved to talk about all of the girls they wanted to
sleep with, and I found it very difficult to feign interest all of the time. I did,
however, more often than not, awkwardly participate in the talks about
girls and sex. However, in the back of my mind was the ever-present feeling
that I wasn't normal, and that I must change. This problem was exacerbated
merely by being placed in the new physical surroundings of high school.
Perhaps it is more accurate to call them "physique-ful" surroundings. My

new, more physically developed age-mates of high school provided many more stimuli to remind me constantly of my feelings about men.

In high school our groups of friends changed. Keith and I started to hang out with the same people, most of whom were male and from the other middle school in town that we did not attend. Some played with me on the soccer team. Others swam with me during my one-season career on the swim team. I attribute my brief swimming career to the many distractions that the swim team offered. The only thing more brief than my career with the swim team was the "brevity" of the team's uniform. I barely made it all season without any very embarrassing moments.

My female friends were generally the same as those from middle school. In general, I never had any problems getting along with girls in school. I just never "got anywhere" with them sexually. Today, I am almost never intimidated by any woman, but I am often intimidated by handsome men. I don't know why this is, but I would venture to guess that it has something to do with my desire to be liked by men and my disinterest sexually in women. I am not sexist. This is not a sexist phenomenon; it is deeper and far more fundamental to my personality than any "ism" could be.

Keith and I are opposite in every way. He, as I've said, is a great athlete and a good student; I am a great student and a fair athlete. He loves the Grateful Dead; I love Beethoven. He is an engineering student; I am a liberal arts student. He is a registered Republican; I am a Democrat. He is a conservative thinker (an oxymoron if ever there was one); I am a liberal. He is heterosexual; I am gay. How do we get along? Honestly, I'd have to say that we don't get along. We were never very close except in proximity to each other. We don't agree on anything except that we never agree on anything.

I don't want to be like him in any way. Deep in my heart I feel that Keith is a fundamentally bad person, one who doesn't care about hurting others. I pride myself on my integrity, honesty, and open-mindedness. Keith, in my experience of nearly twenty-one years, lacks these elements of goodness. (He is very similar to my father, whom I will discuss later.) I must make it sound like Keith and I were and are constantly at each other's throats. That is not the case. It is true that we argue occasionally, but more frequently, I choose to avoid any argument by changing the subject at hand, particularly if it is one of the standard liberal vs. conservative questions. I don't like to appear like a "flaming liberal," which in my home is equated with "flaming homosexual." As far as Keith is concerned, our relationship is a farce, a play in which one actor believes he is living his part and the other is simply humoring him. My sexuality, combined with my paranoia about discovery and then rejection, has caused me to isolate myself from my family and anybody else with whom I feel unable to be completely open.

Nowhere were the fundamental differences between others and me greater than at home.

Keith and I are the youngest of six children. All together we are three men and three women. A regular Brady Bunch without the maid. There is a seven-year gap between my youngest sister and Keith and me. (Keith and I were not a product of Planned Parenthood. Instead, I believe that we were the product of the Catholic Church, or worse yet, my parents' ignorance about and inability to discuss sexual issues such as birth control.) Because of this dramatic age difference (thirteen years in the case of my oldest sister) I was never very close with my older siblings. The most time we spent together was when one of them (always one of my sisters) was forced to stay home and baby-sit. When I entered junior high school, my youngest sister was the last to leave home and go to college. Although I was never very close to any of my siblings, whenever we are together we always seem to have fun. Of course, all conversation revolves around very impersonal subjects, except for the standard "Do-you-have-a-girlfriend?" question which I have learned to dodge with great creativity and eloquence. I lie.

I lie because my family is very different than I am. I don't know how to explain this difference, but it has always existed, and I think it always will. It has to do with our fundamental natures, and mine was and never will be like theirs. They are racist. I am not. They care only about themselves and their families. I tend to look at life on a broader scale. This "bigger picture" has caused me to isolate myself from my siblings because I feel that they are unworthy of my attention. I am not going to agree with their racial slurs and homophobic remarks, and until I feel that I can tell them about my sexuality, I am unable to defend myself in the face of such remarks. My brothers and sisters are fun people to whom I would like to be closer, but until I can be honest with them, I will continue to alienate myself from them.

My relationship with my parents is very similar to my relationship with my twin brother. I love my parents very much and I appreciate all that they have done for me. At the same time, I detest their very existence. They stand for everything that I oppose. My relationship with my parents can be divided into two periods: our relationship before I told them that I was gay, and my relationship with them since.

Before I went to college, things between my parents and me were stable and simple. I succeeded. They praised. I did not spend a lot of time with them. Sure, they were proud of me, but, upon reflection, I don't believe that they really know what I accomplished. They were always more concerned about whether or not I needed a car than what pieces the Wind Band, of which I was the president, was playing for the seasonal concert, which they only went to out of a sense of obligation. We never discussed my interest in girls. Granted, it would have been a very short discussion, but they never even showed any interest. My father never had "the talk" about sex with me. I doubt that he has even said the word "sex."

I am grateful that my parents have been such good providers. However, I resent them for filling me with prejudices and hate which I still have to work to combat even today. Blacks are no good. Jews are no good. Puerto Ricans are no good. The English are no good because of what's happening in Northern Ireland. (My mother is a full-blooded Irishwoman who blindly believes that only the English are to blame for all of the violence in Ireland. I've since learned that this is not necessarily true and that my mother knows very little about her "homeland.") Finally, homosexuals are no good. This is what they have taught me through their actions and words. They have taught me to hate myself. I have learned to love myself since I have left home for college.

My relationship with my parents has been more of a farce since I told them that I am gay. Imagine that: raised in a household where the word "sex" was not even uttered, and I've told them that I am gay. I admit that telling my parents when I did was a mistake *for me*, but it has also reinforced my belief that they are fundamentally ignorant people. (I have a perhaps unfair tendency to freely interchange the terms "ignorant" and "conservative.") That was a lonely summer. I had lost Tim in the spring. He was nearly the only person who knew about me. (He had introduced me to a few other gay men, and I had met a few others after we broke up.) Working, eating, and reading. That's how I spent my summer of 1988. I worked all day long at two jobs. I'd come home and make my dinner. I'd then retire to my room where I read books with homosexual themes, like Mary Renault's *The Persian Boy*, Christopher Bram's *Surprising Myself*, and AIDS nonfiction like *And the Band Played On*. I used to leave these books around the house, and although I doubt my parents knew the content of them, I guess I left them out subconsciously hoping that they would get the message I wanted to convey. At the time, I consciously thought nothing of leaving the books out; I didn't want to appear to be hiding anything.

Periodically, my parents would confront me about my self-isolation during that summer. My response was always, "Everything's fine. I'm just tired." Then it happened. I came home from work one night and I was confronted immediately by my father. He said, "We know something's bothering you, and we don't want you to tell us that there isn't. We can't help you unless you tell us what it is that's on your mind. We are your parents and you can tell us anything. What's the problem?"

"I don't have a problem," I answered in a very insincere tone, but I was feeling rather pressured. My dad was getting equally upset. It was more than obvious that I was keeping something from them and that I wanted to let them know, but from where would I muster the courage to do so? I could barely speak. My breathing seemed to stop. I had to consciously remind myself to inhale or else I would find myself passed out on the kitchen floor.

"I do want to talk to you and mom, but I would like to talk to you tomorrow." I needed time to plan what I was going to say, although I had done just that hundreds of times in my head already.

"No. I want you to talk to us now. We are your parents and we don't like seeing you like this."

I was nearly in tears. This was the big one, and I knew it. I had let the cat out of the bag (my parents hate cats), and it was only a matter of time before I would have to let them know. I suggested that we all sit down in the den. My dad turned off the television right away and sat down on the couch. My mom lit a cigarette and settled down in her recliner. I sat uneasily on a futon opposite my mom and next to my father. (I can't believe how all of the uneasiness is coming back to me as I sit here and recall what happened that evening in August. My hands are shaking as I type.) There was an incredible tension in the air, one which created the loudest silence I have ever had to break.

"I don't have a problem really. I just want to talk to you about me. First, I want to say that I love you very much and that what I'm going to tell you will not change that at all. I want things to be the same after as they were before."

"Of course. We love you and always will. You can tell us anything."

"It's hard for me to do this because I know you so well and because I treasure your love so much. I think that you both would agree that I am a good person who has never done anything to embarrass or shame you."

"No you haven't. What are you trying to say, Ben?"

"This isn't easy for me. I want you to understand that I need you and that I don't want this to change your love for me. I haven't always been completely honest with you. There's something about me which I have to deal with, and I want you to know about it too."

By this time tears were streaming down my face. My mother was sniffling as she puffed feverishly on her cigarette. My dad was noticeably shaken and struggling to maintain himself.

"I'm not everything that I appear to be. Er, rather, there's more to me than is apparent. I'm not . . . I'm not exactly what you think, and it bothers me that I haven't been completely honest with you. I'm the same person, but there's something you don't know about me. I'm . . . I'm not . . . I'm not exactly . . . This is very difficult for me to do because I don't want to hurt you, but I also don't want to be dishonest. I'm not . . . I'm not exactly straight."

My God, I said it. It took me a while, but I came out to my parents. The silence was even more deafening than before. This time my father broke it by questioning me.

"What do you mean you're not exactly straight?"

I couldn't believe it. There weren't going to make this easy at all.

"I mean I'm gay." I barely choked that out through my throat, which had contracted to inoperable dimensions, and the tears flooded my face.

"How long have you known this for?"

"For a long time. Since the beginning of high school."

"Why didn't you tell us before?"

"Because I was afraid of being rejected. I don't want to hurt you, but I don't want to lie."

"Why are you telling us now?"

They were making this tough! "I want you to know about me. I don't want to be dishonest with you. I want some support in dealing with this. I don't want it to be something I have to hide or that we can't talk about."

"You say you are homosexual," (Did I actually hear my father say the "H-word"?) "but what do you mean by that?"

"I find other men attractive."

"Sexually?" (Wow! He just said the "S-word," too!)

"Yes, sexually."

"Why didn't you tell us before? We could have helped you."

"I wasn't sure before. Now I am, and I want your support."

Then it happened. For the first time in my life, I saw my father cry. He couldn't keep it inside any longer. He broke down in tears, jumped to his feet and hurried to the bathroom right next to the den. My mother and I sat and listened to him for a few minutes before I said, "This is what I didn't want to do. I didn't want to hurt you."

She choked through her own tears. Shaking, she said, "We're glad that you told us. We only wish you had told us sooner."

My dad returned after blowing his nose. He had pulled himself back together, but was still quite shaken. The inquisition recommenced.

"Have you told your brothers and sisters about this?"

"No, I haven't."

"Do you plan on telling them."

"Yes, sometime."

"We don't think that's a good idea."

"Why not? I don't want to lie to them either."

"We don't think they will be very accepting of it."

"I'm not going to tell them right away."

"We hope that you don't ever tell them, but if you ever do, we'd like you to tell us that you are going to before you do."

"OK." I wasn't about to make things worse by starting an argument. I haven't even considered telling my siblings after this fiasco, so this promise has been very easy to keep. After I graduate, I wonder if it will be as simple. We talked for a long time about me and how I feel and what they can do. My dad felt guilty and wanted to know if he did anything to cause this. I told him of course not, and that is not why anybody is gay. He needed to know why, but I couldn't answer that question myself. After about an hour spent discussing everything from AIDS to the destruction of the American family, my dad was again in tears. My mom had really never stopped. Instead of rushing from the room, this time he stood up and pulled me up to him and hugged me tightly.

"You're my son. We're always going to love you. We could never reject you. We only want you to be happy." This was the first time my father had hugged me in many years. He has only done so on one other occasion since, that being upon my return from my term abroad. My mother stood and joined our hug. All of us were crying. My father ended it and said, "I'm going to bed now." I don't think that anybody slept for about a week after that night.

Things were more than a little bit tense around the house for the next few weeks before I returned to school. We talked about my sexuality once more before I went back to school. They suggested that I not return to school for the fall term, and that I see someone professional in order to try to change my sexual preference. What preference? I told them that psychiatrists can't change people that way, and that I was going to go back to school. I was seeing a counselor there, and I would tell her all about what they wanted.

The theme of this second conversation was "We're only happy if you are happy." I told them that I was happy and that I didn't know if I was going to ever change. They asked me to look into it by reading books and talking to a counselor. I said that I would, but I never did. I wouldn't know how to be anything else except gay. They told me that I had devastated them, but that they would never reject me as their son. They told me that they probably would never accept me as being gay, and that homosexual acts greatly repulsed them. I hate them for saying those things. The last thing I needed from them was guilt. I have to believe that they are not sincere in their claim of happiness in my own happiness, because they were making me very unhappy.

We have only discussed my sexuality on one other occasion during the next two years. It was in the car on the way up to school after my leave term abroad. They basically wanted a progress report on how my conversion to heterosexuality was going. I told them that there had been no progress, but that I had tried (another lie). They were terrified that their son was everything that the stereotypical "faggot" was. I did everything in my power to dispel these unfair and ignorant conceptions. I also told them that it wasn't something that anybody could change. That was the last time we have discussed my homosexuality.

If I had the opportunity again, I would never have told my parents about me. They have not been supportive at all of me and my inner conflict with my sexuality. In fact, it is an implicit understanding that unless I change, my sexuality will not be an acceptable topic of discussion. I am never to bring anybody home with me, as my brother would bring home a girlfriend. They have made it clear as well that unless I change, I will be unhappy and, therefore, they will be unhappy. What they don't understand is that when they ask me to be something which I cannot be, i.e., heterosexual, they cause me to be unhappy. I am happy being gay, and I could not be happy pretending to be straight. I refuse to live a life of self-sacrifice for the sake of my pseudo-happiness and their peace of mind.

My relationship with my parents since I came out to them has been a comedy at which I am not permitted to laugh. They worry about ostracizing me, and for this I am grateful. They do sincerely love me. What I don't like is the extreme overcompensation which occurs when I am around. When we dine out, they never bring up a controversial topic of discussion in fear that their flaming liberal, i.e., homosexual, son will embarrass them by dropping to his knees and performing fellatio on the cute waiter. Our conversations are very superficial, and tend to revolve around what I want to do after I graduate. I have cleverly come up with the interesting topic of law school in order to put their minds at ease. Basically, I am never told "no" anymore, which is nice, but not at all like the parents I had for the first eighteen years of my life.

One good thing has come from telling my parents about me, and from suffering the ensuing inquisition. It has forced me to examine myself and my sexual development in order to better understand why I am what I am today. I now understand why, when my father would take Keith and me to the racquetball club on Monday nights, I would be more interested in showering in the locker room and soaking in the whirlpool than I was in playing racquetball on the vacant courts. I also now understand why I could not help but have an erection when such showering and whirlpooling was accompanied, and please pardon the pun, by other club members. I understand now why I preferred to watch the men's gymnastics and swimming events in the Olympics instead of the women's basketball games.

The impetus for my first taste of sex was the men's gymnastics floor routine competition in the Olympics. (My first taste of sex was solo, so I should clarify myself by using the term "masturbation.") My parents, Keith, and I were watching the Olympics, which were on quite late as they were broadcasting live from Los Angeles. All three had fallen asleep, and I woke them to send them to bed. I, on the other hand, was not sleepy at all. I was glued to the set. In fact, I was mentally conjuring up some very interesting routines for two people. I decided to give one a try. I stripped down to my jockey shorts and watched the screen. Without making a lot of noise or breaking anything, I tried to imitate the more basic rolls and bends that were being performed 3000 miles away. I found myself with an erection. My tumbling was very pleasurable. Soon I discovered that my erection was leaking. As I had never masturbated before, and because of the intense pleasure caused by my movements, I mistook this pre-ejaculatory fluid for an orgasm. I hurriedly cleaned up, got dressed, and went to bed feeling less than completely satisfied.

It would be less than a week later, after several other similarly produced pseudo-orgasms, that I would experience my first true orgasm. It happened while I was asleep, but I still remember everything about my first and last wet dream. I was fantasizing about being at a swim team practice where none of the swimmers were wearing bathing suits. I remember the image of my being carried on the shoulders of one particular swimmer when I orgasmed.

The first sexual experience that I shared with somebody else occurred my freshman fall at school. It happened the night I described at the beginning when I met Tim for the first time in the library. I will never forget that night for as long as I live. I have to believe had Tim not had the courage to approach me that night that I might not be able to write this paper today. In fact, I might still be denying my homosexuality. I'd hate to know the miserable me if I weren't consciously gay.

As I have already said, Tim and I met at the library. We then went to talk in a classroom in the math building. We chatted for just a few minutes, deciding that it would be better to continue in the secured privacy of Tim's room, where we talked for about two and a half hours about each other and being gay at school. The room was quiet for no longer than five seconds when Tim rose from his desk chair and walked over to his bed where I was sitting. Then it happened. He sat down next to me on the bed and asked, "Would it be alright if I kiss you?"

What was I to say? I thought, "I've been waiting for you to do that for the last two hours." I said instead, "Yes."

It was my first kiss, and it was wonderful. The kiss was tender, yet passionate. It lasted only about two seconds, but it has set the standard for a lifetime. Our lips parted and our eyes met again. Tim asked, "Can I kiss you again?"

This time I didn't answer. Instead I brought my face close to his to be understood as an implicit yes. I was still more than a little bit nervous the second time, but I soon relaxed as that kiss developed into many more. It stirred in me what had been dormant forever before. One thing led to another and soon enough we were undressed and in bed together. That first time was very special for me. It helped dispel the ideas that even I held about homosexuality. Homosexuality was not dirty. Homosexuality was not perverse. Homosexuals do care for each other. Homosexuals can be happy. And I was happy.

That night began my longest and most important romantic relationship. I returned to my room in the wee hours of the morning and was categorically questioned by my roommates the next day. "I was studying very late, and I fell asleep in the study room." This lie was just the first of many. Lying was a fundamental part of my relationship with Tim. I did not lie to him, however. Instead, I felt forced to lie to everybody else with regard to my whereabouts and goings on. I have never been a very good liar, but I made it through my freshman year without any unwanted exposure. Such exposure was what I feared most. I was very happy with Tim as long as things were very secretive. My extreme paranoia about exposure forced me to hide my true self from my other friends. I do not blame myself for this paranoia. Instead, I blame the overwhelming ignorance of society, particularly that of the college community, with regards to gays and gay issues. This ignorance continues to instill fear in the hearts of most gays, including myself.

The beginning of my relationship with Tim seems like a fantastic blur right now. I can't even differentiate any particular evening from among the many nights we spent together in bed. I remember them all to be loving and passionate, but I also remember that I wanted more. I wanted to have more than a secret relationship which consisted of my sneaking across campus late at night to get into bed with my lover. I wanted us to be able to do things together, openly, without fear of accusation or embarrassment. I, however, was too paranoid to take that first step towards a more "normal" relationship. I was much too worried about what everybody might ask or think about me and Tim. He assured me, though, that my paranoia would disappear and we would do more together than just talk and have sex in his room.

Our first public appearance together, but alone, was playing racquetball at the gym. For a while we were playing quite frequently, at least three times a week. Other than his fraternity's parties, racquetball, and the very routine, but passionate sex, Tim and I occasionally shared a meal together. Again, I was always afraid that someone would figure it out if they saw us together a lot. He was not as paranoid, but he, too, was concerned about exposure. Though Tim was then a senior, he did not think, as I did, that sharing a meal or playing racquetball with a freshman (even a cute one) would cause suspicion by others that one was gay. But then we began to get bored with each other, and at least we were honest in acknowledging that it was happening. As I said, the sex was very routine, and Tim wanted more. He wanted to have intercourse, and I didn't.

It really hurt me when Tim went on a trip to a gay bar in Boston with a few friends and admitted to fooling around with one of them. He said all that they did was masturbate each other. "Oh, is that *all*?" I asked conveying the message that that was more than enough for me to be more than a little bit upset. This was the beginning of the end, I knew, and Tim must have known as well. I was still desperate to make it last though. I didn't want my love to die or to give up someone who had done so much for me. I tried to bring some more excitement to his bed, but it was very obvious that Tim wanted to have intercourse more than he wanted me.

And so our passionate love died before the end of April of my freshman year. We still share a common love for each other though. He is in California, and I am at school, but we still keep in touch. He knows that he will always be very special to me, and I like to think that I am still significant to him.

After Tim and I broke up, and, particularly after I returned home for the summer break, I was very lonely. I wasn't about to jump all the way into the back of the closet from which I had recently emerged. I wanted to take some steps forward in the right direction—in the only direction which would guarantee my mental health. I decided to speak to a counselor at school. I saw her several times before I went home for the summer. She listened to everything I had to say, and explained to me why, perhaps, I was feeling the way I was. She helped me a great deal, and for that I will always be grateful. I was feeling great when the spring term ended, and with it my visits for counseling.

During the summer, I told my parents that I was gay.

My visits for counseling promptly resumed upon my return to school. I needed someone to talk to and the counselors at school listened to me. My counselor not only listened to what I had to say, but she also reassured me that I was not alone even at school in my efforts to deal with being gay. She explained to me why I was feeling the way I was, and that these feelings were normal and healthy. She offered guidance, but she never told me what I should do. We talked about my parents and family, my relationship with Tim, and my being gay at school. I never left a counseling session feeling worse than I did when I arrived. In fact, I always felt very secure and confident that my being gay was not something wrong with me, but rather, it was a problem of acceptance on the part of others.

I found the cure for my loneliness in my new family: my friends. When I was "dating" Tim, I neglected my other friends quite a bit and did not foster much development of my relationships with them. Upon my return to campus after the "summer of my discontent," I promptly came out to Dan, who would later come to be my best friend. Dan and I got along great. We played racquetball together and had some classes together. We seemed to hit it off rather well when we first met. Dan is a very open-minded, liberal Californian. I thought that I could trust him with my secret, and I needed to share it with somebody.

I invited Dan to my room and asked him to sit down. He was more than a little bit confused. After about thirty minutes of professing my friendship and other beatings around the bush, I told him I was gay. He barely reacted at all. In fact, he made light of the tense situation by telling me that I was the third person to come out to him in the past two weeks. Apparently, he has a bisexual friend at home, and he used to live with a roommate who was gay. He also told me that there was a point in his life when he was questioning his own sexuality. Dan is not gay, however. I was not used to such a sublime reaction, but I most definitely preferred it to the more recent hysterics of home. Dan was very supportive of me and my struggle, even though he was going through a tough time of his own, as his parents were divorcing. I tried to be equally as supportive.

We grew together that term. We were almost inseparable. When we were with our other friends, we used to love to make comments which only he and I could truly understand. They were usually innocuous as far as the others were concerned, but sometimes Dan would try to put me on edge by seeing how far he could go before someone would ask, "What do you mean by that?" There was never any malicious intent — just good, sadistic fun between friends. I no longer have to hide the truth from my closest friends.

The following term, Dan and I went to Spain together on a study-abroad program. Again, we spent nearly all of our time together there. When we traveled we would usually have to share a bed because we chose to pay less for one bed than to pay more for a comfortable two. Having to share a bed with me never bothered Dan. This was a sign of great trust in me. Granted, I don't think he was worried about my making a pass at him, but his efforts to maintain a relationship where my sexuality was not the central issue was very important to me. I have nothing but fond memories of Dan and myself in Spain. We used to spend a lot of time just talking over a beer and a game of dominos in the town square. I have never been as close to anybody in my entire life as I have been with Dan. I shared my deepest secrets and innermost feelings with him. Likewise, he opened up to me quite a bit.

Dan and I decided to live together during the summer term between our sophomore and junior years at school. For the first seven weeks of the term our relationship continued to develop in the same positive way. After that things started to deteriorate. The reason for this is clear to me: Dan got a girlfriend. Stephanie lived down the hall from us. Dan, and I, met her at a party so wild he didn't even remember meeting her that night. Stephanie remembered Dan, though. She came by the next day and threw herself all over him. Before I knew what was happening, they were in bed together (a few days later), and I was now well in the back seat of Dan's life.

My analysis of myself with respect to this situation is twofold. First, I feel that I was very jealous of Stephanie. Secondly, I still feel that Stephanie is fundamentally not a good person. Was I jealous because I was being neglected, or was I jealous at a more fundamental sexual level? I have to admit that it would have pleased me greatly had Dan been gay as well. I think he has a lot of traits that I look for in someone with whom I would like to be involved romantically. However, I am being completely honest when I say that I really am not physically attracted to Dan. Therefore, I have concluded that my jealousy of Stephanie is due to Dan's behavior towards me, and not my sexuality.

Since they have been dating (sleeping together), I have seen Dan replace me with Stephanie. He no longer confides in me like he used to. Instead, he goes to Stephanie. He no longer has as much time for me as I am willing to give to him. These things are natural in relationships, but they hurt all the same. Since Dan gained a girlfriend, I feel I have suffered a tremendous loss. Perhaps my investment in Dan was too great, but I believe that it was reciprocal to Dan's own investment in my friendship. He, as far as I'm concerned, has chosen to invest elsewhere, leaving me feeling more than a little slighted.

I left school the next fall on pretty good terms with Dan. However, a new distance was created between us, this time geographical, when I went to work in the city for the winter months. Dan made little effort to keep in contact with me when I was in the city. I did call him occasionally, but I stopped when it started to feel like I was troubling him when I did call. My life in the city was dramatically different than it is at school, and I wanted to share it with Dan, but, apparently, he wasn't interested in hearing about it. Instead, I found others with whom to share my excitement. At the beginning of the fall term when I was at school, I came out to Jack and Paul. Jack is also from California, and even more open-minded than is Dan. He was very happy that I told him about my homosexuality and has shown a genuine interest in me and my coming to terms with it.

I was a little more concerned about telling Paul. I was worried that he might be intimidated by my homosexuality because I had suspected him not of being gay, but of being confused about his sexuality. I am now positive that he is not at all confused about his sexuality. He is perhaps one of the more "hormonal" straight men I know. I told Paul at the end of fall term after we had decided to share an apartment as we were going to be working at the same law firm in the city. I'll never forget what he said after I told him that I was gay. With a smile on his face and a slight laugh in his voice he said, "Hey, I've always thought that it's kind of hip to know someone who's gay." I almost cried. Paul is the funniest man I know. Living with him in the city, even in the close quarters of our studio apartment, was an experience which I would gladly share with him again. He will always be very special to me because he shared with me the very first period of my life in which I felt at liberty to do that which *I* wanted. With friends like these, who needs the support of an unaccepting biological family?

All of this coming out was in the context of my winter work-term in the city. I really miss the city; not only was it the arena for my coming out to three of my closest friends, but it is also where I first really lived. I secured a position at the law firm at which my sister works downtown where I worked hard and interacted well with everybody I met. My sexuality was not an issue, and I enjoyed what I was doing. If I had any concerns about my sexuality and my work at the firm, they revolved around the fear of my sister finding out about my post-work activities. I imagined a situation in which I would run into an openly gay attorney from the firm at a gay nightspot. He would talk about it at work, and through some indirect way my sister would become enlightened and freak out about it. She would call my parents, and they too would freak out. She would call my other two sisters and they, too, would freak out, until everybody in my family, nuclear and extended, all the way to Ireland and Lithuania, would be freaking out. As I am only concerned about keeping my parents ignorantly blissful, I blame them for my paranoia (and, perhaps, overactive imagination).

Of course, this did not happen, but I did meet one attorney at the firm while out for a drink in a gay video bar with two straight friends. Meeting him was special because I now had an ally in the very traditional and conservative law firm at which I worked. We would occasionally get together and have lunch. It was great to see that he was a gay man who was succeeding in the working world, the legal profession which I wanted to enter. However, it was equally as distressing to listen to him tell me how very closeted he was and how very discriminatory the legal profession is against gays, even though it has a very high percentage of homosexuals in its ranks. Apparently, image is of the essence in the legal profession, and openly gay attorneys do not help create an image of stability and competence which ultraconservative law firms demand.

My most important experiences in the city occurred outside of the workplace. Upon my arrival, I wanted to introduce myself to the gay community. I called the gay students group at several colleges, as well as the city's gay youth group. I went to one gay youth group meeting and found its membership a bit young for me, but I hit it off rather well with some members of another college group. By my second weekend in the city, my new friends in the student gay group took me out to the popular local nightspots. We first went to a downtown video bar. As we went in, I wasn't particularly impressed by the dark and smokey conditions of the noisy bar. My disappointment disappeared as we passed by the coat check and into the other half of the bar. Everybody in this section appeared to be college-aged and very attractive. My whole disposition changed. I was like a kid in a candy store. It had been many months since I had been in a gay establishment, and that was in Spain, which is a completely different world all together. The people with whom I came were talking to me, but I found it difficult to pay attention to anything except the dark-haired and dark-skinned gentleman standing very close to our circle of conversation. It would be a week later and in a different environment that I would meet Rob.

Rob and I were finally introduced at a gay students' meeting. I was very impressed with what he had to say at that meeting, particularly about the topic of that night's discussion: gay promiscuity. After the meeting he told me that he liked what I had to say also. We talked briefly about a dance that was to be held on Friday, and then we said goodbye. He called the next night about the dance and we decided to go together.

That was the introduction to a very important relationship for me; important because of what I learned about myself upon its dissolution. I really didn't love Rob. I even wonder if I really would find him interesting had we not gone to bed together so soon after meeting. I believe, upon reflection, that I was more interested in a relationship than I was in Rob. I lived a charade with him for over a month, therefore breaking my own rules about sexual activity. I have what some people might call an ultraliberal outlook on the topic of sex. I believe that there is nothing wrong with sleeping with anybody you want to sleep with so long as you meet a particular set of criteria. First, and most importantly, both must be consenting adults. Secondly, and following from my first criterion, one must never force another or be pressured by another to do anything in bed that one does not want to do. Maintaining this level of respect for one's partner is important if my third criterion is to be met. Nobody must be hurt, physically or mentally, by the experience. Lastly, and definitely not least of all, everything done must be done safely. It is obviously too dangerous in today's world plagued by AIDS and other diseases not to exercise the utmost caution as far as sexual contact is concerned. From experience, I would also say that sex where there is an emotional bond is incomparable to that without it, but I do not feel, as some do, that it is immoral to sleep with somebody just for fun, as long as nobody is getting hurt.

I was infatuated with Rob; he made me feel very special. It wasn't really until he came up to school with me for a weekend that I realized what the true story was. At school, I was in my element. He was out of his. I wanted so badly for him to fit in with my closest group of friends. He didn't. He didn't even try. I tried to include him in everything, but he just wouldn't get involved. I realized then that he did not meet the standards that I have for someone with whom I would like to spend, if not all, a good part of my life. When I first met him, I was impressed by what he had to say.

That was the last time he ever impressed me. He just isn't an intellectual equal of mine. He isn't even mildly interesting. Again, I found myself with cold feet, and over a very long two-week period, I broke up with Rob. He didn't understand, and for this reason I feel that I have violated the rules surrounding healthy sex; I hurt him. However, I feel that I did the right thing by breaking up with him in order to avoid hurting him more. He told me that he would have liked for me to just have gone back to school and not to have told him how I felt. But I believed that such perpetuated dishonesty would be an even greater infraction of my own rules of sexual conduct.

Upon breaking up with Rob, I started to do some serious thinking about myself and relationships. I had really never had a normal, successful relationship. I have come to the conclusion that there is nothing wrong with this, because it is not written in stone that relationships must work out. In fact, considering my relative inexperience in the relationship game, I would conclude that I have made some very responsible decisions which have helped greater harms from occurring. I think, though, that my standards are too high. I am never going to find someone with whom I am completely compatible. I have to learn to accept people's faults as much as I enjoy their good points, just as they must do the same for me. I'm not perfect, and I shouldn't expect anybody else to be.

My friends provide the criteria for a man to whom I would make an emotional commitment. First, but not foremost, he must be attractive. He must also be sincere and willing to share his deepest secrets with me. He must be funny. He must be intelligent and captivating. I see these traits in all of my close friends. Most importantly, he must be able to tolerate me and my quirks. Perhaps I should not be looking for a man with whom I can make an emotional commitment, but for a gay man with whom I can begin a sincere friendship. Only then, when I am his true friend, will I be able to be happy in a more intimate relationship with him. This may or may not be the answer to my romantic blues, but it makes a lot of sense to me. I still uphold my rules of sexual conduct, but I now would add another to the list. One should not become intimate with anybody one feels the potential for becoming very emotionally involved with, without first becoming their true friend.

I do have a couple of gay friends. One has graduated and the other is graduating. They, however, are not as close to me as any of my straight friends are. Why is this? The answer is twofold. First, I do not select my friends based on their sexuality. Second, befriending gays at school can be a difficult thing to do due to the lack of a visible gay community. The people who are openly gay do not seem to be the people whom I would normally befriend. Also, my fear of exposure keeps me from meeting potential gay friends. I would like to have some close gay friends, but I feel that it is more important to have true friends than it is to have gay acquaintances. I am also not willing to put my privacy at risk when I do not have the independence or support that I feel is needed to face opposition.

I have returned to school wiser but definitely more frustrated. There is a gay community, only a minute percentage of which is "out." There is a gay students group which holds weekly meetings. I went to one meeting during my sophomore fall, when I was still extremely paranoid about being exposed. I was desperate to find some people like me. I did not find them there. They were talking about marching on the Capitol in Washington. I was thinking about how exposed I was in the strange environment of the student lounge. To make matters worse, a random guy stumbled into the meeting unaware of what kind of meeting he was interrupting. He was picking up something he had left in the lounge earlier. I imagined that the first thing that the intruder did was go tell all of his friends (and mine) that he had seen *me* at a gay students' meeting. Now, more than a year and a half later, my views about this unpleasant experience have changed. I feel that it was one of the first steps I took toward trying to live my life as a gay man. True, it didn't work out, and I have not returned, but I feel that it was a step in the right direction. Indeed, it was a step in the only direction for me. I can't imagine what my life would be like now if I still hadn't confronted my homosexuality and begun to develop positively with it. This positive growth began long ago when I was just a freshman.

Where am I now? I'm very comfortable with being gay, but very uncomfortable with having to be gay at school. Why do I feel this way anywhere? I blame my parents. They will not let me be gay. They want me to be happy, but they don't want me to work for my happiness. I know that if I had the spiritual support (or even the complete assurance of financial support) of my parents, I would be, perhaps, one of the biggest gay activists on campus. Until my parents let me be what I am, I will never begin to realize what I really can do. If I had parental support in gay causes, I might feel very comfortable in the face of campus opposition. I might not fear exposure, knowing that I would always have their love and understanding. Instead, I am a member of my school's huge underground gay community. Here, my activism is limited to my close group of friends who do not need to hear my opinions about gays and gay issues. They are not the ones who need to be reached. The result is a community that refuses to come to terms with itself and its varied sexuality.

I am completing my junior year at school feeling like I am unable to make a difference in my life here or in the lives of other gays. My parents cannot possibly be so powerful! However, their financial grip remains on me. I don't want to hurt them either, but their happiness comes second to mine, as far as I am concerned. The opportunity to put my thoughts down on paper is my greatest step towards public advocacy. I feel that my experiences are similar to those of other gays, and by sharing them with them, and others who are straight, I feel that I am making an impact on others. However, I have not even been able to be honest with my parents about this autobiography project. As far as they are concerned, I am just helping a professor at school with some research.

What have I learned about myself? I have learned that I am a healthy gay man. I am happy with myself, although I could be happier in different circumstances. I feel that I am well on my way to living a productive life. I have learned that there are some things about myself which I must examine more closely if I am to live up to my own expectations. Primarily, I am concerned whether or not my dependence on my family is indeed more than financial. Do I really need their psychological support as well as their financial support? Is my love for them stronger than my resentment of their prejudices? Am I going to be the gay activist that I imagine myself being when I am finally free of my parents' grip? I will only know these answers upon graduating from college and dissolving my dependence on them. I suspect that the answers are complex. I suspect, too, that any other aspects of my dependence upon them will not be strong enough to keep me from living my life as I so choose.

Ritch C. Savin-Williams: Being Young, Gay, and Ben: Reflections on Case 8

In his opening narrative Ben reveals that his life has been similar to the lives of many other youths. For example, many of us, whether straight or gay, perhaps grimace or cast a knowing smile as we remember our Ben-like library experiences when we placed ourselves in a position to meet the romantic partner who would sweep us towards moments of ecstasy and stability. In this Ben is similar to millions of other youths across times, cultures, and species. Yet it has been a unique life in that a set of particular developmental dilemmas that Ben has encountered are faced solely by gay youth. Those differences are fundamental to understanding Ben; Ben did not choose them, has little control over them, and they permeate every aspect of his life. In Ben's words, with perhaps a mixture of pride and remorse: "I am gay, I have always been gay. I will most likely always be gay."

Ben's story does not — because it cannot — answer a fundamental question for developmental and clinical psychology regarding issues of sexual orientation: To what degree does sexual orientation by its very nature produce inherent effects in behavior, including social, cognitive, affective, and sensorimotor behavior? If the answer is "very little," then one assumes that differences found among those of various sexual orientations are essentially artifacts of societal or cultural influences affecting the ways in which individuals act, feel, and think. If the answer is "a lot," then biological or dynamic processes are likely causing linkages between sexual orientation and behavior. One of Ben's developmental struggles is to be like every other youth while not giving up being like no other youth. His "minority" sexual orientation, recently experienced on a conscious level as never before during his life, makes the uniqueness a relatively explicit developmental need. But Ben also longs for the "normalcy" of his peers and of fulfilling, despite his protests to the contrary, his parents' wishes. Complicating this dilemma is that Ben acknowledges not only how he fundamentally differs from his straight peers but also how he is at odds with other gay persons, at least as he conceives of other gays in a stereotypical fashion. I will illustrate these issues as well as others in the pages that follow.

There has been strikingly little research on homosexuality during adolescence. This is not because of the scarcity of homosexual behavior prior to adulthood but because as social scientists and clinicians we choose to ignore them, reflecting the wider blindness of our culture. Accounts are either retrospective (e.g., Bell, Weinberg, & Hammersmith, 1981) or limited by researching the fringes (e.g., hustlers, street kids) of gay youth (e.g., Roesler & Deisher, 1972; Remafedi, 1987a,b). Two recent large-scale studies, Herdt, Boxer, and Irvin's Chicago Youth Project and my own of upstate New York youth (Savin-Williams, 1990), are changing the portrait we have of gay youth.

But youths are also reticent to acknowledge homosexual behavior and a homosexual orientation. Only 1 out of 1,067 checked the "homosexual" box in a survey of adolescents (Coles & Stokes, 1985). More adolescents will "admit" to engaging in homosexual behavior, but their number is far fewer than estimates based on scientific sources would lead us to believe (see review in chapter 1 in Savin-Williams, 1990). An additional difficulty is the complexity of defining terms and persons. Not all homosexual adolescents engage in homosexual sexual activity; many heterosexual adolescents experience homosexual activity; and many homosexual adolescents engaged in no sexual behavior. The synchrony between sexual identity and sexual behavior is absent for many youths. The value of Ben's story is his honest, detailed examination of how his homosexuality has affected, is affecting, and will affect his life course. This is a rarity because few youths have come forward with such insight and courage.

Ben knew his sexual orientation before he had sex. In this he is not at odds with most youths, whether gay or straight. He knew what he wanted, and he wanted Tim that freshman night in the library. But Ben was not yet prepared for anyone else to know; he had just begun the process of being able to say this to himself. Ben, similar to most males (I will not speak here of females), did not choose his sexual orientation. He longs to find happiness within the confines of that destiny.

Ben wants respect and acceptance from his parents, peers, and society—not at any cost but on terms he deems acceptable: without sacrificing his basic sense of self. He loves his parents, desires their acceptance and support, and emulates their value system, such as holding honesty as a lofty but frequently transparent ideal. Similar to many youths, Ben feels that his parents do not express sufficient interest in the real issues of his life, that they are not what he wants them to be, and that they embarrass him. Communications with his father are strained; his father acts in a sexist fashion towards his mother; and, similar to many father-son dyads in American society, "the sex talk" never occurred. Ben rebels against his parents but recognizes that he needs them ("treasure your love") and does not want to hurt them. In growing up there was an intense sibling bonding and competitiveness between Ben and his twin brother Keith. Although Ben takes some pleasure in listing their opposites (e.g., Grateful Dead vs. Beethoven), the reader should be impressed by their early attachment; they are fraternal twins, unplanned by their parents, who are "best friends and worst enemies" with fond memories of being together.

Ben begins sexual activity somewhat later than most youths, perhaps because he is, in terms of puberty, a late maturer. His first sexual outlet, a wet dream, occurred at 15 or 16 years and his first sex with another person is as a freshman in college. The delay may also have been enhanced by family values and Ben's desire for peer acceptance; the only sex he was interested in was condemned and forbidden by those from whom he most wanted acceptance. The former, family values, would not be unusual for most youths, while the latter is a struggle faced by nearly all gay youths. By virtue of being a late maturer Ben is out of synch with his peers; his sexual orientation compounds this.

There are other ways in which Ben is similar to many other gay youths and not to straight peers: disliking team sports, feeling different and isolated from an early age, fearing emotional and financial rejection when coming out to his parents, feeling angry at his parents because he never felt free enough to express his true sexual identity, experiencing an inner conflict regarding the nature and social acceptance of his sexuality, being internally homophobic, having no positive gay role models while growing up, and having difficulty managing his career because his sexuality creates severe restrictions.[1] Most straight youths do not encounter these difficulties, whether because of societal heterosexual assumptions and the glorification of a "natural" heterosexual orientation or because of the very nature of heterosexuality. In either case the outcome is the same: the noted contrasts between gay and straight youths. To understand Ben, one must recognize the developmental influence of these experiences and considerations.

There are also developmental processes that Ben shares with few others, whether gay or straight. Some of these occur among some gay youths, but I believe it is best to view these as residing in the intersection of Ben's homosexuality and life circumstances. In many respects they, in addition to the contradictions that Ben presents in his story, are aspects of Ben's life that should generate discussion because of their potential developmental and clinical significance. There are many ways to be gay during childhood and adolescence. Ben does not present us with a "classical" case of adolescent gayness. He is athletic (soccer, swimming) and interested in sports. His first "pseudo-orgasm" occurs while watching the gymnastics in the 1984 Olympics; his first wet dream contains athletic imagery. Ben associates primarily with other males and needs to be accepted by them. Discrepant from stereotypes, Ben is not sexually promiscuous but is a virgin during junior and senior high school. Friends in college seem surprised that Ben is gay, perhaps because he does not act in a stereotypic (effeminate) way. Ben feels he has more in common with straight than gay friends.

Yet, Ben knows that he is feigning interest in heterosexuality (spin the bottle); he feels "abnormal." The homoerotic aspects of swimming threatened to reveal to Ben his homosexuality and so it was placed "on hold" until college. Some "pre-gay" youths assume this stance; others begin homosexual sexual activities prior to puberty and continue at a fast pace throughout adolescence. Their gay identity is firmly rooted—if not always desired— shortly after puberty when homophilia begins to make sexual sense. There is no one route to being gay.

With the first kiss from Tim, Ben's gay identity begins to escalate the internalization process. Their relationship must be secretive, not only to protect themselves from the homophobic world (e.g., Tim's fraternity[2]) around them but also from their own internalized self-derogation. Their relationship is based on lies and ultimately fails because they are unable to be authentic with each other. Ben cannot, although he wants to, perhaps because his own identity is so fragile. With their breakup Ben feels lonely and frightened, cut off from his family and without the security of the relationship. Ben must now face himself and his "disgusting" sexuality. But he is a survivor; Ben knows how to find support. He tells the safest of friends (Dan, Jack, Paul) that he is gay and they respond with support and humor. It is critical during this time that Ben be selective in who he tells and that he maintain control over the coming-out process. Ben learns how to build a relationship with a man (Dan) without the overt aspects of sexuality complicating the emotional, intimate bond. I will leave it up to the reader to decide whether the relationship was really asexual (emotionally and physically); perhaps the jealousy that Ben admits to when Stephanie enters Dan's life is a sexual one. In any case, the relationship with Dan raises questions for Ben and for the reader of what constitutes a homosexual relationship and attraction. If "sexual arousal" is not present, is the relationship not a sexual one? Were Dan and Ben "in love?" What is the distinction between a friendship and a romance?

Ben's gay identity is greatly strengthened when he is able to remove himself from the confines and inhibitions of college. In the city Ben discovers the freedom, perhaps in part because of the anonymity gained, to pursue his gay identity. He is exposed to the complexity and diversity of what it means to be gay and of the forms that homosexuality can assume, from promiscuity to monogamous relationships. Through his first "out" gay relationship (Rob), Ben comes to a better understanding of his sexual self; he is more interested in being in a relationship per se than with Rob as a person. Because he could not date those to whom he was sexually attracted in high school, Ben shares with many other young gays the difficulties of inexperience in matters of love and sex.

Another issue that concerns Ben is a critical one among many gays and, I assume, straights: the distinctions among sex, romance, and friendship. In a relationship Ben believes he wants someone who is "just like me" and who is "completely compatible" with him. Ben confuses friends with lovers. In friends we seek those who share our interests, attitudes, beliefs, and outlook; in lovers we seek those who fill our voids, satisfy our dissatisfactions, and complement our shortcomings. Ben wants a lover who is attractive, intelligent, funny, captivating, and sincere; these are characteristic of Ben and are thus characteristic of his best friends. Ben comes closer to the truth when he writes that he wants a lover who can "tolerate me and my quirks." Only in an idealized, mythic world do best friends become lovers.[3]

Ben's belief that it is "possible to have a healthy sexual encounter in which an emotional bond does not exist" is reconsidered when he wonders if by moving too quickly to sexual intimacy with men that a relationship is precluded. Although Ben finds this may be true for him, many gay men (and straight, I assume as well) who are in long-term relationships had sex on the first or second date. Ben does not appear to question our Judeo-Christian morality that portrays sex as the outcome of intimacy rather than as a means to that goal. Sexual encounters may be one of the best criteria for discovering if an intimate relationship can form. Early sex does not preclude romance. I am cautious in making any general assumption[4] regarding the way in which relationships form. It is probably a very individual matter.

There are several instances in Ben's story of apparent discrepancies, or at least statements that reflect disparities in thoughts and feelings. Ben speaks of inner conflict regarding his sexuality because while growing up he learned his parents' view towards homosexuality. Thus he came to self-hatred; however, Ben maintains that he is "happy being gay." In regard to his parents, Ben says he "detests their very existence. They stand for everything that I oppose." He blames them for teaching him to hate himself. Yet, the story returns time and again to Ben's desire for his parent's understanding and acceptance: "Until my parents let me be what I am, I will never begin to realize what I really can do." Ben believes, on one hand, that he should be autonomous from his parents. He is fundamentally different from his family; they are racist, homophobic, and narrow-minded. On the other hand, Ben realizes that he cannot separate from them. It is as if he cares *too much* what his parents feel about his homosexuality. The reader senses that Ben speaks for a significant part of his own self when he writes that his parents will not let him be gay. When he is with friends such as Paul, he does not need the "support of an unaccepting biological family." But this is more of a statement of desire than of fact: Ben does not want his self-worth and comfortableness being gay to depend on his parents—but they do.

Ben also notes that he was never close to his twin brother Keith; they are "opposites." Feelings are frequently shared but never talked about among siblings; twins may have a need to magnify their difference in order to individuate themselves. The reality may not be so much that Ben and Keith are opposites but that Ben feels so close to Keith that he needs to distinguish himself. At some level Ben may want to be like Keith or envies Keith because of his privileged heterosexuality. They are twins who were "accidents" in the life of their family and in some fundamental way their fates are intimately connected. They are so close that they are competitors, and Keith has the heterosexual advantage. Ben separates himself from Keith by using his ultimate trump card: he withholds the most important, intimate facet of his life, his sexuality. I believe that these dynamics are far more important than "respecting my parents' wish that I not tell my siblings about my homosexuality" in explaining Ben's resistance to being honest with Keith.

Ben's need or desire to "get back" at someone, to punish the person for pain inflicted, is evident in his story. He harshly assesses Rob after the relationship with him deteriorated. Ben asserts that honesty is a key moral value in his life; he is honest with the people who matter to him most. Thus, his most painful punishment is reserved for his parents: because of their silence in regard to his sexual identity he must be dishonest with them during this, the most exciting time of his life. The cost to Ben is particularly severe: loneliness and alienation. Although Ben says that his friends pick up the emotional slack, I am not convinced by the whole of Ben's story. This is not to deny that Ben's friends serve a crucial role in his life; they simply cannot fully compensate Ben's need for parental acceptance.

Perhaps the most moving is Ben's coming-out-to-parents story. It is both a typical and an ideal coming-out process that manages ultimately to fail both Ben and his parents. Ben warned his parents of his homosexuality by "subconsciously" leaving hints (gay books). His parents did not take the hint but they did display a very sensitive awareness when they asked Ben, "We know something's bothering you, and we don't want you to tell us that there isn't. We can't help you unless you tell us what it is that's on your mind." Ben at first denies and then dramatically tells them. Through tears and hugs, reassurances of love and support, and honesty the family appears to be strengthened by the event. Ben says he was "afraid of being rejected" and his father wanted to know if there was "anything I did to cause this." Ben sees his father cry and receives a rare hug. The father says, "You're my son. We're always going to love you. We could never reject you. We only want you to be happy."

From this ideal beginning the love, support, and openness falter and Ben becomes profoundly alienated from the family. It is unclear what happened. Perhaps things were said that should not have been said ("They told me that they probably would never accept me as being gay"), and Ben began lying to them. Both Ben and his parents were far more comfortable not talking about his homosexuality; it was easier to ignore than to understand, to be silent than to discuss.

There are few "perfect times" to come out to one's parents. Ben says if he had to do it again he "would never have told my parents about me." Perhaps far more important than the initial telling is the continued need to come out to one's parents. After the initial shock, time is needed to absorb, understand, and acknowledge present and future implications. Ben attempts to make the best of this reality; it forces him to undertake self-examination and to turn to friends for support. Ben's story illustrates the consequences of an ideal beginning but a disastrous follow-up in the coming out process. Ben went to individual counseling; as appropriate as this was, I believe the family as a unit could have prospered if they had entered family therapy at this time.

Ben's prognosis would appear to be a healthy one. He can find resources, such as counselors, books, friends, and gay lifestyles, to help him in his coming out and identity processes. Ben does not yet have an entirely positive gay identity — he fears exposure by being around gay friends — but he is moving in a healthy direction. His humor and his insightfulness are strong characteristics that are in his favor. Ben understands the critical role that his parents have in his sexual identity process and that he is emotionally dependent on them. He blames his parents but wants their support; he needs to individuate from their grip without losing his connection to them. Ben understands that "homosexuality is not the cause of my happiness. My acceptance of it is." You may well ask, has Ben accepted it yet? If not, how much further does he need to go? How does he go about it? Can he accept himself without feeling that his family accepts him? Ben may already know the answers to these questions as we read his story.

Notes

1. These and other commonalities among gay youth are reviewed elsewhere in Savin Williams, 1990.

2. My experience has been that collegiate fraternities contain an unusually large number of homosexually inclined men, but such men are extremely closeted and homophobic — both in regard to themselves and as expressed toward others. They are attracted to fraternities as a "cover" and for the opportunities of male bonding.

3. I recognize exceptions, but I believe these are to be rare among persons of all sexual orientations.

4. One example is Ben's notion that friendship must precede romance: "One should not become sexually intimate with anybody one feels that it might be possible to become very emotionally involved with without first becoming their true friend."

PART TWO

Relationships

Theoretical Overview

This section of the book focuses on relationships, specifically family and peer relationships. Psychoanalytic and neopsychoanalytic theories have yielded the most prominent and influential explanations of the processes by which adolescents' relationships with their parents and peers change from childhood to adulthood. Anna Freud and Peter Blos's explication of the process of adolescents' individuation from their parents is well-known (Blos, 1962; Freud, 1946, 1958), as is Harry Stack Sullivan's writing about the development of intimacy through best friend relationships (Sullivan, 1953). Contemporary research has often contradicted these theories, however, or highlighted aspects of adolescent relationships that were not the focus of the psychoanalytic perspective. This introduction touches on some of the most important issues in the study of adolescent relationships that are raised by these theories and research studies and mentions some ways in which the cases in this portion of the book may be used to foster discussions of these issues.

Family Relationships

The psychoanalytic understanding of adolescent-family relationships has traditionally viewed adolescence as a time of profound inner turmoil and outward conflict—a time of "storm and stress." Explosive conflict with family, friends, and authorities was thought of as commonplace. This view was based, to a great extent, on the theoretical work of the psychiatric community in the 1950s and early 1960s (Blos, 1962; Erikson, 1959, 1966, 1968; A. Freud, 1946, 1958). Largely on the basis of their experience with adolescent psychiatric patients, these clinicians and theorists described adolescence as a time that required extreme psychic and interpersonal stress. Emotional crisis and upheaval were viewed as appropriate responses by the adolescent to major psychological and societal tasks required during this phase of life: to dramatically reduce psychological dependency on parents, separate from the family, and form an adult identity. Adolescent turmoil was not only inevitable but necessary for subsequent normal personality integration.

This storm-and-stress perspective of adolescent family relationships is currently perpetuated by the media and widely assumed by the public. However, scholars of adolescent psychology are in the midst of developing a new way of understanding adolescent-family relationships. This new approach to describing and explaining family relationships in adolescence differs from the classic long-reigning psychoanalytic perspective in several ways.

One way the new perspective differs is its contention that adolescents and their families are more likely to negotiate changes in power, responsibilities, and modes of intimacy through a continuous series of minor, although significant, daily "hassles," rather than through tumultuous, warlike conflicts. Data from empirical studies with nonclinical populations of adolescents and their families from the past twenty-five years have led to a radical revision in the psychological community's understanding of how adolescents separate from and remain connected to their families. The majority of research clearly refutes the notion that most adolescents undergo severe emotional stress and family conflict during this period of life. Although experts concur that adolescence is a period of development that requires multiple changes, the current consensus is that adolescence is not ordinarily a time of great turmoil. Various studies using such diverse methods as epidemiological surveys (Rutter, Graham, Chadwick, & Yule, 1976), phone interviews (Montemayor, 1983), and time sampling with electronic beepers (Csikszentmihalyi & Larson, 1984) have shown that for most families with adolescent members, serious conflict and disorganization are not characteristic states (Hill, 1987). Evidence drawn from various kinds of self-reports offered by nonpatient adolescents and their parents provides no support for a picture of dramatic increase in family conflict from childhood to adolescence. In general, the family is not "at risk" for turmoil or disorganization during the adolescent years. The search for greater independence from the family is not usually played out in major battles between adolescent and the parents; instead, current studies look for smaller although still highly significant and lasting transformations in sharing of power and responsibility and the nature of intimacy in the family through daily renegotiations.

This new view does not state that adolescence is a time of no conflict. It would be a mistake to conclude that conflicts between adolescents and their parents or siblings are insignificant or rare and that their presence indicates family or individual psychopathology. All valued human relationships undergo stress at times, particularly times when the relationship must adapt to change within an individual. Adolescents have certainly been shown to value their relationships with their parents, and these relationships do change and adapt as the adolescent becomes an adult member of the family. Although there may not be striking quantitative rises in the intensity of family conflict, the *number* of conflicts does rise to some degree in early adolescence and decrease when adolescents leave home. Conflicts are usually of mild to moderate intensity and are rarely about such dramatic issues as drugs or delinquency (Santrock, 1990; Montemayor & Hanson, 1985). In fact, the vast majority of conflicts in adolescence arise over mundane issues, such as the family chores, curfews, eating practices, dating, and personal appearance.

The case of Betsy (Case No. 9, Becoming Comfortable with Who I Am) illustrates psychologists' changing ideas regarding the "normality" of conflict between adolescents and their families. This case represents the "minor hassles" picture of adolescent family life that psychologists are turning up more and more. The case describes family relationships in ways that significantly deviate from the storm-and-stress model in which developmental advances are the cause of dramatic family conflicts. In the storm-and-stress model a temporary plateau of new independence is reached only after parental capitulation to the adolescent's demands for new levels of autonomy or parental rejection of the "grown up" teenager. Instead, Betsy's family seems to represent a not uncommon adolescent-parent relationship that is characterized by ongoing daily mundane conflicts and compromises that are made possible by Betsy's confidence in the degree of mutual trust and respect in her family, good communication, and a strong desire to maintain parental approval and harmony. This adolescent-parent style is exemplified in Betsy's statement that "in some ways my parents are probably the most protective parents I know, but at the same time they trusted me to do things my friends could never do. . . . I couldn't ride in a car with my friends until they had their licenses for two months, but once I started driving I was allowed to drive into the city sooner than my friends." Her understanding that her parents "trusted me but were worried about the rest of the world" and "their limits were set to protect me, even if I didn't feel like I needed protecting. I trusted them to be fair, and they usually were" is what seems to make this less dramatic style of adolescent conflict resolution possible.

Betsy's case may be used to clarify ideas concerning what an optimal or ideal family for promoting adolescent development would be like. In what ways do Betsy's family relationships foster adolescent independence, achievement, or intimacy goals? What are the problems that might be associated with this low-conflict pattern of family interaction? For example, Betsy raises the question, herself, of whether she is too much of a "goody-goody" for her own development. By her own account, she senses that her strong conformity to adult expectations has been something of a constraint on her peer development. "I would like to say that [a peer friendship experience] helped me relax with respect to following rules. But it didn't. . . . Even after I graduated from high school I was still conscientious to a fault." Perhaps when parents are as reasonable and fair-minded as hers, and a family is so close-knit, it makes it difficult to justify rebelling against such seemingly sound authorities. Cases in other sections of the book may also be useful to study as exemplars of nontumultuous adolescent-parent relationships (see Cases Nos. 5 and 14).

A second important difference in this new approach is that it seeks to encompass the description of a *wide variety of patterns* of family relationships, rather than focusing on explaining one primary picture of how a "normal" adolescent interacts with his or her family. Instead, a wide range of adolescent family behaviors is considered relevant to understanding adolescent adaptive responses to growth in relationships. This new perspective seeks to include more diversity in the adolescents and families encompassed. For example, not enough is known about varieties of adaptive family functioning in African-American, Latino, Native American, Asian-American and other groups of adolescents in our culture. It may be helpful to contrast the family pictures described by adolescents from different ethnic backgrounds (see Chart #1) and by other students in your class. Scholars of adolescent psychology also have an extremely limited understanding at present about adolescents' relationships with their single parents, stepparents, and noncustodial parents.

Identifying different pathways to adolescents' new levels of separation and connection with parents is possible through juxtaposing cases in this section. The family experiences of Betsy can be contrasted with Emily's (Case No. 10, Guilt Was Everywhere Around Me) family experiences of major conflict and turmoil, an exemplar of the less common storm and stress model of adolescent individuation from the family. You might ask yourself which aspects of the tumult in Emily's family are triggered by *adolescent* issues and which are products of a long-standing family system. Her case provides a powerful description of a family under severe stress and one adolescent's extreme strategies for coping with that stress. Clearly, some of these strategies strengthen her resilience (e.g., her perfectionism reinforces her ability to succeed at many demanding tasks, including school), while other strategies, such as bulimia, eventually cause more pain than relief. Emily's case is one reminder of the variety of patterns that lead eventually to successful young adult adaptation and functioning. Cases in other sections of the book may also serve as examples of nontypical family situations leading to more severe stress in adolescence (see, for example, Case No. 4, Someday My Elders Will Be Proud).

A third distinguishing aspect of psychologists' contemporary approach to describing adolescent family relationships emphasizes adolescents' needs for maintaining intimacy and connection with parents and siblings, as well as adolescents' wishes for increased autonomy and independence. The process of separation from the family was the primary focus of earlier psychoanalytic theories. Little is known at present about how adolescents establish new ways of being meaningfully attached and intimate with family members while at the same time negotiating greater independence from the family (Gilligan, 1987).

Results from studies that have observed adolescents' interactions with their parents have indicated the importance of family interaction styles that permit conflict between members in a context of support (Baumrind, 1987, in press; Powers, 1988; Powers, Hauser, Schwartz, Noam, & Jacobson, 1983), acceptance, active understanding from parents (Hauser, Powers, Noam, Jacobson, Weiss, & Follansbee, 1984; Hauser, Houlihan, Powers, Jacobson, Noam, Weiss-Perry, & Follansbee, 1987), and parental expressions of individuality and connectedness (Grotevant & Cooper, 1986).

The first two cases in this section are strong illustrations of the heartfelt need of adolescents to be affectively connected to their families. Emily's case presents particularly significant difficulties in negotiating a sufficient level of closeness and intimacy with her parents. Her story might usefully be contrasted with Betsy's more nonchalant assumptions of parental closeness. The case of Emily may also raise questions for you regarding whether it is more difficult to separate from one's family when a close relationship with a parent is presented with strings attached. Under these conditions an adolescent's attempts to separate from a parent may be seen by the adolescent, as well as the parent, as threatening to the desired family closeness.

Peer Relationships

Peer relationships may include close friendships, cliques, peer groups and crowds, and romantic relationships. There are many cases throughout the book that discuss peer relationships, and the reader is encouraged to look in the theme index (Chart #1) for cases that can be found in other sections but include material on peer relationships. Case No. 4, Someday My Elders Will Be Proud, for example, describes the power of peer pressure when an adolescent's ethnicity and ethnic culture is different from that of the dominant culture. The sections on sexual identity and gender identity are particularly useful for examining romantic relationships.

Close friendships in adolescence may have many facets and functions, such as providing companionship, stimulation, social comparison, and intimacy or affection (Gottman and Parker, 1987; Parker and Gottman, 1989). Ann's (Case No. 11, No "Boring Little Friends") and Rebecca's (Case No. 12, Loving Women) cases present these varied aspects of adolescent close friendship and their developmental transitions throughout early to late adolescence. For example, Rebecca's description of sexual play with her close grade-school friend in private and at slumber parties and the confusion that surrounds it illustrates friendship as an introduction to the sexual aspects of growing up. Rebecca and her friend Kelly show us one example of an early adolescent friendship, whereas Rebecca's friendship with Alexandra occurs in college and is an example of the meaning of friendship at a later developmental stage. Selman's (1980) theory of the stages of growth in friendships may be helpful in contrasting the meaning of friendship to these adolescents at different stages of development. Betsy's case also provides a window through which you may view the importance of close friendships, cliques, and romantic relationships in high school.

Peer cliques and groups may also have a variety of functions in adolescent growth and development. Peers provide a means of social comparison, as well as a source of information outside the family. Both of these functions can be seen clearly in the cases of Betsy, Ann, and Rebecca. The role of popularity, fitting in with desired cliques, or being rejected or neglected by peers is acutely felt by all adolescents included within this section on relationships. Rebecca's and Ann's cases provide particularly good examples of conformity to peers peaking around eighth and ninth grades and then lessening by grade twelve (Berndt & Ladd, 1989).

Current theory and research emphasize the connectedness between the quality of family relationships and the quality of close peer relationships (Parke, 1989; Gold & Yanof, 1985). The cases of Rebecca and Betsy provide the best material for a discussion of the impact of family relationships on the development of peer relationships. Rebecca speaks eloquently about the strain between her father's academic goals and her own and her peers' goals for popularity and the influence of her parents on the development of her sexual identity. Betsy searches for her friendships to stretch her growth in ways that her comfortable family relationships do not.

Another focus for analysis might be the use of Sullivan (1953) and Erikson's (1959, 1966, 1968) theories of intimacy for understanding these cases. For example, how does Rebecca's (Case No. 12, Loving Women) friendship with Kelly exemplify Sullivan's notion of same-sex "chumship"? How does friendship or romantic intimacy contribute to the development of identity? (See Case No. 5, Distilling My Korean-American Identity, for an example of a male's experiences relating to this issue.) Does the research on gender differences in the development of intimacy (Berndt, 1981, 1982; Blyth, Hill, & Thiel, 1982; Buhrmester & Furman, 1987; Burleson, 1982; Coleman, 1987; Diaz & Berndt, 1982; Sharabany, Gershoni, & Hofman, 1981; Youniss & Smollar, 1985; Zeldin, Small & Savin-Williams, 1982) seem to hold in these cases? What are the aspects of a romantic relationship that are valued by the adolescents in this book, and how do these values change as these adolescents mature? In this section, Rebecca may be used as one example of romantic values at the college age, whereas Emily, Ann, and Betsy each provide examples of romantic values during high school.

CASE 9

Becoming Comfortable with Who I Am

This author presents the reader with a study of adolescence as it occurs within a happy, supportive network of family, friends, and mentors. Betsy describes her involvement in school drama as a place where she finds adult and same-age peers and a sense of self. She rarely questions her positive relationship with her parents, but her confidence in who they are and how they see her is temporarily shaken when they prevent her from traveling with friends on a carefully planned trip. She also describes her relationships with adult and same-sex friends, and reflects on how these help her find or recognize another piece of herself. While her story does not fit the "storm-and-stress" model of adolescent development, it does illustrate some of the normal stressors of adolescence that are the result of developmental growth.

When I was 16, I got to sing my first solo in the school's spring musical. I also got to do my first stage kiss, which also happened to be my first real-life kiss. It took me much longer than my girl friends to be interested in boys. In ninth grade I went to lunch with my gym class. My friend Sarah, who was in the same class, loved it. We ate surrounded by the football players, and Sarah flirted with a new one everyday. I did my algebra homework with one hand and ate my sandwich with the other. Once in a while, one of the guys would try to get me to talk to him. But I was sure that he was only making fun of me, and he almost always smelled sweaty and stale. I would answer with a shrug and a smart comment, and he would turn back to Sarah.

In ninth grade this didn't bother me. I got my homework finished during school, and this left the whole afternoon and evening to read books and write letters to my friends in Morocco. During my eighth-grade year, my family had lived in Morocco because my father, who was a history professor, was doing research there. My younger sister and I had gone to a private English school. I loved it. I hated weekends because I wanted to get back to my friends and teachers. I loved the British ritual that was a part of the school day. We started in a big hall lined up by forms. The head master came in and said "Good morning children," and we answered, "Good morning Mr. Simmson." We stood in line outside the classrooms before the teachers came, and then they led us in. Everything was so formal and neat. The British accents were so much cleaner than the Southern drawl that I had grown up hearing. I tried to copy one, and wished with all my heart that my parents had been British.

I hated leaving at the end of the year. But I slowly began to see the merits of an American public high school, and I started to make new friends. In my tenth grade year I auditioned for the school musical. I had loved musicals ever since I saw *Brigadoon* when I was 10. Auditioning terrified me, but to my amazement and delight, I got a part in the chorus. Now I had something new to throw my enthusiasm into. I got to every rehearsal early, volunteered for every set day, and learned the whole musical by heart in the first few weeks.

By eleventh grade, I started to feel like a real part of the drama crowd. Getting to do a solo and a stage kiss made me one of the important upperclassmen. Doing the kiss on stage embarrassed me a little and pleased me a lot, but I was still not overly interested in boys. My obsession with British schools was gone, but now every spare moment of my time was spent at rehearsal, or shopping for costumes with our drama teacher, or planning activities for the drama club. I simply did not have time to devote to talking about, dressing for, and impressing the guys.

In my senior year that changed. Partly because of pressure from my friends, and partly because I really did like him, I developed a crush on Kevin, the same boy I had kissed the year before in the musical. I was excited when he offered to drive me home from the drama club Christmas party. It was my very first date, and we went to McDonald's for cokes and then drove around town for a while. Unfortunately I spent the whole drive wondering if I was supposed to kiss him when he dropped me off. I wanted to, but I didn't know if he wanted to, and I didn't want him to know that I wanted to if he didn't want to. Being busy wondering about all this, I didn't keep up my end of the conversation very well, and soon we were back at my house. When he stopped the car, I panicked. If he did want to kiss me, I wasn't sure I knew what to do, in spite of my practice in the musical. Rather than let him know that, I decided to get out of the car fast. As soon as I got inside, I was positive that I had done the wrong thing. I should have stayed and talked to him for a while, and then seen what happened. The next day at school I was afraid to look at him and his friends because I was sure that he had told them all that I was a goody-goody and a prude. I knew that I was the laughing stock of the twelfth grade.

It turned out that he wasn't laughing, and a week later he came over to study chemistry. This time things worked out better. I was $17^1/_2$, and it was the first time that I had ever kissed a boy, except on stage, which didn't count. We went out a few more times, and then the romantic part of our relationship petered out without either of us really ever saying anything about it.

I didn't really date anybody else in high school. I did get more practice kissing, though. I got the "kissing roles" in the two plays we did in my senior year, and at our drama cast parties we played spin-the-bottle and truth-or-dare. I had fun, but much to my disgust, I was never more than friends with the guys in our group. I compared notes with my girl friends about the various merits of different boys, but the few times that I knew there was a mutual interest on his part, I was too shy to let him know, and nothing came out of the relationships except for conversations in the hall at school.

I'm not really sure why I was so late to discover boys. Maybe part of it was that it took me so long to adjust from coming back from Morocco. I had had very different experiences from the other students, and because I didn't know how to fit in, I stayed on the fringes of the crowd in my ninth- and tenth-grade years. I was convinced that my high school was not as good as the English school, and I was happier dreaming about what I didn't have than dealing with what I did. In my junior year when I did begin to fit in, I hadn't had the practice liking boys that all my friends had. Even though I wanted a boyfriend by then, I didn't really know how to go about getting one. Another part of it was that I had several time-consuming hobbies and interests that occupied me after school. In the first part of high school these included writing to friends in Morocco, taking piano lessons, playing tennis, and reading. Later I got involved with school-related activities like drama and yearbook. I didn't have time to go home after school and watch soap operas and TV sit-comedies or read *Seventeen* magazine like my friends did. Without some of these powerful reminders of how males and females are supposed to react to each other, I was happy to go about my life relatively unaware of and uninterested in boys long after my friends were involved with boyfriends.

I have always been concerned about approval. In ninth grade I received three compliments about my looks within several weeks of each other, and I replayed them often in my mind. The first was from the mother of one of my sister's friends. I overheard her telling my Mother that I got prettier each time she saw me. After that, whenever she came to our house to drop off her daughter or pick up my sister, I made sure that I looked nice, and then hung around in hopes of impressing her again.

A little later my neighbor told me that I looked like a young Ingrid Bergman. I watched all the Ingrid Bergman movies I could get ahold of and looked for comparisons between us. I tried fixing my hair in Ingrid-like styles, and waited to see if anyone else would notice the similarity. No one did.

The third compliment that I remember vividly from this time was from an artist mother of one of my friends who said that she would like to paint me. For a while I hoped when I saw her that she would follow through and ask me to sit for her. Then I saw some of her other portraits and was not impressed by their beauty.

Almost all the compliments that I can remember from the early part of high school were from adults. My friends would comment on a pretty article of clothing or say that my hair looked nice on a particular day, but that was the duty of friends. My curly hair wouldn't fit into the feathered style that all the girls wore, and I didn't like wearing makeup. (This was still my British boarding school stage, and the English girls weren't allowed to paint their faces.) I didn't want to look like everyone else, but I didn't feel attractive around people my own age. Adults approved of me. I was quiet and polite, I made good grades in school, and I didn't adopt the current teenage fads like listening to rock music or talking on the telephone for hours on end. I sought approval from adults as a substitute for popularity among my peers.

I was always conscious of how other people saw my reactions. It was as though there were two of me. One part was living my life—feeling happy and sad, excited and disappointed. The other part was outside of me watching and noting my effect on others. The outside part enjoyed getting sympathy, attention, and praise. It could romanticize even the worst situations. It put me in the place of the injured heroine from the movies. It was the part of me that imagined what people would say about me if I were to die, and wished to be involved in tragedies for the effect of it. The inside of me did the feelings. It was what made me grieve when my Grandmother died, squirm with pleasure at getting a part in a play, and react naturally to daily ups and downs.

I don't think that in high school I could have put into words how these two different aspects of my personality reacted with each other. I sometimes worried that my thoughts didn't seem nice or proper. It seemed morbid to like the attention I got when something bad happened to me. But it wasn't that I wanted tragedy. I was generally a happy person, and I think that a part of me couldn't accept that things could get so bad that there was nothing left to enjoy. I felt a lot of things very deeply, and romanticizing what was happening to me was a way to lighten up sad thoughts.

My high school drama teacher, Susan, and her husband, Ron, didn't have any children of their own, but they have spent their lives "adopting" other people's children. I had the good fortune to be one of those children.

Susan reveled in surprises and doing special things for other people. During the musicals she would ask a couple of us to go along with her to shop for costumes. I loved these afternoons. Susan would come and pick us up in her huge old blue Cadillac. It was no longer a fancy car, but the seats were smooth and comfortable, and two people could sit up in front with Susan. There were stores near home that we could have looked in, but Susan liked to go farther afield to check out the discount outlets and used-clothing stores. The stores were cluttered and had the musty smell of an old attic. Sometimes there would be bins of old shoes or boxes of scarves for fifty cents. Some days things were sorted by style, some days by color or size, and some days there was no apparent logical order at all. We mixed and matched skirts, blouses, and jackets to create period pieces and tried on dozens of hats to find the one that would look just right. I liked Susan's approval when I came up with a good idea and the attention that was paid especially to me when looking for my costumes. When we finished with our shopping, our bags would be deposited in the trunk of the car, and Susan would almost always say, "There's a wonderful little restaurant around the corner. How would you like to try it out?" We went to The Grill, a hamburger place that still served malted milkshakes from the frosty metal cup that they were mixed in. Another time it was The Dessert Place, which served nothing but desserts. We all agreed that the cream cheese brownie with ice cream, hot fudge sauce, and whipped cream was the best. It didn't really matter where we went. There was a cozy, relaxed feeling of belonging. Susan and Ron spent hours of their free time with us. They took us to weekend-long drama conferences, and invited us all to parties at their house. Susan coached a group of us for the literary meet in my senior year and took us to the competition. Ron came to help when we built the sets for plays, and we all learned how to use a power saw and a ratchet properly.

The day before I graduated, Susan stopped by my house in the morning before school and left an envelope. Inside was a silver bookmark and a letter to me. Susan had been given the bookmark by her favorite teacher when she graduated from high school, and now she was giving it to me. The letter told about Susan's high school experience, and about her teacher who had done for Susan what Susan had done for me. Like me, Susan had been a shy, quiet student, and her teacher had encouraged her and helped her get involved and have confidence in herself. I felt very lucky and touched that Susan had decided to give the bookmark to me, and I vowed to keep it to pass down to someone special in my future.

Having older friends who weren't relatives was important to me. No matter how much I loved and confided in my parents, it was good to be listened to by someone else. They sympathized when I got into arguments at home, but they also had more perspective on how my parents felt than my loyal same-age friends. They would be supportive of me, but also helped me to see my parents' side of things. I could take suggestions from them without the resentment that I would have shown my parents.

One of my other teachers became another close adult friend. She was an interesting, extremely shy woman who had a hard time making conversation on the superficial chatty level. But she liked hearing what students were thinking. Her solution was to require a weekly writing assignment of one page on any topic that a student chose. In addition to being good writing practice, it allowed her to get to know students without the awkwardness of conversations. This is how I got to be friends with her. I was frustrated with being one of the few liberal democrats in my classes. It was important to me to have people know my political and ethical views, but I was tired of always having to defend and stand up for what I believed in when I was in the minority. There were several guys in my classes who liked to start political discussions, and when I joined in, they would all jump on me with loud, defensive arguments. Several times I came close to tears of frustration with these fruitless conversations.

After one such discussion, I wrote a passionate paper saying that I would never speak up again, because there wasn't any point in it. My teacher returned my paper with a page full of comments. She had had the same kind of experience, she said, and she knew how I felt. She went on to talk about the difference between discussions where people tried to understand others' view points and ones where the purpose was to congratulate oneself on one's own good judgment. I learned a lot from her about my own reasons for joining these arguments. I also started to realize that I wasn't going to change the views of my classmates on most issues, and that while a one-on-one discussion was often interesting and beneficial to both people, it wasn't worth it to rise to the bait of three or four people who were eager to squelch opposing views.

Whenever I most needed someone to reinforce my ideas, I would write to her, and the next day I would get an answer that agreed or at least sympathized with me. It was like having my own personal "Dear Abby." I continued to write to her when I was no longer in her class, and we became good friends. There were other things we shared besides political views. Taste in books was one, and she would bring in books for me to read, and I would lend her my favorites. Since we met by writing, it seemed most natural to keep writing, and although we always greeted each other warmly when we passed in the hall, most of our conversations were in written form.

Getting involved in drama was the beginning of the end of my shyness and lack of involvement in school and friends. Susan, my drama teacher, played a major role in this change, and the other drama students did the rest. In particular was my friend Angela. Before I auditioned for my first play, I knew Angela only as a gregarious, friendly person who was president of our class. She was always in the front row of pep rallies full of school pride and class spirit. I sat in the middle of the crowd hating the noise and thinking that the whole idea of pep rallies was stupid. Once I even brought a book and stopped up my ears with my fingers as I tried to read. I didn't like or dislike Angela. She was just another classmate, and I didn't see much in common between us.

Then we both got parts in the spring musical, and I started to get to know her. We were both drama rookies and were often grouped together for warm-up or set day. We thought that the same things were funny, we liked and disliked the same people, and by my junior year we were good friends. That ended my role as an observer at school functions. Angela just expected that everyone was as spirited as she was, and I found myself coming to school early to decorate the halls for Christmas, and making signs for the football games. And her enthusiasm was infectious. Soon I did start to get excited about the things we did. I really did care when we won a football game, or when the junior class won the spirit stick.

Angela was popular, but not in the same way that the cheerleaders were popular. She was genuinely interested in other people, and people liked her because she made a point to find out about them. She wasn't only concerned about school-related activities, and she and I went to things like the art museum and concerts together. She didn't care that my family didn't go to church. Neither did she, and that was unusual in our conservative Baptist county.

The other students in drama became good friends too. It was a place for people who didn't quite fit into the mainstream. They were a little more liberal, and a lot more accepting of differences than the other students at school. I found a niche with them, and by the time I graduated I felt at home with them and like a leader instead of a follower.

In some ways my parents are probably the most protective parents I know, but at the same time they trusted me to do things that my friends could never do. I still had a bedtime in ninth and tenth grade, but on weekends I didn't have a curfew as long as they knew where I was. I couldn't ride in a car with my friends until they had had their licenses for two months, but once I started driving, I was allowed to drive into the city sooner than my friends.

Most of my parents' rules were based on the fact that they trusted me but were worried about the rest of the world. When I wasn't allowed to do something, it was usually because they were worried about my safety or health. I would often get furious at them for a rule that kept me from doing something with my friends, but I did know that they weren't trying to be mean, and that their limits were set to protect me even if I didn't feel like I needed protecting. I trusted them to be fair, and they usually were.

I could talk to my mother about almost everything, and although I shared some of my problems with my friends, in those relationships I was usually content to be the listener. My mother gave me more satisfactory advice than my friends, and I could count on her not to spread around what I told her. I was equally close to my father, although our conversations generally focused on discussions of future plans, political problems, or whatever we were doing together. For a long time, even into early high school, he would read aloud to me in the evenings before bed. We liked to play tennis, frisbee, or croquet together.

The biggest and most shattering argument I ever had with my parents was in my senior year. Angela's parents had a condominium in Florida, and we were planning a senior trip for the week after school was out. Angela and I and two other girls were going, as well as three guys who were friends of ours. When I asked my parents if I could go, I told them who was going and what the arrangements were. I was sure that my parents trusted me enough to know that I would be sensible and responsible. At first my parents were reluctant to give me permission, but we got out a map and found a route that was all on the interstate. They knew that Angela and Jeremy, the two drivers, were cautious, and the trip would be very inexpensive. They finally said yes, and we went ahead with the plans. For a week the trip was all we talked about. What to bring, what to wear, what we would do, where we would eat. Angela and I and Anne had study hall and lunch together and every minute was filled with plans. We'd write notes during class when an idea couldn't wait. Then one evening about half an hour before I had to leave for play rehearsal, my parents called me into the living room. They looked serious, but I couldn't think of anything that I had done wrong, and I was looking forward to rehearsal, so I wasn't concerned.

My mother said, "Daddy and I have talked about it for a long time, and we're not happy with the idea of you being away alone for so long."

I didn't get it. "What do you mean?"

"We don't want you to go to Florida."

"What? But you said I could go."

"I know, and we are very sorry. We know it's unfair, but we don't want you to go."

I couldn't believe it. It was like their words were floating around in the air and weren't reaching my brain. I knew they couldn't mean it because they had already said it was okay and my parents didn't break promises. I tried to keep my voice from shaking, "But we already planned everything. Angela is counting on me to help pay my share. And you promised." I came back to that.

"You can tell Angela that we will still pay for your share of the rent. The more we thought about it, the more we didn't want you driving that far without an adult. If something were to happen to one of you down there, it would be hours before a parent could get there to help. We are very sorry, but you can't go."

I was crying now. "Please Mommy, I have to go. We've been planning it for weeks." And then finally shouting at the top of my lungs. "I hate you. It's not fair. You said I could go and you lied."

I ran from the room and ran upstairs, stumbling as I went. I slammed the door as hard as I could and a little piece of plaster fell off of the wall. Lying across my bed I sobbed, "I hate you, I hate you." I cried until my head hurt, my eyes stung, and my sleeve was soaking from my tears and runny nose.

I had to go to rehearsal, so I got up and went into the bathroom. Still crying, I washed my face and blew my nose, but my face was red and blotchy and my eyes were bloodshot. I drove to school and the road was blurry. I wanted to be in an accident. If I were dead or hurt, they'd see what they'd done. But I got to rehearsal without event. I was a few minutes early, but I waited in the car until warm-ups started so that I wouldn't have to talk to anybody. I finally went in, and stood in my place with my head down. I tried to keep my mind blank, but I couldn't keep the tears from coming to my eyes. At break Angela asked me what was wrong. I couldn't tell her. I didn't know what to say. I knew she would feel sorry for me, and I couldn't handle that.

For the next three days, I tried again and again to change their minds. I'd start in a reasonable voice and end up screaming at them as I saw they were truly set in their opinion. In between pleading with them, I ignored them, spending most of my time in my room, coming down to eat silently or go to rehearsal.

I still didn't tell Angela. At school when we had study hall, she'd start to make more plans, and I just couldn't tell her that I couldn't go. It got worse everyday. I'd resolve to tell her, but when the time came, I'd keep quiet, and go home and plead again. Finally my mother said that if I didn't tell her, she would call Angela herself. So I took a deep breath during study hall and said, "Ange, I can't go with you guys. My parents are being jerks. They'll pay for my share, so don't worry about the money." I answered their questions as lightly as I could, trying desperately not to let them see how much I cared that I couldn't go. I said that they'd better send me post cards, and that I still wanted to hear all the plans.

It was several weeks before I spoke to them normally again, and even then when I thought about the trip, I got mad. When I look back, I can understand why my parents didn't want me to go, and I know how hard it must have been for them to tell me I couldn't. As a parent I might have felt the same way. But what was so hard for me to accept was that they went back on their word. My parents, who were supposed to be fair and trust-worthy, had said one thing and then changed their minds. If they had said no in the first place, I would have pleaded to go and argued and gotten angry, but I would have been on solid ground. I wouldn't have felt as if the floor beneath my feet was suddenly gone. This argument had shaken up my trust in them, and it took a long time before I trusted them again. Even now almost three years later, when I've forgiven them and taken another trip to Florida with the same people, I can still remember the disbelief and shock I felt at my mother's words, "Daddy and I have talked about this for a long time. . . ."

Although the senior-trip argument was a major disagreement, on the whole I had a good family life. My college roommate refers to my family as a "Brady Bunch" family. I have a little trouble with the analogy since, as my dad said when I told him, "We're not a reconstituted family, and Mommy doesn't have blond hair and wear short skirts." But I do know why she said it. My family does things together. We sing songs on car trips, and we make baskets on Easter morning to put on the doorsteps in the neighborhood. We go for walks together, and eat dinner together when everyone is home.

I don't mean to sound as if we are a wonderful, happy, too-good-to-be-true family. We aren't, and often the things we did together didn't go the way we planned them. Either my sister or I would be sullen and uncooperative about whatever we were doing, and Mommy and Daddy would end up annoyed and disgusted. Elizabeth and I got along well when we were alone together, but when the whole family was doing something, we vied for attention. We would take on opposite roles. If Elizabeth was complaining and whining, I would be interested and helpful, and if she were having a good day, I would be the one to ruin the mood. It's not something we did consciously. It's just how things worked out.

Our family does a lot of laughing and teasing. My father has a quiet, observant sense of humor. He understates the obvious, and mutters funny comments under his breath. My mother's humor is sillier—the kind that sometimes prompted her to answer the phone "Downstairs Maid." My sister and I inherited some from each of them.

Sunday mornings were one of my favorite times, and still are when I am home. Mommy or Daddy would be cooking breakfast as Elizabeth and I trailed into the kitchen in our pajamas. The newspaper would be scattered around, and the dog and cats would be underfoot asking for food or chasing each other. After we ate, we would sit around the table for a while talking, and it would usually end up in a bout of silliness as we teased someone. It was a good time to be together. It was unplanned, and everyone was relaxed.

My family provided a good base to come back to. When things weren't going right at school, I could always tell them. We did have arguments, sometimes big ones like about my senior trip. But except for that one time, they weren't earth-shattering, and didn't last very long. One of the animals would do something cute, or something funny would happen and we'd end up laughing. Someone would apologize, or we'd just forget what we were mad about. I like and respect my family as well as love them, and I can count on them.

The summer after my junior year I went to the Governor's Honors Program (GHP). It was a six-week academic program for high school students, held on a college campus. I studied drama and loved every minute of it. We did trust exercises where we told other people things that we had never told anyone before. Most of our work was on ensemble pieces. The class depended on working with everyone else in the group, and we grew very close. There was no one who didn't fit in, and everyone had a place.

My roommate was a girl whose major area was drama, so we started out with a common interest. We met at the hall meeting after our first dinner, and started talking immediately. Her name was Margaret, but since there were several other Margarets on the hall, she decided to call herself "Megs," and then christened me "Germie" because I also studied German. The names stuck, and that is how we were referred to for the rest of the summer. We got along from the first day.

It was a time of being very self-concerned, very full of the importance of our deep thoughts. Megs and I stayed up until 3:00 in the morning and talked about life. She was the first person outside my family whom I told that I didn't believe in God. We also compared experiences with guys, and hers were as negligible as mine. She too was very involved in drama, and had little time for anything else. Her family life was much different from mine, not as stable and happy, and I felt privileged that she told me all she did about it. When an old man whom she was close to died, she cried on my bed. One night when I woke up terrified from a nightmare, she was there to reassure me. At the end of the summer we cried and vowed to write forever. I wrote once, and she wrote once, and then we both just stopped.

There was something special and isolated about that summer. Not just for Megs and me, but for all the friends I made there. By the end of the six weeks I would have said that they were the best friends that I had ever had. But in the fall when school started, they seemed to fade away like the nicknames we had used all summer. I think that we all outgrew each other. That was the summer when I first solved all of life's big questions. Soon I realized that my solutions were only the beginnings of the answers.

It was a stage for all of us where closeness was vital. If you didn't tell your friends everything about yourself, you were holding back — not being honest. And so we did share everything. That may have been what made us drift apart later. When the thoughts and secrets that we had related to each other so passionately weren't important or true anymore, then the need for the friends who knew those things faded out, too. If I had met the same people in the course of my ordinary life at school, I might have gradually become friends with them. But there wouldn't have been the same urgency that there was about our six-week summer. GHP is described as an intensive learning experience, and it was. The stimulation and concentration from our subject areas was carried over into our relationships.

When I was in first grade, I came home from school with headaches because "the other kids were so noisy and bad." I hated seeing others misbehave, and I even felt responsible for them. I would try to be extra good and cooperative so that the teachers wouldn't think that it was their fault that things were out of control. On my report cards the comments would range from, "A delight to have in class," to "A studious pupil," to "Has good ideas, but needs to learn to speak up more." The slant of the particular comment depended upon whether the teacher was desperately glad to have an obedient student in a disruptive class, or whether she felt that each student should be encouraged to participate and contribute. I would try to comply with whichever behavior was valued. Luckily, over the years I had enough of the encouraging, creative teachers to overcome my shyness and by tenth grade I was no longer embarrassed to speak out in class and express my ideas.

I still felt a responsibility towards my teachers, though, and even when they were boring and dry, and especially if they were trying too hard to reach the students by telling dumb jokes and sitting on the edges of their desks, I wanted them to know that their efforts were appreciated. It was hard work. I'd sit in the front row and smile at their attempts at humor, and be attentive and ask questions while most of my classmates passed notes or tuned out. I wasn't a brown-noser, although it may have looked to some like I was. I just couldn't stand a teacher to feel like he or she was doing a bad job. Most of my friends were also good students, and although they weren't as concerned about encouraging bad teachers, they looked benevolently on my attempts to do so. The people that I didn't know so well wrote me off as a brain and a book worm, but they weren't people I cared about impressing.

I was also extremely concerned about following the rules, being on time, and being prepared for things. I could not feel comfortable loitering in the hall after the warning bell rang, and then rushing to class at the sound of the second bell. I hated leaving homework till the last moment, and I didn't really even like holding a place in the lunch line for someone else, although I conceded to this small breach of the rules. I worried about these little things, but I didn't want to do it openly because even to my best friends it would appear too "goody-goody." I became skilled at thinking of excuses for getting my classmates to comply with the rules with me without actually showing that I was worried about breaking them. I'd think of something to show them in the classroom so that they would come in with me before the bell rang, or I'd chatter constantly while we were walking so that they wouldn't notice that I was hurrying to get us somewhere on time. I became pretty skilled at this manipulation, and although it was sometimes a strain, it was a more attractive alternative to me than breaking the rules or openly admitting that I didn't want to break them.

My conscientiousness was partly instilled in me by my parents. They have high moral standards, and Elizabeth and I were always taught that dishonesty was unacceptable. Although they were not pushy parents, they also motivated me to do well in school and in my extracurricular activities. I learned that it was important to try my hardest, and since I was capable of making good grades and generally succeeding in what I did, these things became very important to me. I liked the approval I got both from my family and other adult friends when I did well. So I followed the rules, studied hard, and did what was expected of me.

In twelfth grade, though, I met my match. It was second semester, and I had Drama I sixth period. My friend Kristen and I had both had enough experience that we were doing Drama II during this period. This meant that most of the time we were sent off to work on our own, rehearsing scenes or doing errands for Susan. This would have been fine except that Kristen had the worst case of "senioritis" that I have ever known. She was sick of school. She had already been accepted to the college she wanted to go to. And she did not want to be in school rehearsing scenes for drama class.

Susan would give us an assignment to work on or an errand to run and a hall pass, and we would be turned loose to work on our own. I liked Kristen a lot, but she intimidated me, and I was afraid to suggest that we should actually do what Susan was expecting us to do because that was obviously not what Kristen had in mind. None of my subtle tactics worked very well on her either. So I spent sixth period every day of spring semester of my senior year following Kristen around the school hoping that Susan wouldn't find out that we weren't quietly rehearsing our scenes. Kristen and I sat in the sun in the senior court yard. We went and bothered Mr. Jason, the yearbook teacher. And she wrote our initials and graduation year in magic marker on the walls outside the school! Since we were both known as good students, no one questioned our activities. Everyone just assumed that we were being responsible and mature. The fact that we were betraying their trust obviously did not make me happy. But I cared too much about being Kristen's friend and companion to protest too loudly. There was a silent struggle between us. I would tentatively suggest that maybe we should at least go over our scene once in case Susan asked to see it, or that we really should get the xeroxed copies that Susan had asked for. Kristen would concede, but would drag out the task to take the whole period so that we wouldn't have to go back to class. I tried to keep us on track and Kristen provided the entertainment.

I would like to be able to say that this experience with Kristen helped me to relax with respect to following the rules. But it didn't. My sense of duty was too deeply ingrained to be relaxed by one semester of bending the rules. Although I lived with Kristen's antics, even after I graduated from high school I was still conscientious to a fault. I now worry about slightly different things like getting papers done, studying for exams, and paying the rent. I cannot skip classes with a clear conscience, and I cannot enjoy myself if I have any unpleasant task hanging over my head. In some ways this causes me unnecessary anxiety, and I envy people who can be carefree and unconcerned all the time. But it has also given me the discipline to work hard at school and my jobs. I do have fun and relaxed times—they just come after my work is done.

In some ways I still feel very close to my high school years. I have been surprised at the amount of emotion I still feel in remembering things that I have not thought of for a long time. In other ways I am able to realize things about myself now that I couldn't see at the time. I can see the change that I went through as I struggled to find friendship and support without compromising myself and my values. I was different from many of my conservative Southern classmates since I had been brought up by Northern liberal parents. Consequently many of my basic values were contrary to those of the people that I went to school with. This made relationships difficult because I often felt that I had to choose between getting along with others and being honest about my real feelings.

In ninth grade I didn't know how to deal with this conflict, and as a result I was shy and awkward. When I got involved in drama, I met people who were also a bit out of the mainstream. They helped me to feel comfortable in saying what I really felt when it was important. But I also learned that it was not necessary to always agree with someone in order to be friends, and that sometimes concentrating on similarities was better than worrying about differences. I think that I came out of high school with a stronger sense of myself because I had been exposed to such a variety of attitudes different than my own.

I made a speech at my graduation, and as I spoke in front of my class, and our parents and friends, I felt comfortable with who I was, and who they were.

I was grateful that I hadn't been sent to a British boarding school.

CASE 10

Guilt Was Everywhere Around Me

This author examines her struggle to survive and grow in a family that undergoes crises of health, money, and disintegrating relationships. She describes the overwhelming anxiety, guilt, and responsibility she feels for holding her family together and shares the coping strategies she developed during this time. As she explains, some of these methods of coping, such as bulimia, had devastating effects on her, while other more positive strategies, such as seeking friendship support, were instrumental in leading to her current sense of herself as a young woman with many strengths.

There are so many things in my life that make me feel guilty: wanting to be on my own; wanting to live in my own place; wanting to have my own room, my own furniture, my own money to spend on myself. I know that these are normal thoughts, wants, and desires for a 21-year old. I know this. But I feel selfish, especially because of my mother. She has done so much for me and my sisters, and all we do is think about ourselves and complain. But it's not that bad, it really isn't. My mother does her best. Why make it worse by complaining?

Being a Resident Assistant my senior year is keeping me busy. I am in charge of thirty-two women on my floor. I put all my energy into everyone else's problems so I won't have to deal with my own. I make sure that I keep helping others, but I know that someday I will have to help MYSELF. I think of my mother who has helped other people her whole life. Now she has no one but herself to help. She stares into the mirror in front of her; she must face herself now. But she breaks down and sobs because she realizes that she doesn't know who that woman in the mirror is or ever was. I cry for her, but I cry deeper inside for both of us. When I look into the mirror I see my mother's reflection instead of mine.

I want to make decisions for ME. I want to lead my own life. I know I am part of a self-destructive family, but I can't walk away from them. I love them. I feel so guilty when I think about what I should do and what I do do. These feelings make me angry, and I turn around and take it out on my mother, which causes more feelings of guilt and the cycle starts all over.

When I was in high school I used to stay home on weekends to avoid the guilt I felt when I went out with my friends. I felt guilty because I knew my mother wanted me to stay home. Of course, she never told me that, but I felt it. That made me angry, but then I'd think about the fact that the feelings were my fault, not hers, and I'd begin to feel guilty again. I took my anger out on my mother with silence and occasional deeply meaningful "I'm just tired" remarks. When I did go out with my friends, I dealt with the guilt and anger by telling my mother I would clean, dust, and vacuum the next day. I'd make a list of things to do before I left, and I'd feel better. Sometimes. Now that I think about it, the only times I didn't feel guilty about going off somewhere with my friends was either after I had just cleaned the house, or when Mom was off doing something fun, too. I just couldn't leave if I knew she'd be home slaving over that house.

When I was a junior in high school, my mother, who is a registered nurse, was hurt on the job. She had to have surgery and was in the hospital for quite a few weeks. That's when I became Mom. I remember waking up at 5:30 every morning, making breakfast or packing lunch for my two younger sisters, cleaning up the house, driving them to school if the bus was late, and zooming off to make the 8:05 bell in my homeroom. I played field-hockey three hours every day after school and worked at a supermarket. By 6 or 7 almost every night I was back home to cook dinner and clean the house. On the nights that my father worked late or was visiting my mother, I became responsible for taking my sisters to the basketball games, roller skating, or whatever may have been planned for the evening. I usually attempted my homework when everyone had gone to bed and somehow managed to remain an A/B student. I love my mother so much, I just wanted to make her happy, which she would be knowing the house would be kept spotless and my sisters well taken care of.

I learned how to be a perfectionist from my mother. I had no idea, however, the extent to which this perfectionism influenced me until I ran the household myself. A picture with dust on it meant "a dirty, unkempt house." I would then dust the entire house, ranting and raving the whole time. Mud on the floor meant "old, dirty floors and unvacuumed rugs." So the floors would be mopped and the rugs vacuumed.

I never understood why my father and younger sisters couldn't see the dirt and the dust in that house. Why couldn't they see the cat fur on the couch, or the burnt popcorn kernel in the kitchen corner? I was convinced it was not that they just *didn't* see these things, but that they *wouldn't* see them. I remember all the times my mother mumbled about something not being cleaned up and directed her comments toward my father. He would always get so frustrated with her. "I didn't see the coffee mug in the sink!" he would say. This would undoubtedly begin a major battle. I must have heard thousands of times, "I am a slave. I'm a piss-poor nigger!" These words verbatim, I must add, began and ended every argument that concerned the "filthy, rotten, hell-hole we live in!" It amazed me that I learned to see the things my mother would have seen. My sisters hate that part of me.

The truth is, we lived in a fairly large, beautiful home in an upper-middle class estate. Our house was immaculate. We hardly ever wore shoes in our house, and a military sergeant performing a white-gloved inspection couldn't have soiled the tip of his finger. Inside the closets in our bedrooms were wrinkle-free shirts and pants, all ironed with the creases "just right," first three buttons buttoned, no overlapping clothes one upon another, every pair of shoes neatly lined up, sweaters folded the same way and piled on the shelves above the shirts. Inside our drawers, every sock was paired and every piece of clothing folded. My mother would stay awake until 2 or 3:00 in the morning ironing, and I learned never to approach her during these times. I was convinced she was working so hard to make me feel guilty, and she would be in a bad mood if I interrupted her. Guilt was everywhere around me.

Behind a family living together in crisis are individuals living alone in chaos. Although everyone is affected, each person reacts in a different way. My father lies and makes up stories that seem to make him feel like a better man. My middle sister can block out her feelings and appears completely unaffected, although I know she's full of emotion. My youngest sister at age 16 rebels completely; she can become cold and frigid at the drop of a pin, and literally runs away from the family. Like my mother, I concentrate on helping everyone else — family, friends, peers, anyone — as long as I don't have to face ME. People tell me they think I'm such a strong person, but I'm not. I'm always confused. I always feel guilty. Worst of all, I can't face myself, and it's been this way all my life. During my senior year in high school, all my confusion and frustration built up to a climax: I became violently bulimic.

Bulimia was not a way for me to control my weight, it was a way to control my thoughts and feelings. With this control I could block out every thought, all the confusion, all the guilt, and the pressure and tension in my life would ease. My mind would become numb — temporarily, at least. I began bingeing every once in a while in my house when no one was at home or everyone was asleep. I would open up the fridge and grab the milk, then eat as much as I could. In order to hide the amount of food I was taking, I used strategies like cutting a cake into squares and placing the pieces on a small plate so it looked like there was a lot of cake leftover. It worked very well. I could eat half of the cake and no one would notice. During a binge I would eat a large variety of food instead of all the Oreos or an entire cake. This way, no one missed the food.

My binges consisted of only sweet food and a lot of milk. Binges lasted anywhere from fifteen minutes to an hour or more before I ran to the toilet, turned on the faucets full blast to drown out the noise, and jammed my fingers down my throat. Early on, I only went on a binge once or twice every few weeks, and I was very secretive about it. The open faucets made enough noise to cover up the sound of my vomiting, and I always flushed the toilet at least three times. Sometimes I'd even take the phone off the hook during a binge/purge cycle so that I wouldn't be interrupted. Interruptions made me very anxious. The binges were always triggered by the overwhelming feelings of tension in the house when I walked in. It felt like the walls were closing in on me, and I would become anxious and overwhelmed with stress. Then I'd need my release.

When I was a freshman commuting to college, my mother went into the hospital again for her back. Everything about it was upsetting. I hate hospitals. My mother was always in pain going into the hospital and always in pain coming out. I was angry and upset for her. If the doctor hadn't screwed up her first back surgery, she wouldn't be in the pain she was in. I knew she might never work again and that she'd always be in pain. Didn't he know she was a hemophiliac? Didn't he know she'd spend the rest of her life with nerve damage to her leg and back?

Old stresses reentered my life: my desire to keep the house clean to perfection; the need to run the family flawlessly. I took over every responsibility I could find to keep myself busy. I took a job, I ran errands, I cleaned the house from the moment I came home from classes until I went to bed at night. Even when I was just sitting at the kitchen table I was constructing some kind of list of things to do or thinking about what to add to the list I already had. Anxiety built.

When my mother came home from the hospital about a week after Christmas, I knew immediately that she was different. I had tried to make everything so perfect. The house was spotless, the clothes were all washed, the fridge was packed. We had a special electric hospital bed set up in our family room so she wouldn't have to go up and down the stairs. Even the dogs were bathed and groomed. In a selfish way I was glad she was home because although I missed her so much, I had her back to help me carry out the household responsibilities.

She slowly climbed into bed, and we gave her her medication, but she hardly spoke. Later, when I tried to talk to her she snapped at me about the house "going down the drain" because we would be in school all day, and there would be "so many things to do." I felt so sad and worthless. By the end of the next week I couldn't handle the pressure or the tension any more. I packed my bags and went to my best friend's house. I lasted one sleepless night. "How can I walk away? We need to work this out! I want this to be like it used to be!" What had happened to my mother? I didn't know that she had always thought of me as a terrible person. It hurt so much to hear her harsh words.

It was very hard to maintain a stable relationship with my mother during that period of time. The anxieties in my life were enormous. So I'd binge. Binge. Binge. Binge. Some days my sisters would be at school and my father would be at work. Alone and anxious, I'd start eating. Faster and faster, more and more—until I was forcing myself to vomit between fifteen and forty times a week.

I was tired and unhealthy. Sick. I knew it, but it just wasn't important. The bulimia wasn't a concern or a priority.

After a while, I began to realize that if something happened to me, there would be no one to take care of things. I was wasting food that my parents paid for. I began to feel guilty for being so weak—not just in my physical strength, but in mind, too. Everything I was doing was affecting my family. I was just adding another problem to our family crises. A few months later I told my best friend and my mother about the bulimia. It was so difficult for me to admit my problem to them because I felt like such a failure.

My mother set up an appointment for me with a psychiatrist. Every week I sat in a chair and talked about my family. When my therapist asked me to talk about ME, I would simply start crying and say, "I don't know," until the hour was up. Eighty dollars an hour—what a financial strain for my family—and it was all my fault. After six months of what I felt was wasted money for no progress, my therapist started me on antidepressants. I flushed them all down the toilet a few days after I picked up the prescription. Yes, they did slow me down, but nothing could stop me from thinking about all the chaos in my family, and the anxiety and guilt I felt as a result of it.

Bulimia wasn't my priority, and my psychiatrist recognized this. Around the eighth week of my therapy, he presented me with an ultimatum: "Make this eating disorder come first in your life, or you will be admitted to a hospital for the summer." That meant I would have to leave my family. I had to stop. I set goals to break what had become a self-destructing habit. One day—no bingeing. Two days—no bingeing. Eat one cookie. Stop. Feel the tension build—take a walk. Drive over to see a friend. Anything. It was so hard, so hard that it took three years before I completely stopped bingeing and purging. Living at school helped because the bulimia seemed only to exist at home. I wanted to be there to take care of my family, but home was the source of the anxiety, the guilt, the tension, and the numbness that made me need to run from the chaos.

During the treatment for my bulimia, about five months after my mother had come home from the hospital for the second time, I said to her, "I can't believe how we were when you came home from the hospital. You hated me for so long." She replied, "Honey, I don't know what you're talking about. We've always had such a wonderful relationship." She talked all afternoon that day, and it was only then, five months after the fact, that I was told she had developed water-on-the-brain during surgery. It was the result of a drug which had been given to her to counteract the problems she had due to hemophilia. Six pounds of fluid on her brain had caused her to have short-term memory loss, a change in personality and severe depression. No one had ever told me, and for five months I lived thinking something terrible had changed my mother forever. And she didn't even remember those first few days home from the hospital.

Throughout it all was my group of friends who kept me going. We met in third grade and by our freshman year in high school the eleven of us were inseparable. There were times when our friendships with the guys in the group were so deep, we confused them with love. Sometimes we crossed over the line, but it never worked. It was like kissing your brother. There is some bond that holds us together unlike any relationship any of us has ever had with a person not from our group. We have a kind of uniqueness that our peers wish for and envy, our parents love and adore, and our teachers respect and admire. Our new friends will never, ever understand it. I feel so much emotion and passion when I think about them that I don't think I could ever express it in words. Only we know how lucky we are to have each other, and one hug, one kiss, one touch says it all.

My friends were there for me during all the crises in my life, even my pre-teen years, which were pure hell. Every part of my body seemed to need some sort of treatment. Not only did I have to wear braces on my teeth, but also a brace on my back to treat my scoliosis, curvature of the spine. In the same year I was also diagnosed as having Juvenile Rheumatoid Arthritis, for which I had to take eighteen to twenty aspirin every day. The aspirin were needed to decrease the inflammation in my knees, but I hated taking them. I became very aware of teachers and students watching me pop pills all the time, and there were times when I didn't even take half as many pills as I was supposed to. I felt guilty for not taking the prescribed number of pills, and I remember crying the nights before my aspirin-level blood checks.

During my senior year in high school my boyfriend was killed in an automobile accident. I had dated David for four months when it happened. He had attended my high school a few years before me, and had gone straight from high school into the Army. I was introduced to him shortly after he returned. Although we hadn't been together long, I had already begun to feel that the relationship had the potential to get much stronger. It was exciting and thrilling to be with him, but I never really let him know. I put up my defenses to protect myself from losing control and letting myself fall in love with him. Something inside told me not to let him cross over into my world. I was so afraid of falling in love, of relationships, of potential serious commitments. Why? Was it him? I wasn't sure what it was, and it frustrated me.

The phone call about the accident came one morning after a party that I had gone to without him. I had wanted to see him later in the evening, but I hadn't been able to find him. And now on the other end of the phone, his family was telling me he had been in an accident and was in critical condition at the hospital. I think about that morning now and wonder if maybe it wasn't the easiest part of the tragedy — things gradually worsened throughout the day.

David's sisters called me from the hospital that afternoon and told me that he had been placed on a respirator. With every twitch of a toe or slight movement of a finger, they would call to tell me he was alive. They called me four times that day. It was 11 p.m. and I was sitting in my basement with three close friends when the telephone rang once more. "Come to the hospital. Mom told David you were coming and he squeezed her hand! We're all counting on you. Bring him back to us." The pressure I felt at that moment was unbearable. My heart crumbled and I prayed to God that He would let me wake from this bad dream.

A while later I was walking down the hospital corridor approaching a waiting room full of nieces and nephews, sisters and brothers, grand-parents, and parents. I had never met any of these people in the short time that David and I had been seeing each other, and now they wanted me to bring their child back to them.

At 3:00 in the morning, I was called into the room where I was with David for the last time. I remember walking down a long hallway, holding my friend's hand so tightly that my clenched fist left small bruises. We stood together staring at the doors in front of us. I could feel Death waiting to smother me. My heart pounded against my chest. I had to go in. I forced myself to completely shut down. I closed my eyes and opened the doors. . . .

Deep, dark, deadly blue. Blue air, blue people. People who seemed no longer human. "Breathing machines" made of tubes and flesh. One of them was once my boyfriend, yet this lifeless body couldn't be. This man barely had a face from the bridge of his nose down to his chin. His body was white, almost transparent. I cannot describe more of what I saw that night. I cannot put it into words. I took his ice cold hand in mine and held it for almost an hour. His mother and I prayed for a shiver, a jolt, a twitch. But there was nothing. I held that hand every night in my dreams for over a year.

That night members of his family told me that he had been much more serious about me than I had ever known or wanted to know. It was also that night that his family, whom I had just met, forced me to become the only living part of David for them to hold on to.

Throughout the summer and into my first year at college, his mother would send me anything she could find concerning David. She sent copies of letters he had written to her while he was in the Army, poems about his death she had written and sent into the town newspapers, accident reports, and finally, an autopsy report. (I never read it.) Before I left for school she gave me a beautiful, delicately-thin, gold necklace and told me David had gotten it for me as a graduation present. She would often call and make sure that I was still wearing it.

The pressure they imposed on me soon became unbearable, but I felt guilty about trying to break away from them. They needed me. It took a year and a half for me to put aside the guilt I felt for wanting to free myself from them. I did care very much about David, but I felt that his family wanted me not only to join their family, but to become a living part of David for them. One night I wrote to his mother: "I can no longer bear the pain and relive the tragedy each time I hear from you, each time I see you. I love you and your family, but it is a love I have for you that has grown out of death and never a minute before. I can't take the pressure or the pain any longer. Understand that I must do this for myself. Please also understand that I did care for David, but I did not, nor did I ever give myself the chance to, fall in love with him. I learned to love him more after his death, and this is just not right for any of us. I'm sorry."

That was the last I heard from the family with the exception of a phone call here and there, and on my birthdays.

Meanwhile, my own family's problems were trying enough. I think our biggest problem is money. My family's life revolves around money. Every problem, every argument—MONEY. I worried about my hospital appointments because of money. I felt terrible on Christmas because my parents spent so much money buying presents. It seems as though we've always had money problems, or at least I was always hearing about them. I didn't really think there was a real problem, though. Mom made good money as a Registered Nurse and Dad owned and managed a huge furniture store. When I was in junior high, I even got teased for living in the wealthiest section of town. I had the "perfect" family.

Almost three years ago, we began to lose everything. My father sold his store and worked for another store. He was unhappy working for other people, so he quit his job and opened up his own furniture store. All we knew was that the business wasn't doing well and we were losing a lot of money.

I found out from a few of my male friends that my father had called them up and asked them to help clear out his store of anything that could have been considered "odds and ends." I didn't understand why this had to be done in the middle of the night, and I was embarrassed and ashamed that he brought my friends into the situation. The next day I figured out bits and pieces, and my mother filled me in on what she knew. My father hadn't been paying rent and the man he owed the money to had a warrant out for his arrest, or was ready to kill my father himself. In the next few weeks we got phone calls every day, finding out about debts of thousands of dollars that my father owed to banks, advertising agencies, and even some of my parents' friends.

My parents' marriage had never been anything spectacular, but this was the icing on the cake. I thought my mother was going to have a nervous breakdown. We had to sell the cars, some furniture, and cut back on everything but the bare necessities. I applied to transfer to a very inexpensive college, as compared to the one I was attending, and began at the new school as a second-semester sophomore. The day I had to leave my first college I just packed up and drove away. I don't regret that I had to leave that school. It made me feel good to know that we were going to save money and be able to pay off some of the debts. I would finally be able to feel comfortable knowing that this was a big help to my parents.

Unfortunately, it wasn't enough, and we had to sell our house. We moved to another town about an hour away. My mother used to say that all she had for herself was her health, her house, and her dog. She had lost her health to the back accident, and now she had to lose the house that she'd slaved over for thirteen years. She loved that house, and she lost it all at the expense of my father's lying and mismanagement of money. Even the dog died a few months after we moved. I felt so bad for her, but there was nothing I could do.

It's very difficult for me to say exactly what I think of my father. He's a very nice man. He's never raised his hand to me and hardly ever raises his voice in my presence unless I've caught him off guard, arguing with my mother. I get very confused with my feelings towards him because I'm not sure whether I hate him for what he's done to our family, or whether I love him simply because he's my father. I tell him that I love him, then my mother tells me about more problems he's caused us, or horrible things he's told her, and then I feel guilty for not being on my mother's side and standing strong with her. I know of so many lies he's told my mother, and I feel so used by him. I gave him all the chances in the world to prove himself a caring father, but only my youngest sister saw through him to the lying, cheating, and deceit — and was able to walk away from it.

Many problems in my family stem from a lack of communication. It's not that we don't talk about our feelings, but we don't talk about them directly to the person involved, and the interpretation of the feelings and facts ends up causing battles. In my family we play "operator." Tell Mom the sky is blue and by the time it gets back to you, Dad says Mom said you said it's raining.

I always got caught carrying the messages back and forth between my parents, and whenever there was an argument, I got blamed. Eventually, I learned to have my parents write down exactly what was to be said to the other person, so that their problems couldn't be blamed as a "misunderstanding" on my part. Everyone wonders why my parents didn't just sit down and talk these things out. I don't know. Psychologists, marriage counselors, family therapists, no one could help. We'd walk out of a session completely frustrated and scream, yell, and cry all the way home. But at least we tried.

I guess I wasn't too shocked when my father told us this summer that he'd been having an affair and was moving in with "her." I had known for the past three years that my parents' marriage would end in divorce. My father told me all the time that he wasn't happy, but he just couldn't afford an apartment if he moved out. He stayed out late. He used to run down the street to get milk and not come back for an hour or two. He'd go away with friends frequently. On Father's Day he was away with a "friend" and showed up for the holiday dinner three hours late.

He used to talk about how unhappy he was. We joked about how bad the marriage was. I joked about it with my mother. She seemed to know that someday this would happen; being together was tearing them apart. I guess my mother never thought that after he'd already taken so much away from us he could do more. She was wrong. I guess I was, too. He could have at least waited until they were divorced.

While I was home from school a few months ago, my mother and I became enraged over something. We lashed out at each other like never before. I screamed and hollered and we basically told each other to go to Hell. I left the house to blow off some steam and clear my thoughts. The laundry machine was broken, so I took the clothes to the laundromat. It was the perfect excuse to walk away from the argument. It was the first time I had refused to stay and talk it out. I'm always the one to turn around and want to make things better. This time, however, I just left! It felt good in a way. I had total control of the situation. I just didn't want to deal with it, so I left!

When I was sitting there on top of the folding table watching the dryers shrink all our clothes, I started to feel like I had made a mistake. I mean, I didn't just leave—I had the laundry! What am I saying? There I was, doing the laundry. I didn't just take off to get out of the house, I brought some of it with me.

Another revelation: I probably DID feel guilty for leaving so I compensated by doing the laundry. So much for the "new me." I haven't changed a bit. And for a minute, I was actually going to begin explaining my feelings of guilt, the feelings of guilt that had begun and how I blocked it out! Oh, well. Try, try again.

When I came home a few hours later, there was a note on the counter from my mother. She explained in the note that she was afraid, not afraid that we were not getting along because of the problems in the family, but because we were seeing eye to eye. Adult to adult. She went on painfully to describe her conflict. She wanted me to be home with her, as her child; but she knew I was grown up and independent and she wanted me to have my own life and live and be happy. We don't see each other as much as we used to, or at least as we want to. Yet my mother knew how much I wanted to be home. And she knew how much I wanted to be away. At the same time, my own inner conflict existed as well. We speak to each other now as friend to friend, and as mother to daughter. Sometimes I just don't want to grow up. I want her to read over my papers for school, or call my boss when I don't feel well enough to work, and tell me to take the day off. Often, I call her on the telephone just because I know she'll say what I want to hear and I love it. But sometimes I want her to see me as an adult with choices and decisions to make about my life. I don't know how she does it. She knows exactly what I need: she'll be one or the other, or both when I need her to be. But sometimes we want different things from each other, and the conflict becomes real. It's okay, though. She made me realize that this is what happens sometimes between a mother and a daughter.

I look into a mirror and I see my mother, and she is crying. I can't help her. I can't see myself; I only see my mother. I'm not sure who I am but I know I am a good person, otherwise I wouldn't deserve the people I have in my life. But I can't help my mother. I feel guilty. Okay, I have a lot of things to sort out. I understand I can't change anyone, they can only change themselves. Wonderful, so I don't have to take care of everything and everyone anymore! Here's only one person I am responsible for now—me. I have to face myself. Take care of myself. Rescue myself.

I think about all the things we've been through. It's not so bad, though. It's just that everything seems to happen all at once. It'll get better. We'll start new. We are stronger and we are survivors. I know that I will have to face the fact someday that I must learn to look into the mirror and see ME in the reflection. I know that I will have to face and deal with my fear of food and my fear of becoming a co-dependent woman like my mother. I know that I must learn to control my anxiety and my guilt. I have all the love and support I could possibly have from my friends and family. I will use the strength they give me to find the strength in myself.

Someday.

CASE 11

No *"Boring Little Friends"*

This writer describes the key high school friendships that helped her deal with issues of control, identity, and sexuality in early adolescence. Despite her role as the oldest and most responsible in a family of eight and her success in school, she finds herself looking for friendships and adventures that will help her rebel against the comfortable and known sense of self these accomplishments gave her. She and her friends hang out in bars, sneak out of their houses at night, and fantasize together about men and sex. Her actual love life consists of many unfulfilled crushes early on, masturbation that makes her feel guilty and sinful, and eventual experimentation with men who return some of her feelings. Her early adolescent years seem full of unmet desires: the words "I want" appear again and again in this case as she reflects on the role of male and female friendships in her life.

I was funky. Dana was sophisticated. Liz was crazy. We walked to school together, went for bike rides, cut school, got stoned, talked on the phone, smoked cigarettes, slept over, discussed boys and sex, went to church together, and got angry at each other. We defined each other with adjectives and each other's presence. As high school friends, we simultaneously resisted and anticipated adulthood and womanhood.

Seven years later I am still a little funky, living in New York City, and working and writing. Liz is still a little crazy—she lives in London now with her Portuguese rock-'n-roll boyfriend, and works at a hotel. I think Dana is in the Army, but we have lost touch. She was never that sophisticated, but she was a model and incredibly beautiful and went out with lots of boys. So she seemed sophisticated to Liz and me who were busy clunking into each other in front of our lockers.

Today I am in love with a man I have been seeing for over two years. I love him and he loves me. Simple—and yet incredible and unexpected and as wonderful as I had hoped. At age 15 I never thought a man that I loved would ever love me. All my personal experience had proved quite the opposite.

What was possible at 15 and 16? We still had to tell our parents where we were going! We wanted to do excitingly forbidden activities like going out to dance clubs and drinking whiskey sours. Liz, Dana, and I wanted to do these forbidden things in order to feel: to have intense emotional and sensual experiences that removed us from the suburban sameness we shared with each other and everyone else we knew. We were tired of the repetitive experiences that our town, our siblings, our parents, and our school offered to us. The realization that *our* world was actually a very small part of *the* world hit us when we were 15. The real world looked bigger, brighter, and much more fun.

The friendship between Dana, Liz, and myself was born out of another emotional need: the need for trust. The three of us had reached a point in our lives when we realized how unstable relationships can be, and we all craved safety and acceptance. Friendships all around us were often uncertain. We wanted and needed to be able to like and trust each other.

In the following story, I talk a lot about myself as a high school student. I call myself a "good girl" a few times. To me that means I didn't get kept after school for talking in class. I didn't fail classes. I was not fresh to my teachers or to my mom and dad. Mostly, I didn't do any of those things because I was successful and happy when I was a "good girl." I got good grades, didn't get hassled too often by my folks, and had a bunch of friends. I really wanted to go to college, and go away to school, and I knew my parents didn't have much money, so I figured that I'd need a scholarship if I wanted to go someplace challenging. With that understood, I resolved to do well in school.

Although I was "good," underneath the surface I felt wicked, or at least hypocritical at times. I smoked in the bathroom, but I made sure I did not get caught. I had a fake ID, but when I went to bars I did not get drunk or into trouble. I had a few drinks and laughed with my friends and looked at boys. I was a pretty cautious teenager.

I was also responsible, partly out of caution, and partly because I really wanted to get things done the right way and not fool around with failing or losing out on an opportunity. I have a pretty competitive streak (I think from growing up with siblings all very close in age), which pushes me to do things even when I'm not that inspired to do them. Like if I thought I might win an essay contest, I would write something. Just to do it.

I think the other reason for my responsibleness is that I was brought up to be aware of other people's needs. I was/am the oldest girl (woman) in a family that continued to grow and change while I was in high school and college. As new kids were added and little ones grew up I think I developed the aptitude to see what needed doing. Then I would do it, often just to cut down on household strife — or to help out my mom, who I am very close to and sometimes felt bad for because she was so busy. I liked helping out. It always felt good to contribute.

My parents' lives are not carefree. They have money worries, and worries about my other siblings, and worries about their own private lives. I was always reluctant to add to their burden. On the other hand, they sometimes seem especially good at making me feel that that is just what I am doing. Most of the time I get along well with my parents. Most of the time everyone in my family tries to be supportive and giving to other family members. But my parents seem to have a fear of losing control over me and my two younger sisters. My older brother has almost always done what he wanted to do whether my folks liked it or not. I was always more obliging. I liked it when they were proud of me.

In the suburban area where I grew up, many people are extremely conformist and preoccupied about money. My family really went against this money-as-most-important model. We didn't have a lot of money. I didn't always have the right kind of jeans or sneakers. I wore clothes from thrift shops before it was cool and trendy.

I went to East Middle School, which had the reputation of being run like a Catholic school — very tight control. The kids from West had reputations as loud-mouth rich kids. Many of them lived, not in town, but in the Harbour, where there were no sidewalks or 7-11s. Many of the West girls wore designer jeans and expensive sweatshirts. These girls also talked extensively about who they had fooled around and gone out with, what guys liked them, how far they had gone with guys, and how many times they had gotten drunk or stoned. Most of the West girls weren't like that; but the cliques from West were much stronger and less fluid than the cliques from East.

At the beginning of ninth grade it was amazing how quickly it was established that the "cool" West girls and the "cool" East girls were supposed to somehow be friends. It was also quickly established that the West girls were really the coolest. They were the richest and the toughest and the loudest. I was a "cool" girl in East, but not because the guys liked me, or I was really pretty, or because I had great clothes. I was the editor of the newspaper, the valedictorian, friends with all the teachers, and on basketball, volleyball, and softball. So I was cool for basically unexciting reasons — the girl people could refer to when their parents weren't going to let them do something; "Ann's going. . . ." I was also pretty perceptive and even-handed for a junior high school kid. So people usually trusted me, telling me things about themselves and their lives and other people because I either gave good advice or could keep a secret.

I was always pretty insecure with the "cool people," though. I saw so much back-biting and lying and name-calling and dropping of friends that somewhere inside I was always nervous that I would be pushed out; maybe people would stop calling me or inviting me to parties. When I entered high school, my preoccupation with the "cool people" heightened. Suddenly there were so many more people to keep up with, and new ideas of what was in or out. In the first two years of high school I was quite popular—mostly for the same reasons I was popular in junior high school. I was cool enough not to be a geek, nice to lots of people, and was also productive. I could run for president of the class, or chairperson for sports night, and get elected. My "popular" friends really pushed for my election (making posters, etc.), probably because they would get some "fringe benefits" out of it too; they would get to be on committees where they didn't have to do anything, but could still get out of going to class. I guess I felt like an outsider because my popularity always seemed quite precarious—it seemed so connected to external factors. I remember feeling that others were inherently popular—while I had to work at it.

In ninth grade I worked pretty hard at being popular. By the end of the year I felt smug about my popularity, but by tenth grade this smug attitude turned to impatience. Popularity was not always fun; it was often unsettling—or boring. Tenth grade was a year filled with "Sweet Sixteen" parties that were actually competitions: who had the best party, who wore the best outfit, who bought the best gifts, who got invited to the most parties. One time a girl hated another girl because she had bought an identical outfit to wear to the same Sweet Sixteen party. I remember being down in someone's basement during tenth grade (a whole bunch of girls were hanging out after school), and the girl who got the outfit first got on the phone to "bawl out" the other girl for buying the same outfit. Then all the girls there took turns getting on the phone to say nasty things to her, telling her she was a slut, or stupid, or that they never really liked her. I sat there for about a half hour getting angry and embarrassed. I was ashamed that I was actually *debating* about leaving. Finally I did get up and said, "This really sucks." And I left.

I walked out. I kissed them all off. I walked home, in the rain I think, really mad at them for hassling—demoralizing Donna about a stupid outfit. I was also incredibly nervous all night that my phone would ring and they would be on the phone bawling me out for something. I was also afraid that I would be labeled uncool and idiotic and blacklisted from parties and lunch tables and weekend plans. When I went to school the next day I found out that the girls decided they "respected" me for leaving.

The phone call was made from Liz's basement. She had been much more "in" than me in junior high and grade school. Short, cute, and incredibly funny, Liz was a daring loudmouth. When I had moved to town in fourth grade, on the first day of school Liz asked me if I was a boy (because I was tall, had short hair, and a pencil case with my brother's name on it) and I hated her for months. Liz and I had become really good friends during Freshman year. She and I hung out with the same kids and walked home from school together almost everyday. During the walk we moaned about boys and school and popularity and the pressures we felt from our parents and our group of friends. We reassured each other. I confided in Liz my multitudes of crushes.

During ninth and tenth grade I constantly fell in love with older boys I knew only slightly and shy boys my own age I knew well. I never went on dates with these boys; I just thought about them a lot. I knew some older guys from school government and committees. They were nice to me. Some flirted quite a bit with me. But I never went on dates with the older guys because they never asked me out. They usually had girlfriends who were Seniors. The shy boys my own age were not quite ready for dating. While I was thinking about true love and romantic walks through the park, I think they were thinking about video games, Pink Floyd, and sex with girls from Budweiser ads. I never quite felt much like "dating material." I was tall and liked school and talked a lot in class. I wore weird clothes and wrote articles for the school newspaper about local political candidates. Sometimes bizarre boys who wanted to be comic strip heroes or felt as stifled as I did by our relatively small town would confess their true love for me. These incidents never led to sexual relationships with these boys. I would tell them that I knew how they felt, seeing that I had a few unfruitful crushes of my own. I never liked any of the boys who liked me.

Perhaps Liz and I became good friends because we were both incredibly sensitive to the propensity of the "popular group" to just drop people, to turn on them for no apparent reason. We were both afraid and angered by this possibility. Perhaps we bonded because we walked home the same way, or because we were in the same confirmation class in seventh grade, or because we put each other into hysterics, mimicking people we knew and writing sordid letters back and forth about teachers at school we pretended were having illicit affairs with each other. We loved to talk about Dr. Ruth Westheimer. Neither of us had any sexual experience (beyond kissing) until eleventh grade, but we both had dramatic imaginations.

I also unburdened my family problems on Liz as we walked home, stopping to sit on the curb before we parted. I was the oldest girl in a family of eight. My two baby brothers drove me crazy—I was responsible for them quite often. I had an older brother and two younger sisters too. It sometimes embarrassed me to have so many siblings. People always seemed so surprised and compelled to say rude things about birth control and ask if my family was Catholic. We were, in fact, Catholic. I went to religious instruction until eleventh grade or so. So did Liz. We hated it sometimes, but enjoyed getting out of our houses on a school night. Liz, my brother, and I would go to lectures at church and then go to Carvel and hang around for another hour and laugh or talk about our lives. Liz told me about her family problems too—about her cousin Susan who had died of cancer the previous summer; about her "perfect" older sister; and about her older brother who was emotionally disturbed—he was four years older than Liz, but lived in his own world where he was king and spoke his own language.

I think high school and her changing body crushed Liz's spirit. Suddenly she was supposed to stop wearing painter pants and start blow-drying her hair. She was supposed to wear makeup, start French-kissing guys, and stop being loud and crazy, because, "God, Liz, you really intimidate guys when you act so crazy like that. . . ." A gymnastics accident forced Liz to be relatively sedentary, and she gained weight as she started developing breasts and hips. I remember her period was (and still is) terribly painful. She took the Pill for a while too, and hated the side effects of bloating. We talked about it a little bit in a joking way—how she ought to find someone to have sex with while she was "protected." I think taking the Pill was really embarrassing for Liz. It seemed premature in light of the rest of her life. Womanhood was like one big punch in the face to Liz—it really spoiled her fun.

By the end of ninth grade, my friendship with Liz had solidified. We each trusted the other's loyalty. We probably began hanging around with Dana out of a desire for other solid, loyal, caring friendships. Liz and I both knew Dana from grade- and junior high school. She had always been incredibly prissy, cute, and quiet. She brought tuna fish and crackers to lunch every day because that's all she would eat. Boys and teachers loved her. She wore cute little skirts and had blond hair and blue eyes. I had been friends with her off and on, and so had Liz.

The three of us had gone through the same religious instruction, and Dana and I each had a brief connection to a Catholic youth group. Liz stopped going to mass when she got her period. I think she must have felt that there was no God, or that God was abandoning her—since growing up seemed so difficult. Painful and unattractive bodily changes like cramps and pimples, coupled with her sadness about her cousin Susan's death, made Liz lose faith. Soon the youth group made me want to throw up; it was as cliquey as high school, except here it was cool to be depressed and pathetic. In my opinion, the youth group was less interested in spiritual growth than group therapy. Dana stopped going after all the guys there were in love with her. Although I continued to go to mass and believe in God, by the time I was in tenth grade the admonitions of the nuns and religious instruction teachers to think holy thoughts began to fade from my conscious thoughts, which were filled with boys and sexual fantasies and worries about school.

In ninth grade Dana was itching to emerge from her circle of (as Liz and I nastily had characterized them) "boring little friends." She began to model in high school and the "popular crowd" was suddenly eager to embrace her. It didn't hurt that many beautiful senior guys were in love with her. The popular crowd believed in coolness by association. By the end of tenth grade the three of us knit together in an effort to be "real" friends for each other. The "popular crowd" became less and less important as we became more important to each other, depending on each other for support and social life.

I think it was our personality differences, as well as our common desire for true and loyal friends, that made our friendship initially exciting. Dana was somewhat devious, manipulative, daring, and exciting. As a professional model she enjoyed the attention her appearance got her. But sometimes she despaired over her "looks" in melodramatic evenings where she would sit on the floor of her room, stuffing her face with pretzels and ripping up her modeling pictures. Liz was "the clown," always the loudest and funniest. (Later, in eleventh and twelfth grade, Liz had weeks of depression where she wouldn't come to school or answer the telephone. In tenth grade, however, Liz was still able to put on the act of crazy woman without too much strain and inner contradiction.) My personality was not as overtly extreme as Liz or Dana's. I always felt boring in comparison to the two of them. They were always getting into trouble at home and in school, while I was getting good grades and having a relatively peaceful time at home. I always got along pretty well with my brothers and sisters. I got along well with my parents overtly, but I spent much of ninth and tenth grade lying to them about where I was going and what I was doing.

My days were full of fantasies. I wanted to get out of my town, my family, and my life. They were all so boring and safe. I wanted to go on trips, live in England for the summer, and have a love affair. I really wanted to fall in love. More than that, I wanted someone to fall in love with me. I wanted a taller, older, smarter, more worldly boy (more everything than the boys I knew) to be in love with me. I wanted that kind of boy/man to help me experience the world more fully. I read a lot of books, which no doubt perpetuated my idea that a relationship would complete me and increased my desire for a boyfriend or a love affair. Reading always reminded me of the worlds that I was not part of. It reminded me how boring my life was. Magazines like *Seventeen* and *Teen* helped me to connect self-worth to whether I held a man's sexual attention. My father and brothers paid attention to me. So did my uncles and grandfathers. And my male friends. But I wanted to feel sexually desirable. I wanted everything right away and simultaneously felt as though it would never happen. I wanted to go and see and do and experience the world. Instead, I was in Eastview, babysitting, riding my bike, and going to the beach.

I was always much taller than everyone in my classes until high school. By junior high school I was even taller than some men teachers, which embarrassed me greatly. My body size influenced me in two important ways. I think people felt that I was very mature and responsible, and they treated me that way—so I did assume a lot of responsibility from my teachers and my parents. At the same time, I think my physical body did mature earlier than other kids' did, and this seemed to be a social drawback to me. I never felt cute or desirable. I always felt too big, too much like a boy. I think I missed out on the girlishness of adolescence. At least I never felt that I was desirable to boys my own age, although I was comfortable with them socially, to be friends and hang out and talk. Sexually I always felt out of place. I was the size of a woman, but not the age of a woman. I had the life of an adolescent without the right physique or mentality.

I remember intense waves of desire as early as seventh grade—sexual feelings I didn't know what to do with. Perhaps it was due to my early-developed body. I remember distinctly the first time I masturbated—the night after a sleepover party in seventh grade. Though I consciously had crushes on "nice boys," I fantasized that night about a boy I felt was really sleazy and sexy. Sexiness and sleaziness were completely interwoven to me—as indoctrinated as I was by my religious instruction classes: "Don't read your horoscope! Abortion is always killing a baby! Sexual desire is bad news! Feel guilty if you start to think lustful thoughts! Repent if you are looking at dirty magazines or reading dirty books!"

During seventh grade I said my rosary every night before I went to sleep. I got up every morning to go to mass before school during Lent. I also masturbated at least once a day. It was during seventh grade that I became a part of a dirty book swap, where girls I knew and I would find books loaded with sexual passages and trade them before volleyball practice. One of my friends had two brothers in college and we found *Hustler* magazine in their room. The pictures, and more than the pictures, the stories, sexually excited me. The images and words in the magazine were so strong and enticing. The pictures showed naked men and women having sexual intercourse. It was incredible to see nude bodies. It was amazing to see a man's penis. I was very curious. The stories were filled with images of women who were weak and submissive. They loved the sex that was forced upon them by overpowering men. Many of the stories told of once innocent women who suddenly became nymphomaniacs after being raped. The magazines were an unending source of fascination. I thought about the stories and pictures even when the magazines were not in front of me.

It is amazing to recall that all this sexual turmoil coincided with playing volleyball, singing in the chorus, writing for the newspaper, and getting awards when I graduated from middle school in eighth grade. I felt incredibly guilty about masturbating until about the eleventh and twelfth grade, when I began dating, and began to debate about whether or not to have sex with the boys I went out with. Suddenly masturbation seemed innocent when compared to my new, more horrible and dangerous desire to actually have sex.

During the tenth and eleventh grade, the friendship I had with Liz and Dana made me happy, but it never pushed me to explore these incredible contradictions within myself. Liz, Dana, and I were sympathetic to each other. We encouraged each other to feel what we were feeling. However, in retrospect, we were not that honest with each other. I had these incredible contradictions in my life about who I appeared to be, and how I actually felt inside; but on the outside I was tame compared to Liz and Dana. Both were frequent class-cutters, school-skippers, family haters, and shoplifters. In contrast, I went to my classes, didn't steal, and didn't have screaming matches with members of my family. It may have seemed as though my confusion and despair did not reach the depths of Liz or Dana's, but it did. I didn't act like Liz and Dana because it really was not my style. I could not judge their actions as bad because I really didn't think they were. I agreed with them that their family life was hard. I didn't care that they stole. I just didn't want them to get caught. The manifestation of my confusion was perhaps more internally directed. I was enormously confused by the contradictions I experienced. I desperately wanted someone to help me break out of my boring life. I wanted someone to fall in love with me. I realize now I wanted a boyfriend during early high school so badly because his presence would somehow validate the sexual urges I was having. I know I felt my appearance would be validated if someone else appreciated it—I felt that if someone liked my face and my body, perhaps I could too.

I realize now that for the years I was in high school I was pretty obsessed with my weight. In almost every single journal entry I have written, "I need to lose at least five to ten pounds." Sometimes at night before I went to sleep, or if I couldn't sleep, I would eat. I would eat much more than I needed to, more than I even wanted to, sitting at the kitchen table at two o'clock in the morning. I just kept eating because somehow the food did comfort me, fill me up, helped me to relax and sleep. Often I would go on a diet. In ninth grade, when I was planning to get pictures taken to bring to a modeling agency at my aunt's suggestion, I dieted strictly for four solid months. I would eat a slice of bread with no peanut butter and drink a glass of water with it for lunch. I exercised in the basement everyday. I lost at least fifteen pounds. I remember being pretty skinny, but never feeling like I was thin enough to look good.

When my mother told me I couldn't model and be a chairperson for class night (a position to which I had just been elected), I went immediately to the bakery and bought two chocolate-covered custard donuts and ate them one after the other. My attempt to get away from my house, to get away from the control of my mother and dad, to live an exciting, non-high-school-ish life, which I thought having a modeling career would accomplish, was foiled. I wanted to be grown up. I wanted to be an adult, to divorce myself from my parents, to not care about what they thought or said.

During the summer before eleventh grade, Liz went on a bike trip to the West Coast. While she was gone, Dana and I hung out almost every day. We went to the beach one day with three boys we knew. I was in love with Randy, and Tom was in love with Dana, and Bill was this weird guy we didn't know (who has ended up being one of my best friends from high school). I remember feeling that Randy liked Dana and not me, and I painfully remember coming home on the train and seeing him rub Dana's calf "because it was so smooth." It made me feel dead inside that he was attracted to her. She was so much more sexually appealing than I was.

Being with Dana made me want to be more desirable and made me actively confront the importance of appearance. Dana and I would go into New York City; Dana wanted to take me to her modeling agency so I could model too. Sometimes we went to the city dressed in her modeling clothes. We went to bars and got propositioned by old men. It was simultaneously gross and exciting. Only now do I realize what it must have looked like, two 16-year-olds in low-cut sweaters hanging out in seedy bars too close to Penn Station. But then it felt exciting and even slightly dangerous.

When Liz came back from the West Coast, the three of us hung out together. We lied to our parents regularly. If we got dropped off at the movies we went around the corner to the Ticktock Cafe and used our fake proof (bought in the city) to drink whisky sours and tom collinses. We smoked pot in the bathroom of the movie theater before we saw *The Muppet Babies*. When Dana's parents went away to bring her older sister to college, Liz and I slept over. We pulled down the shades, drank beer, smoked cigarettes and pot, and took the train into the city at 2 a.m. to buy pretzels on Seventh Avenue. We also rode our bikes to the Bay almost every night after dinner, pretending we were on the shore of France, or England, or Spain. Liz and Dana would take off their shirts in the twilight and ride with just their bras on, though I was never that nervy.

While Liz and Dana were similar in rowdiness and spunk, Dana and I shared a common interest in men. Since we were both tall we were often mistaken for being older than we were. Liz was much shorter and cuter — most of the time she could not pass for anything over her age, 15. Dana and I were competitive about attracting men. I think this was a phase propelled partially because Dana was a model and had met a lot of people who informed her about the power of her appearance. This mindset, along with the images thrust upon us by *Seventeen Magazine,* made us all think a lot about how we looked. Boys did like Dana more than they liked me, and it made me jealous, and I think that also put a competitive edge to our friendship. At that time Liz was not interested in flirting. Dana and my barhopping adventures in NYC made her feel excluded. She *was* excluded, to the extent that we were interested in men on a level that she was not — or could not be. Liz looked and acted too "childish" to even toy with going to bars and flirting with older men, and I know this bothered her even though she thought Dana and I were idiots to be so obsessed with appearances and men.

Dana actually had boyfriends. I didn't have a boyfriend until the middle of eleventh grade. During ninth and tenth grade my "love life" consisted of crushes. I can't believe now how many crushes I had on boys during junior high and high school. Reading my journal from that time period is amazing. I entertained thoughts of three or four boys simultaneously, and would write about my "progress" with each of them, in my journal: "Harry danced with me four times at the party. I always thought he was stupid, but maybe he's just shy." "I talked to Donald in Spanish. He gave me a piece of gum." "Sonny keeps touching me in lab." "I think Dan has a girlfriend." During ninth and tenth grade I didn't "go out" with anyone. My crushes on older, inaccessible guys always faded away after a few months. My crushes on guys my own age never amounted to anything either — perhaps because my crushes were on guys who were not yet interested in dating. I felt, however, that no one was interested in dating me because there must be something wrong with me. I was too tall. I was too fat. My hair was ugly. I was too loud. I wore weird clothes. Maybe I smelled.

I often felt uneasy about always "being good" when Liz and Dana went on stealing sprees or cut school, but I consoled myself by thinking that I was often the only thing that stood between them and juvenile court. It did not make me feel too "out of it" when Liz and Dana were "bad" together. Men were much more intriguing and powerful than theft by the time we were 15 and 16. Because Liz felt she could not participate, or in a sense, win, when she competed, she often felt left out of conversations and men-meeting sprees. I think that Liz began to resent both Dana and me, and thought that we were silly and stupid for "acting like 21-year-olds." Often Liz would remind Dana and me of our age and complain that we were no longer any fun. Liz began to resent men as well. For her men became adversaries who challenged her for (and often won) Dana's and my attention.

Liz, Dana, and I differed greatly in our rebellions that summer. Liz and Dana waged all-out wars, fighting daily with their parents, running away, and stealing. Although I participated by lying to my parents, smoking pot and cigarettes, and going to bars, my "rebellion" was actually a period of intense internal confusion. On one level I felt good about my school work and social life and friends, and on another level, I knew I was an unattractive loser doomed to be controlled by my parents forever. I wanted so many things: to have fun, to be smart, to be free, and to be desired. It was a dramatic time of life—it was difficult to feel and want so much and to actually be so limited.

New friendships with women which I developed in college did not replace or mimic the relationships I had with Liz and Dana, but there are elements of sameness. I see my relationships with women as continuing to be places where I develop and define myself, where through interaction and shared experience I become more and more comfortable with who I am, where I have come from, and where my life is going. I am supported in these relationships; in them I feel comfortable and safe and loved.

In eleventh grade, I started really dating guys. My first boyfriend was an exchange student from Greece. He was very good-looking and charming—he brought me roses, champagne, and perfume. In some ways I loved to be with him; we went out to dinner and basketball games and movies. We took bike rides and made out. But after a while, his height (he was a whopping two inches shorter than me) and our lack of communication began to bother me. He really didn't speak much English—and I spoke no Greek. So we broke up. Even while I was going out with Evan I had a huge fixation on a guy a year ahead of me who just wanted to be friends, but he (I felt at the time) really led me on, led me to believe he did want to go out with me. By the end of eleventh grade I was pretty sick of having pointless crushes on guys.

During the summer before twelfth grade I met lots of guys and went out on a few dates here and there. At the end of the summer I started dating a friend of a friend's brother. He was older, very handsome and smart. He wanted to have sex with me, and he quickly moved (away from me) when he realized that I was not going to sleep with him. At the time I didn't really see this. I thought there was something wrong with me. Later that year I met another "older guy" at a dance club who I then dated for over a year. I really fell in love in that relationship. Don was very good for me and to me. He came from a background similar to mine, and was able to help me through difficulties with my family and friends. He was very understanding and sensitive. He did not push me (very much) about sex—he was pretty good about waiting until I was ready. We had lots of fun together, I think because we were both open and giving. We broke up mainly because he wanted a big commitment (like marriage) and I was still in my first years of college. I was learning different things. I wanted to become a person at least a little different from our parents and I felt that although he wanted to, he was just too hung up about life and his family. It just got too hard to reconcile what we both wanted.

In college lots of guys had crushes on me. I think it was because I was nice and friendly. I have a warm personality. This was fun for a while, and then it got to be a hassle to tell guys I only liked them as friends, etc. I actually felt, at times, eager to be in a relationship with a man to avoid having guys telling me they liked me. Perhaps the crushes reminded me too much of my own painful crushes—that I had begun to see as immature and selfish.

Now I am involved in a committed long-term relationship that really might go anywhere. . . . My wariness in this relationship (I think) stems from not wanting to "waste time." I guess I have learned lots of lessons about men and relationships through the difficulties I have had with them; but for a long time I felt pretty humiliated by my propensity to feel so much unwarranted feeling for guys who didn't *really* care about me.

My high school years seem incredibly far away. I feel as though I have grown a lot since high school, and I'm sure my growth has a lot to do with leaving home and making my life at college my own. Moving away from home has helped me to make decisions without needing my parents' approval. I have learned that they love me even if they don't agree with my decisions to live away from home with my friends for a summer, or go on a trip with my boyfriend. I think I've learned a lot from friends in college who have had family experiences very different from mine. I have also learned about myself, my identity, through the actual process of making decisions.

Because I have graduated from college this year, I am at another extended moment of indecision and anxiety about who I am and what I am going to do with my life. So maybe I shouldn't be writing about my adolescent feelings as though they are something of the past. I am still in the process of defining myself as my own person. However I now see this "self definition" more as a lifetime process that involves what I will do more than who I am. I feel confident that my life will straighten out. I don't spend days lying on my bed listening to the same song over and over. I've been through it all before. Life and love and sex are no longer great unknowns.

CASE 12

Loving Women

This author describes the evolution of her sexuality from childhood sexual play through heterosexual relationships to her present identity as a lesbian. She was close to her father, who encouraged her intellectual interests, until she finds that in junior high school she needs to discount her intelligence and shun academic success in order to be popular. The resulting breach with her father is never repaired and seems to be a turning point; if the price of a man's love is conformity to being what he wants you to be, she can live without it. Toward the end of high school her troubled boyfriend overwhelms her with his emotional needs and reinforces the sense of emptiness and not being fully understood in heterosexual relationships. In college she develops close platonic relationships with women in which she feels for the first time appreciated for her intellectual and emotional strengths. She finds that being comfortable with herself is most possible in intimate relationships with women.

When I think of my pre-adolescent years and who I was, I seem to remember myself being much the same as I am now. I remember the same moments of standing still, listing adjectives that located me in my world. I'm sure that my list changes, as my context has surely changed and shaped me with its changes. Yet I have remained remarkably similar in my method of taking stock. I start by sitting alone either in my bed with my fan or my clock, or outside on some type of rhythmically moving object — a swing or something. I like a regular beat. I first describe in detail, to myself, the physical surroundings and the time frame that I'm in. I guess it gets me into an observant framework.

After I establish the framework, I recount each of the relationships that are crucial to me at the time, usually concentrating on their expectations or perceptions of me and following with expectations or desires of my own. If I'm feeling strong joy, resentment, anticipation, or confusion, I try to list or chronicle the events or tensions that led to these feelings. If I think that I want to cry or scream, I definitely do it now — I find that I can't *really* cry spontaneously or in front of anyone else, unless it's my mom or my brother and I'm frustrated or angry—loneliness or heartbreak crying happens when I decide I'm ready for it. Finally, I think about myself as a part of a bigger structure—sometimes I ask myself if I'm believing in God at the time, and that varies. If I am, I first do the Catholic prayers that I learned growing up, very quickly, followed by a very slow analysis of them. For instance, I say, "Our father, who art in heaven, hallowed be thy name. Thy kingdom come, thy will be done. . . . Is God a father, is he like my father? Can He be in Heaven, is Heaven a different place from this one, how is it different? And is God's will what is done? Who is to know what He wills and how to do it, especially when it seems so improbable that everything priests say that God wills should actually be done?" It goes on like that, which is the only way that I can eke meaning out of it.

In the last few years, I've articulated to myself a direct challenge to my idea of God—that is, when I'm believing in God. I do not believe that God is actually a He. Now my mother thinks that I'm crazy to be so concerned with the male-oriented language of prayers. She tells me that I can, of course, imagine a genderless God. But this isn't really true, or at least it's not that simple. It's not just a product of intellectual acceptance of feminism and the fact that I've learned to criticize anything produced out of a patriarchal system. It's that I honestly can't pay attention to praying in any religious language that I've learned. I fall dead asleep at night when I try to pray in any form that I associate with Catholicism. And I'm sure that it's because I've incorporated the image of God as man—not a physical man like that trite grandfather image, but just someone who doesn't understand women, or at least me. Someone distant and very analytical and fair, but in a strident, formal way. I guess God just doesn't appeal much to me as "He" is constructed by the church.

My next step in the debriefing process is to bring it back into myself. I list the things that have always been true of me—most of them having to do with how I interact with others, but not all of them. I'm smart, I'm motivated, I'm eccentric, I'm honest (blunt), I'm caring. I'm high strung, I'm independent to the point (sometimes) of being selfish or claustrophobic or cold when pressured. I take stock of myself physically, describing myself as if I see me walking down the street. I end up with my mom and my dad—how I'm so like both of them and how I am also so different that they could not have anticipated how different I would be.

The first real memories that I have of myself outside of my familial role are based in what I remember of the descriptions and actions of my first best friend, Kelly. Apart from my family, who obviously contributed most to my sense of myself, she really shaped a lot of my view of me. She told me a lot about what she thought of me, but she also modeled attitudes for me, which I either absorbed or rejected. She introduced me to the idea of sex, of romantic relationships, and of physical maturation, all of which dramatically affected my own feelings toward approaching adolescence.

I met Kelly when I was in second grade, and the school that I moved into was a very small private school for girls. We had only thirty girls in our grade, and the academic and social roles were already well established when I came into the middle of second grade. These roles barely shifted in the six years that I attended the school, with the notable exception of Kelly's leading role in both areas. I don't remember how we established the best-friend-ship, but I do remember it happening almost immediately. I am pretty sure that it had to do with academic success. Kelly was the "smartest" when I got there. Within one or two weeks, I was her rival. She made the overtures, and we started an intense and very competitive relationship. We were always together, and we were always competing. We wrote plays, and we did extra math in our playtimes, racing with each other to finish the exercises.

Kelly told me once that I was smarter than she was, and it completely floored me. My immediate reaction was to protest vehemently that it was she who was the smarter, because I had always sensed a territorial tone and aggressiveness that had been the precipitating factor of our entire competitive dynamic. It seemed to me that our friendship worked on the premise that she was the dominant mind and I was her most worthy challenger. I was comfortable in the role. It was worthwhile to me to be second if it secured our friendship. A mutual friend told me that Kelly had said that she had always envied my intelligence — that she had always had to work harder than I did to end up at the same level. It made me feel displaced from the friendship all over again.

Kelly was the first person who made me aware that I was intelligent. She was the first person who showed me how dangerous intelligence, especially intellectual comparison and competition, can be to a friendship. She was also a positive precedent, however, for future friendships based on intellectual compatibility.

Kelly told me that I would get my period, which meant that I could have babies. She told me that I'd bleed a lot, uncontrollably, and that it would happen every six months and it would keep on for weeks. She told me that it would happen any day now (we were eight years old), and that when it did happen everyone would know because my breasts would get big and I'd have to wear a bra. I was incredibly distressed about all of this. I cried and cried and spent hours pressing my chest in to keep it from growing. I dreaded the blood and somehow I connected it to growing old and separating from my mom. I was too ashamed to tell her what Kelly had told me. Finally I had a nightmare and she figured out what had happened and then set it straight for me, trying to convince me that menstruation would be a wonderful event and that it probably wouldn't happen to me for a few years. I felt a little better, but never entirely confident that I would adjust to it all.

Kelly told me a lot about sex. In fact, she told me everything that I knew about it until late in fourth grade. Kelly's parents had given her some information about the actual act of intercourse early in second grade. I guess that they told her about male and female genitalia, which I already knew, but also about how intercourse actually works. They also told her that intercourse takes place in heterosexual romantic situations, and that they did actually have and enjoy sex themselves. This blew my mind.

Kelly explained to me all about the penis and the mature vagina and told me that I would definitely want a penis in my vagina, that I would have a boyfriend or a husband, and that this would be something I would do. She also explained something about being sexy, which was certainly nothing I had thought about before. She had all these old *Playboy* magazines from her Dad's closet which gave us very explicit ideas about both the act of intercourse and the sexy woman. I remember being very excited about all these pictures, but very sure that all of this was a big sin. Still, my admiration for Kelly and her vast knowledge won out over religious restraint and it became our secret fund of coveted information.

Kelly first suggested that we play games based on sex in third grade. She would always act the man's part—she'd be my boyfriend. I was supposed to be sexy and receptive, and she'd seduce me. We tried to switch it around, but that never seemed to work. In retrospect, I guess it was because Kelly was always dominant in our friendship. She made up the rules for these games, and she had to be the one to control their progress. We would lock the door to our rooms, take off our clothes and try to figure out how to pretend to have sex. We were really scared of getting caught, especially me.

Kelly publicized our expertise and her magazine store. We were already leaders among the girls, so we kind of started a trend. Third and fourth grades were the slumber party years, so Kelly set forth a slumber party game which became sort of routine. We would all get dressed and made up, designate judges, put on music, and have strip shows. These became more and more elaborate, despite the risk of parents figuring it out. That was the extent of it—we never got as physically close as Kelly and I did. There were some girls who were really into it, and some who weren't, but we all did it. I never let on that it was really exciting to me; I always acted nonchalant and waited for Kelly to suggest it.

In fifth grade there was a huge turn of events. The whole attitude of the class toward academic achievement changed dramatically. All of a sudden, with the increased attention to boys at other schools, a new *type* became popular. It was not at all cool to be smart, nor was it cool to be at all involved with teachers. It was cool to be making bad grades, to be disrespectful to teachers, to smoke and to drink. The best thing to do if one was smart was to deny it. To be "modest" — in other words — I deprecated myself constantly, in hopes of remaining popular. It was a constant struggle to continue to please myself and my teachers, which I wanted to do, and to please my peers. The main connection here is that Kelly refused to deny her intelligence and she remained openly assertive about what was important to her — pleasing her parents and teachers and making good grades. Everyone turned against her, and the weapon of choice was the accusation of lesbianism, which fit conveniently with everyone's newfound interest in boys. I was incredibly relieved when Kelly switched schools in sixth grade, because I had been afraid that she would tell them what we had done. She was a constant reminder of something I wanted to forget.

My self-image, although influenced in key ways by my peers in my early adolescence, was always colored by my perceptions of what my father thought about me. Throughout my childhood, my father was my role model. I remember spending a lot of time with him until I was about 8 or 9. He was funny, interested, and challenging for me during those years. He was always intent on hearing what I had to say and encouraging me to express my ideas. It isn't surprising that I imagined growing up and practicing medicine as he did, and he certainly did encourage me to believe that I could accomplish whatever I wanted. He told me that I was very intelligent when I was about 7 or 8 years old, and I understood him to mean that I was like him, that we shared a special and elite bond. I asked him how he knew, and he told me that he could tell by my ability to converse.

For as long as I could remember, we had had intellectual play — we worked together constructing plastic models of the human body, and he would take me to the lab on Saturdays so that I could work with the lab equipment to run experiments. I remember researching and writing a twenty-page report on the cell just for fun, to give him as a present. It was understood that I was to excel in school; he certainly ascribed to a competitive model of assessing academic success. He always knew which other girls in my class were my rivals, and he was very interested in my comparative analysis of all of our performances. My mother had a problem with this, and Dad and I kind of went underground with the commentary sessions, sort of forming an alliance against Mom, who clearly didn't understand the importance of all of these measurements. I was impressed by my father's obvious intelligence, and I trusted that he was absolutely right to push me as hard as he did. I felt no resentment at that time, only admiration. I think my father picked me out to succeed, to fulfill his hopes, and this is why he never harped on the negative impact that being female would have on my chances. I'm glad of that, even if I resented the extreme pressure, since I feel it gave me strength as a female that many of my female friends never developed.

My interests started to diverge from those of my father in fifth or sixth grade, when academic success or ambition became taboo for the girls in my peer group. In our setting, a small private girl's school, peer opinion was crucial, and deviants from the accepted trend were treated very cruelly. There were no alternative social groups in our class of twenty-five, so it was adapt or be absolutely miserable. The girls devised ingenious tortures, which really scared me into line. Name-calling, mostly, but sometimes they would steal lunches, or write on lockers, or call up the boys who would be, I supposed, appalled at these academic statistics.

The only acceptable reaction was public, intense self-deprecation and real deference to the loudest ringleaders (inevitably not those making good grades) in every extra-curricular group event. Sometimes, we were even required to cheat for them in tests and homework. Above all, tattling or visible signs of distress were reactions that were punishable by being ostracized from the group. I managed to stay in with the "popular" girls and, perhaps more amazing, to convince myself that I was happy at the school and in their group. I missed test questions on purpose, though never enough to seriously jeopardize my grade. I just wanted to avoid the announced list of A+ tests. I was really torn. I had always looked up to my teachers, and they liked me. And my father, of course, was fit to be tied. He sensed, as did my teachers, that I was purposefully decreasing my academic standards.

Over the course of these three years, my feelings about the kind of interaction I had always had with my father changed dramatically. Instead of enjoying the intellectual exchange, I shied away from it. I don't think my dad could understand why this happened. He's very "logical," very driven, and very emotionally distant. I never felt comfortable discussing anything personal with him; I felt he thought my friends were really silly and unworthy of his or my time. It wasn't until I switched schools in that first year of high school that we were able to reestablish any connection at all.

I had strong friendships in high school, but none of them had as much impact on my current view of myself as my first real "love" relationship. At the very end of my senior year of high school I became involved with Jason. It lasted throughout my first year of college, and it has conditioned my responses to love relationships since. I suppose, in retrospect, that it was very serious or intense, although it really crept up on me. I had always intended to avoid the dependence that eventually developed on his part, yet I seemed to miss obvious clues, or at least to avoid confronting them straight out.

Jason was two years older than me, and although I had been vaguely aware of him in high school, I never planned or even anticipated getting any more involved with him after he graduated. He initiated the dating, and when he came home for the summer, he avidly pursued both my time and my emotional involvement. Because I had just recovered from a breakup with a guy who didn't have the inclination to be committed at all, Jason's attention came as a welcomed change of pace. He was very charming, very attentive, very interested in my family, and very interested in finding out about things I enjoyed — books, plays, whatever it was that I wanted to do. Within a month we were together constantly, and he was saying that he loved me. I thought that I loved him too, although I knew that I was attracted to him because of the way that he felt about me. He came across as very glib, witty and carefree — people were drawn to him. I felt privileged to penetrate that act — as if that was what intimacy was all about. In a bizarre way, I was really attracted to the disturbed, depressed side of his personality, which often came out when we were alone; I loved feeling as though I could help him.

I felt like I was a crucial source of positive energy for him. He would confide in me — he was angry with his father; he was worried about the alcohol and drugs on which he depended; he couldn't see any positive future for himself post-graduation; he was convinced that he couldn't be happy on his own; he would rather die than be alone. I would listen to him cry, and I would tell him that there were things worth doing — emotional and intellectual. I would tell him that we would do them together, and that then he would be okay on his own. I guess that I started feeling stifled after this scene replayed over two months, but by the time I noticed a desire to spend time alone and the need to rethink the benefits of all these pursuits, I was already inextricably involved with Jason. I worried that he needed me to help him find some self-esteem. He had mentioned suicide enough for me to feel a heavy responsibility. Probably worse, nobody could believe the seriousness of his depression, since his carefree social demeanor was so well constructed. My mother and my friends thought that I exaggerated, and I knew that his friends would never believe it. It seemed completely impossible, since he was manic in public. This increased my sense of being isolated in a relationship which was only real to the two of us. I considered it selfish of me to want to be alone or away from him, so much so that I rarely consciously articulated the desire to do so. Instead, I just felt frustrated.

I made the decision to have sexual intercourse with Jason in the middle of that summer. I decided then that the intense attachment and need I perceived and felt must be love, or the strongest feeling that I was capable of at that point in my life. I discussed this in depth with Jason and also with one of my best girl friends. It was an extraordinarily difficult decision to make, especially because I knew that I would not be able to discuss it with my mother. Both of my parents are serious Catholics and had always taken a firm stand against premarital sex. I remember thinking that I might never be involved in something so serious again, although I don't remember thinking that I'd be involved with Jason forever. He did not directly pressure me to have sex with him, but he made it clear that he thought that sexual intimacy was a natural step in our already intensely developed emotional relationship. We went through God, sin, lying to my parents, birth control, and my fears about the actual act countless times. I went to Planned Parenthood with my best friend and cried the whole way home after the physical and the Pill lecture.

I definitely decided to have sexual intercourse because it seemed important to him. I had never been very involved in the sexual aspect of our relationship. I was completely alienated emotionally from the physical interaction, so I never really had any physical response worth mentioning. I certainly never had an orgasm, and he didn't ever ask if I had or, if not, why I hadn't. It never crossed my mind to care—I just assumed that the sexual dimension of the relationship wasn't important to me in itself. The actual act, which I had never really planned for, didn't impress me as very different from the foreplay stuff that we had been doing all along. I don't remember disappointment; I hadn't been expecting anything amazing. Intercourse seemed inconsequential compared to my reaction.

My response seemed completely bizarre to Jason, but to me it made complete sense. I kicked him out of my bed (my parents were out of town) and I started reading all of my old letters and journals from camp and high school. I played my favorite tapes and informed him that I wanted to cry alone. After he was gone, I cried about leaving my mom and my room and my high school routine. I cried about growing up, which I had never wanted to do. I didn't feel guilty then, although I knew that I had been rationalizing my way into a sexual relationship that I had learned was sinful. At the time, I just felt old. It wasn't horrible. It was just the event that I needed to release all of the separation anxiety that I was feeling before leaving home for college. It definitely didn't have much to do with Jason.

As soon as I left for college, Jason broke down. He called daily and cried on the phone; he was usually so drunk that I had to call his friends at home to tell them to go pick him up at the fraternity. So, feeling guilty about my responsibilities to Jason and the resistance it evoked in me, and simultaneously attempting to rationalize some sort of separation from him, I started in on myself with a guilt trip about my sexual relationship with him. I had nightmares about Hell and I told him that I wanted to break off the sexual aspect of our relationship, or at least the intercourse. He reluctantly agreed. The guilt culminated at Christmas time, when I decided that I should confess the whole thing before Christmas Day.

I hadn't been in a confessional since eighth grade, but I managed to drag myself in and tell the very old priest that I had had sex with my boyfriend. He said, "Fornication!?! How many times? Less than 50? You are very lucky that you have come for forgiveness, for you were going straight to Hell. Do you steal too?" Needless to say, I barely made it through the prayers, and when I emerged shaking, my mom asked me why.

I couldn't tell her, and that made me cry. The religious guilt served both to reinforce my sense of desperation to get out of the relationship and my anger at myself for arriving at that point. It gave me an impetus or even an excuse to leave Jason, even if it left me more confused about the place of sex within intimate relationships.

It took the rest of the year to get out of it. Jason wasn't willing to let me loosen it up at all; he definitely fought it. I told him that I would not see him until summer, when we would discuss it again. I started seeing someone else, which ended with him calling at all hours of the night to make sure that I was in my room alone. His friends called me to yell at me. I told him in May that I wasn't even willing to try to work it out over the summer. He pulled out every insecurity that he knew that I had and tried to throw them in my face. He took my confidences about my family — my fear that I was really selfish with them, even unable to move out of myself in dire situations when Mom (especially) really needed my support — and used them to retaliate. I remember him telling me that he was the best that I would ever have, that he knew that deep down I was too selfish to ever care for or love anyone, and that no matter who tried to tell me otherwise, he knew me better, and he knew the truth. I was afraid for a long time that he was right.

This relationship precipitated a screening process which is just starting to break down in my final year of college. I find myself unbelievably conscious of my own emotional independence, almost to the point of being incapable of sustaining any "love/romantic" — type relationships once they require a commitment. As soon as I detect any signs of a lover's "neediness," I start to back out of the involvement. I am reluctant to become involved with anyone who seems emotionally inconsistent; I'm very wary of tears or "melodrama." And I'm definitely reluctant to become involved with any men sexually. I like to have my physical space to myself — I have since refused any sort of cohabitation with my male lovers. I'm not sure how much of a correlation there is between my lack of interest in intercourse and the associations I have from its role in my relationship with Jason, but I'm sure that it is connected. Often that guilt which seems to be religion-based emerges in these situations. I think, though, that this guilt marks a reaction to being pressured by the men with whom I am involved, and from whom I would like to break away. I think that this guilt serves as an easier route away from oppressive relationships than confronting the claustrophobia I feel directly.

In the winter of my first year I took my first Women's Studies class. It was challenging, and it provided the first real professor-student contact that I had had at the college. I had been surprised at the distance I had felt from my professors first term. In high school, I knew all of my teachers well. I spoke often in some classes, depending on how the boys treated me. For my first term at my college, I hadn't spoken in class nor had I spoken to any of my professors outside of the classroom. The Women's Studies class was very small, discussion-oriented, and my professor insisted on seeing each of us in her office for conferences. She encouraged me to continue taking Women's Studies, and she gave me a sense of confidence about my academic work.

I also came into contact with some of the more active feminists on campus through the class. I began to be aware that there were women and some men on campus who were interested in the issues that interested me; I became somewhat involved in the counter-mainstream politics on campus, especially with (mostly white) women's issues groups. I also began to develop and articulate the unstated concerns, especially about stereotyping, that I had had during high school, and even before then. I learned more about feminist theory, and I developed a framework for the arguments I had always had with the way that I had been treated. I began to feel stronger, more concrete about my ability to be actively in discord with an institution or group or society that made me feel marginal. Looking back, I know that I depended a lot on rhetoric to develop this stronger stance; I don't think that issues of differences among women had made an impact on me then. But I know that it was a time of expansion for me, intellectually and socially. I knew that I had a lot to learn, but I was so excited that academics could offer me something that seemed to have to do with me and my experiences.

I still hadn't found a real group of peers with whom I felt comfortable enough to expand and act on these feminist issues. I was going to meetings, but I was still tentative and concerned about how to make personal connections with these very impressive but intimidating women. My best friend and roommate, Jane, was involved along with me, but we were both in a similar spot — reserved, shy, but very interested. The pivotal connection occurred my sophomore spring, when I took a history class on national liberation movements in Third World countries. I was grappling with issues of racism and cultural imperialism for the first time, which really complicated but expanded what I had been learning in Women's Studies classes that I had been taking. I remember being overwhelmed by the information; I was almost immobilized by the impact of information so radically different from anything in my world. I met Alexandra in this context. She was in the class, and she was very vocal and very intelligent. She was also beautiful, a physically engaging presence. The amazing thing about her was her ability to express all of the anger that I felt while also including all of the facts, and clear, pointed analyses of the situations. She clearly believed that she could channel all of her conviction into some effective action. As we were preparing to write our first paper, she asked me about how I was going to approach the question. We had an involved discussion, and we made plans to write the paper together at the computer center. I surprised myself at my own ability to debate with her; I think that I gained confidence because she obviously considered my thoughts intelligent and worth hearing.

That was the start of a very involved intellectual friendship. We spent the remainder of that class conferring over paper questions, our own questions, and questions raised by active members of the political left whom she knew. She was involved in feminist issues, but also very involved with the radical left of the international students association on campus. She constantly challenged me, and she constantly involved me in protest actions on campus. I made the transition that I had held back on for my first one and a half years — I became a visible member of the college's political left. I was nervous because it meant being recognized and often ignored or treated with hostility. Alexandra took me on as her protegé. She had such a sense of mission, and I was so impressed and awed by her, that I jumped into anything that I could be involved with.

At the end of that term, visible feminists were being harassed by "anonymous" hate mail from hostile conservative campus groups. Also, many women students had been sexually harassed in dorms, and while members of the women's issues group had heard about it through the grapevine, none of the incidents were being reported because there was no clear protocol or support system for these women. A group of us took these incidents to the college president and received little active response. So the group decided to sit in pairs, wearing gags, passing out statements about how women were silenced on campus when they tried to speak out about harassment. I was afraid to "sit in" in front of the fraternities, in the dean's office, and the ultra-conservative newspaper's offices, but because Alexandra encouraged me, I did it. I remember that she told me that I was brave, and I remember thinking that it was worth being petrified and being verbally abused to be in the middle of a direct, anti-authority action with her. I felt stronger and more effective than I had ever felt.

As my friendship with Alexandra progressed, we moved out of the intellectual somewhat. I realized that I was dying to be included in her personal life. If she called me to come over and hang out, I was thrilled. I loved listening to her talk about her women friends — they were entertaining, smart, politically impressive, and always involved in some scandal or other. I liked it when she confided in me about strains or stresses in her group; she thought I was perceptive and that I offered a good perspective on what she would tell me. But I hated it when she told me about her lovers. I didn't really formulate why I hated it then; I just felt frustrated.

Sometime over the course of my junior year in England I realized that I was infatuated with her. I got used to the idea of being attracted to, even infatuated with, a woman through trying to figure out why I felt so strongly about Alexandra. I knew that I wanted to be her confidante — her intimate friend. But as I tried to imagine what it would be like to be one of her most preferred friends, I also admitted to myself that that wouldn't be enough. I knew that I would still feel disappointed. I was both emotionally and sexually attracted to her; I couldn't separate those two impulses at all in my feelings for her. It was the sexual attraction that I uncovered slowly. It had not been a conscious element throughout the process of getting closer to her. Also, I had never related personally to lesbianism. I was interested in my homosexual friends, and I had been politically involved in gay and lesbian issues at my college. But I had never felt as if the word or concept *lesbianism* had anything to do with me. Part of this was, I'm sure, that I had never had any models. I never encountered a single person who was openly homosexual until I came to college. The only contact I had had was with Kelly, who was labeled *lesbian,* derogatorily, by our peers.

I came back from London into my senior year having decided, after thinking about Alexandra, that I would be open to a lesbian relationship if someone who interested me came along. This decision was monumental, for once I admitted it to myself, I developed a resolve that I knew would back me if I did get into a situation that seemed to require it. I was scared, but I was proud of myself for making this mental step. Since Jason, I had been involved with two other men, and both of my relationships with them ended similarly to my relationship with Jason. We would start dating, and in what seemed an inappropriately short amount of time, the men would be emotionally involved to a degree which seemed unwarranted, frightening, and claustrophobic to me. Also, the sexual aspects of these involvements, although not oppressive, were not crucial or even consistently satisfying for me. I liked these men a lot before I got involved with them — both were good friends with whom I had similar political and intellectual interests. Both were sensitive about my emotional and sexual needs, but I had the same feeling of distance and constraint that I had felt with Jason, only to a lesser degree that was not frightening, only frustrating.

After Alexandra, I decided that part of the reason that these relationships were occurring was that it was always a man with whom I was involved. I thought that the emotional nurturance that I was providing and rarely receiving had to do with a communication gap or a difference in emotional expectations somewhat rooted in gender. I hadn't had trouble in the numerous close relationships that I had had with women friends. I had two wonderful women friends with whom I could consistently communicate and reciprocate emotional needs. Then, Alexandra tilted the balance by introducing both a sexual desire for a woman combined with a real drive to be totally immersed in her life. I had the resolve; the mental preparation had occurred. However, I didn't think that I would get involved in a lesbian relationship at my college. The lesbian community here was so small, so catty, and so prominent that I couldn't imagine wanting to get in the middle of it.

I met Marie fall term. I had known that she was gay, although she had graduated and was somewhat removed from the lesbian undergraduate community. She was intelligent, experienced, and wise — she had been through so much more than I had encountered in my sheltered life. I was impressed at her strength and her self-possession. She was interested in me; I suppose she sensed that I was open to the idea of a gay relationship. We talked about it extensively, and she was amazed that I had mentally prepared myself before ever making any actual steps. We got involved in a romantic relationship, although I wasn't in love or in awe as I had been with Alexandra. We developed a close bond, and I concentrated on the differences that I perceived between this relationship and my previous ones with men. I felt that I had a sense of proximity, or sexual familiarity, that I had never had before. I attributed this to the fact that we were both women. We had a much more similar approach to sex than I had had with the men I had dated. I felt that sex was much less goal-oriented, much less alienating, and much less demanding. I was more comfortable about it than I had been, and I didn't experience the guilt repercussions that I had in the past. I never felt like I should feel ashamed for enjoying it. We had an easier time relating to each others' views about feminism and, more importantly, we had a better understanding about how to talk about things on which we didn't agree than I had had in past relationships with men. Instead of defensive or aggressive counteracting of my feelings, she was able to honestly set out how she felt, and I could usually find a correlating or analogous feeling in my experience. I was looking for something which could integrate a sexually satisfying relationship with the comfortable, open communication I had had with my women friends. I got closer to this with her than I had in the past.

However, after some time I felt constricted. I tried to confront this feeling with Marie because we had established an open channel of communication. Although we tried to work with giving me space while allowing for her desire to be with me often, we couldn't seem to find a resolution. It was really hard for me to face the feelings of claustrophobia again, when I had hoped that it would not recur if I were involved with a woman. But it did, and I think (in retrospect) that I have some understanding of why it did. First, it was very hard for me to integrate this relationship with the relationships I had established with my other women friends. My friends were initially very supportive, and in theory they were all prepared to accept that I had a woman lover. But Marie's obvious attention and possessiveness interrupted the well-established dynamic. My friends, especially my two closest friends, felt sad, jealous, and somewhat displaced. Instead of asking for support as I probably should have done, or even taking more time just to talk about Marie with them, I tried to play it down for them. I was constantly trying to compensate for my relationship with Marie. Of course I ended up denying any of my own need for support and also hurting these friends as they sensed that there was so much that I wasn't sharing with them. This took its toll on my enthusiasm for the relationship with Marie.

Second, and perhaps more disturbing, I felt some of that demand for intense emotional sustenance similar to what I had felt in previous claustrophobic relationships. I didn't think that I could handle what I perceived to be serious demands on my time, space, and emotional availability. I had to acknowledge that this pattern in my relationships was entirely due to me. However, it did teach me something about my own space and time limits and the importance of my friends as they affect my love relationships. I knew that I would have to be clear from the start about what kind of interaction made me feel threatened or constrained. Anyone with whom I would get involved would have to be able to deal with my wariness, which would probably require a lot of patience. And I would have to be very careful not to compromise my relationships because of my women friends, and also not to alienate my women friends from my relationships with women as lovers. Challenging, but worthwhile. I did feel that to become involved with women as lovers was a positive move. The feeling of proximity in both communication and sex convinced me that it was an important step in ascertaining what I want in a love relationship. I know that it doesn't bypass every relationship hitch. But it makes a positive difference for me.

The only really disturbing aspect of identifying myself as a lesbian is that I worry about my family. I have not told my parents or my sister, and although I did tell my brother, he has not given me any support or feedback. This decision has been a major turning point in my life — even though I worry about my family and sometimes about my future, I feel better about myself now than I ever have. I have learned a lot about my own needs, likes, and dislikes in both love relationships and friendships. I have a new relationship now, and I feel for the first time the ability to get over this pattern that has felt inevitable at times in the past. She is the first person with whom I have been able to relax and share space comfortably, and I feel that even though there is a strong physical attraction and emotional involvement, I am not threatened or claustrophobic. I think that this ease derives in part from an understanding of my limitations and also my abilities, mostly newfound, to be comfortable in an intimate emotional, communicative, love relationship. She is very independent, very motivated, and very concerned with listening to me and expressing herself clearly. She is able to cultivate an emotional side to a very comfortable relationship without setting up what I perceive as a need too great for me to handle. Also, I have learned how important it is to be straightforward and thorough with my women friends, especially Jane, my best friend through all of my college career. I really love her, and it has been hard to let her know that I will always be with her despite the fact that I will have women lovers. We have learned, however, that it is best to talk to each other about exactly how we both feel about our relationship and about our relationships with lovers, no matter how painful it may be. I think that the intimacy is worth the painful moments.

PART THREE

Challenges

Theoretical Overview

There exists within the field of adolescent research a controversy over whether adolescence is typically a period of storm and stress, of alienation and separation, or a more harmonious evolution in which positive feelings about self and family are extended into the larger realms of peers and society. The purpose here is not to debate these differing perspectives. Each has merit and accounts for the different individual circumstances and coping styles of a complex period of human development. One point of agreement in this debate is that, stormy or halcyon, adolescence is a period of major transformation of the physical and psychological self. Even under the best of circumstances adolescents travel an exquisitely poignant journey through difficult developmental terrain. Finding one's way would be challenge enough. But when the ground is continually shifting with the ongoing physical, emotional, and cognitive growth of this period, the journey becomes full-time work for most adolescents. Add to that additional challenges and one can see the outline of important risk factors for healthy development.

Our notion of "challenges" implies obstacles or special difficulties that must be negotiated in addition to all the more "typical" preoccupations of adolescence. These are important both because of what they tell us about adolescents' coping strategies in general, and because many adolescents face such challenges at some point. If we add up all the adolescents who must deal with such challenges as physical disabilities, serious illness, divorce, the death of a parent, sibling, or close friend, physical or sexual abuse, unwanted pregnancy, racism, substance abuse, or mental illness, we can see that significant challenges, whether acute or chronic, represent, if not the norm, at least a sizable subsample of all adolescents.

Each of the three cases included in this section represents a distinct challenge to healthy psychological growth at three different developmental periods: (1) a serious physical disability from birth, (2) a severe stutter and serious sexual abuse in early childhood, and (3) the emotional crisis surrounding an abortion in adolescence. Taken as a whole, these cases highlight both what is unique and universal, at least for Western culture: Unique, in terms of the specialized issues these problems raise for adolescent development; universal, in that the cases highlight the way in which the tasks of adolescence remain relatively constant even in the face of powerfully destabilizing events. The emergence of adolescence represents both a difficult context in which to bring preexisting problems, and a new opportunity for overcoming some of the more debilitating psychological effects of these issues.

Self-understanding is one of the more important aspects of emerging adolescent abilities for overcoming serious challenges. Prior to adolescence, childhood is characterized by the embeddedness of the child in his or her family and the strong tendency, whether for better or worse, to identify with persons and norms within the family. The increasing importance of the peer world and the simultaneously evolving capacity to see parents as less powerful and more fallible are conducive to a loosening and diversification of earlier identifications. This capacity facilitates the healing that can occur through important substitute relationships such as teachers, mentors, peers, and families of friends. Such healing may be necessary when families have not been sufficiently nurturant, protective, or enhancing of self-esteem. While these family relationships may be important at earlier periods, the adolescent can now, through the eyes of those important others, see new possibilities for himself or herself and adjust his or her persona and behavior accordingly. There has long been recognition that this emergent ability to gain self-knowledge through interaction with others—this "looking glass self" (Cooley, 1902; Mead, 1934)— helps explain why positive relationships can have such a restorative effect on the damage of earlier events. This "mirroring" becomes especially salient in peer and romantic relationships during this time (Sullivan, 1953; Erikson, 1968) as the adolescent learns to take a perspective on himself or herself by gradually modifying the self-image he or she sees reflected in the eyes of peers.

Self-understanding has been shown to be an important "protective factor" (Beardslee, 1989) in ameliorating the risk to healthy psychological development from serious life stressors. Ideally, self-understanding should lead to action that transforms one's adaptation to circumstances, or changes the circumstances themselves. It is only when insight leads to new and better means of coping with life's challenges that we can say the individual is rising to the challenge. Indeed, insight without action can reflect a profound sense of hopelessness. The cases presented here all reveal the adolescent biographers to be reacting to serious stress by developing insight and then taking steps to make things better.

There is an emerging field within developmental psychology devoted to studying individuals who are *resilient* or seemingly *invulnerable* to serious risks and stresses that have been shown to affect negatively the mental health and long-term adjustment of many children. This new field represents a significant historic shift from studying almost exclusively those individuals who succumb to developmental risks to those who are equally exposed but who overcome the risk and remain healthy. Among factors shown to place children at risk are: serious mental illness of a parent, physical or sexual abuse, serious marital discord, poverty, emotionally unsupportive relationships with parents, foster-home placement, and parental alcoholism (Rutter, 1975, 1979; Werner, 1989). While different studies find differing degrees of relative risk for each of these and other factors, it does appear no single risk factor is determinate. Rutter's studies mentioned here found that, when only a single risk factor was present, the probability that a child would suffer from a psychiatric disorder was no greater than for a child in a family without any of these risk factors. However, two risk factors produced a fourfold increase in the chances of a psychiatric disorder in the child; four risk factors produced a tenfold increase in risk. It would seem that most children can cope with a certain amount of stress stemming from these risks, but when overloaded with multiple stresses, they become exponentially more likely to succumb. Many children and adolescents, however, do not succumb even under such stress. And therein lies a hopeful avenue for understanding how some children are protected, or protect themselves, against the vicissitudes of serious stress. And we might speculate that, whatever these protective coping mechanisms are, they are promotive of good mental health in general and could be helpful even in low-risk individuals.

Three of the most important protective factors appear to be (1) personality features such as self-esteem, (2) family cohesion and lack of discord, and (3) external support systems that encourage and reinforce the child's efforts to cope (Garmezy, 1985; Masten & Garmezy, 1985). Protective factors are not fixed attributes; they are subject to development or reduction over time within the same individuals, and those that may aid in coping at one time may not work at another. Thus these factors should be seen as dynamic; the resilient individual is one who can adapt his or her coping strategies to changing situations. In this sense, protective factors should not be seen as fixed traits of the individual or circumstance, but rather as interpersonal and interactive. This is what Rutter (1987) refers to as protective *mechanisms* or *processes* that the individual may apply or modify as needed.

The cases that follow reveal a variety of risks and developmental vulnerabilities, as well as a number of protective coping mechanisms. These mechanisms are employed to secure important emotional needs, and with development these needs themselves undergo transformation. For example, in *Forever an Awkward Adolescent* our physically challenged autobiographer describes how he used to experience closeness with his father by allowing him to do virtually everything for him, including helping him dress each morning up until high school. He states that as adolescence and his desire for independence emerged, better late than never, he began to insist that his father restrain "his legendary penchant for interfering." His need for independence, however, didn't obliterate his desire for closeness with his father; it caused him to redirect it along more age-appropriate lines, like shared ideas and interests. We can see how the developmental tasks of adolescence, here for greater autonomy, have similar transformative effects on parent-child relations for a severely disabled adolescent as they do for any other. The difference is that it is adapted to those particular circumstances. For an unchallenged adolescent the same task of autonomy might lead to a demand for greater privacy or a right to choose his or her own clothes.

In addition to the press of developmental tasks, our autobiographer's coping is enhanced by the remarkable self-understanding he demonstrates in his attempts at adaptation. He repeatedly stresses his own responsibility for his adjustment and happiness and the need to find some means of "fitting in" with his able-bodied peers lest they give up trying to relate to him and leave him to his " 'default' pigeonhole . . . of a short, oddly postured disabled kid." And he writes repeatedly of having to create "a persona I could live with" by mirroring himself in the eyes of his peers. This search for identity by means of acceptance and validation by his peers is another important task of adolescence. Thus he demonstrates the interaction of developmental tasks and protective factors, here identity formation and self-understanding, respectively, which together serve to compensate for the risks of isolation and dependence his physical disabilities represent.

In the case of a sexually abused adolescent, *The Simple Beauty of a Conversation,* we read how a severe stutter during childhood and adolescence (which may or may not have been related to his abuse) devastated his self-esteem and his relationship with his parents. This devastation had a profoundly negative impact on his social relations. But the functional needs and possibilities of adolescence propelled him into new relationships—warm mentors at work, and an accepting and affirming girlfriend—which gave him belated self-confidence to overcome the more debilitating effects of his stutter and abuse. In this sense, the functional tasks of adolescence became for this young man more than something merely to be achieved on the road to adulthood; they became his single most important opportunity for redressing the developmental damage incurred in his childhood. Each phase of life, therefore, not only provides extra obstacles for adolescents with special challenges, but also represents a fresh chance to redirect the inexorable movement that phase will require. His ability to seek and utilize the support and encouragement of adult mentors, as well as his self-understanding, are the protective mechanisms that may account for his resilience against the vulnerabilities from his abuse and speech problem. These mechanisms and the developmental task of romantic intimacy that emerge in adolescence combine here in a powerful protective partnership.

The two cases just mentioned represent long-term challenges, whereas the case concerning adolescent abortion, *Proud of the Strength I Had,* involves an acute crisis that results in an extended period of depression, anxiety, and guilt feelings. The resulting effect on this autobiographer's self-esteem, attitude toward sexuality, and capacity for intimacy represent risks to her healthy transition to adulthood. A variety of studies find that many women who undergo abortions experience periods of depression, regret, and guilt (Cvejic, Lipper, Kinch, & Benjamin, 1977; Ford, Castelnuovo-Tedesco, & Long, 1971; Smith, 1973), but that these feelings are typically mild and abate in the short term without negatively affecting general functioning. Other studies have found that the primary response to abortion is relief (Adler, 1975; Ewing & Rouse, 1973; Monsour & Stewart, 1973), and that in the case of adolescent abortion in particular it "is neither psychologically harmful nor in other ways damaging to the patient" (Olson, 1980, p. 440).

However, adolescents are found to have somewhat more negative emotional responses than adult women, though not severely worse (Adler, 1975; Bracken, Hachamovitch, & Grossman, 1974; Margolis, Davidson, Hanson, Loos, & Mikelson, 1971; Payne, Kravitz, Notman, & Anderson, 1976). This seems to reflect the experience of our autobiographer who describes somewhat more lasting negative feelings. Perhaps because she was a middle-adolescent at the time, she was unable to fully anticipate her sense of loss and to prepare for it psychologically as older adolescents appear better able to do (Hatcher, 1976). The inherent stress of an unwanted pregnancy in adolescence was exacerbated by this writer's sense of betrayal and isolation; her former boyfriend offered no support other than to pay for the abortion, and she felt unable to tell her parents or even her twin sister. She describes how this crisis led to her later participation in a college support group for other students who had terminated pregnancies. The emotional catharsis and gradual understanding of her feelings led to active participation in reproductive-rights events and close friendships with other women who shared the same experience. We can see here the integration of self-understanding and action as central to her eventual success in managing this stress and recovering from her depressed feelings. This emerging insight also brought into focus her family's inability to communicate emotionally and her determination to redress this constriction of her own emotional openness. When her younger sister thought she might be pregnant, our author took this opportunity to soothe her own feelings of isolation and abandonment by providing the type of support she wished she had. Thus the opportunity to reflect on the linkage between how she became pregnant—"not being able to talk about sex and contraception" with her boyfriend—and her family's emotional silence—"I grew up in a family that stuffed their feelings and never talked about anything, including sex"—led to an important self-understanding about the ways she wanted to change. This crisis illuminated an underlying and ongoing challenge to her happiness—her family's dysfunctional emotional communication.

The developmental vulnerability of an unwanted pregnancy is itself reflective of the adolescent tasks of balancing intimacy, identity, and sexuality. In this case we can witness the painful beginnings of learning how to develop and employ protective mechanisms—sharing intimate feelings with trusted friends, providing the type of support to others she now knows she needs, searching for an ideology that gives meaning and purpose to her experience, and actively identifying with other women who assert their feelings. Her moves in this direction are tentative, but she seems to have a solid understanding of the cause of much of her unhappiness and the means of redressing it. Similar to the lessons of the other cases, the challenge to her emotional development is met by interaction of protective mechanisms and developmental tasks.

These cases reveal much about the opportunities of adolescence for growing stronger through challenge. Unfortunately, not all such challenges are met so successfully. However, these autobiographies are representative of the reality that most adolescents who face such circumstances do somehow find a path to productive lives. The following cases give us an intimate look at how it might be done.

CASE 13

The Simple Beauty of a Conversation

This author's shocking discovery of his speech impediment in first grade leads him to feel insecure and self-conscious regardless of academic and social accomplishments. His "identity as a stutterer" makes him give up in school, because it is "easier not to attempt something than to fail at it." He plagiarizes and cheats his way through high school without being caught, as much a rebellion against his parents as a way of getting by. His religious faith, a close friendship, and his work in the library help him through some of the most difficult years, providing support and contributing to a growing sense of himself as a valued person. He experiences a setback when, early in college, his girlfriend is raped, an experience that causes memories of his own early sexual abuse to surface for the first time. He feels like a stronger person now, "standing on his own two feet." His stutter reappears only occasionally, reminding him of the difficulties each of us has in our lives.

As I started high school many teachers and friends held high hopes for me, but by the end of my senior year there was a question as to whether I was going to graduate or repeat the year. My academic problems did not all stem directly from my learning problems. The most accurate description would be to say that I was burned out. I desperately wanted someone to recognize that I was having problems and to offer help. That never happened and I continually failed at all attempts to get myself on track. It became easier not to attempt something than to fail at it. I could see no future for myself. I never even tried to think about what I wanted to do after graduation. I couldn't handle the present, so trying to plan my future was an impossibility.

I got by the best I could. High school was very painful and difficult for me, and as a way of protecting myself I pretended that I didn't care about the school or my classes. If I had let myself feel that high school could be a very positive experience for me if I was successful, then the pain would have just been worse. I did very little homework, cheated on almost every test, plagiarized all my critical papers, and skipped school as often as I could get away with it.

I need to go back to my early childhood to explain all the problems I had with school. At the age of 5 I went through kindergarten. I enjoyed it and as far as I knew I was just like all the other kids. However, I found out that while all my other friends were going on to first grade, I was going to go to another kindergarten class. No one ever explained to me why I was repeating kindergarten. When I got to the new class I was with a bunch of other kids who were pretty normal. For 1 hour a day, however, I was taken aside with a special teacher who came to the class just to work with me. I didn't mind because I remember thinking she was pretty. She would show pictures and ask me to tell her what I saw. For example she would show me a picture of a dog and I would say, "dog."

"No, that's not right. Try it again," she would often say.

I had no idea what I was doing wrong. The picture was very obviously a picture of a dog and as far as I knew I was saying the word "dog." This would happen with pictures of trees, cats, farm animals, and many other simple items. I would tell her what it was and she would say, "No, try again." She never told me what I was doing wrong.

The other kids in class must have picked up on what was going on because pretty soon they all started calling me names like "retard" and "moron." I didn't understand this either. I went home crying to my mother one day and asked her why I was being called these names. I can remember the most pained expression I have ever seen come to her face and she said simply, "Because they're not very nice children."

I made it through that year in pretty good shape, all things considered. In first grade the same teacher came to see me every day again. We would go to a small office in the basement and do the same things we did in kindergarten. I know it was unintentional, but one day she did one of the most cruel things I have ever experienced. I went to see her that day and we went through the same routine. This time, however, she had a tape recorder. She recorded the answers I gave to the pictures. Then she rewound and played the tape back to me. I'm not even sure how to describe my reaction to the tape. I was about 6½ years old and like every other little kid I wasn't all that self-conscious or worried about the differences between myself and other kids. But that tape crushed me. The voice I heard was absolutely unintelligible. The voice was stuttering terribly and all the pronunciation was completely off. I couldn't even recognize what it was saying. The voice didn't even sound human. I was sure that I had said "dog" but when the tape got to the point where the word should have come, something completely foreign, not even resembling "dog," came out. I started crying and screaming, "That isn't me! You put another tape in there! That isn't me!" She couldn't calm me down.

I guess everybody assumed I was aware of my speech problems because they were so severe. At the very least I must have been aware of my stutter. But I wasn't aware of it at all. As I've said, no one, my parents included, had ever talked to me about it before.

That tape had an immediate effect on me. I became very withdrawn and would hardly talk to anybody. I particularly avoided talking to my parents both because I didn't want them to hear me speak the way I did and also because I felt betrayed; I wanted to hurt them with my silence. That might sound like a lot for a 6 year old but it is very true. Everything that had happened — staying back in kindergarten, the special teacher, all the kids making fun of me — became clear to me and I became very bitter towards my parents for having never talked with me about it. I really hated them. Over the next 10 or 11 years I spent much of my time finding little ways that I could hurt them and get back at them for the way they had failed me.

My relationship with school didn't fare much better. Soon after the tape was played to me, the special teacher told me that she was transferring and that we wouldn't be working together any more. I have no idea if the tape incident had anything to do with her decision, but I am sure now that it did play a part in my parents' decision not to get any more help for me. They couldn't deal with the pain, and I think they felt that the best thing to do was to ignore my problems and hope they would disappear with age. So I no longer went to any special classes. In the regular classes I did everything I could to keep from having to speak in front of the class. I didn't want the other kids to hear how I talked. Through the rest of grade school every teacher I had just about killed himself or herself trying to get me to apply myself more. They all felt I had great potential if I would be more outgoing. I resisted all these efforts. While my pronunciation improved somewhat, my stutter had not improved at all by the time I entered junior high.

It is very difficult to discern how much my stutter affected my image of myself and how much it affected others' image of me. Trying to look back objectively, I would say that for the most part it had its greatest influence on my own self-image. When I was growing up it sometimes seemed that everybody was laughing at me and pointing me out, when in reality probably only a few did so. There are some events that make me realize now that my friends and classmates must have held me in fairly high regard. In the fourth grade I was elected class president. In sixth I was given awards for sportsmanship, leadership, and math ability. In the seventh grade I was chosen as the "Most Intelligent" out of a class of about 150. Still, these did very little to raise my self-esteem, so sensitive was I of my stutter. The effect of these positive reinforcements was minimized to the extreme by my self-consciousness. The only identity I had for myself was as a stutterer. None of my other accomplishments came close to having the effect on me that the fear of stuttering and speaking incorrectly in front of others did. I felt that no one else knew who I really was because I had become so proficient at hiding my speech problems. I saw myself as hiding who I really was from others. To some extent this was true.

In junior high my self-esteem reached its lowest point. My outlook on everything was dictated by my view of myself. I built a reputation at school for being able to get away with cheating, skipping classes, forgery, and other things like that. During lunch at school a lot of kids would come to me looking for help. I'd make a cheat sheet, sell an essay, or do whatever the occasion called for. This was my first niche in junior high and freshman year. It was fun at first because it was novel and it got me a lot of attention. Sometimes it was more innocent and sometimes it was of a much more serious nature. For example, I went through the honors English sequence in high school and plagiarized almost every critical essay I was assigned to write. Some other students were caught doing this but I never was. I learned how to choose obscure, yet valid, sources and how to change things around just enough so that there was very little chance of getting caught. I cheated on almost every test I took and spent a minimal amount of time on homework.

I was shy with girls and doing things like this created opportunities to talk with them. This was very important. I've been attracted to girls as long as I can remember. My first kiss was in kindergarten — the second year that is. I was embarrassed afterwards and I was afraid the girl would start telling the other kids that I had kissed her, so a couple of days later I went back to her house and beat her up, which sounds worse than it was. I had my first opportunity to have sex when I was in the sixth grade. The girl was in the eighth grade and I'm pretty sure she was drunk. We were behind some bushes in the church playground across from my house. She came over to me and took off all her clothes. She kept saying, "Come on over and lay me." I had never done more than kiss a girl at that point and I didn't know what "lay me" meant. I went over to her and she stuck her hand down my pants. I ejaculated as soon as she touched me. She laughed at me and said she wanted me to do that again but this time while I was "porking" her. I didn't know what that meant either. To be honest, I had no idea what to do at all. We fooled around for a while but we didn't actually have sex because I didn't know what to do. She kept laughing at me the whole time. I put my clothes back on and left her lying in the bushes. Immediately after this experience and for the next few days, I felt awful. I was cold and shivering all the time and I couldn't stand to have anyone closer than a few feet away from me. I didn't understand why I felt this way but then I didn't understand anything to do with sex at that time.

I went through puberty at an early age. By the end of the sixth grade I had had a couple of wet dreams and I was masturbating often. The incident with the first girl made me curious about and interested in girls. A friend and I used to climb trees in our backyards together. It started a few years earlier as an innocent childhood pastime and we just kept on doing it. One late afternoon during the summer after sixth grade, we were sitting up in the tree talking quietly when we saw a light go on in my neighbor's house. It was the bedroom of a girl who was about a year older than we were and who was my sister's friend. My friend said to me half jokingly, "Wouldn't it be awesome if she changed and didn't pull her shade down?" I agreed of course, but we really didn't expect anything. But then she did change into her bathrobe without pulling down the shade. We sat for a while without saying anything. I think we were both embarrassed to talk or to move because we both had erections and didn't want the other to know.

One day later in the summer the girl we spied on, Jean, stopped by to see if my sister was around. I was home alone that day and told her so. She came in for a while anyway and we started talking. I got an erection and since I was wearing my bathing suit it wasn't long before she noticed, although I tried to hide it as best I could. At first I was embarrassed, but pretty soon we started talking dirty. We kept daring each other to say dirtier and dirtier things and to shift our clothes around to reveal more. Eventually we went into the shower and I lost my virginity. I think it was her first time also, but I'm not sure.

The time in the shower felt pretty good to me but I don't think Jean enjoyed it very much. She looked like she felt very guilty. Nevertheless she started coming over often when I was alone. We fooled around and tried a lot of things. She must have known more than I did because I really didn't understand how girls got pregnant, but after the first time in the shower she never let me penetrate again. Instead we did other things. At the time we did it I liked it, but I always felt dirty after she had left. Every time we fooled around she would ask for a few of my father's beers to take back home (he never kept track of them). One day she came over with a *Penthouse* and read some of the letters to me. She said she would try those things if I could get her a full bottle of wine. My father had one and I gave it to her. I had heard about prostitutes in church and what it meant if you got into that stuff. I started thinking that what we were doing was almost the same thing. I had a terribly guilty conscience, but every time she came over the same thing would happen.

There was something more than just a guilty conscience though. I couldn't bear having people being physically close to me. If I ever was in a crowd, such as in a mall, I would get lightheaded and have dizzy spells. I also hated to have anyone stand behind me. If I was in any line I would stand a little off to one side to prevent people from being directly behind me. I thought that maybe these feelings had something to do with what Jean and I were doing but I didn't understand them.

When school started again, Jean stopped coming over. We never talked about what we had done again and I think both of us really wanted to forget it. I have never bragged about these experiences to anyone. There are just too many painful feelings and too much confusion connected with it for me to be able to talk about it lightly. As a Catholic I felt what I did was morally wrong, and then there were all those other feelings which I couldn't figure out. In college I told the first girl I slept with that I was a virgin. She said she was too (and she was probably telling the truth) and that it made it more special because it was the first time for both of us. I've only slept with one other girl since, and I told her that my only experience was with the other college girl. Right now I just don't feel comfortable letting anyone know about what happened.

After the summer with Jean I entered junior high school. That's when most kids start dating, but I became very shy with girls. I knew what sex was like but I had a lot of trouble talking to girls. Each day I was becoming more and more self-conscious about my stutter; I felt that no girl would ever go on a date with a guy who talked like I did. As a result I didn't have any dates in junior high or high school, although I did begin to talk to girls more. I had other problems then as well. I've mentioned what my academics were like. My grades were respectable but they were not earned honestly. My parents and I were moving further apart. About the only time we ever talked was when we were fighting.

As a result of my problems with my family and in school, I needed to find a place I could find some solace and security. Actually, I found three areas: religion, friends, and work. I was raised in a fairly strict Catholic manner. My mother took me to church every Sunday and we fasted before and after mass. I went to classes preparing me for all the sacraments and attended service on every holy day. Sometimes the tedium and monotony of these rites would get to me but overall I have always been a religious person. Often prayer and hope for the future has been the only outlet I have had when times have been really bad. I have never had a serious question about my belief in God and the scriptures, and for most of my life I have prayed every day. While my religion is and always has been an important part of my life, I have often questioned the attitudes of the Catholic Church itself. Nevertheless, I do have strong faith and I try to follow as best I can the teachings of forgiveness, forbearance, and humility. I take pride in my faith.

When I was a sophomore in high school, a priest in my parish, a person whom I really admired, came to me and tried to convince me to enter the priesthood. I actually considered this for a time. In the end I decided against it. But that is not the significance of that incident. This was the first time that someone I really admired let me know he saw some value in me. He was seeing good in me that I couldn't see myself. It had a profound effect on me. I didn't turn myself around in a day because of it, but I did have my first thoughts of where I was going and the person I was as opposed to the person I was capable of being. These were brief, very scattered thoughts but the seed had been planted. It was the encouragement of other people like him that helped me learn that many people saw me in a better light than I saw myself. I had very little self-respect so I had to get it from others, most of whom have been very religious. At least they are religious in my estimation of how the religious should be; they practice their faith and they show their belief in how they treat other people rather than by preaching to them. And they are secure enough in their faith that they can accept faiths that differ from their own. I have a lot of respect and admiration for these people. I learned from them that a strong belief in the self often goes hand in hand with a strong belief in a set of principles and precepts.

The Catholic Church requires public worship and professing of faith, but I was always very private about it. In that sense I made a poor Catholic. In fact, along with most of my friends, I denied holding any beliefs. I made jokes about the church and about older adults who were very religious. It's also true that I outwardly denied my faith because my mother was Catholic and worship was an integral part of her life. I didn't want to be anything like my parents, and it was a form of rebellion. But, still, inside I found it a source of comfort and hope. As I grew older I started understanding the readings at Mass more and saw that they could be applied to my life. I often looked at myself as a modern day Job. I suffered through trials and hardships as a test of my faith. Not only my faith in God but also my faith in myself and my ability to keep hope alive in my breast and work for something better. I had occasional thoughts of suicide, and three times I made concrete plans to go through with it, but there was always something inside that wouldn't let me give up on myself. Religion helped add to my sense of identity, but that still wasn't enough. There was only so much I could get through my private contemplations and beliefs; I needed experience on a more social level.

This leads to the other two areas — friends and work. I had enough friends that I didn't feel like an outcast, but I had only one really close friend, the one who was my peeping-Tom partner. The two of us had met when we were 5 and had been best friends ever since. The strength of our friendship cannot be overstated. We never pressured each other into doing anything (like trying drugs) and we could share our secrets and problems. My friend, Bill, had a much better relationship with his family than I did, so I adopted his family as my own in a way. I didn't look up to or respect my parents, but I did his. Their opinions had more weight with me than my own parents' opinions. I don't mean to imply that my mother and father were failures as parents, but I held hard feelings against them and looked to Bill's parents for guidance.

Bill and I did everything together. We liked the same shows and music and hung out together all the time. In fact, it wasn't uncommon for teachers and other kids to get the two of us mixed up. There was a great amount of security in that relationship for me. I felt that Bill accepted me for who I was; he was the only person who I wasn't afraid to stutter in front of. Bill and I were (and still are) blood brothers. When we were very young, probably 7 or 8, we slit our thumbs with a knife and rubbed our bleeding fingers together. I assume that isn't done much today. We took everything from swimming lessons to guitar lessons together.

Our parents all worked and much of the time we were left to ourselves. During the summer we spent most of every day unsupervised. Some of our activities were questionable. For example, there was the summer that a moose was spotted in our town. A moose had not been seen in our town for over a hundred years so the news stirred up some fear along with the curiosity and fascination. Only a handful of people had seen the animal, and it was assumed that it had just moved on out of town. One afternoon Bill and I came up with a brainstorm. Our local paper had carried a picture of the tracks left by the moose so we cut that out. Next we got some wood and cut out models that resembled the prints. We tied the models to the bottom of our sneakers and walked in the backyard. Sure enough, we left tracks in dirt that were very similar to those in the picture. The next few nights we snuck out of our houses and went to the swampier areas of town. We put the moose feet on the bottom of our sneakers and walked in the mud of several backyards. A couple of days later we read in the paper that the moose was back and, the paper said, it was possible now that there was more than one. The police had been placed on alert. Aside from our terror of being found out by the police, we loved the whole episode. We had fooled the adults again.

The two of us did everything together and continually made future plans. In the long run this may have come close to hurting me; I relied too much on Bill's friendship and didn't try to be more outgoing and build my confidence. On the other hand, if I hadn't had Bill and the security of our friendship, I never would have learned how to function well socially.

The summer before high school I got a job at the town library, and I was excited about starting work. I had spent a lot of time at the library (it was very close to my house) and I knew several of the librarians. My immediate boss, Mrs. Johnson, turned out to be one of the most special people I have ever met. She was kind, friendly, intelligent, always quick to praise but also ready to point out mistakes in a constructive way, and an all-around lovely person. She could discern everybody's personality. She must have known that I needed a place where I could feel I belonged because she soon gave me many important responsibilities that were within my capabilities. This helped my confidence tremendously. I felt everyone there wanted to see me succeed, and when I made mistakes they treated them as very minor in comparison to all the other things I had done right. It wasn't long before I was working very hard at my job. I would do everything they wanted done — and more if I could find other little jobs. If they needed someone at an awkward time on short notice, I always volunteered. At first it was simply that I wanted Mrs. Johnson and the others to keep giving me praise and that their good opinion was very important to me. Eventually, though, I began to realize that to do a task with integrity and diligence was important and was its own reward. Before working at the library I had never felt what it was like to accomplish something that I had spent much time and effort doing. There was great satisfaction in it. It was a long time before I applied this to schoolwork, but that would come.

I worked at the library for about 6 years. It's hard to summarize all I learned and all the feelings connected with the library and the staff, but there are a few key points. First is the dedication of the staff. Many of the full-time employees held a Master's degree in Library Arts and yet were making under $22,000 a year. They unfailingly did their best to work for the community in what was often a shamefully thankless capacity. I admired their dedication. I felt I wanted to emulate that, and often now when I feel I'm unfairly overloaded with work and responsibilities I think of those people and remember that I should appreciate what I have going for me. The other staff — the part-timers, custodians, and such — were the same. They all did their jobs well and created an enjoyable atmosphere for everyone. Sometimes I wondered how so many good people could be concentrated in one small place. Maybe I'm a naive optimist but I came to the conclusion that it was the atmosphere, the congenial and supportive feelings around us all that was responsible for it. Most people have it in them to be their best but the circumstances surrounding them are not as favorable. And where did this atmosphere come from? I think it came from Mrs. Johnson and a couple of others there who were much like her. They were very supportive, generous, and kind to everyone, and so everyone else began to emulate and encourage this attitude. I don't know how well I have succeeded, but I have tried to hold this attitude and to project it to those I come into contact with. I've learned that how you treat people can really make a difference. Sometimes a kind word from the right person at a certain time can make all the difference in the world.

Another aspect of the library that was very important to me were the patrons, whose questions and requests for help had a great influence on me. I felt I held a certain power. If I knew the answer to a question, then I could solve a person's problem. Perhaps if a person was particularly nasty I could purposely misdirect that person (I never did that but I was aware that I held the power). It really built my confidence. I was given certain responsibilities and I was living up to them. This was something I couldn't find in school.

After a couple of years of working at the library, I noticed that many people recognized me outside of the library. For a very shy person this really fed my ego. One of my favorite memories happened right in the library. A mother brought her little girl to check out some children's books. The girl was no more than 3½ years old. She could walk and talk only a little bit. Her mother sat her on the counter as I checked out her books. I was talking to the girl like I usually did with little children; I asked if she enjoyed reading or if her mother read her stories at night. When I was done checking out the books and the mother was taking her off the counter she smiled and said, "He's a nice man, isn't he, Mommy?" Her mother agreed. I felt about 10 feet tall the rest of the day. I knew from my experience at the library that I wanted to work in some capacity with people.

The problem was always that I couldn't seem to apply myself to anything outside of working at the library. I matured a great deal while working there, but I needed to extend that to other areas. I continued cheating on tests and papers throughout all of high school, but after freshman year I stopped advertising it. I quit helping my friends cheat and bragging about my crooked accomplishments. I wanted to become a more serious student, but I wasn't secure enough in my abilities to give up cheating. I felt I needed to cheat to get good grades. It was also partly force of habit; I was accustomed to cheating — not studying — and that was hard to break. I was still very withdrawn in class and did not participate. I avoided all high school social events. Overall, high school did not have a great effect on me because I put so little into it. What I did outside of class was of greater consequence.

When I wasn't working and my friend Bill wasn't around, I spent most of my time by myself feeling very lonely. Only those who have experienced extended periods of loneliness know what it can do to you. Fortunately, I had enough interests to occupy some of my time. For example, I was very interested in astronomy, and early in July there is a meteor shower that appears every year. One summer I decided to get up in the middle of the night to watch it. I had never seen a meteor shower before and I was not expecting it to be anything too spectacular. I got up around 1:00 in the morning and went outside the house. It took a while before I could discover the section of the sky in which it was taking place, but when I first saw it, I was frozen in place. Every few seconds a bright streak would shoot across the sky and disappear. Each one couldn't have lasted more than a second, but the power they seemed to display left me awestruck. They sped over the sky so quickly that they were hard to follow and I got dizzy from turning my head so quickly.

Then I decided I wanted to enjoy this more. I went inside and made a couple of sandwiches and got a drink. On leaving the house I caught a glimpse of my father's old pipe. It was a big, awkward thing but it seemed to match the moment perfectly. I had never smoked before — I had never even considered it — but I grabbed some tobacco and some matches and went outside with my little package. When I got outside I wasn't satisfied with my view. My house is on a hill but the house next to mine was taller and was blocking my line of sight. Nothing was going to get in my way of enjoying this show so I decided to climb up my neighbor's roof. I had scaled the side of their house several times before a few years earlier (to peek in their windows) but I had never been on the roof. The house had a fairly sturdy drain pipe so I tied my things in a bundle around my waist and climbed up to the roof. It was an old house with a lot of nooks and crannies in it so I found a good comfortable spot which couldn't be seen from the ground and sat down to rest. Lighting up the pipe took a few tries, and when I did light it at first I felt sick from the smoke. After a while I got used to it and started on the sandwiches. There was no moon that night and the sky was very dark. I looked upward and watched the lights streak from one side to the other.

I was all alone. I could see no one and no one could see me. The darkness of the sky was very soft and deep and the warm yellow streaks painting a path across the backdrop every few seconds were both magnificent and calming. My troubles were all below me and the show I was watching seemed to put everything into its right place. This was so much larger than anything else I had ever seen. How many trillions of miles and billions of years had these meteors travelled only so I could watch them burn out in flame? Everything else seemed insignificant. There were no happy families, no unhappy families. No good students and no bad students. There were no words locked inside my head refusing to come out right. All of us were little and of no importance to what I was witnessing. A quote from Dickens floated over me and didn't seem as harsh as when I first read it: "The universe makes a rather indifferent parent." I stayed on the roof for a couple of hours and for that time all was right in the world. Unfortunately, that was only a passing moment — no matter how good it made me feel, it didn't help me deal with everyday life.

After barely graduating from high school, Bill and I went together to a community college. It was something of a joke academically; my high school classes were more difficult. In spite of skipping a lot of classes we ended up with A's and B's and decided to transfer to a technical college. A couple of weeks into the semester I realized engineering was not for me and decided to transfer again in order to become an English major and live at school. It meant separating from Bill the next fall, but I felt it was time for me to try going out on my own.

That summer I met a girl named Ellen and soon started dating. Everything seemed perfect—almost too good to be true. We understood each other's feelings and problems and were able to give support to each other. For example, one day we were talking and I stuttered a little bit. She asked me directly about my stutter. No one had ever done that before. People had avoided mentioning it because they thought it would embarrass me. That attitude carries the implication that there is something wrong with having a stutter. Ellen asked me about it very straightforwardly. I realized that she accepted it as simply a part of me—just like my hair is brown and my eyes are blue. It had a great influence on me and I felt myself falling for Ellen. I took her to her prom and we saw a lot of each other during the summer.

So much happened that summer it's hard, even in my own mind, to organize it all. Most was due to Ellen's influence and the nature of our relationship together. She was the first girl I ever developed an intimate and supportive relationship with. We shared our secret hopes and dreams and could rely on each other if we wanted to talk over problems we were experiencing in our lives. We each knew that we could depend on the other. We took things very slowly as far as a physical relationship went. When I think back to the time we shared, I think my favorite memories were when we went to the park and had a picnic. We would lie on the grass, sometimes I would lay my head on her lap, and talk or just sit quietly. There was something very special about being able to spend quiet time with someone as close to my heart as she was. All the days we spent together seemed to be sunny, happy, and fulfilling. I'm probably romanticizing our time together, but that is the quality of my memories of Ellen. Being able to build a relationship like that, particularly since Ellen and I were so well matched, resulted in my maturing a great deal.

I can't give a surefire explanation for it, but my stutter was decreasing markedly. By the end of the summer stuttering had become a rare incident whereas before it had been the norm. Perhaps it was because I was at the age when men finally stop growing. My metabolism may have changed slightly. Maybe it was because I was maturing mentally and emotionally. By the end of the summer I was almost speaking normally. I am determined never to forget, however, what it was like having a problem such as that and what it was like to have people judge me and put me down for something over which I had no control. I'm very fortunate to have experienced that and to have had it corrected for whatever reason. I work with the mentally handicapped now, and it's always surprising to see how far they can go beyond what is expected of them. I've learned never to place restrictions on the abilities of other people, and more important, on my own abilities.

Ellen was going to a school about 1500 miles away. We could have made a commitment at the end of the summer, but we both thought that we should go off to school with full freedom and then see how we felt. It was difficult because we were both very much in love by that point. It was a good decision though, and we promised to keep in touch. Without Ellen's support, I don't think I would have had the confidence to leave my home and all my established friends and go off to an unfamiliar environment. She was never even aware of that. It was one of the ways she helped me without knowing it.

We left for school and, as promised, we kept in touch. I wrote her every day, and she called me often. After 3 weeks we found it very hard to be apart. We kept on saying how much we missed each other. Towards the end of September, Ellen said that she was coming home in a couple of weekends. She wanted to get together and spend a day with me. I'm pretty sure we were both ready to make a commitment — we were going to become engaged to become engaged, so to speak. Ellen hinted that she felt ready to begin a sexual relationship. We started talking on the phone more often, and Ellen began thinking about transferring to a school in my area so we could see more of each other. I was on top of the world.

Friday night around 11:00, about a week before Ellen was to come home, I was in my room studying when I heard the phone ring. It was Ellen and she sounded upset. She said she had been assaulted that afternoon and described what happened. When she had finished, I said, "Ellen, you keep saying that you were assaulted but I think it's important that you admit outright that you've been raped."

It was a painful phone call for both of us. We talked for an hour or so; I said I knew a place I could call to get some information and I would call right back. I called a rape crisis hotline and found out all the medical, legal, and physical aspects I could. I called Ellen back and we decided to fly her up here, take her to a hospital, and see what she wanted to do as far as pressing charges. She felt she couldn't tell her parents what happened, so I had to help her on my own. I did what I could for her, but I don't know how much help I was. I was very upset. It was an extremely difficult weekend. She went back to her school in a couple of days, which was probably the hardest thing of all. I wanted to keep her with me and protect her. But she had more courage than I did and went back to finish the semester.

I was in a bad state after she left. I didn't eat for a total of 6 days and when I did start eating, it was only in little bits. I couldn't sleep, and when I did I was having terrible nightmares. I would dream of people chasing me and then setting me on fire; people surrounded me and hacked at me with knives. The nightmares were bad, but I wondered why they were always about me. Ellen was never in any of these dreams. I felt very selfish, like I didn't really care about her. This brought on a tremendous feeling of guilt.

Soon the dreams started to change and seemed to reflect something that had actually happened. I couldn't put my finger on it, but each time I woke up I seemed to be close to recalling something I hadn't thought of in years. Bits and pieces started coming together, and it just got worse and worse. I began calling back memories in my waking hours. For over 13 years my mind had withheld these incidents and blocked them from coming forward. However, now with Ellen's experience, it all came back. I remembered being a small child and a man I knew brought me into a bedroom. I remembered him laying me on my stomach and his hot breath on the back of my neck and the pain as he pushed down on me. It happened more than once; he did things that I didn't understand then but I understand now. I can't say how many times he did this because they are all blurred together. The experiences had been locked in my memory for years—I had never recalled or spoken about them to anyone before. I must have been afraid at the time to tell anybody, including my parents, what was going on.

By the end of the semester, I was a mess. I was in a crisis situation and my grades were horrible. I did pull through it, but the next semester I decided to get counseling. I started understanding a lot of things. I understood now why I hated crowds and having people stand behind me. I understood why the experience with sex brought up so many confusing emotions. What I have never learned to understand is why some people will use other people weaker than themselves to satisfy their own selfish wants. I still know the man who did the things to me and it really seems he doesn't remember it at all. Maybe he does and is suffering with a terrible conscience, but I don't think so. I have been watching him since to find out if he has been doing it to any other child. I don't think he has. If I find out that he is, I'm not exactly sure what I would do. Most likely I will kill him if I think I can get away with it. I don't have violent feelings towards most people, but if someone like him keeps hurting innocent people in that way, I don't think he should live. I want people who do things like that to know that they are in a lot of danger.

The relationship between Ellen and me was never the same. We stopped dating. She wasn't able to continue a physical relationship with me, or start one with anyone else at that time. It wasn't a complete loss because we developed a very strong and supportive friendship. I eventually told her what had happened to me as a child, and we helped each other in many ways. Our friendship became something very important to each of us, and we have both benefitted from it. I learned from her what love and generosity in the face of pain really is. Since then we have both gone on to date successfully and are both happy and contented people. We both had something horrible done to us, but neither of us is guilty of ever hurting another person.

I have found a role for myself. It was very painful growing up, but through the pain and all my mistakes I have learned a lot. I do very well in school, and I'm working my way towards studying counseling psychology in graduate school. I earn A's and a few B's now, and I'm finally the student that I've always wanted to be. In fact, I'm more successful in college than anyone else in my family. I'm not spiteful and bitter and don't rub it in my family's face, but I do like the feeling (and the place in the family) it gives me. I find that even now I tend not to participate in class discussions as much as I could, but that is more from old habits than from shyness. I date girls, but I haven't dated steadily since Ellen. I guess I'm guilty of comparing every girl to her and the quality of the relationship we had. A friend who is studying for her doctorate in psychology and knows my history with Ellen would like to see me get into counseling men who physically and sexually abuse women. I can't consider that right now because I still have very violent feelings toward these people and I know that is wrong. Maybe sometime in the future I'll be able to think about it.

Some days I go through mood swings. In the morning I can be the most cheerful optimist and yet come back in the evening seeing red with rage. However, it has been a long time since I've experienced any sort of depression, and I think that is the important thing. I simply write off my mood swings to my Irish temperament. Besides, these mood swings are so minor compared to my former depths of depression that I can joke about them.

Recently I became very ill and spent several days in the hospital confined to a bed and connected to an IV tube. For the next several weeks I was very weak. During this time my speech regressed terribly. It made me realize that my problems had not gone away, but rather I had learned to compensate for them. When I was weak and fatigued I didn't have the concentration necessary to maintain my methods of compensation. I was at first upset and felt once again that I was very different from others. Soon, however, I came to the conclusion that it was a good thing. It would come back every once in a while to make certain that I didn't forget where I came from and how far I've come. I would be reminded from time to time that we all have our strengths and our weaknesses and it is important to accept both from all people. I would be reminded of the simple beauty of a conversation.

Altogether, I have been very fortunate in my life. Some terrible things have happened to me, but then I have also been lucky enough to come into contact with many wonderful people. These people have shown me what it means to be a caring and responsible person. They've allowed me to make all my mistakes without placing any judgments on me. I have learned from them that the way you treat other people really can make a difference for the better. Treat everyone with the dignity and respect they deserve and it will always come back to you. Stand by others when they're in need because when you're in need you'll find you have a lot more friends than you thought you had. But most of all, learn to stand on your own two feet. If you can't help yourself, there is little that others can do for you. Everyone is going to experience pain and hardship at some point in their life, and that is when we learn the depth of both our own strength and of our relationships with others. If we have planted strong roots, we should be able to withstand much of what comes our way. At the library, there was a saying on the bulletin board which I have always liked: *Be optimistic even when you feel desperate.*

Robert Kilkenny and Gil Noam: Opportunities for Recovering Reflections on Case 13

This life story is a compelling portrayal of the emotional and developmental aftereffects of psychological trauma in childhood. From the beginning there is a central question of why an apparently popular and intelligent child would feel so hopeless, insecure, and unworthy. Our author, whom we shall refer to as Ray, describes a childhood marked by self-imposed isolation from both parents and peers. His despair seemed to grow worse with time, eventually causing him to plan several suicide attempts in adolescence. The indigenous psychologist in us all searches to know the cause of so much pain and wasted potential; we seek clues to solve the central mystery of why a life so promising should prove so unsatisfying. But our author takes pains to make clear that for him there is no single explanation for his unhappiness. Our analysis here will emulate Ray's approach by slowly and carefully peeling back the layers of shame, guilt, and depression that protectively cover the truth.

As we struggle to understand another's life, we want to account for why it has progressed in one way and not another. No single course of development is strictly inevitable; there are too many variables and opportunities for overcoming. So, in looking at this case there is no simple cause and effect between experience and outcome. Many other children with severe stutters do not experience the same degree of shame and despair, which is not to say that it isn't an additional burden to maintain self-esteem in the face of so apparent a handicap. Something has happened to destroy Ray's childhood but he won't reveal exactly what. Clues are dropped (he has a bad stutter) and hints given (his parents let him down) but the mystery remains until he reveals his sexual abuse at the hands of an adult male known to him. But even then Ray does not make an explicit link between his childhood problems and his sexual abuse. So it is left to the reader to decide what, if any, connection his abuse had on his symptoms of depression, alienation, and poor self-esteem, and most importantly on the course of his overall development. The temptation in such a case is to attribute to the most serious trauma the causation of all subsequent difficulties. This line of analysis might lead us to speculate that some symptoms have symbolic value, i.e., that his stutter represents an inability to speak the unspeakable truth of his sexual victimization. And though such an analysis would elegantly tie together many loose ends, it may not be what is really important here. What matters more is listening carefully to what meaning the author constructs from his experiences.

Initially, our author offers a two-part explanation in which his stuttering is described as the main problem. First he says that his shock at discovering his stutter through a tape recording of his speech therapy led to feeling "bitter toward my parents for never having talked to me about it. I felt that I really hated them. Over the next ten or eleven years I spent much of my time finding little ways that I could hurt them and get back at them for the way they had failed me." Though that serves to account for the seeming lack of closeness with his parents, it is such a prolonged overreaction (6-year olds don't typically hold 10-year all-consuming grudges against their parents) that we wonder what else might account for a rage and alienation so severe that he would cut himself off from the most likely source of love and comfort in his life. However, it does offer the important insight that he felt his parents had somehow failed him in their obligation to protect him from devastating emotional pain. It raises significant questions about the nature of his relationship with his parents and indicates an ambivalent attachment at best.

When Ray finally relates the fact of his having been sexually abused, we see the trauma that shaped the troubled outlines of his development, either as primary cause or as a corrosive catalyst to an already shaky self-esteem. Research on the effects of child sexual abuse reveal that there is a wide variation in its developmental effect (Van der Kolk, 1989). Risk factors thought to affect outcome include age at which abuse occurs, physical force or violence, threats to the child, age difference between victim and perpetrator, length of abuse, closeness of relationship between victim and perpetrator, whether the abuse is disclosed and the circumstances under which it is, whether the child is believed, reaction of parents, consequences for the perpetrator, and availability of expert professional services for the child and family. In general, children's vulnerability to psychopathology is magnified by multiple stressors so that, typically, no single factor is determinate. As one would expect, the more severe and numerous the stressors, the greater the risk of lasting psychological impairment. The relative contribution of each risk factor to psychological outcome is not yet fully understood and is probably complexly mediated by individual, cultural, gender, and other differences. Risks can be counterbalanced by protective factors which buffer the stresses (Garmezy, 1987). These may include: (1) personality features such as self-esteem, self-understanding, and social competence, (2) supportive relationship with parents and lack of family discord, and (3) external support systems such as adult mentors, school experiences, and peer support.

In Ray's case, what information we have on his risk factors is not hopeful, though he appears to have a number of protective factors. We know that he was repeatedly subjected to forced anal intercourse by an adult whom he knew. Though we don't know the nature of the relationship with the perpetrator, he apparently knew Ray well enough to have ongoing access to him, which at that age implies someone he probably trusted. And since Ray stated he is still in a position to observe this person closely enough to determine whether or not he is abusing other children, it seems plausible that the perpetrator could even have been a member of his family. The popular notion of child molesters as strangers is not supported by research. Most studies find that the majority of sexual abuse is perpetrated by either relatives or other adults known by the child (Finkelhor, 1984, 1987). What this points to is an increased likelihood that Ray was abused by someone close enough to him to cause him to feel betrayed and to have subsequent difficulty in forming trusting relationships. The combination of force, betrayal, apparent silence, lack of timely professional help, etc., all conspire to create a constellation of vulnerabilities that go a long way toward explaining the serious nature of Ray's sense of shame, isolation, depression, etc. It makes his subsequent success and movement toward recovery all the more remarkable and important to understand.

The efforts to overcome the after-effects of childhood trauma often reach far beyond the early years, as we have seen in Ray's case. This fact raises the question of how adolescents and adults experience traumatic events differently from how children do, and how these different developmental eras produce new opportunities for recovery from traumatic events. In this case, the emerging adolescent abilities and desires for intimate peer and romantic friendships, vocational exploration, separation from family, and intellectual development are used by Ray to full advantage in addressing and undoing some of the damage to his self-esteem and social confidence in his childhood.

Instead of focusing only on the maladaptive aspects of repeating trauma, our theoretical perspective (e.g., Noam, 1988) emphasizes how each revisiting of the traumatic event always has a "healing intention." Each time old anxieties and symptoms are reawakened, there is an implicit hope that the effects of the trauma can finally be overcome and the painful thoughts and feelings can be put in a new perspective. Though some theorists take a similar approach to trauma, we have found one key to the potential recovery from traumatic events in the normal sequence of social, cognitive, and emotional development (e.g., Noam, Powers, Kilkenny, & Beedy, 1990). Many clinicians report – and we have found this phenomenon to be consistently present in our own clinical work – that those forces that produce hopelessness and despair can become the seeds for future opportunity and vitality. We think the best approach to understanding these capacities for psychological recovering is to begin with a framework of normal developmental transformations and to explore within each transformation a new opportunity and strengthened ability to rework some of the debilitating effects of psychological trauma.

Before returning to Ray, we want to briefly address two developing capacities, evident in our own adolescent research, that can contribute to overcoming trauma: (1) the development of intimate relationships, and (2) the continued evolution of self-understanding or insight into self and relationships. These two capacities define in essential ways that we are social beings who cannot achieve our full humanity without interpersonal bonds and that we are all essentially epistemologists in that we give meaning to our experience and our relationships. Gaining insight into painful relationships of the past has the potential to modify the power of the traumatic experience. But thinking, without strong feelings, remains shallow and intellectualized. In intimate relationships, where it really counts, we make ourselves vulnerable, and thus the earlier hurts inevitably reemerge. It is only in the context of relationships that the capacity for insight has the opportunity for transforming feelings and behavior resulting from a self-protective reaction to trauma. Full recovery requires that new insights somehow transform old behaviors and feelings. Important relationships are the context within which this can happen – indeed, where it often must occur to preserve the relationship.

There is, in fact, a great deal of evidence for these ideas from research with at-risk children. Those children who successfully master their development in the face of grave adversity (e.g., schizophrenic or depressed parents) are the ones who have had some positive and sustaining relationships (e.g., Garmezy, 1985; Rutter & Quinton, 1984). It is these important relationships that form the backdrop against which later relationships can be formed. But even when these resiliency-producing relationships do not exist, adolescent and adult intimacy can provide new opportunities for recovery.

With this brief theoretical background we will return to Ray. On both counts, a history of intimate relationships and an ability to generate insights about these relationships and his life, Ray demonstrates great strengths. In terms of the former, he has had enduring friendships in childhood. His childhood chum was a source of continuous strength and support. Ray tells us: "Bill and I did everything together. We liked the same shows and music and hung out together all the time. In fact it wasn't uncommon for teachers and other kids to get the two of us mixed up. There was a great amount of security in that relationship for me. I felt that Bill accepted me for who I was. . . ." His ability to make such a friend is an important sign of psychological resilience, or ability to maintain aspects of health in the face of serious stress. He was able to reach outside his family for the nurturing he needed, despite the fact that he had been so deeply and consistently hurt by important people in his life. His ability to maintain this long and strong friendship, or in the terms of Harry Stack Sullivan (1953), a "chumship," is an important factor in buffering the damage done to his self-esteem and ability to trust others: "We could share our secrets and problems." It was his primary means for staying connected to the world of peers and finding validation in the process. Significantly, his best friend's family became an important resource for trusted support: "I adopted his family as my own. . . . I didn't look up to or respect my parents but I did his . . . and as a consequence I looked to his parents for guidance." He views his life path as one great attempt to escape the non-nurturing experiences with his parents and teachers, who harmed him deeply. We are not concerned here with what they actually did, but with his experience of them as most unhelpful and even undermining of his emerging self-esteem. For many people, life becomes the attempt to overcome these early hurts.

Turning to the second protective process, the development of insight or self-understanding, Ray gives us many examples of his strength in this area. In the process of his development, Ray begins to define himself in opposition to the people he does not respect or trust (parents, teachers). We can see his chronic lying and cheating as manifestations of his alienation from adult authority and as a problematic assertion of his own will and autonomy. In a positive sense, it is his way of being less of a victim of incompetent authority. His own abuse had, after all, occurred within the scope of his parents' own, at best, ineffectual authority. Instead, he is beginning to build his own identity, asking himself who he is in the face of all the experiences that shaped him. This case itself is a beautiful example of a developmental shift to a greater degree of personal, ideological, spiritual, and professional complexity and commitment. Throughout, Ray is introducing his voice and making sense of the relationships that have been important. And in the process he is asserting his own power over his life — a very important step in undoing the feelings of helplessness and powerlessness that come with being victimized as a child.

We often identify this search for self with adolescence. But we forget that depending on the cognitive, social, and emotional developmental level, adolescents pursue these goals quite differently. At earlier developmental levels adolescents tend to blame others for their fate and are quite impulsive and self-protective in their responses. Many of those adolescents who remain at these less mature developmental positions for prolonged periods of time have been abused or come from homes impoverished on a number of levels.

The developmental shift described earlier is from what we call the *mutual-inclusive* level to the *systemic-organizational* level (Noam, Powers, Kilkenny, & Beedy, 1990). At the mutual-inclusive position the self is defined through important identifications with significant others. A self so tied to external sources of validation is particularly vulnerable to the actions of others and feelings of inadequacy and responsibility for problems in the relationship; e.g., "People would treat me better if I were a better person." If these important relationships are abusive or nonsupportive, a negative self-concept and/or social isolation may result. On the positive side of this equation, however, Ray's ability to form warm mentoring relationships with adults at the library where he worked is a positive example of his ability to meet these crucial developmental needs for building trust and confidence in himself through other means. He tells us what he needed in the relationship with an adult: support, care, encouragement, but also an honest guidance and critique based on the firm foundation of acceptance. Some people are lucky enough to receive this kind of treatment from their parents, but many people have to find these relationships with mentors and friends outside the immediate family.

Further development is no guarantee toward positive self-experience. But in the move toward the systemic-organizational perspective the person can stand back somewhat from his or her identifications and begin to question and thereby modify them into a new sense of identity. It allows one to think of oneself in biographical terms, as a life with multiple influences and turning points. Influences are seen as formative but not necessarily deterministic; the self can reshape itself if it knows what and how it has come to be. With this multiplicity of perspectives on the self emerges the potential for mourning the injuries afflicted by trauma in a new way: the trauma does not need to define self and relationships anymore. Instead, the traumatic experiences can be objectified and be given the proper place in development. Ray provides us with excellent descriptions of how the evolving abilities for self-reflection at the systemic-organizational level provide a means for recovering. Simplifying our developmental account considerably, we view Ray as describing a fundamental shift of perspective about himself and important relationships. Statements like "I had very little self-respect, so I had to get it from others" demonstrate hard-won psychological insight and the development of a complex understanding of human motivation. At many points he takes a biographical point of view, tracing how the past has shaped the present (e.g., "I need to go back to my early childhood to explain all the problems I had with school. . . ."). In fact, this autobiography would not be nearly as interesting or informative were it not for these abilities to reflect upon the manner in which otherwise disparate influences converge to shape his life.

In spite of these evolving protective processes, there remain unresolved thoughts and feelings that cause Ray to operate simultaneously on less evolved psychological levels. When Ray talks about the man who abused him, the complexity of cognition and emotions collapses. He states: "If I find out that he is (sexually abusing another child), I'm not exactly sure what I would do. Most likely I will kill him if I think I can get away with it. I don't have violent feelings towards most people but if someone like him keeps hurting innocent people in that way I don't think he should live. . . ." It is perfectly understandable that Ray feels like killing the man who abused him, but in other areas he has demonstrated considerably greater abilities to explore the consequences of his ideas and actions. We can feel the pent-up rage he still feels and also realize that he has not had the fifteen years since the event to process these feelings and gain some emotional distance from them because he has only relatively recently allowed these facts to reemerge to conscious awareness. So his insight and ability to integrate these feelings into the rest of his thinking and feeling is still limited by his reawakening and reliving of his trauma and its effects. This is a phenomenon we call "encapsulation" in which certain developmental aspects of the self, often connected to previous trauma, lag behind the general psychological development of the individual in other areas.

Overall, Ray provides us with an excellent example of how present experiences evoke unworked-out issues from the past, and how they can be readdressed with new information and emerging developmental abilities. Here, his girlfriend's rape is an assault of him as well. He is extremely upset, as any one would be whose intimate friend were attacked. But in Ray's case it leads to a return of many memories that had been hidden from consciousness. Having described nightmares of being chased and hurt, he relates the coming into conscious awareness of his own rape.

> Soon the dreams started to change and seemed to reflect something that had actually happened. I couldn't put my finger on it, but each time I woke up I seemed to be close to recalling something I hadn't thought of in years. Bits and pieces started coming together and it just got worse and worse. I began calling back memories in my waking hours. For over 13 years my mind had withheld these incidents and blocked them from coming forward. However, now with Ellen's experience, it all came back. I remembered being a small child and a man I knew brought me into a bedroom. I remembered him laying me on my stomach and his hot breath on the back of my neck and the pain as he pushed down on me. It happened more than once; he did things which I didn't understand then but I understand now. I can't say how many

times he did this because they are all blurred together. The experiences had been locked in my memory for years—I had never recalled or spoken about them to anyone before. I must have been afraid at the time to tell anybody, including my parents, what was going on.

The agony of the return to those feelings that he had carried with him for so long and that have made him so vulnerable are quite typical for any person who has the courage to readdress the trauma "head on." With the help of his girlfriend, Ellen, he can now gain some control not only by working on his own abuse history but by giving her support. It is this "passing over," helping others with what has been most dangerous to the self, that creates a grammar, a language, for what before had been unspeakable. To make one's own vulnerabilities the source of helping others is at the heart of most clinical practice. Most therapists have experienced some trauma or problem that they were able to work through. It is also at the heart of intimate friendships. It is not the vulnerabilities that are the problem in relationships—they are to be expected—it is the shared willingness to work on them and move beyond them that distinguishes productive from stagnant relationships.

Ray's relationship with Ellen served as both the stimulus and the means for his courageous confrontation with his own past that some precocious part of him had kept secret even to himself until the circumstances were right. His closeness and deep empathy for his girlfriend made her rape such a powerful emotional provocation that his own rape experience broke into consciousness. However, this relationship served as more than the mere stimulus for his reawakening. It also helped him recover to the point where he now had the strength and courage to finally address his own trauma. Prior to this he understood his stutter to have been the core problem around which his life had revolved. But this understanding of the problem would face a new challenge, as his stutter virtually disappeared in the context of his girlfriend's love: "she accepted it as simply a part of me—just like my hair is brown and my eyes are blue. It had a great influence on me and I felt myself falling for Ellen." Whatever the underlying cause of his stutter, one psychological purpose it served—the primary explanation for his depression and alienation from his parents and peers—was no longer serviceable. Since he no longer stuttered, he would have no explanation for the lingering feelings from his own rape. His improved speech did undoubtedly ease the burdens on his self-esteem. But it couldn't also be expected to address his own rape-induced feelings. His conscious understanding of his unhappiness as solely based on his stutter, was being destabilized by the press of his own healthy development in the areas of intimacy, self confidence, and self understanding.

Also at this time just prior to his breakdown, his relationship with Ellen was about to become sexually intimate: "Ellen hinted that she felt ready to begin a sexual relationship. We started talking on the phone more often and Ellen began thinking about transferring to a school in my area so we could see more of each other. I was on top of the world." Though part of him was on top of the world, his other sexual experiences with girls had left him feeling dirty and ashamed, a frequent outcome of sexual abuse. The unfinished business of his own past meant that he was not yet ready for a sexually intimate relationship with someone he truly loved. Their love for one another led to the prospect of sexual intimacy, and that same love made her assault his assault. Their relationship had boosted his confidence in himself as an attractive, sexual young man who was now strong enough to face the major source of his enduring anguish. It was love that empowered him: his love and empathy for her, and the effect of her love on his own belief in himself. This is an example of using the developmental opportunities of adolescence for forming intimate romantic attachments to redress the damage done in an earlier developmental period to that same ability for attachment.

Ray's story illustrates two important features of human development, one discouraging, and the other heartening. First, we can see the devastating effects of sexual abuse in childhood. It is worth each of us contemplating how utterly devastating an event would have to be for us to expend daily the energy required to totally suppress something that was having such an effect on our lives. We all know the simple phenomenon of trying to put a tune or phrase out of our minds, and the more we try to suppress it the more forcefully it jumps to consciousness. If that is true for something of no consequence, imagine the psychological energy Ray had to expend, unknowingly, to keep from awareness this most influential event in his life. This suppression reflected the devastating strength of the trauma and affected the suicide-tinged ruin of his childhood. The recognition of despair that he states at the conclusion of his autobiography: "Be happy even when you feel desperate" represents an ongoing challenge to his recovery. And if we extrapolate Ray's suffering and despair to the prevalence of child sexual abuse we have a sobering view of the developmental struggle of many children and adolescents.

More optimistically, however, we also have an example of the way in which life presents opportunities at each developmental level for healing and transformation. Ray demonstrates that one can find important parts of what one needs in close relationships and other contexts for learning. His chumship and "adoption" of his best friend's family, his willingness to be mentored and nurtured by his supervisors at the library, his eventual openness to intimate-romantic relationships—coinciding with the remarkable disappearance of his stutter—and even his ability to allow his empathic reaction to his girlfriend's sexual assault to break his suppression of his own abuse, are all powerful examples of relationships as the primary developmental context for healing. But not all such cases show such progress toward psychological recovering. An important part of the reason for Ray's success is Ray himself — his thoughtfulness, ability to reflect on himself, and courage to face the truth. It is this combination of his predispositions to self-understanding and to seizing the developmental opportunities for relationships that, taken together, explain Ray's impressive progress. These two forces for healing — relationships and insight — are at the center of our clinical-developmental theory and are poignantly captured in Ray's description of his reaction to the parish priest asking him to consider the priesthood:

> This was the first time that someone I really admired let me know he saw some value in me. He was seeing good in me that I couldn't see myself. It had a profound effect on me. I didn't turn myself around in a day because of it, but I did have my first thoughts of where I was going and the person I was as opposed to the person I was capable of being. These were brief, very scattered thoughts, but the seed had been planted. It was the encouragement of other people like him that helped me learn that many people saw me in a better light than I saw myself.

These are important words of reminder that for most people the process of recovering from serious psychological trauma happens not in the clinic but in the context of warm and caring relationships. Ray demonstrates courageously the possibilities that exist within us and around us.

CASE 14

Forever an Awkward Adolescent

This is the story of a young man born with serious physical disabil-ities. He describes the tension between his parents over how high their expectations for his autonomy should be. His father's "legendary penchant for interfering" results in his doing everything for him, whereas his mother, having "less patience with incompetence," expects him to learn to do for himself. College becomes a new opportunity for forming close female friendships and for academic achievements, but these are tainted by doubts over whether he is held to the same standards as his peers. And he asks, "What is to become of my sexuality?" and envisions "a 35-year-old with the sexuality of a 14-year-old, and the prospect does not please me." As he plans to begin graduate school for a career in media, he will not accept society's narrow expectation that he should practice his profession as a repre-sentative of the disabled because "I do not think of myself as a disabled person."

My first clear memory is from nursery school. When I was 3 years old my parents sent me to a small nursery school for about three or four hours about twice a week. It was in the basement of a local church, and I distinctly remember being carried down a long corridor past beautifully colored stained-glass windows. Someone was carrying me and pointed out the colored shapes which were on the opposite wall as the sun shone through the windows.

I should note that at this point I had not yet learned to walk. I still think of it as "learning" to walk, but this is not quite accurate. Because I was born with physical disabilities, the first three to five years of my life were interspersed with multiple operations, where the doctors tried to stretch my hamstrings surgically. After each of these operations I was put in a plaster cast—at one point, both legs up to the waist. It was all in an effort to un-club my feet so that I might someday be able to walk. Everyone was very excited when I finally did, spontaneously, while waiting with my father in a doctor's waiting room. My parents and all their good friends were in tears, I guess, because the professionals had been about evenly divided on whether I'd ever walk at all. I don't remember this important occasion, however, which is one of my peculiar tricks of memory—I never seem to understand the full implications of various "remarkable" events in my life.

I don't have a lot of clear early memories of my parents. I always took them for granted, at least until I began to figure out ways that I might lose them. Like when I began to realize that their marriage wasn't that great. They really should have divorced twenty-five years ago. Except then, they wouldn't have had me! Even so, they are very unsuited to each other, and their arguments and periodic leavings and returnings were a bit of a cloud in my childhood.

I am sometimes embarrassed and worried about how little their sour relationship has seemed to affect me. I have had moments of tears and fear during particularly bad patches but, by and large, I have never had those self-blaming feelings that everyone says kids have when their parents have problems. I think it is a testament to my parents that despite their trials, life at our house always had a sense of security and permanence. I don't know if they did it on purpose; more likely it was their conservative view of how one conducted ones' life that did it. Breakfast was always there. Dinner was always at 6:30. Everything was predictable. At the time, I came to envy my friends' younger, more adventurous parents (they went to movies — we never did), but now I think that it was better for me to have parents who took refuge in routine. I never really worried that I wouldn't be taken care of, that I wouldn't be loved.

I entered adolescence (and eighth grade) at about the time we made a cross-country move. Thinking back on that period, I am certain that the move was good for me. For one thing, my best friend had moved away the year before, at a time when our relationship was becoming difficult. We first became friends, at age 5, because we shared a disdain for the crowd. We weren't joiners. For me, this trait was determined by my disabilities; I had had to learn how to entertain myself. The fun I had was sedentary: matchbox cars, model planes, books about WW II fliers, and television — which spent a great deal of time catering to the imaginations of would-be fighter pilots and space travelers. My friend also liked these things, but more by choice. After a while, we reinforced our reclusive tendencies, and as we grew older we grew farther and farther apart from our peers who were either getting into sports or getting into trouble.

Predictably, as puberty struck, my friend and I began to reevaluate (separately) where we stood. I suspect that my friend began to see that others his age were having a lot of physical fun, horsing around in ways which seemed impossible, or at least improbable, for me. Suddenly, going over to each others' houses to play with Legos no longer sufficed to sustain our friendship. I, too, began to identify with other peers, people who also stood out, but who seemed to have made the transition from Legos to a kind of makeshift intellectualism. When a group of us began reading *The Lord of the Rings,* my best friend did not join in. Soon after this, he moved away.

For my family, the move across country was very traumatic, though they tried to act as though it was an adventure. My main concern was whether I would be able to survive in the new public school I would be entering. Having spent all my grade school years at an "experimental education" school on a college campus in my home town, I was not used to a "structured" school environment. The realm of real schools was a mysterious and sinister one in the lore of this "campus school," and I'm afraid I bought into the horror stories of academic rigor and regimentation which passed for information on public schools among my 12-year-old schoolmates. I think that entering middle school in the new town, far from any familiar people or places, was the best way for me to get into regular schooling; kind of like being thrown into a pool as a way of learning to swim. As it turned out, it was all right. I gained confidence in my academic abilities by having my intelligence confirmed for the first time by grades. The teachers there were every bit as human as in my other school, and the kids were far more numerous, so I could hide in anonymity. At least, that is what I thought. Actually, because of my disabilities I was almost instantly known, or known of, by everyone in the school. I was also treated with uniform kindness and curiosity from the first day, but even then I wondered, as I do now, how much of that kindness was actually pity for me because of my disability.

Since I have been physically disabled all of my life, I have managed to cope with the purely practical problems arising from this with a minimum of fuss on my part; I felt no loss, because I had no feelings of "normality" to compare with. One of my physical problems is that I am short, about four feet, two inches tall. Until I began growing whiskers on my face and driving a car, I was constantly mistaken by strangers as being a little kid. It's a hell of a pain for a 16-year-old boy to be handed a kiddie's menu every time he enters a restaurant. It is even worse when mere coherent speech is greeted with awe. If explaining to the old lady in church that I am taking five classes in high school provokes an assumption that I must be terribly smart, how am I supposed to know whether I really am or if everyone is just impressed that I don't drool on myself? I have high standards for myself, perhaps not as high as many straight-A college students, but I am always impressed when I witness, say, good writing and intelligent conversation in others, and

I aspire to such standards of intelligence. During my teen years it was a constant nagging irritation that everyone around me had what I felt were extremely low expectations. I never knew where I stood.

Almost everybody treats me well, whether or not they really know me. In fact, I gained a reputation among some of my high school peers for being really smart, even though plenty of students within my range of ability (such as those with whom I went through an Honors English program) had better grades and study habits than I did. After awhile, I began to realize that people were predisposed to treating disabled people with extra kindness. Perhaps, I thought, my "smart kid" reputation, which I considered to be disproportionate to my actual abilities, was part of this extra kindness. Supporting this notion was my observation that many people who had known me for a long time, even some members of my extended family, tended to express admiration for my accomplishments with an enthusiasm far beyond what I considered to be appropriate. I was able to gauge this by comparing my parents' response with that of my brother and certain close friends, all of whom had gotten used to the fact that, indeed, I had learned to walk and talk and go to school like any normal kid, and hence, responded in a more subdued fashion to what were, after all, fairly minor accomplishments on my part.

My desire to do well academically did not, oddly enough, compel me to become an especially studious student. My parents never really put the pressure on me to get straight A's, and when I came home with report cards that were mixed A's and B's, they seemed to feel these were fairly wonderful. Either they were too old to understand grade inflation, or they were falling into the same trap I explained above—being glad that I was still alive and walking and apparently intelligent. I tend to think that it was a little of both, which means that I have been guilty, on occasion, of taking advantage of the very tendency which I despise. I have often allowed myself to rest easy in others' low expectations. This is something which I continue to fight in myself. Still, it was terribly important to me that I never got less than a B. I constructed a sort of artificial line of performance below which I told myself my parents would be disappointed. For some reason, I was never too concerned about what my teachers or my friends thought about my grades; I looked solely to my parents for approval on that score.

If, as I surmised, peoples' expressed admiration of me was exaggerated by the issue of my disabilities, then how could I be sure exactly how much of that praise and admiration had been earned and how much was phony or misplaced? Naturally, as I moved through adolescence, I cared more and more about where I stood in the grand scheme of things. Since the whole business of looks and sex appeal was entirely outside my league, my only arenas for competition and comparison were in academics and in "being likable." I tended to look to everyone I met for approval, and conversation was my weapon. At first, I was just naturally inclined to have an odd sense of humor, and to express both this humor and my interest in history and politics in conversations with adults and with as many interested friends as I could find. After awhile, though, around my senior year in high school, I began to sense that being able to carry on a conversation about a wide range of topics was not just fun but an asset, too.

I have long thought that one of the real handicaps of having congenital disabilities is that one often grows up isolated from all the trivial things that adolescents banter about. Music, girls, cars, clothes, films, television, magazines — the whole range of popular culture is a special language which the adult world too easily dismisses as unimportant. But for the teenager cut off from this language, relating to peers who are already leery of him or her because of a disability, is doubly difficult. The good will most people have to "give it a try" with the disabled teen may be there at the beginning, but unless the teen is able to "run with the ball" and "fit in" at least by speaking the same language as his or her peers, the good will will quickly turn to embarrassment, and then the disabled teen will be ignored. If it were up to me, people who counsel disabled kids and their parents would stress the importance, often denigrated in "normal" kids, of "fitting in."

In retrospect, I think that a lot of what I was doing in high school was constructing a character, a persona, I could live with. Most adolescents do this, but for me, it was doubly important because the character I had, my "default" pigeonhole in the eyes of others, was that of a short, oddly postured, disabled kid. I wasn't sure at the time, and I'm still not positive, just what kind of persona I want to have. This has made constructing myself an ad hoc process. For the most part, however, I think I have been able to impress others enough with images other than disability. When I get scared, though, when I think about it too much, I wonder if it's all my imagination. Does everybody still think of me as a disability, and not as a person? I don't know. I'll never really know for sure, because I am always suspicious of others' response to me. I guess that I function from day to day on a veneer of faith; I survive with happiness and pride by assuming that other people see me as I see myself.

My parents are two people whose reactions to me I have trusted. From my mother I get a cartload of political convictions, or perhaps prejudices, because at times I think that her convictions are as much prejudice as they are considered opinions. I count among the greatest gifts of my college years the ability to critique and analyze my own political and social beliefs. By and large, I inherit from Mom a respect for what good can be done by government, along with a profound and unquenchable skepticism which prevents me from ever being satisfied with what government or any other authority is doing. I realize, because I have seen it in my mother, that this is a frustrating way to approach the world. Always having to "bitch, bitch,

bitch," not because it's right or good or a citizen's responsibility, but because I can't contain myself, is a burden — especially in a society which frowns upon excess in expressing one's views.

Having lived, for the most part, away from my mother for four years, I have found that I still care deeply about what she thinks of my actions. I don't think I could ever pursue a career, for instance, that violated her standards of morality. This cancels out a lot of possibilities, but fortunately, I have no desire to become a stockbroker. Nevertheless, as I pursue graduate studies in mass media and popular culture, I find myself wondering about how she would feel about my being an advertising copywriter, or a television producer, or network reporter. I tend to think that as long as I stay true to my own standards, I will not run afoul of hers, but sometimes I am not sure, and that worries me.

One of the peculiar dynamics of my relations with my parents has been growing up in an atmosphere thick with a history of Dad's legendary penchant for interfering. When I was much younger this didn't bother me, because I sought the security he provided. He was always the provider, the caretaker. In fact, he even helped dress me in the mornings right up till I entered high school. He was always looking for ways to make my life easier. Of course, the problem with this is that it retarded the development of my self-sufficiency. Mom was dead set against this. It wasn't that Mom was uncaring, it is just that she had less patience with incompetence.

In the long run, she was right; it was more help to me to force me into doing things myself than to smooth out any remotely rough areas of day-to-day life. As I got older, Mom became increasingly adamant that Dad was now an abnormally doting parent. She felt that perhaps it was more selfishness on his part — his need to feel needed and in charge — than a true concern for my welfare, which kept him so involved in my physical challenges. Eventually, she began to suggest to me that I ought to resent his "interference" as much as she did. In a way, this was good, because it finally caused me to increase and jealously guard my self-sufficiency. At first for Mom's benefit, but eventually for my own, I began to oppose my father's instinctive moves towards helping me dress, get in and out of cars, put on jackets, etc. He knew that it all was for the best, and I no longer saw him as my guardian for life. Instead, I began to see him as a friend, a father, and sometimes a pain!

Our relationship has since changed for the better. We now have more arguments than we used to, but they are adult-type arguments. And on the whole, we share a mutual interest in each others' lives. I am sure that he harbors more than a little "controlling interest" in my life, but if he does, he at least is honest enough to admit it, and often interrupts himself in mid-sentence, chuckling at his own tendency to criticize and worry the joy out of new adventures.

Other people, too, have influenced me in less vital, but no less endur-ing ways. I think that I first got a taste of the joys of discussing politics from the high school librarian. He was a balding, middle-aged man with a bit of a paunch, and a wonderfully dry sense of humor. A fan of George McGovern, he introduced me to the blessings of "Norwegian charisma" while we both watched Walter Mondale stumble through the 1984 cam-paign. I would come in after lunch and wander over to his office, where we would swap political stories we had heard or read about.

Here was a man, as well educated and articulate as my parents, and with similar political stripes, who actually enjoyed watching the "march of folly" that politics provides. It was a liberation for me. There were very few of my peers with whom I could talk about politics, either because they didn't care or because my views were hopelessly out of sync with theirs. For two years, then, I was able to spend at least an hour of every day just yakking away about anything that popped into my head. In fact, from testing my wings with him, I was finally able to spar with my parents on political topics.

I suspect that this kind of jabbering contributed as much as anything else to my interest in editorial journalism. When I approached the journal-ism advisor about taking the journalism class (thereby becoming a member of the paper staff), I remember that I had a goal in mind of writing a column. My work in his English class impressed him, so he helped me convince the editor that I should have my own column. In retrospect, I am sure that part of his admiration of me was that damnable tendency I mentioned earlier—to see any accomplishments by a disabled person as a miracle—but I guess I didn't really mind it that much if, in the end, I received recognition purely on my own merits.

I am sure that is one reason why I loved writing that column and the one I wrote for four years in college. In college, I began my column before very many people knew who I was. Consequently, when I got favorable comments from strangers, it was all the more special to me. For the first time in my life, I could be sure that I had earned every bit of the praise I got. I am a person who has never been short of expressions of approval from others, but anonymous praise is like gold to me. This is why I look forward to continued writing of this nature—hopefully, as a career.

There is one incident from my adolescence which has had perhaps the greatest impact on my outlook. During the long drive from the West Coast to what would be my college in the East, I became seriously ill. At this point, the most severe aspect of my disability stemmed from the effects of severe scoliosis on my lung functions. As I grew, my spine curved even more; the more it curved, the more it applied pressure on my lungs. Hence, my breathing capacity was getting progressively smaller. While a spinal fusion operation at age 10 prevented this from becoming fatal, as it turned out, the procedure left enough room for worsening to make it nearly so.

Knowing that the high altitudes we would have to endure on the drive east would make me uncomfortable, my doctors prescribed an oxygen tank which I could use whenever I got too tired by the lack of oxygen. Unfortunately, this did not solve the physical problem of actual breathing, and the result was a potentially deadly spiral; the more oxygen I breathed in, the less my brain was induced to stimulate breathing—the less I breathed, the less I was able to expel carbon dioxide. By the time I had reached my destination I was unable to sleep, because I would stop breathing and wake up.

At one point, I was told that I would never recover fully from this malady—as, in fact, I have not—and that I had about five years to live. The only alternative was to surgically install a permanent tracheostomy so that, in addition to using extra oxygen at night, I could have the help of a respirator in breathing. We waited a few weeks in the vain hope that somehow I would spontaneously pull out of this hole, and during this time I continued to prepare for my first day of classes which was less than two weeks away.

Most of the people around me, my mother and father in particular, saw my entering college as a fantasy. After all, I did look pretty bad, and I could barely cross a room on foot, much less walk to class. Only my older brother seemed to think that they were all overreacting. For all of my life he had lived with the constant and recurrent threat that I would die, that I would never walk, that I could never do thus and such. Every time I had taken a turn for the worse he had been told that "you'd better come and see him, it could be the last time." Every time I had "proved them wrong," as he put it to me. While he was particularly worried with this incident, he still felt that as long as I was certain I would start college on time, there was hope.

To hear him tell it, I am some kind of brave hero for having kept my faith in my own ability to recover. From my point of view, it wasn't bravery or faith. I never really realized how serious my condition was. All along, my mind refused to accept the gravity of the situation. Instead, I whiled away these "sick" hours thinking about how I'd decorate my dorm room, and what classes I would take. Finally, it got bad enough that it was decided to do the tracheostomy. Within a week I was going to my first class. To me it seemed natural. It was what I'd planned all along. I was feeling much better, the oxygen with the respirator at night left me quite healthy during the day, and I was doing what I wanted to do.

In a number of ways, this incident is typical of my outlook as I have grown up. First, it shows how I have generally dealt with adversity: I ignore it. I refuse to accept it. I do not think of myself as a disabled person. While this has helped me thus far, it may not continue to do so. Out there in the nonacademic "real" world, disabled people, like any minority group, have to organize and vocally assert their rights. I have always shied away from doing this. For one thing, my relatively privileged family background has, to a large extent, smoothed my path. I have not had to advocate strongly for myself because money and my father's position as a doctor have advocated for me. Besides that, though, I simply do not want to be labeled. I take no particular "pride" in being disabled, even though I have as much reason to do so as any disabled person. It all comes back to that nagging problem— how can I earn praise and self-esteem without having my disability in the equation?

But as I inch towards a career, perhaps in journalism, certainly in some kind of media, I am finding that I will have to fight society's tendency to view me primarily in terms of my disability. In my chosen field, there is a tendency to pigeonhole people. Blacks report on race issues. Women report on feminism. I don't really want to be a writer or producer of columns or programs about disability. I understand that people see in me a useful tool; articulate, intelligent, and poised disabled people are hard to come by because so many of them have social disabilities which come with their physical problems. Some would say that it is my duty to serve society in the most natural way possible to me, to become an advocate for disabled people. While I accept the logic and morality of this, I simply don't want that!

In addition to calling my attention to this desire in me to be seen in my own terms, my near-death episode also made me more aware than I had ever been before of how important my relationship with my brother is. He was 14 when I was born, and I am pretty sure that he got short shift because of the all-consuming problems of my infancy. Although he may harbor some resentment towards me, he also has a devotion to me which I always find surprising. Most importantly, he has supported and challenged me consistently throughout my life—from the time he set out to teach me to get up after falling down, to the times he questioned my opinions and forced me to take steps towards independence and maturity which I was unwilling to take. While others let me grow up somewhat spoiled and lazy, he insisted that there was no reason why I couldn't do dishes or cook dinners. During my years at college, the longest time I have ever lived near him, my brother has had a major role in helping me grow up.

By far the richest time in my life has been my four years in college. The intellectual benefits have been enormous, not so much in the amount of stuff I have learned, but in the atmosphere. My college and I were peculiar matches. Traditionally a very athletic campus, it nevertheless fits my personality in that its students have tended to opt for a kind of athleticism which emphasizes the enjoyment of the sport over outright achievement. I, too, get most of my enjoyment out of activities that have no intrinsic value, no tabulation of results.

Socially, college would have been a waste for me had it not been for my fraternity. It is a cliché that fraternity members learn as well as party in the frat, but it really is true in my case. Of course, mine was an atypical one; for fifteen years coeducational, it has for an even longer time been a contradiction, a fraternity for nonjoiners. Because some of the members had the courage to invite me to rush in the spring of my freshman year, I was able to live for two full years in a house with eighteen men and women who considered themselves a true family. We cooked together, studied together, and fought with each other over how to take care of our family and the structure that housed it. Because I lived with these people, they had plenty of time to get to know me.

Far from shutting me up in a closed community, my fraternity experience gave me the confidence to branch out and become better acquainted with others on campus. When people met me, I was identified with my newspaper column and with my fraternity. Thus, I was more than just a disabled student; I had other identities to start me off. I used them as a launching pad from which to make other people understand who I was in a deeper way.

Before writing this meditation on my adolescence, I was asked, among other things, "What makes you want to get up in the morning?" I think that my first answer would be "whatever it is I have to do on that particular day." This illustrates an important tendency of mine. All my life I have done what's been put in front of me to do. Kids go to school, so I went to school. After that, in my family, you go to college, so I went to college. After college, you either get a job or continue your education, so I will attend graduate school. I pay my bills. I do my reading. I grade papers. I cope. I get along. At the same time, however, I am motivated by a need for approval from others.

Some aspects of adolescence are harder to cope with than others. I often wonder what is to become of my sexuality—I cannot envision (except in erotic dreams) a time when a woman would find me attractive enough to spark a long-term love relationship. I have read of other people far more disabled than I am who have found both love and sex with compatible, willing partners. Yet, a paraplegic is, if immobile, still normal in appearance. I am not. I am short, my back curves severely, and because of my rapid metabolism and restricted abdominal cavity, I am skinny to the point of being emaciated. I have had many female friends, but what could possibly provoke them to see me and be sexually attracted to me?

I have tried on two occasions to move closer to two different female friends. In both cases, this consisted of my acting as comforter and patient listener in time of crisis or stress. On both occasions, they appreciated it and the friendships deepened. But in both cases, I suspect, they had no idea that I had any other motive than a friend's concern. And in each instance I felt like a beast, because I knew that I had ulterior motives. I know something of the dangers of a male/female relationship based on the weak and emotionally distressed woman and the strong "I'll take care of you" man, and I have no desire to become a "co-dependent"—with or without sex.

I look at the future of my sexuality, and I see a 35-year-old with the sexuality of a 14-year-old. In this area, I am likely to be forever an awkward adolescent—and the prospect does not please me. At the same time, I hope that the sense of humor, the curiosity, and the weightlessness of carefree adolescence can be preserved, to some extent. I look around me and see many people in both journalism and culture studies who seem to have retained these characteristics. Perhaps I can, too. I hope, finally, that I do not ever really grow up.

In sum, I have come a long way. Because of me and those who have supported me, I have accomplished many things and done a lot of growing up. I am still an adolescent, though. Only an adolescent has the audacity to hope for what I hope for, which is—everything.

CASE 15

Proud of the Strength I Had

This writer describes her experience of teenage pregnancy and how she copes with its effects on her emotional and social development. Without the support of her former boyfriend or the knowledge of her parents, she decides alone to have an out-of-state abortion soon after her high school graduation. She shares her struggle to find meaning in her actions and to redefine her own identity. In college, she finds support from a campus women's group that helps her make sense of her experience and understand herself better. She begins to examine her family life and the impact of those relationships on her feelings about men and the coping styles she has developed. She also comes to acknowledge her own strength and courage in dealing with this extremely difficult adolescent experience.

It was a week or so after high school graduation. The air was musty and the cement floor was cold. I played nervously with the phone cord and traced its path to the door with my eyes. The garage was the safest place, but I prayed that no one could hear me. It's funny how you suddenly believe in God when you think something bad might happen.

The woman on the other end of the line finally found my records. "Let's see," she said, "Oh yes, your test came out positive!" She sounded excited. I wasn't. I almost dropped the phone. My stomach felt like lead. I couldn't believe her.

"Are you sure?" I barely managed to utter. "Yes, isn't that what you wanted to hear?" Was she stupid? She had to look up my name for the results, didn't she know I was only 17?

"No," I said. She gave me the name of some abortion clinics and I hung up the phone.

On August 18th I had an abortion. In September I left for college. My grades were never affected; in fact, I got a 4.0 my first semester. Studying kept me from thinking too much. Six months after my abortion I saw a sign for a support group for women who had had abortions. I knew that I needed to go. Shaking, I called the number, and they told me where and when it would be.

In this group I began to let out some of the feelings that I had kept bottled up for months. Listening to the other women taught me that I was not alone, although many told stories and expressed feelings that were different from my own. Sometimes I left the group aching with the pain I felt from reclaiming all those feelings I'd pushed to the back of my mind. Other times I was amazed at how well I connected with these women, how much I learned from them, and how much I looked forward to this meeting every week. In the journal I kept, things came out on paper that I never could have said aloud.

March

My boyfriend and I had just broken up when I found out. He wouldn't even speak to me so that I could tell him, but eventually I cornered him. He didn't care, and he didn't want to help. All he could say was, "Jesus Christ, are you sure?" I reminded him that it was his problem too, and he said he would give me the money, but he wouldn't go with me. He assumed, as I did, that I would have an abortion. My Mom would hate me for it. She had always condemned abortion, saying that it was killing a baby. Maybe it is; maybe I did.

After a few phone calls I found out that you have to be 18 to get an abortion in my state without parental consent. I was just four months too young. Eventually I made an appointment with a clinic in a nearby state. The woman I spoke to was very supportive, but I had to figure out how I would get there. A week went by before I asked a friend to take me. Then a few more weeks of wishing I could tell someone and trying to hide the hurt and tears. I guess I did a good job, because no one noticed. The worst part was when I saw my half-brother, an adorable 3-month-old. I couldn't hold him or look at him without thinking that I might as well be killing him.

April

I live constantly in two worlds. One is where I can talk or write about it and show my real emotion — when I'm alone and cry, when I'm with the few friends who know, or when I'm with the support group, the only people who really understand. The other world is all the other times. Then I have to pretend that I am okay. I have to conceal my feelings. If someone reminds me, I can't share the hurt inside. Nor can I when some guy makes a joke or comment about a girl who had an abortion, when Amy eats a peanut butter and banana sandwich and Jean asks if she's pregnant, or when everyone giggles at the jokes, even me, but they don't know what's going on in my head. The pain is when there is an editorial in the paper about abortion and Mary says, "My friend at home had one—I'll never forgive her. She could have given it up for adoption; I was adopted." If only she knew. The pain is when I walk by a poster advocating reproductive rights that someone has scribbled "Fetus-Bashers" on in red magic marker. I want to scream at the person who did it, but they aren't there. I want to rip the poster down, but I don't. I want to tell the person I'm walking with how upset I am, but she won't understand.

May

Mom,

I know you'd hate me if you knew. To you it's disgusting, it's killing. I'll never be able to tell you. Maybe I'm hurting myself or our relationship by not telling you. I would have liked your support. I needed your help, but I couldn't tell you, and I still can't. I never wanted to hurt you.

Sometimes I wish you had guessed somehow. But you would have wanted me to have the baby; you wouldn't have let me make my own decision. Maybe it was a bad thing to do, maybe it wasn't the "right" thing to do. But I don't want a baby, and I don't want to give birth to one only to give it away. I wanted to go to school and learn and have fun, not be trapped in my own body for nine months. I didn't want to be stared at by mothers who warn their teenager at their side: "She can't be more than 16; I hope you never do a stupid thing like that!" I didn't want my sisters to be ashamed of me. I didn't want my friends and teachers to think I was a bad person. Because as we all know, girls who have sex are bad, and girls who get pregnant are stupid.

When I read these journals over again, I remember feeling so isolated and scared that everyone would hate me if they knew. When I did start telling people, I felt terrified of what they might think or say. But the more people I told the less it hurt to retell and the more confident I felt that I was right. The decision I made was a good one, and it was mine to make. I felt proud of the strength that I had to make it through this crisis on my own and stick to what I really wanted to do.

Experiencing for myself the inaccessibility of abortion for teenagers and going to the support group both pushed me to explore feminism and identify with it. I joined a pro-choice group on campus, went to protests against Operation Rescue, and wrote an article for a women's newspaper. I told my closest friends and even some not so close. My experience with abortion was becoming an integrated part of my life. But I also felt disillusioned by "the feminist movement." The political group I joined talked about "rights," and I didn't feel comfortable talking about my abortion, or talking at all, for that matter. It was hard for me to talk about abortion without including my own experiences. But I continued going because I had to make sure that abortion didn't become illegal, or in my case, more illegal. Being involved politically made me feel like maybe I could make a difference.

The pro-choice group organized rides to Boston for the protest against Operation Rescue which was trying to close down clinics there. I rode down the night before with Sarah, another woman in the group, and we stayed at my dad's house. I don't remember when exactly I met her, or if we knew before that ride that we'd both had abortions, but for two and a half hours we talked about our experiences. It was amazing how close I felt to her; she made me feel even stronger. We found that we both felt alienated from the political group, and we talked about it a lot. She told me that she was in the support group that I had been in the semester before. I realized how much I missed talking about my abortion with women who understood.

It was an emotional weekend and maybe one of the best ones in my life. Talking with Sarah and being with her at the protest made it seem that much more important to me. I felt so good and real and so passionately involved. This was something I believed in like I never believed in something before. It was an incredible feeling facing, inches away from me, the people who believed I was a murderer and wanted to take away my right to control my own body.

After the protest I saw little of Sarah outside the pro-choice meetings, until another semester later. She called and asked if I wanted to help her start a support group, or what we later decided to call a consciousness-raising group, for women who had had abortions. We both missed and needed those discussions. We put signs up and met the people who answered in a café on campus. Soon we were a group of eight, and the first night we met I found myself in tears, realizing how much I still needed to talk about it and how much was still left unresolved. I wanted to piece my life together. Why had all this happened to me? Can I go on hiding it from other people, from my family? At the fourth meeting I decided to tell my whole story. I didn't just talk about my abortion, I talked about my whole life. I was trying to make sense of it all. I began to identify some reasons behind my getting pregnant. One was my family. I told the group: "No one ever talked about anything in my family. My dad left when I was 13 and my mom told us not to tell anyone. My twin sister and I never said a word to each other about it. When my dad told us he was leaving we cried. Actually she cried, I didn't. I went upstairs to my room and closed the door. And that was the end of it, no one ever talked about it again."

The second explanation that I alluded to was my early sexual relationships with men. I described myself during that time as very insecure: "In school I wanted desperately to be liked, and boys actually seemed to like me. When some guy asked me out, I couldn't believe it. I'd say yes. I didn't know what else to say, even if I didn't like him. I dated a few guys and each time one of us got scared off and then avoided each other. Then Rick asked me out." I had difficulty talking about him even with this group of women. I tried to describe him and our relationship. "God, I don't know why I ever went out with him. He was . . . so awful. And we had a nine-month 'relationship.' After the first month I just wanted to break up with him, but I couldn't do it. I didn't want to hurt his feelings and I was afraid of what he'd do. He was always trying to get me to sleep with him. I was only 15. He ended up basically raping me."

Rick said he wanted me to be his girlfriend. There were guys I liked a lot more than him, but no one had asked me out before like that. He was nice and funny and said he loved me. Though I soon found him annoying and pushy, I couldn't break up with him, even after he raped me. I was scared that he might kill himself. I was afraid he might freak out and hurt me. I was attached to him and the attention he gave me. And I didn't even know I had been raped. "I just thought I was a horrible person because I couldn't keep him from touching me. I felt horrible, but I didn't know why. I thought I'd done something wrong. I just cried. I didn't even think of saying anything to anyone; I wouldn't have known what to say. I couldn't believe that I'd just had sex with someone; I couldn't even say the word. My parents never talked about sex either, except my mother's little innuendoes about it being bad. So I thought I was the worst person in the world."

I finally broke up with Rick, but I often felt pushed into later sexual experiences as well. I said to the group, "I slept with Chris too, or he convinced me to sleep with him. That's what it always seemed like. I didn't want to do it, but I would give in. It was always like the guy was trying to convince me and I never really wanted to, but I always would." With Chris, part of me did really want to sleep with him, but I was unsure and I didn't know how to talk about it. I think most of the time I didn't want to was because I was afraid of getting pregnant, and I didn't know how to talk about birth control either.

Chris and I broke up when he went to college, partly because he was going away, and partly because I was interested in someone else. I was 16, almost 17, and a senior in high school. Darren was a junior, but I thought he was the greatest. He drank a lot and did some drugs, and I hated both. But for the first time I really felt comfortable sleeping with someone. To Sarah and the other women I said, "Birth control was just never an issue for us." It was the first time I had admitted it, but it wasn't completely true either. It was an issue, but we never talked about it. I didn't ask him about it and he didn't ask me about it. It was really strange because I was terrified that I was going to get pregnant. I always thought about it, worried about it, but I couldn't do anything about it.

Although we didn't use contraception, and we didn't talk about it, I thought about it constantly, and I was scared. I even wrote a paper about teenage pregnancy for a psychology class. I remember working on it, thinking, "This could be you, you have to do something about this." I remember having this feeling that I HAD to talk to him about it, but I couldn't. It seemed easier not to say anything and put it out of my mind, to try to forget about it.

At one point I thought I was pregnant, and I told him. He couldn't believe it and he said something about me being on the Pill. I said, "No, I'm not, where did you get that idea?" But inside I felt relieved that the subject finally came up. He said that he just figured that I must have been, since I never seemed worried about it. It seems almost funny now, but it wasn't then. How could he have thought that all this time, when for me it hurt so much to pretend it wasn't a problem?

It turned out that I wasn't pregnant. He was so happy and I was relieved. We talked more after all that, we started using condoms "most of the time," and I worried about it less. Then he started to drink more and got more into drugs, and he wanted to be with his friends and not me. He tried to break up with me, but I took a fit. "You can't leave me, Darren," I cried, "I love you, I can't believe you are doing this to me, you said you loved me!" Finally he gave in and said he still did, but he kept away from me and finally he broke it off completely. I was still hurt, but I knew I didn't like the drinking and our disagreements around it, so I didn't argue this time. Two or three weeks later I worried that I was pregnant again. I tried to call him. He was never home, and his brother once just said, "He doesn't want to talk to you." Finally I got in touch with him and told him. He just said, "Jesus Christ, I can't believe this!"

My mother is totally anti-abortion. I knew if I said anything to her, I would be having a kid. I only told one of my girlfriends; she was the only person I thought I could trust. I did one of those home pregnancy tests; I hid it behind the books in my bookcase when you have to let it sit for a couple hours. I totally freaked out when I looked at it and it came out positive. My friend was more clueless about what to do than I was. I turned to another close friend, this time a guy. I asked him to drive me to the hospital so that I could have a real test done. I didn't tell him why I was going, and he drove me, no questions asked. I was convinced that this test was going to be negative, that the first test was wrong. I was sure of it. The next day the woman on the phone told me it was positive.

Meanwhile I started getting involved with someone else. Todd and I started spending a lot of time together. We weren't going out yet, but we were close. One night I told him about it. He said he'd been through it with a girlfriend, but she turned out not to be pregnant. He said he'd take me for the abortion appointment. I was so relieved. I told my mom and my boss that we were going shopping for the day; Mom even let Todd take her car.

When we got there he just dropped me off, he didn't come in with me. At the time it was exactly what I expected, but now it seems strange that I didn't want him there for support. It didn't even occur to me to ask him to come in with me. I think I felt that it wasn't his responsibility and it was something I wanted to do on my own. I am still in awe of the idea that I went through this all by myself.

I walked in alone with my $250 check from Darren. I was nervous, but I felt better once I was inside. The woman on the phone warned me that there might be picketers, but no one bothered me. Most of the people in the waiting room had someone with them, but it didn't bother me too much at the time. I was so relieved to actually be there. I started to get scared waiting, but I still couldn't believe that I had made it there and that I was going to be okay.

The first thing they did was counseling, or at least that's what they called it. It's just when they describe the procedure in detail. I went into this room with the counselor and a 30-year-old woman who was there for the same reason but seemed totally relaxed. The counselor started to explain to the two of us exactly what happens with the doctor and the instruments. Suddenly I was terrified and I started to cry. I couldn't help it. I was scared of how much it would hurt, of what it would be like. The counselor and the other woman were like "Oh my goodness, what's wrong?" as if there was no reason whatsoever for me to be the least bit upset.

What bothers me about the whole thing is that no one ever talked about it, I mean really talked about it. They were all robots, just doing their job, describing the procedure, taking blood, giving out pills, acting like it was no big deal. It seems like it wouldn't have been so scary if we could have talked about it more. If someone only said, "I've been through it too. It's okay to be scared, but you will be okay."

Someone sent me to get changed and directed me to the next waiting room. I was there for two hours in my gown. Or maybe it was just an hour, or only twenty minutes, but it seemed like forever. There were around five other women there, and a woman came in to call a name once in a while. The chairs were arranged in a circle around the room. We sat there facing each other and no one said anything. Everyone seemed scared except the older woman who flipped through a magazine and made comments here and there. But the person who really stuck out in my mind was a girl who looked no older than 13. I felt so terrible for her—she looked so scared. I just wanted to reach out to her, and tell her everything was going to be okay.

Finally they called my name and I followed a woman to another room. Another woman was there to talk to me and to hold my hand during the abortion if I wanted to. The doctor said, "So you are going to college in the fall? So what's your major?" I couldn't believe he was asking me about college; I could barely answer, I was so terrified. But I guess it was better than him not saying anything at all. It was so painful. I remember screaming and crying, literally. Afterwards I wondered if anyone heard me. They said it would hurt some, but this was the most painful thing I had ever felt. It hurts to think about it.

Afterwards I went into a room with other women who were recovering, lying down with blankets and eating slices of oranges and crackers. After about fifteen minutes I felt a lot better, so they said I could leave even though you're supposed to stay for longer afterwards. I started to get cramps after about fifteen minutes driving home. We stopped and bought some pain reliever but it kept getting worse. They said that cramps were normal, so I didn't really worry about it. I didn't realize how bad it was until the next day when I got up and got ready for work. I was still bleeding heavily. I knew I should call the clinic. According to the information sheet they gave me I should have called them if this happened. I thought about it, but I knew they'd want me to see a doctor. I don't know if I was more scared that something was wrong with me or that my mother would find out. For three days I was in agony and then finally it stopped.

My experience with abortion and the support groups I've involved myself in have allowed me to experience a great level of intimacy with other women that I never felt before. But it also seemed to pull me away from my family. It was something I couldn't go to any of them to talk about, something I hid from them. I hate that they can't really understand a part of me. The people I'm closest to don't know my deepest secret, my deepest hurts, and the greatest motivation for some of my interests. Sometimes I feel guilty about not sharing it with them. I'm afraid that one of my sisters may have to go through the same thing one day and she wouldn't tell me either. She would have to deal with the same silence I did. But last year I realized that I hadn't hidden everything from them. One day my 17-year-old sister called me at school. She was scared that she was pregnant and didn't know what to do. Even though she didn't know I'd had an abortion, she knew how I felt about it. She said, "I can't have it. School and field hockey, I just couldn't." I told her it was okay and she didn't have to do anything she didn't want to do. I told her where she could go for a test and that she could call me anytime she wanted. If she was pregnant I told her: "I'd know what to do, it's alright." I was scared for her, but I was happy that I could be there for her. It made me feel good that she wouldn't have to go through it alone.

I know I will never tell my mother, and that's okay now, but sometimes it still makes me sad. We are still very close, though. I'm probably closer to her than any of my sisters. We talk a lot about boyfriends (both of ours), school, jobs, and my dad. I know she's not the best listener in the world, but I like to be there for her. Sometime she really surprises me and gives me good advice, but she has trouble just listening. One of my greatest fears is that she will find out and it will ruin the relationship we have. I think she'd hate me for a while, and she'd feel guilty too. I'm sure her love for me would overcome it, but I just don't want to put her or myself through it.

I want to tell my twin sister. It is absolutely bizarre to me that she doesn't know this about me. Although we fight and still compete, we've shared a lot more since we've been at school and I feel pretty close to her. I told her about being raped and we talked about that often. But I can't seem to tell her about my abortion. I want to. I'm not afraid of what she will think of me anymore because I've had one, but I'm afraid of what she will think of me for not telling her. I'm afraid that she will really freak out. That she wouldn't believe me anymore or she'd hate me for not telling her. I'm afraid of totally shocking her.

Recently my mom said to me while looking at an old picture of the four of us kids, "You were always so happy as kids, laughing all the time, having fun." I had a really weird feeling when she said it. I never remember being happy as a kid. Scared of my own shadow might be a better description. I couldn't bear to tell her that, I just nodded and smiled.

I remember all of us kids fighting a lot. I remember my mom yelling a lot. I don't remember my dad being home much. I remember him coming home at 1:00 in the morning. I remember them yelling a lot on weekends. We bought a sailboat, but it was mostly just another place to fight. I remember a teacher that I loved in seventh grade. We wrote in journals in her class. Once I wrote about one of our boat trips, only I left out the bad parts, the fighting. When I got the journal back she wrote, "Sounds wonderful!" I felt like she liked me and what I wrote, but I also felt horrified. I had a sick feeling in my stomach, like I knew it wasn't true; it wasn't wonderful.

In the autobiography I wrote my senior year in high school I identified my dad leaving as one of the two events that had the greatest effect on me (the other was being a twin). The hurt was fresher then, and I was angry and jealous. Those feelings certainly haven't gone away, they just aren't so strong. Then it seemed I wanted so badly to believe that my family was perfect before the day he destroyed it all and left. Now I tend to think of the bad times, all of the fights, and I can't remember the good stuff. Now I see that something was very wrong with my family before he left. No one communicated, but everyone fought. I guess my dad just wasn't happy, and he spent less time at home and more at work, and then my mom became unhappy. Or maybe it was the other way around. I don't know how it really happened or whose fault it really was.

To me then it was all my dad's fault; he did everything that hurt me. But sometimes I think my mother's reactions, as well as our own, made things worse for us. No one in the house talked about it, except my mom, who was an emotional wreck. She'd try to pry information out of us after we'd been to my dad's. She told us, begged us, to ask him to come home and to tell him that we loved him. She said he'd come if we did. We couldn't tell him how much it was hurting us; we just went to see him and tried to be "good." But mom telling me this made me feel even more like it was all our fault. She also told us not to tell our friends; she didn't want anyone to know. Until we moved two years later, I told my friends he was on a business trip when they came over.

I don't blame my mother for any of these things, even though they hurt me. I feel thankful that she survived and didn't just give up. As for my dad, I try to see him as much as I can. We can have fun together, but I feel like he can't ever be there for me emotionally. It still makes me sad. For the most part, I'm not bitter anymore. But he still tries to get away with giving my mother as little money as possible and he pays almost nothing toward our college bills. Though they've been divorced for years, the hurt still seems to drag on. Mom still makes comments about his wife and kid. I understand her hurt, but I'm still caught in the middle.

I have tried here to explain my inability to deal appropriately with sexual relationships as being the result of my not having been able to talk about sex and contraception. The feelings from the beginnings of my adolescent sexuality were of being scared, not having control, and not having a choice. I now know that this is related to having grown up in a family that stuffed their feelings and never talked about anything, including sex. My family always avoided subjects that were upsetting, embarrassing, or controversial. So when it came to talking about contraception with my boyfriend, I had no basis to deal with it and felt it was beyond my control. My way of coping with the inevitable crisis of a pregnancy was not to practice contraception, but to put it out of my mind. That was easy; I had practiced that all my life.

Notes on Contributors

Andrew Garrod is Associate Professor of Education at Dartmouth College, Hanover, New Hampshire, where he teaches courses in adolescence, moral development, and moral education. His recent publications include an essay review, "Making Moral Youth," with Robert Howard, in the *Harvard Educational Review,* an edited book entitled *Learning for Life: Moral Education Theory and Practice,* and a two-volume anthology edited with Janet Webster, *Worlds Unrealized: Short Stories of Adolescence in Canadian Fiction.* His research interests include adolescence, moral development, and moral education.

Carol Gilligan is the author of *In a Different Voice: Psychological Theory and Women's Development* and Director of the Harvard Project on the Psychology of Women and Development of Girls. As professor of Human Development and Psychology at the Harvard Graduate School of Education, she works collaboratively with students, colleagues, clinicians, and teachers. The work of the collaboration appears in *Making Connections,* edited with Nona Lyons and Trudy Hanmer; *Mapping the Moral Domain,* edited with Janie Ward and Jill Taylor; and a series of working papers.

Robert Kilkenny is Associate Director of the Hall-Mercer Laboratory of Developmental Psychology and Developmental Psychopathology at McLean Hospital and Harvard Medical School. He has most recently published an article in the Life Span Development Series with Gil Noam, Sally Powers, and Jeff Beedy on developmental aspects of adolescent relationships with parents and peers. His current research interests include delinquency, moral development, and risk and prevention in developmental psychopathology.

Gil Noam is Director of the Hall-Mercer Laboratory of Developmental Psychology and Developmental Psychopathology and Assistant Professor of Psychology at the Harvard Medical School at McLean Hospital. He has published widely on adolescent development and clinical developmental lifespan psychology and teaches courses at the Harvard Medical School and Harvard Graduate School of Education in child and adolescent development. He is currently working on a longitudinal study of the process of recovery in the development of adolescents and young adults.

Sally Powers is Associate Professor of Psychology at the University of Massachusetts, Amherst, and instructor of psychology at Harvard Medical School. She has published numerous articles based on her research on family interaction and its relation to adolescent development and psychopathology. She recently received a career advancement award from NSF for her research. She teaches courses in adolescent development, psychopathology, and child and adolescent psychotherapy and is currently working on a longitudinal study of rural adolescents and their families.

Ritch Savin-Williams is Associate Professor in Human Development and Family Studies at Cornell University. He is the author of *Gay and Lesbian Youth: Expressions of Identity* and *Adolescence: An Ethological Perspective*. His research interests include exploring the diversity of developmental patterns that gay men, lesbians, and bisexuals undertake in achieving a gay, lesbian, or bisexual identity, with a particular focus on the adolescent years.

Lisa Smulyan is Associate Professor and Acting Director of the Program in Education at Swarthmore College, Swarthmore, Pennsylvania, where she supervises student teachers and teaches courses in educational foundations, adolescence, women and education, curriculum and methods, and the writing process. Her publications include a book, co-authored with Sharon N. Oja, entitled *Collaborative Action Research: A Developmental Process*. Her research focuses on classroom-based research with teachers and the use of life/career history as a basis for understanding school practice and providing effective staff development.

Selected Bibliography

Adelson, J. and Douvan, E. (1975). "Adolescent friendships," in Conger, Mussen, and Kagan (eds.), *Basic and Contemporary Issues in Developmental Psychology*. NY: Harper and Row, pp. 277–290.

Adelson, J. and O'Neil, R. (1975). "Growth of political ideas in adolescence: The sense of community," in Conger, Mussen, and Kagan (eds.), *Basic and Contemporary Issues in Developmental Psychology*. NY: Harper and Row, pp. 53–70.

Adler, N. (1975). "Emotional responses of women following therapeutic abortion." *American Journal of Orthopsychiatry,* 45:446–456.

American Psychological Association: Interdivisional Committee on Adolescent Abortion (1987). "Adolescent abortion: Psychological and legal issues," *American Psychologist,* 42(1):73–78.

Aristotle (1941). *Rhetorica.* New York: Random House.

Bakan, D. (1972). "Adolescence in America: From idea to social fact," in Kagan and Coles (eds.), *Twelve to Sixteen: Early Adolescence.* New York: W.W. Norton, pp. 73–89.

Bardige, B. (1988). "Things so finely human: Moral sensibilities at risk in adolescence," in Gilligan et al., (eds.), *Mapping the Moral Domain.* Cambridge, MA: Harvard University Press, pp. 87–110.

Baumrind, D. (1987). "Developmental perspectives on adolescent risk-taking in contemporary America," in Irwin (ed.), *Adolescent Social Behavior and Health.* San Francisco: Jossey-Bass, pp. 73–125.

Baumrind, D. (in press). "Rearing competent children," in Damon (ed.), *New Directions for Child Development: Child Development Today and Tomorrow.* San Francisco: Jossey-Bass.

Beardslee, W.R. (1981). Self-understanding and coping with cancer. In Koocher & O'Malley (Eds.), *The damocles syndrome: Psychosocial consequences of surviving childhood cancer.* New York: McGraw-Hill.

——— (1989). The role of self understanding in resilient individuals: The development of a perspective. *American Journal of Orthopsychiatry, 59* (2), 266–278.

Bell, A.P., Weinberg, M.S., and Hammersmith, S.K. (1981). *Sexual Preference: Its Development in Men and Women.* Bloomington, IN: Indiana University Press.

Benedict, R. (1950). *Patterns of Culture.* New York: New American Library.

Berndt, T. (1981). "Relations between social cognition, non-social cognition, and social behavior: The case of friendship," in Flavell and Ross (eds.), *Social Cognitive Development: Frontiers and Possible Futures.* Cambridge: Cambridge University Press.

————— (1982). "The features and effects of friendship in early adolescence." *Child Development,* 55:151–162.

Berndt, T.J., and Ladd, G.W. (1989). *Peer Relationships in Child Development.* New York: John Wiley.

Berndt, T.J., and Perry, T.B. (1990). "Distinctive features and effects of early adolescent friendships," in Montemayor (ed.), *Advances in Adolescent Research.* Greenwich, CT: JAI Press.

Berry, G.L., and Asamen, J.K. (eds.) (1989). *Black Students: Psychosocial Issues and Academic Achievement.* Beverly Hills: Saga Focus.

Blos, P. (1962). *On Adolescence: A Psychoanalytic Interpretation.* New York: Free Press.

————— (1972). "The child analyst looks at the young adolescent," in Kagan and Coles (eds.), *Twelve to Sixteen: Early Adolescence.* New York: W.W. Norton.

Blyth, D., Hill, J., and Thiel, K. (1982). "Early adolescents' significant others: Grade and gender differences in perceived relationships with familial and non-familial adults and young people." *Journal of Youth and Adolescence,* 11:425–450.

Bracken, M., Hachamovitch, M., and Grossman, A. (1974). "The decision to abort and psychological sequelae." *Journal of Nervous and Mental Disorders,* 15:155–161.

Bracken, M., Klerman, L., and Bracken, M. (1978). "Coping with pregnancy resolution among never-married women." *American Journal of Orthopsychiatry,* 48:320–333.

Brown, L.M. (in press). "Telling a girl's life." *Women and Therapy.*

Buhrmester, D., and Furman, W. (1987). "The development of companionship and intimacy." *Child Development,* 58:1101–1113.

Burleson, B. (1982). "The development of comforting communication skills in childhood and adolescence." *Child Development,* 53:1578–1588.

Chodorow, N. (1974). "Family structure and feminine personality," in Rosaldo and Lamphere (eds.), *Women, Culture, and Society,* Stanford, CA: Stanford University Press. pp. 43–66.

————— (1989). *Feminism and Psychoanalysis.* New Haven, CT: Yale University Press.

Clark, R. (1983). *Family Life and School Achievement: Why Poor Black Children Succeed or Fail.* Chicago: University of Chicago Press.

Coleman, J.C. (1987). "Friendship and the peer group in adolescence," in Adelson (ed.), *Handbook of Adolescent Psychology.* NY: John Wiley, pp. 408–431.

Coles, R., and Stokes, G. (1985). *Sex and the American Teenager.* New York: Harper and Row.

Cooley, C.H. (1902). *Human Nature and the Social Order.* New York: Scribners.

Côté, J., and Levine, C. (1987). "A formulation of Erikson's theory of ego identity formation." *Developmental Review,* 7:273–325.

Cottle, T.J. (1972). "The connections of adolescence," in Kagan and Coles (eds.), *Twelve to Sixteen: Early Adolescence.* NY: W.W. Norton, pp. 294–336.

Crockett, L., Losoff, M., and Peterson, A.C. (1984). "Perceptions of the peer group and friendship in early adolescence." *Journal of Early Adolescence,* 4(2):155–181.

Csikszentmihalyi, M. and Larson, R. (1984). *Being Adolescent.* New York: Basic Books.

Cvejic, H., Lipper, I., Kinch, R.A., and Benjamin, P. (1977). "Follow-up of 50 adolescent girls two years after abortion." *Canadian Medical Association Journal.* 116:44–46.

Diaz, R., and Berndt, T. (1982). "Children's knowledge of a best friend: Fact or fantasy?" *Developmental Psychology,* 18:787–794.

Dickinson, E. (1960). *Complete Poems.* Boston: Little, Brown.

Elder, G. (1980). "Adolescence in historical perspective," in Adelson (ed.), *Handbook of Adolescent Psychology.* New York: John Wiley, pp. 3–46.

Erikson, E.H. (1959). "Identity and the life cycle." *Psychological Issues,* 1:1–171.

―――― (1964). *Insight and Responsibility.* New York: W.W. Norton.

―――― (1966). *The Challenge of Youth.* New York: Anchor Paperback.

―――― (1968). *Identity: Youth and Crisis.* New York: W.W. Norton.

―――― (1975). *Life History and the Historical Moment.* New York: W.W. Norton.

―――― (1980). *Identity and the Life Cycle: A Reissue.* New York: W.W. Norton.

Ewing, J.A., and Rouse, B.A. (1973). "Therapeutic abortion and a prior psychiatric history." *American Journal of Psychiatry,* 130:37–40.

Finkelhor, D. (1984). *Child Sexual Abuse: New Theory and Research.* New York: Free Press.

―――― (1987). "The sexual abuse of children: Current research reviewed." *Psychiatric Annals,* 17(4):233–237.

Ford, C., Castelnuovo-Tedesco, P., and Long, K. (1971). "Abortion: Is it a therapeutic procedure in psychiatry?" *Journal of the American Medical Association,* 218:1173.

Fordham, S. (1988). "Racelessness as a factor in Black students' school success: Pragmatic strategy or pyrrhic victory?" *Harvard Educational Review,* 58(1):54–84.

Fordham, S., and Ogbu, J. (1986). "Black students' school success: Coping with the burden of acting white." *The Urban Review,* 18(3):176–206.

Fowler, J.W. (1981). "Adolescence," in *Stages of Faith: The Psychology of Human Development and the Quest for Meaning.* San Francisco: Harper and Row, pp. 69–77.

Freud, A. (1946). *The Ego and Mechanisms of Defense* (C. Baines, Trans.). New York: International Universities Press.

―――― (1958). "Adolescence," in *Psychoanalytic Study of the Child,* Vol. 13. New York: International Universities Press.

Freud, S. (1962). "The transformations of puberty," in *Three Essays on the Theory of Sexuality.* NY: Basic Books. pp. 73–96.

Fritz, G.K., Williams, J.R., & Amylon, M. (1988). After treatment ends: Psychosocial sequelae on pediatric cancer survivors. *American Journal of Orthopsychiatry, 58* (4), 552–561.

Garmezy, N. (1985). "Stress-resistant children: The search for protective factors," in Stevenson (ed.), *Recent Research in Developmental Psychopathology.* Oxford: Pergamon Press.

―――― (1987). "Stress, competence, and development: Continuities in the study of schizophrenic adults, children vulnerable to psychopathology, and the search for stress-resistant children." *American Journal of Orthopsychiatry,* 57(2):159–174.

Gibbs, J.T. (1984). "Black adolescents and youth: An endangered species." *American Journal of Orthopsychiatry,* 54(1):6–23.

Gilligan, C. (1977). "In a different voice: Women's conceptions of self and morality." *Harvard Educational Review,* 47(4):481–516.

———— (1982). *In a Different Voice.* Cambridge, MA: Harvard University Press.

———— (1987). "Adolescent development reconsidered," in Irwin (ed.), *Adolescent Social Behavior and Health.* San Francisco: Jossey-Bass, pp. 63–92.

———— (1989). "Teaching Shakespeare's sister," in C. Gilligan, N. Lyons, and T. Hanmer (eds.), *Making Connections.* Cambridge, MA: Harvard University Press.

———— (1990). "Joining the resistance: Psychology, politics, girls and women." *Michigan Quarterly Review,* 19(Fall).

Gilligan, C., and Murphy, J. (1979). "Development from adolescence to adulthood: The philosopher and the dilemma of the fact," in D. Kuhn (ed.), *Intellectual Development Beyond Childhood.* San Francisco: Jossey-Bass, pp. 85–99.

Gilligan, C., Brown, L.M., and Rogers, A. (1990). "Psyche embedded: A place for body, relationships and culture in personality theory," in Rabin, Zucker, Emmons and Frank (eds.), *Studying Persons and Lives.* New York: Springer.

Gilligan, C., Lyons, N., and Hanmer T. (eds.). *Making Connections: The Relational Worlds of Adolescent Girls at Emma Willard School.* Troy, NY: Emma Willard School.

Goethals, G.W., and Klos, D.S. (1976). *Experiencing Youth: First Person Accounts.* Boston: Little Brown.

Gordon, S., and Gilgun, J.F. (1987). "Adolescent sexuality," in Van Hasselt and Hersen (eds.), *Handbook of Adolescent Psychology,* NY: John Wiley, pp. 147–167.

Gottman, J.M., and Parker, J.G. (eds). (1987). *Conversations with Friends.* New York: Cambridge University Press.

Grotevant, H.D., and Cooper, C.R. (1986). "Individuation in family relationships." *Human Development,* 29:81–100.

Hall, C., and Lindzey, G. (1978). *Theories of Personality.* New York: John Wiley.

Hall, G.S. (1904). *Adolescence: Its psychology and its relations to physiology, anthropology, sociology, sex, crime, religion, and education.* New York: Appleton-Century-Crofts.

Hatcher, S. (1976). "Understanding adolescent pregnancy and abortion." *Primary Care,* 3:407–425.

Hauser, S.T., Houlihan, J., Powers, S.I., Jacobson, A.M., Noam, G., Weiss-Perry, B., and Follansbee, D. (1987). "Interaction sequences in families of psychiatrically hospitalized and non-patient adolescents," *Psychiatry,* 50:308–319.

Hauser, S.T., Powers, S.I., Noam, G., Jacobson, A.M., Weiss, B., and Follansbee, D., (1984). "Familial contexts of adolescent ego development." *Child Development,* 55:195–213.

Havighurst, R.J., Bosman, P.H., Liddle, G., Mathews, C.V., and Pierce, J.V. (1962). *Growing up in River City.* New York: John Wiley.

Hill J.P. (1987). "Research on adolescents and their families: Past and prospect," In Irwin (ed.), *Adolescent Social Behavior and Health.* San Francisco: Jossey-Bass, pp. 13–31.

Hollingshead, A.B. (1949). *Elmstown's Youth.* New York: John Wiley.

Jackson, J.S., McCullough, W.R., and Gurin, G. (1981). "Group identity development within black families," in McAdoo, *Black Families.* Beverly Hills, CA: Sage Publications. pp. 252–263.

Jordan, D. (1971). "Parental antecedents and personality characteristics of ego identity statuses." Unpublished doctoral dissertation. State University of New York at Buffalo.

Josselson, R. (1987). *Finding Herself: Pathways to Identity Development in Women.* San Francisco: Jossey-Bass.

Kohlberg, L., and Gilligan, C. (1972). "The adolescent as philosopher: The discovery of the self in a postconventional world," in Kagan and Coles (eds.), *Twelve to Sixteen: Early Adolescence.* New York: W.W. Norton.

Lewin, K. (1939). "Field theory and experiment in social psychology: Concepts and methods." *The American Journal of Sociology,* 44:868–897.

Lewis, C.C. (1987). "Minors competence to consent to abortion." *American Psychologist,* 42(1):84–88.

Lyons, N. (1983). "Two perspectives: On self, relationships, and morality." *Harvard Educational Review,* 53(2):125–136.

Manaster, G.J. (1989). *Adolescent Development: A Psychological Interpretation.* Itasca, IL: F.E. Peacock Publishers.

Marcia, J. (1966). "Development and validation of ego identity: Status." *Journal of Personality and Social Psychology, 3:551–558.*

——— (1967). "Ego identity status: Relationship to change in self-esteem." *Journal of Personality,* 35:118–133.

——— (1980). "Identity in adolescence," in Adelson (ed.), *Handbook of Adolescent Psychology.* New York: John Wiley.

Margolis, A.J., Davidson, L.A., Hanson, K.H., Loos, S.A., and Mikelson, C.A. (1971). "Therapeutic abortion: Follow-up study." *American Journal of Obstetrical Gynecology,* 110:243–249.

Masten, A.S., and Garmezy, N. (1985). "Risk, vulnerability, and protective factors in developmental psychopathology," in Lahey and Kazdin (eds.), *Advances in Clinical Child Psychology,* Vol. 8. New York: Plenum Press.

McAdoo, H.P., and McAdoo, J. (1985). *Black children: Social, Educational and Parental Environments.* Beverly Hills: Sage Focus.

Mead, G.H. (1934). *Mind, Self and Society.* Chicago: University of Chicago Press.

Mead, M. (1930). *Growing Up in New Guinea.* New York: W. Morrow.

——— (1958). "Adolescence in primitive and modern society," in Maccoby, Newcomb, and Hartly (eds.), *Readings in Social Psychology.* New York: W.W. Norton.

Miller, A. (1983). *The Drama of the Gifted Child.* NY: Basic Books.

Miller, J.B. (1976). *Toward a New Psychology of Women.* Boston: Beacon Press.

Monosour, K., and Stewart, B. (1973). "Abortion and sexual behavior in college women." *American Journal of Orthopsychiatry,* 43:803–814.

Montemayor, R. (1983). "Parents and adolescents in conflict: All families some of the time and some families most of the time." *Journal of Early Adolescence,* 3:83–103.

Montemayor, R., and Hanson, E. (1985). "A naturalistic view of conflict between adolescents and their parents and siblings." *Journal of Early Adolescence,* 5:23–30.

Mosley, D.T., Follingshead, D.R., Harley, H., and Heckel, R.V. (1981). "Psychological factors that predict reaction to abortion." *Journal of Clinical Psychology,* 37:276–279.

Muuss, R. (1988). *Theories of Adolescence.* New York: Random House.

Noam, G., (1988). The Theory of Biography and Transformation: foundation for Clinical-Developmental Therapy. In Shirk (Ed.) *Cognitive-developmental approaches to child therapy.* New York: Plenum.

Noam, G., Powers, S., Kilkenny, R., and Beedy, J. (1990). "The interpersonal self in life-span developmental perspective: Theory, measurement and longitudinal case analyses," in Baltes, Featherman, and Lerner (eds.), *Life-span Development and Behavior,* Vol. 10. Hillsdale, New Jersey: Lawrence Erlbaum Associates.

Olson, L. (1980). "Social and psychological correlates of pregnancy resolution among adolescent women: A review." *American Journal of Orthopsychiatry,* 50:432–445.

Parker, J.G., and Gottman, J.M. (1989). "Social and emotional development in a relational context: Friendship interaction from early childhood to adolescence," in Berndt and Ladd (eds.), *Peer Relations in Child Development.* New York: John Wiley.

Payne, E.C., Kravitz, A.R., Notman, M.T., and Anderson, J.V. (1976). "Outcome following therapeutic abortion." *Archives of General Psychiatry.* 33:725–733.

Perry, W.A. (1970). *Forms of Intellectual and Ethical Development in the College Years: A Scheme.* New York: Holt, Rinehart, and Winston, pp. 45–56.

Peterson, L. (1989). Coping by children undergoing stressful medical procedures: Some conceptual, methodological, and therapeutic issues. *Journal of consulting and clinical Psychology, 57*(3), 380–387.

Piaget, J. (1972). "Intellectual evolution from adolescence to adulthood." *Human Development,* 15:1–12.

Plato, (1921). *Republic.* Oxford: Clarendon Press.

Powers. S.I. (1988). "Moral judgment in the family." *Journal of Moral Education,* 17:209–219.

Powers, S.I., Hauser, S.T., Schwartz, J., Noam, G., and Jacobson, A.M. (1983). "Adolescent ego development and family interaction: A structural-developmental perspective," in Grotevant and Cooper (eds.), *Adolescent Development Within the Family.* San Francisco: Jossey-Bass.

Pritchett, V.S. (1971). *Midnight Oil.* London: Chatto and Windus.

Remafedi, G. (1987). "Adolescent homosexuality: Psychosocial and medical implications." *Pediatrics,* 79:331–337.

———— (1987). "Male homosexuality: The adolescent's perspective." *Pediatrids,* 79:326–330.

Roesler, T., and Deisher, R. (1972). "Youthful male homosexuality." *Journal of the American Medical Association,*

Rogers, A. (in press). "A feminist poetics of psychotherapy." *Women and Therapy.*

Rosen, R.H. (1980). "Adolescent pregnancy decision-making: Are parents important?" *Adolescence,* 15:43–54.

Ruddick, S. (1989). *Maternal Thinking.* Boston: Beacon Press.

Rutter, M. (1975). "Attainment and adjustment in two geographical areas. I: The prevalence of psychiatric disorder." *British Journal of Psychiatry,* 126:493–509.

———— (1979). "Protective factors in children's responses to stress and disadvantage," in Kent and Rolf (eds.), *Primary Prevention of Psychopathology: III: Social Competence in Children.* Hanover, NH: University Press of New England.

———— (1987). "Psychosocial resilience and protective mechanisms." *American Journal of Orthopsychiatry, 57*(3):316–331.

Rutter, M., and Quinton, D. (1984). "Long-term follow-up of women institutionalized in childhood: Factors promoting good functioning in adult life." *British Journal of Developmental Psychology,* 18:225–234.

Rutter, M., Graham, P., Chadwick, O., and Yule, W. (1976). "Adolescent turmoil: Fact or fiction?" *Journal of Child Psychology and Psychiatry,* 17:35–56.

Santrock, J.W. (1990). *Adolescence,* 4th ed. Dubuque, IA: Wm. C. Brown.

Savin-Williams, R.C. (1990). *Gay and Lesbian Youth: Expressions of Identity.* Washington, DC: Hemisphere.

Selman, R. (1980). *The Growth of Interpersonal Understanding.* New York: Academic Press.

———— (1979). "A structural-developmental model of social cognition: Implications for intervention research," in Mosher, (ed.), *Adolescents' Development and Education.* Berkeley, CA: McCutchan Publishing Corporation, pp. 123–132.

Sharabany, R., Gershoni, R., and Hofman, J. (1981). "Girl-friend, boy-friend: Age and sex differences in intimate friendship." *Developmental Psychology,* 17:800–808.

Sisson, L., Hersen, M., and Van Hasselt, V. (1987). "Historical perspectives," in Van Hasselt and Hersen (eds.), *Handbook of Adolescent Psychology.* New York: Pergamon Press, pp. 3–10.

Slater, E.J., Stewart, K.J., and Linn, M.W. (1983). "The effects of family disruption on adolescent males and females." *Adolescence,* 17(72):203–214.

Slaughter, D. (1972). "Becoming an African-American woman." *School Review,* 299–318.

Smith, E.M. (1973). "A follow-up study of women who request abortion." *American Journal of Orthopsychiatry,* 43:574–585.

Spaulding, J.G., and Cavenar, J.O. (1978). "Psychoses following therapeutic abortion." *American Journal of Psychiatry,* 135:364–365.

Sullivan, H.S. (1953). *The Interpersonal Theory of Psychiatry.* New York: W.W. Norton.

Surrey, J. (1984). "The self-in-relation," in *Work in Progress.* Wellesley, MA: Stone Center for Developmental Services and Studies.

Taylor, R. (1976). "Psychosocial development among black children and youth: A reexamination." *American Journal of Orthopsychiatry,* 46(1):4–19.

Taylor, R. (1989). "Black youth, role models and the social construction of identity," in Jones, (ed.), *Black Adolescents.* Berkeley: Cobbs and Henry.

Van der Kolk, B.A. (1987). *Psychological Trauma.* Washington, DC: American Psychiatric Press.

Ward, J. (1989). "Racial identity formation and transformation," in Gilligan, Lyons, and Hanmer. (eds.), *Making Connections: The Relational Worlds of Adolescent Girls at Emma Willard School.* Troy, NY: Emma Willard School.

Werner, E. (1989). "High risk children in young adulthood: A longitudinal study from birth to 32 years." *American Journal of Orthopsychiatry,* 59(1):72–81.

Youniss, J., and Smollar, J. (1985). *Adolescent Relations with Mothers, Fathers, and Friends.* Chicago: University of Chicago Press.

Zeldin, R., Small, S., and Savin-Williams, R. (1982). "Prosocial interactions in two mixed-sex adolescent groups." *Child Development,* 53:1492–1498.

Film Reviews

A Little Romance (1979), directed by
George Roy Hill

An adolescent love story about the son of a taxi driver and the daughter of a wealthy American actress who run off to Venice to kiss under the Bridge of Sighs. The trouble and opposition they encounter along the way make their fantasy a reality with a bittersweet ending.

A Separate Peace (1972), directed by Larry Peerce

Two prep-school roommates during the Second World War learn some difficult lessons about adult emotions and moral compromise in this film. We watch the conflict between the two parallel internal conflicts each feels and see how each young man chooses to resolve the problems in his own way.

A Sure Thing (1985), directed by Rob Reiner

A wry look at two college students falling in love. They are not shy, not modest, not insecure, and through circumstance are forced to share experiences and rely on each other. The main characters learn to share their doubts and uncertainties about life, and they experience sex as an accompaniment to respect and love.

American Graffiti (1973), directed by George Lucas

An innocent, romantic, and humorous look at American life in the early 1960s. For the high school students in this film, the future is uncomplicated. Their decisions include whether to go to college, get a job, or just cruise around in the car and listen to the radio.

Anne of Green Gables (1987), directed by
Kevin Sullivan

The story of Anne Shirley, an irrepressible, determined, and feisty romantic. This film charts her progress from the struggles of early adolescence to developing womanhood, showing how she gains her independence and learns about love, friendship, and what it means to be a part of the family that adopts her.

Another Country (1984), directed by Marek Kanievska

This film provides a sensitive portrayal of students in an English public (private) boarding school in the 1930s. It focuses on the experiences of two boys who are "different" and who refuse to accept the rules and regulations of the school. The film explores the developing homosexuality of one of the boys and the awakening political consciousness of the other.

Birdy (1985), directed by Alan Parker

The story of two friends from South Philadelphia. Inseparable as children, they grow apart in high school as they pursue different kinds of birds; Al is a slick Romeo but "Birdy" is obsessed with birds of the feathered variety. They both go to fight in Viet Nam and are wounded, but Al's wounds are physical and Birdy's are internal. Their personalities undergo tremendous changes as they struggle to help each other.

Bloodbrothers (1978), directed by Robert Mulligan

An emotional story of an Italian-American family living in the Bronx. Richard Gere plays a rebellious teenage son and nephew of construction-worker brothers who fight, drink, and pursue women.

Born on the Fourth of July (1989), directed by Oliver Stone

A graphic account of a young soldier's personal Viet Nam. The film shows his development from a sporty teenager to a hardened and cynical man, mentally and physically paralyzed, struggling to survive in his changed and hostile world.

The Breakfast Club (1985), directed by John Hughes

This film shows what would happen if a jock, a dropout, a brain, a beauty, and a rebel were put together in school detention on a Saturday morning. As they learn to talk about their lives in and out of school, they come closer to understanding each other and the social structures that help to keep them apart.

Breaking Away (1979), directed by Peter Yates

This film explores some of the issues for a group of boys coming of age in Bloomington, Indiana. Four local boys, just out of high school, are spending one final summer having fun before going off to jobs, college, and the army. Their final summer marks the end of some dreams and beginning of others, as they annoy parents, friends, and everyone else in an attempt to assert their individuality.

Brighton Beach Memoirs (1986), directed by Gene Saks

This is the story of a 12-year-old boy, Eugene, whose life is governed by a desire to see a woman naked. His home is crowded with relatives, and his experiences are seen within a continuous pattern of family interactions.

Class (1983), directed by Lewis John Carlino

What happens when you find out that you are having an affair with your roommate's mother? What happens when she finds out? And what about your roommate? This film answers these questions, taking everyone's feelings and sexual insecurities into account. There is also an amusing look at the relations between boys and girls at adjacent boarding schools.

The Chocolate War (1988), directed by Keith Gordon

Establishing your independence in the face of apparently insurmountable opposition is part of growing up. Jerry makes the decision to stand alone against his teachers, his peers, and the traditional authority of the school when he refuses to help his school through financial problems.

Dead Poet's Society (1989), directed by Peter Weir

This film deals with the effects of an unconventional teacher on a group of boys in an ultraconservative private school. The teacher encourages individuality whereas the administration favors conformity. This film is also about adolescent desires in the face of parental opposition: one boy tries to get the girl of his dreams and another wants to be an actor. Ultimately tragedy strikes, and the teacher is blamed for sowing the seeds of discontent.

The Diary of Anne Frank (1959), directed by George Stevens

The true-life account, seen through the eyes of an early adolescent, of a Jewish Dutch family forced to hide from the Nazis during the Second World War. Anne's concerns—her relationship with her parents, siblings, and young men; her sense of what is fair and just; and her view of the world—are those of many early adolescents, but the context makes us aware of the effects of culture and history on youth.

Diner (1982), directed by Barry Levinson

Women are strange, threatening, and mysterious to this group of 1950s young men who are growing up slowly. The Diner serves as a focus for recharging their emotional batteries. As they talk about football and eat fries, they develop the courage to venture into romantic and sexual adventures.

East of Eden (1954), directed by Elia Kazan

This is the story of two American brothers living on a lettuce farm in California in the years before World War I. Violent and diffuse, this film conveys the frustration of the young, confused hero, James Dean. His alienation from his mother is also an important theme.

The Getting of Wisdom (1977), directed by Bruce Beresford

A poor young girl goes to an affluent boarding school and has trouble fitting in. Her clothes, her hair, and her tastes are all wrong. Desperate to excel, she embarrasses herself by playing music hall numbers on the piano, while everyone else is playing Beethoven. She then attempts to conform by shunning another girl who wants to be her friend.

Gregory's Girl (1982), directed by Bill Forsyth

A low-budget, highly sensitive film set in Glasgow that focuses on same-sex and romantic peer-group relations. Gregory, the "hero," loses his place on the football (soccer) team to Dorothy, with whom he falls immediately in love. Their friends provide a range of support in the romantic process that ensues.

Fast Times at Ridgemont High (1982), directed by Amy Heckerling

A very graphic high school sex-romp. It centers around a confused girl who sleeps around and is humiliated and hurt in the process. Perhaps this film is valuable for discussion of its unpleasantly sexist portrayal of women.

Hairspray (1988), directed by John Waters

This amusing story is set in the 1960s and focuses on a teenager's concern with appearances. Tracy wants to look good, not despite being fat but because she is fat. She earns a place on a local television dance show, models clothes from the Hefty Hideaway, and gets the guy she wants. She also has time to espouse anti-segregation in between her love affairs with dancing and the hairspray can.

Hoosiers (1987), directed by David Anspaugh

Small schools have problems when they have to play basketball in the state finals. In this film, despite a shortage of players and a disillusioned coach, a small school makes it and faces the problems the best it can. There is a fairy-tale feel to this film, along with an amusing illustration of small-town politics, as teachers, parents' groups, and the coach clash.

I Never Promised You a Rose Garden (1988), directed by Anthony Page

The central character in this film is a mentally ill 16-year-old girl. She lives in a fantasy world, to which the viewer is privy, and is hardly aware of the outside world. Her struggle toward sanity, assisted by other patients, revolves around her allowing reality into her life. This is a disturbing film but one that provides insight into world of someone labeled "insane."

Last Picture Show (1971), directed by Peter Bogdanovich

In West Texas in 1951, time seems almost suspended, and this film evokes the resulting sense of stagnation and sterility. Adventure for the teenagers in this setting involves leaving home, even if only to go fight (and die) in Korea. The film creates an unromanticized portrait of the American Southwest.

Lords of Discipline (1983), directed by Frank Roddam

A tense drama, set in a Southern military academy, where a secret society of student cadets resorts to psychological and physical torture in an attempt to drive out the only black student. The film deals with corrupt codes of honor, hypocrisy, brutality, and the courage of the few students who stand in opposition.

Mask (1985), directed by Peter Bogdanovich

This warm film portrays the feelings of the central character, Rocky, with great poignancy. Rocky has a disease that misshapes his face, and his handicap is handled with humor and sensitivity. It is an absorbing story that follows his close relationship with his mother, his interest in baseball cards, and a growing awareness of girls.

My Bodyguard (1980), directed by Tony Bill

Although high school students may look different, they often share the same anxieties. Clifford, a charmingly average boy, hires a large, supposedly violent classmate, Linderman, to be his bodyguard. A friendship develops between the two boys as Clifford learns that while Linderman may look like the incredible Hulk he is just as vulnerable as anyone else.

Ordinary People (1980), directed by Robert Redford

The matter-of-fact world of suburbia is closely examined when an ordinary family loses its older son in a boating accident. Each surviving member, especially the remaining son, is forced to reassess his or her own role as a member of the family, to test the strength of the love that still exists. The film explores their individual roads to self-discovery and healing and the effects of that process on family relationships.

The Outsiders (1983), directed by Francis Ford Coppola

In this film teenagers in Tulsa in 1966 come in two types: a "soc," who has it all—cars, money, and a future—and a "greaser," who is an outsider with nothing but friends and dreams. The film provides an intense portrayal of adolescents caught between the innocence of childhood and the disillusionment of adulthood.

Peppermint Soda, directed by Diane Kurys

An engaging film that chronicles two teenage sisters as they face the unfamiliar issues involved in growing up. Their age and personality differences lead them to respond to love, parents, friends, and each other differently, yet the sibling warmth helps each through some difficult times.

Picnic at Hanging Rock (1980), directed by Peter Weir

This puzzling film, set in an amazing Australian landscape, examines the disappearance of three young girls on a trip. The mystery of their disappearance is not solved, but the viewer is asked to consider the role of their awakening sexuality in the process.

Portrait of the Artist as a Young Man (1978), directed by Joseph Strick

An excellent adaptation of James Joyce's autobiographical novel in which Stephen Dedalus explores his Irish-Catholic childhood and adolescence as he attends Trinity College, Dublin. Through the story, Stephen begins to question the absolute authority of his upbringing and is compelled to leave school in search of freedom and truth.

Puberty Blues (1981), directed by Bruce Beresford

This film set in a Sydney, Australia, suburb, focuses on two high school girls who worry about popularity, fall in love, and learn about relationships the hard way. The film uses warmth and humor to examine the issues in adolescent girls' lives.

Rebel Without a Cause (1955), directed by Nicholas Ray

A classic James Dean film of teenage angst and the problems that teenagers must deal with in the 1950s and, to some extent, today. Parental arguments, peer pressure, and misunderstandings lead to a sense of desperation and isolation. Both violence and romance provide an outlet for needs and emotions.

River's Edge (1987), directed by Tim Hunter

This film is a study of despair and moral breakdown among ordinary teenagers who are heavily involved in drugs and alcohol. When one of them kills his girlfriend, he takes his friends to see her body. No one calls the police, and they conceal the crime; human nature becomes desensitized.

Romeo and Juliet (1968), directed by Franco Zefferelli

These star-crossed lovers are not the first to experience parental opposition and familial obligations, and they certainly will not be the last. On the threshold of adulthood, Romeo and Juliet fall in love but fail to find a place for themselves in the face of unyielding parental resistance.

Rumble Fish (1983), directed by Francis Ford Coppola

A somewhat surreal story, derived in part from Greek tragedy, that portrays the disillusionment of a teenage boy when he watches his idolized older brother "fall." The film focuses on street survival, and its dreamlike direction heightens the tension and adds poignancy to the isolation of the boy and the breakdown of his family life.

Running Brave (1983), directed by D.S. Everett

Robby Benson stars as Billy Mills in this factual account of the first Native American athlete to win a gold medal at the Olympics. The film deals with prejudice and Billy's fight for acceptance and struggle for self-expression in a hostile environment.

Running on Empty (1988), directed by Sidney Lumet

The Popes, a married couple, were forced underground because of their political activities in the 1960s. In this film, we see how their children adapt to this life, the only one they know. Problems arise when the children adapt to this life, the only one they know. Problems arise when the children reach adolescence and need to stop running from their parents' past and make their own lives.

Saturday Night Fever (1977), directed by John Badham

In this now classic film, we follow the fortunes of Tony Manera, a Brooklyn adolescent, on the dance floor and in the back seat of cars. He faces his first big problem when he meets Annette. Although he likes her, he never respects any girl he sleeps with. After becoming Annette's dance partner, he begins to face some of the sexism and racism that have characterized his actions to this point.

Say Anything (1989), directed by Cameron Crowe

This is a warmhearted romantic comedy about honesty and dishonesty in relationships. It explores the trusting relationship between a girl and her straightforward, dependable father and her complex feelings for a fellow student who is very different from her in both background and aspirations.

Sixteen Candles (1984), directed by John Hughes

Your sixteenth year could be the most awful year of your life, or it could be your best. The central character of this film is a 16-year-old girl who copes with crushes, "geeks," annoying family, and sexual tension. The comedy in this film is based on real, rather than impossible, situations.

Smooth Talk (1986), directed by Joyce Chopra

In this film, the main character's everyday routine of hanging out at the mall, arguing with parents, and teasing boys is threatened with the beginnings of real sexual experiences. Arnold, an outsider, brings adult sexuality into the world of casual flirtation. This film is shocking without being sensational when dealing with loss of innocence and the reality of the adult world.

Splendor in the Grass (1961), directed by Elia Kazan

This film deals with the frustrations of teenage love when parents interfere. These parents are stereotyped as mean, intolerant, and unforgiving monsters. They deny the sweethearts' love and watch the disastrous consequences of their interference.

Stand by Me (1986), directed by Rob Reiner

Based on a Stephen King novel, this film is about four 17-year-old boys who set out on a thirty-mile journey to see the undiscovered corpse of a boy killed by a train. For the main character, Gordy, the trip is an obsession, because his older brother has just died and his parents seem to wish that Gordy had died instead. He says, "That was the summer that I was the invisible boy." Chris, one of his friends, encourages him to write and to value himself, and they form the closest friendship of their lives.

Summer of '42 (1971), directed by Richard Mulligan
A romantic and nostalgic view of the coming of age of a young boy during one idyllic summer. He develops a friendship with and love for a young married woman, and his experience is almost untouched by the War, which exists beyond his own world of sand dunes and summer beach houses. When tragedy strikes, and the reality of the War is brought home to him, he must accept the responsibilities of love, grief, and loss.

Tex (1982), directed by Tim Hunter
This film examines what it is like to be poor, young, and living a rough-shod life without any parental control or influence. The two brothers have already lost their childhood innocence by having to deal with the adult world, yet their attitudes, language, dreams, ideals, and youthful aspirations illuminate the film.

Walkabout (1971), directed by Nicholas Roeg
When a brother and sister are abandoned in the Australian Outback, an Aboriginal boy rescues them and leads them back to civilization. A relationship develops between the girl and the Aboriginal boy. This is a romantic portrayal that raises questions about what constitutes civilization and wilderness.

Wish You Were Here (1987), directed by David Leland
The heroine of this film is a young girl of uncrushable spirit. England of the 1950s is rigidly conservative, but she rebels against the hypocrisy that exists in the provincial seaside town in which she lives. By exploring her own sexuality she learns about herself.